The Use of Exodus in Hebrews

Studies in Biblical Literature

Hemchand Gossai
General Editor

Vol. 142

PETER LANG
New York • Washington, D.C./Baltimore • Bern
Frankfurt • Berlin • Brussels • Vienna • Oxford

King L. She

The Use of Exodus in Hebrews

PETER LANG
New York • Washington, D.C./Baltimore • Bern
Frankfurt • Berlin • Brussels • Vienna • Oxford

Library of Congress Cataloging-in-Publication Data
She, King L.
The use of Exodus in Hebrews / King L. She.
p. cm. — (Studies in biblical literature; v. 142)
Includes bibliographical references and index.
1. Bible. N.T. Hebrews—Relation to Exodus.
2. Bible. O.T. Exodus—Relation to Hebrews. I. Title.
BS2775.52.S54   227'.8706—dc23   2011018762
ISBN 978-1-4331-1381-9
ISSN 1089-0645

Bibliographic information published by **Die Deutsche Nationalbibliothek**.
Die Deutsche Nationalbibliothek lists this publication in the "Deutsche
Nationalbibliografie"; detailed bibliographic data is available
on the Internet at http://dnb.d-nb.de/.

The paper in this book meets the guidelines for permanence and durability
of the Committee on Production Guidelines for Book Longevity
of the Council of Library Resources.

© 2011 Peter Lang Publishing, Inc., New York
29 Broadway, 18th floor, New York, NY 10006
www.peterlang.com

All rights reserved.
Reprint or reproduction, even partially, in all forms such as microfilm,
xerography, microfiche, microcard, and offset strictly prohibited.

Printed in Germany

Contents

Figures ix
Tables xi
Editor's Preface xiii
Acknowledgments xv
Abbreviations xvii

Part One: Descriptive Use of Exodus in Hebrews

Chapter One. Introduction 3
   Need of This Study 3
   Contribution of This Study 6
   Summary 9

**Chapter Two. Descriptive Analysis of Significant Exodus
Citations and Cultic Vocabulary in Hebrews** 11
   Starting Point 11
   Rhetorical Context of Hebrews 12
      Identity of *Auctor*'s Audience 13
      Nature and Purpose of Audience-Oriented Criticism 17
      Authorial Reading in Light of Christ as Yahweh 19
         Theological Reason 20
         Rhetorical Reason 21
         Covenantal Reason 25
   Significance of Apostasy in Exodus 31:18-34:35 to Hebrews 27
      Literary Significance of Exodus 31:18-34:35 to Hebrews 28
      Theological Significance of Exodus 31:18-34:35 to Hebrews 29
      Hermeneutical Significance of Exodus 31:18-34:35 to Hebrews .. 31
   Auctor's Use of Exodus 25:40 in Hebrews 8:5 33
   Auctor's Use of Exodus 3:14 in Hebrews 11:6 35
   Auctor's Use of Cultic Vocabulary from Exodus 37
      Auctor's Use of Sanctuary and Tabernacle from Exodus 38
      Auctor's Use of Priests and Sacrifices from Exodus 39
   Summary 48

Part Two: Prescriptive Use of Exodus in Hebrews

Chapter Three. Presuppositions of a Prescriptive Analysis in Hebrews 53
    Theo-Onto-Logical Structure of Reason 53
    Comparsion of Two Ontological Grounds 54
    Methods 60
        General Method of Inquiry 60
        Hermeneutical and Theological Approach 62
        Intertextual Approach 64
    Summary 67

Chapter Four. Prelude to Prescriptive Analysis in Hebrews 69
    Goal of Prescriptive Analysis in Hebrews 69
    Overall Process of Prescriptive Analysis 70
    Ontological Context of *Auctor* 72
    Ontological Context of Modern Readers 73
    Ontological Context of *Auctor*'s Intended Audience 77
        Comparative Analysis 78
        Description of Biblical Pedagogy 80
    Biblical Analogy of Being 83
        Analogy of Being in Ontological Context 83
        Analogy of Being in Theological Context 84
    Summary 85

Chapter Five. *Auctor*'s Attitude toward the Old Testament in Light of the Christ Event 87
    Introduction 87
    Auctor's Philosophy of History 90
    Auctor's Theology of Revelation 94
        Need for Philosophical Deconstruction 95
        Theological Models 97
        Survey of Relevant Studies 99
    Auctor's Christocentric Exegesis of the Old Testament 104
        Auctor's Exegesis Is Christocentric 104
        Auctor's Belief in Christophany 106
    Summary 109

Contents

**Chapter Six. History of the Interpretive
Influence of Exodus in Hebrews** 111
   Auctor's Ontology 112
   History of the Interpretive Influence of Exodus 3:14 113
   Comparative Analysis 115
   Toward a Prescriptive Analysis of Exodus in Hebrews 120
      Two Important Corollaries 120
      Use of the Prescriptive Power of Exodus in Hebrews 120
   Auctor's Pedagogical Use of Exodus 3:14 123
   Summary 125

**Chapter Seven. *Auctor*'s Typological Use of Exodus in
Light of the Christ Event** 127
   Auctor's Christocentric-Typological Use of Exodus 25:40 127
      Grammatical Significance of *Ton Hagion* in Hebrews 8:2 127
      Typological Use of Exodus 25:40 in Hebrews 8:5 130
   Prescriptive Significance of *Auctor*'s Metanarrative 137
      Support for the Continuity Model 138
      Comparative-Prescriptive Analysis 138
      Prescriptive-Descriptive Analysis 143
   Summary 147

**Chapter Eight. Hermeneutical Methodology Employed in the
Use of Exodus by *Auctor*** 149
   Comparative Analysis of *Auctor*'s Hermeneutic 150
      Auctor's Doctrinal Center in Relation to Its Ground 151
      Autopistic vis-à-vis Axiopistic Hermeneutic 155
   Comparative Analysis of *Auctor*'s Hermeneutics 158
      Scholars' Valuations of *Auctor*'s Hermeneutics for
         Constructing Christology 159
      Ontological Significance of Exodus 25:40 for
         Constructing Christology in Hebrews 162
   Summary 166

Chapter Nine. Conclusion 169
   Summary of Descriptive and Prescriptive Analyses 169
   Correct Interpretation of Hebrews 9:22–23 171
   Suggestions for Future Research 174

Bibliography 175
Subject Index 201
Author Index 209

Figures

Figure 1. Dynamic of Ritual Worship 46
Figure 2. Foundation of Classical Theology 58
Figure 3. Cognitive Epistemological Revelatory Sources from
    Exodus in Hebrews 71
Figure 4. Context of Axiopistic System before the
    Contribution of Immanuel Kant 73
Figure 5. Context of Autopistic System after the
    Contribution of Fernando Canale 73
Figure 6. Modern Pedagogy 74
Figure 7. Classical Pedagogy 74
Figure 8. Modern View of Nature and Supernature 76
Figure 9. Classical View of Nature and Supernature 76
Figure 10. Biblical View of Nature and Supernature 80
Figure 11. Biblical Pedagogy 80
Figure 12. *Auctor*'s Overall Index of Reality 112
Figure 13. Index of Reality for Classical Christian Doctrinal System 117
Figure 14. Mosaic-Biblical Metanarrative of *Auctor* 134
Figure 15. Spatiotemporal Sanctuary Operating in the
    Past, Now, and Future 141
Figure 16. Spatiotemporal Sanctuary Operating in the
    Mosaic, Extended, and New Exodus 145
Figure 17. Structural Outline of Hebrews 152
Figure 18. Significance of Psalms 2 and 110 in Hebrews 154
Figure 19. Levels of Cognitive Specificity in Connection with the
    Theological Precondition 170
Figure 20. Non-Spatiotemporal Heavenly Sanctuary according to
    Classical Pedagogy 172
Figure 21. Spatiotemporal Heavenly Sanctuary according to
    Biblical Pedagogy 173

Tables

Table 1. Diversity of Theological Positions Reflected by the Various Interpretations of Heb 9:22–23 4

Table 2. Comparison of Two Ontological Presuppositions 55

Table 3. Summary of Relevant Studies 100

Table 4. Scholars' Valuations of *Auctor*'s Ontology Reflected by Descriptive Analysis of His Use of Exod 25:40 in Heb 8:5 121

Table 5. *Auctor*'s Hermeneutical Methodology in Light of His Use of Exodus 150

Table 6. Autopistic vis-à-vis Axiopistic Hermeneutic 156

Table 7. Scholars' Valuations of *Auctor*'s Hermeneutics and Hermeneutic 163

Table 8. Scholars' Valuations of *Auctor*'s Pedagogy Reflected by the Various Interpretations of Heb 9:22–23 171

Editor's Preface

More than ever the horizons in biblical literature are being expanded beyond that which is immediately imagined; important new methodological, theological, and hermeneutical directions are being explored, often resulting in significant contributions to the world of biblical scholarship. It is an exciting time for the academy as engagement in biblical studies continues to be heightened.

This series seeks to make available to scholars and institutions, scholarship of a high order, and which will make a significant contribution to the ongoing biblical discourse. This series includes established and innovative directions, covering general and particular areas in biblical study. For every volume considered for this series, we explore the question as to whether the study will push the horizons of biblical scholarship. The answer must be *yes* for inclusion.

In this volume King She has sought to fill a void in the manner in which scholars have interpreted the Books of Hebrews. She notes that the preponderance of studies on Hebrews have focused on what he views as a "descriptive analysis of the Old Testament citations in Hebrews and have not yet moved toward a prescriptive one via ontological analysis of reason conceived by *Auctor*." The author focuses on Heb 9:22–23 as the basis for his arguments noting that the use of *analogia entis* by *Auctor* is principal in the construction of a biblical Christology. While She does not see the descriptive interpretation as the final approach to the text, he does acknowledge its importance and builds on it to construct his argument. This study is certain to generate widespread discourse, particularly in evangelical scholarship, and will not only further expand the biblical horizon, but will do so in a direction that invites further conversation.

The horizon has been expanded.

Hemchand Gossai
Series Editor

Acknowledgments

This book represents a revision of the doctoral dissertation defended by the author in September 2008 at Dallas Theological Seminary in USA. It is a result of much effort and a great deal of time. The biggest thanks should go to my Lord Jesus Christ who made possible the completion of this book. The Lord saved my mother prior to my study in seminary so that she could support me financially and in prayers during my four-year master's program. Then, He provided a godly wife to encourage and support me throughout doctoral studies.

The Lord has also supported my family through many brothers and sisters, especially those from Cornerstone Chinese Bible Church of Texas. I especially want to thank Dr. Heidi Burns and Dr. Hemchand Gossai for accepting this book into Studies in Biblical Literature series. I wish also to express my appreciation to the Chinese Department at the Melbourne School of Theology for paying the publication expenses.

I thank the inter-library loan officer of Dallas Seminary, Debbie Hunn, for her unrelenting effort to secure numerous significant dissertations for this study. I also thank Dr. Fernando Canale for his hospitality when I conducted a long interview with him on January 8, 2008 in his office at Andrews University. I simply could not have completed this study without the spiritual "fruit" I gathered from the personal interview and many subsequent communications via emails.

The faculty of Dallas Seminary has earned my deepest gratitude for service and friendship. Great thanks with due appreciation should go to my dissertation readers for their expertise, careful supervision, and encouragement. They are Dr. Ronald B. Allen, Dr. James E. Allman, Dr. W. Hall Harris III, and Dr. Harold W. Hoehner. I also thank God for providing me with several competent readers during various stages of this writing. They are Monica Sargent, Robby McCollom, and Dr. Henry Clary. Their love for me is obvious for they were willing to work diligently within a very small window of time to polish my expression.

Hesed and Jedid, my two little boys, have prayed for their dad's dissertation without understanding what dissertation really means. After completion, they continued to pray for the work to be published. I should appreciate their faith in Jesus. Finally, I dedicate this book to my faithful wife, Keh, whose "husband has full confidence in her and lacks nothing of value" (Prov 31:11).

Abbreviations

AB	Anchor Bible
ALGHJ	Arbeiten zur Literatur und Geschichte des hellenistischen Judentums
AUSDDS	Andrews University Seminary Doctoral Dissertation Series
AUSS	*Andrews University Seminary Studies*
BETL	Bibliotheca ephemeridum theologicarum lovaniensium
BHS	*Biblia Hebraica Stuttgartensia.* Edited by K. Elliger and W. Rudolph. Stuttgart, 1983.
Bib	*Biblica*
BIS	Biblical Interpretation Series
BKC	*Bible Knowledge Commentary.* Edited by J. F. Walvoord and R. B. Zuck. 2 vols. Wheaton, 1983-1985.
BSac	*Bibliotheca sacra*
BTB	*Biblical Theology Bulletin*
BU	Biblische Untersuchungen
BZAW	Beihefte zur Zeitschrift für die alttestamentliche Wissenschaft
BZNW	Beihefte zur Zeitschrift für die neutestamentliche Wissenschaft
CBET	Contributions to Biblical Exegesis and Theology
CBQ	Catholic Biblical Quarterly
CBR	*Currents in Biblical Research*
ConBNT	Coniectanea biblica: New Testament Series
CRS	Commentary Reference Series
CTJ	*Calvin Theological Journal*
CTQ	*Concordia Theological Quarterly*
DOTP	*Dictionary of the Old Testament: Pentateuch.* Edited by T. D. Alexander and D. W. Baker. Downers Grove, 2003
DRCS	*Daniel and Revelation Committee Series.* Edited by F. B. Holbrook. 7 vols. Silver Spring, 1986-1992
DTIB	*Dictionary for Theological Interpretation of the Bible.* Edited by K. J. Vanhoozer. Grand Rapids, 2005
EBC	*The Expositor's Bible Commentary.* Edited by F. E. Gaebelein. 12 vols. Grand Rapids, 1976-1992
EvRT	*Evangelical Review of Theology*
EvQ	*Evangelical Quarterly*
EvT	*Evangelische Theologie*
FB	Forschung zur Bibel

FRLANT	Forschungen zur Religion und Literatur des Alten and Neuen Testaments
GDR	Gorgias Dissertations: Religion
GTJ	*Grace Theological Journal*
HTR	*Harvard Theological Review*
ICC	International Critical Commentary
IBS	*Irish Biblical Studies*
JATS	*Journal of the Adventist Theological Society*
JBL	*Journal of Biblical Literature*
JETS	*Journal of the Evangelical Theological Society*
JSNT	*Journal for the Study of the New Testament*
JSNTSup	Journal for the Study of the New Testament: Supplement Series
JSOTSup	Journal for the Study of the Old Testament: Supplement Series
KEK	Kritisch-exegetischer Kommentar über das Neue Testament (Meyer-Kommentar)
KSUM	Korean Sahmyook University Monographs: Doctoral Dissertation Series
LXX	*Septuaginta: Id est Vetus Testamentum graece iuxta LXX interpretes*. Edited by A. Rahlfs. Stuttgart, 1979
MNTS	McMaster New Testament Studies
MT	Masoretic Text
MTS	Marburger theologische Studien
NA^{27}	*Novum Testamentum Graece*. Edited by Barbara and Kurt Aland, Johannes Karavidopoulos, Carlo M. Martini, and Bruce M. Metzger. 27th rev. ed. Stuttgart, 1993
NAC	New American Commentary
Neot	*Neotestamentica*
NICNT	New International Commentary on the New Testament
NIDNTT	*New International Dictionary of New Testament Theology*. Edited by C. Brown. 4 vols. Grand Rapids, 1975–1985
NIDOTTE	*New International Dictionary of Old Testament Theology and Exegesis*. Edited by W. A. VanGemeren. 5 vols. Grand Rapids, 1997
NIGTC	New International Greek Testament Commentary
NovT	*Novum Testamentum*
NovTSup	Supplements to Novum Testamentum
NS	*New Scholasticism*
NT	New Testament
NTL	New Testament Library
NTM	New Testament Monographs
NTS	*New Testament Studies*

NTTS	New Testament Tools and Studies
NZSTR	*Neue Zeitschrift für systematische Theologie und Religionsphilosophie*
OT	Old Testament
OTNT	Ökumenischer Taschenbuchkommentar zum Neuen Testament
PRS	*Perspectives in Religious Studies*
SBL	Society of Biblical Literature
SBLDS	Society of Biblical Literature Dissertation Series
SBLSPS	Society of Biblical Literature Seminar Papers Series
SEAJT	*South East Asia Journal of Theology*
SHS	Scripture and Hermeneutics Series
SJT	*Scottish Journal of Theology*
SNT	Studien zum Neuen Testament
SNTSMS	Society for New Testament Studies Monograph Series
SPS	Sacra pagina Series
SupJSJ	Supplements to the Journal for the Study of Judaism
TynBul	*Tyndale Bulletin*
TCICD	*Three Central Issues in Contemporary Dispensationalism: A Comparison of Traditional and Progressive Views.* Edited by H. W. Bateman IV. Grand Rapids, 1999
TDNT	*Theological Dictionary of the New Testament.* Edited by G. Kittel and G. Friedrich. Translated by G. W. Bromiley. 10 vols. Grand Rapids, 1964–1976
TDOT	*Theological Dictionary of the Old Testament.* Edited by G. J. Botterweck, H. Ringgren, and Heinz-Josef Fabry. Translated by J. T. Willis et al. 15 vols. Grand Rapids, 1974–2006
TJ	*Trinity Journal*
TRu	*Theologische Rundschau*
TS	*Theological Studies*
TWOT	*Theological Workbook of the Old Testament.* Edited by R. L. Harris, G. L. Archer Jr. 2 vols. Chicago, 1980.
TZ	*Theologische Zeitschrift*
VF	*Verkündigung und Forschung*
WBC	Word Biblical Commentary
WMANT	Wissenschaftliche Monographien zum Alten und Neuen Testament
WUNT	Wissenschaftliche Untersuchungen zum Neuen Testament
ZAW	*Zeitschrift für die alttestamentliche Wissenschaft*
ZNW	*Zeitschrift für die neutestamentliche Wissenschaft*

Part One: Descriptive Use of Exodus in Hebrews

• CHAPTER ONE •

Introduction

After reading Hebrews, many students of the Bible would easily notice that *Auctor* is clearly one of the greatest Christian systematic theologians of the NT age.[1] They usually come to this conclusion by assessing how *Auctor* strategically activates citations (i.e., quotations and allusions) from the OT to support *his* theological argumentation in light of the Christ event.[2] This valuation focuses on *Auctor*'s rhetorical skills whereby he aptly articulates the Hebrew Scriptures to ensure that his first readers will value the new form of Christian liturgy or worship actualized by the death of Christ. In order for *Auctor to* teach this new heavenly liturgy of Christ to his audience, he must have already systematically intergrated the cultic notions of covenant, tabernacle, priests, and sacrifices both in Mosaic and Christological terms via faith whereby the reality in the heavenly homeland can be seen. This dimension of *Auctor*'s genius as theologian to interpret and *describe* the reality of God and His creation in relation to the heavenly liturgy of Christ has been well noted and studied extensively by scholars.

Need of This Study

However, this work argues that another dimension of *Auctor*'s greatness as theologian has gone unnoticed. That is, *Auctor*'s unparalleled scriptural knowledge to *prescribe* the correct interpretation about the reality of God and His creation. It is the correct interpretation because presumably, at least, the first readers of Hebrews were able to identify and share the same ontological

---

[1] "Auctor" means "originator, source, author." P. G. W. Glare, ed., *Oxford Latin Dictionary* (Clarendon Press, 1982), 205. Hurst is the originator of the term *Auctor* for the scholarship of Hebrews. L. D. Hurst, *The Epistle to the Hebrews: Its Background of Thought*, SNTSMS, ed. G. N. Stanton, vol. 65 (Cambridge: Cambridge University Press, 1990), 4.

[2] *Auctor* is masculine in light of διηγούμενον in Heb 11:32. See William L. Lane, *Hebrews 9–13*, WBC, David A. Hubbard and Glenn W. Barker, vol. 47B (Dallas, TX: Word, 1991), 381, n. b; contra, R. T. France, "The Writer of Hebrews as a Biblical Expositor," *TynBul* 47 (November 1996): 246, n. 4.

ground presupposed by *Auctor* to understand the reality of God and His creation in relation to the the heavenly liturgy of Christ properly.

Historically, previous studies in Hebrews reflect at best a descriptive analysis of the OT citations in Hebrews and have not yet moved toward a prescriptive one via ontological analysis of reason conceived by *Auctor*. When we interpret the Bible, we have already consciously or unconsciously presupposed a certain ontological ground to understand the biblical texts. The key feature of descriptive analysis is that scholars come to the Scriptures with a specific view of reality (ontology) and then posit the exegetical or apologetical meaning of the biblical texts as well as their understanding of *Auctor*'s biblical theology in light of the interpreted intertextual connection between the Old and New Testaments. In other words, various theological or pedagogical frameworks are used to interpret the reality of God so as to propose various descriptions of the biblical *theologies* of *Auctor*.

In order to highlight the difference between the descriptive and prescriptive analyses, let me use the following example in Hebrews to illustrate how descriptive analysis creates an intellectual impasse. In Heb 9:22-23, *Auctor* says:

> Indeed, under the law almost everything is purified with blood, and without the shedding of blood there is no forgiveness of sins. Thus it was necessary for the sketches of the heavenly things to be purified with these rites, but the heavenly things themselves need better sacrifices than these. (NRSV)

Table 1. Diversity of Theological Positions Reflected by the Various Interpretations of Heb 9:22-23

Scholars	What are those "heavenly things" needing to be purified?	How should one understand the reality of the heavenly sanctuary?
Harold W. Attridge	Human conscience, mind, and heart	Metaphorical (immaterial) sanctuary
F. F. Bruce	Human defiled conscience	Presence of God in heaven
Peter T. O'Brien	Consciences of God's people	Metaphorical (immaterial) sanctuary
Ceslas Spicq	"without sense"	Cannot be understood
Hugh Montefiore	"unhappy comparison"	Cannot be understood
Alberto Treiyer	Heavenly sanctuary and its content	Spatiotemporal sanctuary
Kevin Conner	Heavenly sanctuary and its content	Spatiotemporal sanctuary

From Heb 9:22-23, scholars have raised two related and important questions: (1) what are those "heavenly things" needing to be purified? ; (2) how should one understand the reality of the heavenly sanctuary? Table 1 summarizes the answers to the questions from seven scholars who are selected to illustrate the diversity of theological positions reflected by various interpretations of Heb 9:22-23.[3] This theological diversity is a crisis of faith because believers are unable to identify *the* theological position prescribed by *Auctor* for his first readers. In the final analysis, reason itself is unable to choose among these idiosyncratic *theologies* of Hebrews suggested by scholars.

Though many would readily accept the interpretive diversity of Heb 9:22-23 as normal in this postmodern world where people are so accustomed to the notion that the absolute truth or theology does not exist, I agree with Martin and Edward Farley calling this intellectual phenomenon *the* crisis of faith. From the perspective of Christian education or pedagogy, Martin succinctly describes this crisis of faith in the context of ontology and epistemology as follows:

> Farley is right to say that the crisis of faith is primarily an intellectual one; however, I would prefer to narrow our focus by saying that the problematic of belief is fundamentally *epistemological: how can we know that our knowledge of God might be knowledge of something real?* If we are searching for epistemological validation for our belief in something real, then we are ultimately concerned that our knowledge is grounded ontologically in what Martin Heidegger called, being-itself. In order for Christian belief in God to make sense we need a way of understanding how our knowledge is connected to ontology and how ontology is connected to God. If we make the connections between epistemology and ontology, and between ontology and divinity, then we will be able to assert finally that in some way we can know the reality of God. I will argue in this monograph for a change in consciousness, an alteration in the conceptual structures of our mind, a new pair of spectacles if you will, so that we can see the realities before us. *Faith in God requires a rational framework that values the type of knowledge that religious knowledge is.* But this requires a different understanding of rationality.[4]

---

[3] These seven scholars are: Harold W. Attridge, *The Epistle to the Hebrews: A Commentary on the Epistle to the Hebrews*, Hermeneia, ed. Helmut Koester (Philadelphia: Fortress Press, 1989), 262; F. F. Bruce, *The Epistle to the Hebrews*, New International Commentary on the New Testament, ed. Gordon D. Fee (Grand Rapids: Wm. B. Eerdmans Publishing Co., 1990), 228-29; Peter T. O'Brien, *The Letter to the Hebrews*, Pillar New Testament Commentary, ed. D. A. Carson (Grand Rapids: Wm. B. Eerdmans Publishing Co., 2010), 337-38; Ceslas Spicq, *L'Épître aux Hébreux*, 3d ed., Etudes bibliques, ed. Th. Camelot, P. J. de Menasce, and V. Ducatillon, 2 vols. (Paris: J. Gabalda, 1952-1953), 2:226; Hugh Montefiore, *A Commentary on the Epistle to the Hebrews*, Harper's New Testament Commentaries (New York: Harper & Row, 1964; reprint, Peabody, MA: Hendrickson Publishers, 1987), 160; Alberto R. Treiyer, *The Day of Atonement and the Heavenly Judgment: From the Pentateuch to Revelation* (Siloam Springs, AR: Creation Enterprises International, 1992), 428; Kevin J. Conner, *The Book of Hebrews* (Vermont, VIC: KJC Publications, 2002), 333.

[4] Robert K. Martin, *The Incarnate Ground of Christian Faith: Towards a Christian Theological Epistemology for the Educational Ministry of the Church* (Lanham, MD: University Press of America, 1998), 10-11.

Imagine a rhetorical and pedagogical situation where even the first readers of Hebrews were uncertain of *Auctor*'s view of the reality of God, then how could *Auctor*'s audience identify and understand his theological teaching? Would a great theologian and effective orator like *Auctor*, who envisions the danger of apostasy among his audience, communicate his theological argument with such a state of indeterminacy?

It is obvious that the heart of Hebrews is Christology. If the answer to the foregoing question is affirmative, this means that there seems to be no definitive clue provided in Hebrews to direct *Auctor*'s intended audience to understand how he utilizes the cultic languages from the Hebrew Scriptures and the Christ event to construct his Christology in a proper ontological context. In other words, the intended audience is "lost" amidst the forest of various ontological perspectives cooked up by individual imagination. This scenario does not fit coherently into the vision and faith of those who uphold a high view of Scripture, including the Book of Hebrews: that is, the Scriptures are the inspired and authoritative revelation from God to guide lost humanity into the salvation of Christ and His kindgom.

If our answer is negative, there should be some conspicuous textual signposts which could be recognized immediately by the first recipients of Hebrews, yet these ontological clues are easily overlooked by subsequent readers who are "possessed" by their contemporaneous reason(s) and traditions. This scenario seems to provide a case for Paul to exhort believers "not be conformed to this world, but be transformed by the renewing of your mind, that you may prove what the will of God is, that which is good and acceptable and perfect" (Rom 12:2, NASV). Since mind and reason are inseparable, the best way to renew our mind seems to be a criticism of theological reason and this is the key feature of prescriptive analysis.

Contribution of This Study

Hebrews 9:22-23 is chosen as the illustrative text because it clearly reveals *Auctor*'s use of analogy of being (*analogia entis*) or logic to explain Jesus' priestly ministry in heaven. Indeed, *Auctor* has used *analogia entis* to construct Christology in light of his interpretive relationship between the Old and New Covenant systems of worship which involves the comparsion of two sanctuaries, two priesthoods, and their related sacrifices. Scholars generally recognize the existence of such an analogy in Hebrews and the complexity of how to understand *Auctor*'s religious language of analogy ontologically. However, in my knowledge, nobody has ever conducted a criticism of *Auctor*'s use of analogy of being and logic via prescriptive analysis of his use of Exodus.

A complete analysis of how *Auctor* utilizes Exodus to construct his Christology necessitates that a prescriptive analysis be conducted for two biblical Books: Exodus and Hebrews. During the literature review stage for this research, I was very fortunate to discover that Canale already did a prescriptive analysis for Exodus in 1983.[5] Without the contribution of Canale's dissertation, the scope of the present work would be well beyond the limit of any monograph. What Canale has done in his groundbreaking dissertation on the prescriptive analysis of Exodus serves as a paradigmatic model for the present work.

Though the present work is the first study focusing on the prescriptive analysis of Hebrews in the history of interpretation, this study cannot be done in isolation from descriptive analysis. Descriptive analysis is important because it is a text-oriented and rhetorical study whereas prescriptive analysis is a pedagogy-oriented and ontological study. Descriptive analysis articulates the meaning and significance of biblical texts *within* the logic of a certain theological precondition or tradition whereas prescriptive analysis examines the logic of various theological preconditions critically to identify the correct ontological meaning and significance of the texts. When one is doing biblical exegesis within the logic of a certain theological system, he simply will not cast doubt against his own tradition and a criticism of theological reason is always beyond the scope of any descriptive analysis.

This work will progress from descriptive analysis to prescriptive analysis. The reason is twofold. First, descriptive analysis is text-oriented whereas prescriptive analysis focuses on reason or pedagogy. Hence, the starting point should be the biblical text, that is, the revelatory source. Second, text has a higher level of cognitive epistemological specificity than logic (reason). In other words, descriptive analysis is more determinative and specific to one's theological precondition in terms of cognitive specificity. Hence, prescriptive analysis should be preceded by descriptive analysis. It is probably these foregoing strengths of descriptive analysis that have rendered such an approach so attractive to biblical scholars that no one has ever done a prescriptive analysis for any biblical book until 1983.

Despite the significant contribution of Canale's 1983 dissertation, I am very surprised to discover that scholarship in Hebrews has not yet moved toward a prescriptive one. I will validate this claim by checking the current state of relevant research about the study of Exodus in the NT.

Writing in 1957, Otto Piper said, "As far as I can ascertain, nobody has ever made a special study of Exodus in the New Testament."[6] Piper's observation is dated and is no longer entirely accurate. After 1957, some have focused on the study of Exodus in the Gospels, Acts, Pauline Epistles, and

---

[5] Fernando Luis Canale, *A Criticism of Theological Reason: Time and Timelessness as Primordial Presuppositions*, AUSDDS, vol. 10 (Berrien Springs, MI: Andrews University Press, 1987). This work in its unpublished dissertation form was completed in 1983.

[6] Otto A. Piper, "Unchanging Promises," *Interpretation* 2 (January 1957): 3.

Revelation.[7] However, to my knowledge, no one has yet attempted to isolate and thoroughly study the use of Exodus in Hebrews.[8]

On the other hand, several recent doctoral dissertations are considered significant and relevant enough to deserve a careful analysis because they have advanced the general knowledge about the use of Exodus in Hebrews in varying degrees.[9] Even so, these relevant works reflect, at best, a descriptive analysis of Hebrews and have not yet moved toward a prescriptive analysis.

---

[7] After Piper's work, there have been only two special studies of Exodus in the NT: by John Charles Kirby, "The Exodus in the New Testament" (S.T.M. thesis, McGill University, 1957); R. E. Nixon, *The Exodus in the New Testament* (London: Tyndale Press, 1963). Nevertheless, Nixon's and Kirby's analysis of Exodus in Hebrews accounts for only 3 pages (ibid., 25-27) and 18 pages (Kirby, "Exodus in NT," 156-73) respectively. This observation does not include dissertations focusing on Exodus in one or more NT Books. These dissertations are: Edward Craig Hobbs, "The Gospel of Mark and the Exodus" (Ph.D. diss., University of Chicago, 1958); George L. Balentine, "The Concept of the New Exodus in the Gospels" (Th.D. diss., Southern Baptist Theological Seminary, 1961); Jay Smith Casey, "Exodus Typology in the Book of Revelation" (Ph.D. diss., Southern Baptist Theological Seminary, 1981); Stephen Hre Kio, "Exodus as a Symbol of Liberation in the Book of the Apocalypse" (Ph.D. diss., Emory University, 1985); Rikki E. Watts, "The Influence of the Isaianic New Exodus on the Gospel of Mark" (Ph.D. diss., Cambridge University, 1990); William J. Webb, "New Covenant and Second Exodus/Return Theology as the Contextual Framework for 2 Corinthians 6:14-7:1" (Th.D. diss., Dallas Theological Seminary, 1990); Sylvia Christine Keesmaat-de Jong, "Paul's Use of the Exodus Tradition in Romans and Galatians" (Ph.D. diss., Worcester College, 1994); David Wei Chun Pao, "Acts and the Isaianic New Exodus" (Ph.D. diss., Harvard University, 1998).

Also, according to a recent work by Mills, under the topic of "exodus," there is only one entry out of the total of 1110 bibliographic references listed for biblical research in Hebrews. This is Watson E. Mills, *Hebrews*, Bibliographies for Biblical Research: New Testament Series, ed. Watson E. Mills, vol. 20 (Lewiston, NY: Mellen Biblical Press, 2001), 61. Mills only refers to Albert Vanhoye, "Longue marche ou accès tout proche? Le contexte biblique de Hébreux 3,7-4,11" *Bib* 49, no. 1 (1968): 9-26.

[8] Apart from some relevant doctoral dissertations listed later (infra, n. 9), the most relevant minor works (like Kirby's thesis and Nixon's book, supra, n. 7) are done by Oudersluys and Thiessen. Richard C. Oudersluys, "Exodus in the Letter to the Hebrews," in *Grace upon Grace: Essays in Honor of Lester J. Kuyper*, ed. James I. Cook (Grand Rapids: William B. Eerdmans Publishing Company, 1975), 147-51. Matthew Thiessen, "Hebrews and the End of the Exodus," *NovT* 49, no. 4 (2007): 353-69.

[9] They are Streeter Stanley Stuart Jr., "The Exodus Tradition in Late Jewish and Early Christian Literature: A General Survey of the Literature and a Particular Analysis of the Wisdom of Solomon, II Esdras and the Epistle to the Hebrews" (Ph.D. diss., Vanderbilt University, 1973); James E. Reynolds, "A Comparative Study of the Exodus Motif in the Epistle to the Hebrews" (Th.D. diss., Southwestern Baptist Theological Seminary, 1976); Martin Emmrich,

Summary

The goal of this work, then, is to unveil those textual and ontological signposts in Hebrews by studying *Auctor*'s use of Exodus via both descriptive and prescriptive analyses. After the discovery of these signposts, I will utilize them as the ontological benchmark of *Auctor*'s doctrinal system to decide which theological positions of scholars are ontologically consistent or inconsistent with *Auctor*'s system. It is not difficult to acknowledge that the correct interpretation of a particular passage in Hebrews must be ontologically consistent with *Auctor*'s theological system.

In summary, the thesis that will be defended here is that the state of indeterminacy created by descriptive analysis in Hebrews can only be overcome by a prescriptive analysis of *Auctor*'s pedagogy (reason) and the function of Exodus in the theology of Hebrews.

The conclusion of this work is likely to be that a proper understanding of how *Auctor* utilizes the canonical revelation from Exodus can provide readers with an epistemological lens from Exodus to identify the correct interpretation of Heb 9:22-23. As a result, the state of indeterminacy for Heb 9:22-23 is resolved and the crisis of faith is overcome. Since our ability to identify the correct interpretation of a particular passage necessitates the application of a certain ontological ground to make such judgment, we can also apply the same ground to resolve other areas of doctrinal indeterminacy such as the identification of the correct view concerning the relationship of the Old and New Covenants in Hebrews.

"Pneumatological Concepts in Hebrews" (Ph.D. diss., Westminister Theological Seminary, 2001); Russell E. Miller Jr., "The Doctrine of Rest in Hebrews 3-4 and Its Implications for Liberation Theology's Use of the Exodus" (Ph.D. diss., Bob Jones University, 2004); Kiwoong Son, "Sinai and Zion Symbolism and the Hermeneutics of Hebrews: Heb. 12:18-24 as an Interpretative Key to the Epistle" (Ph.D. diss., Brunel University, 2004); Gabriella Gelardini, "«Verhärtet eure Herzen nicht» Der Hebräer, eine Synagogenhomilie zu *Tischa be-Aw*" (Ph.D. diss., University of Basel, 2004).

• CHAPTER TWO •

Descriptive Analysis of Significant Exodus Citations and Cultic Vocabulary in Hebrews

Only some significant citations and cultic vocabulary that are drawn from Exodus by *Auctor* will be discussed here. The reason why they are important will be evident later. Citation from the OT in the NT is usually classified as either quotation or allusion. Though the number of quotations and allusions cited in Hebrews is debated, I adopt the assessment of NA[27] for the purpose of this study. NA[27] is chosen because it represents the scholarly consensus upon the use of OT in the NT. NA[27] indicates that two quotations and thirty-two allusions are drawn from Exodus by *Auctor*. Among these thirty-four citations, the most important quotation and allusion are Exod 25:40 (Heb 8:5) and Exod 3:14 (Heb 11:6) respectively.

The citations are examined within the argumentative context of Hebrews to show the rhetorical significance of Exodus in Hebrews. I **boldface and italicize exact parallels** between the LXX and Hebrews and <u>*cognate parallels or lexical parallels that differ morphologically*</u>. Other nonlexical but significant parallels will not be marked but will be discussed if necessary.

Starting Point

Since descriptive analysis is text-oriented, it points to Scripture as the starting point of this study. Grier writes:

> Every system has a self-referential starting point that cannot be validated by an authority. It must simply be accepted as self-referential. This starting point will have *metaphysical* implications as well as ethical implications.[1]

---

[1] James M. Grier Jr., "The Apologetical Value of the Self-Witness of Scripture," *GTJ* 1 (Spring 1980): 75, emphasis added.

Contrary to other philosophical and/or general literary studies, Canale rightly argue that the "starting point for the Christian interpretation of the God principle is Scripture."² When Scripture is acknowledged as the assumed source for epistemological access to the ontology of God, it is necessary to presuppose that the *Vorlage* (i.e., parent text or underlying text) for *Auctor* is the Septuagint (LXX). *Auctor* appears not to have utilized the Hebrew text or the Masoretic Text (MT) as his *Vorlage*.³

For the sake of this study, the LXX is the assumed *Vorlage* used by *Auctor* as his epistemological access to the ontology of God. The text of the Hebrew Bible is quoted from *Biblia hebraica stuttgartensia*, ed. K. Ellinger and W. Rudolph, 4th corrected ed. (Stuttgart: Deutsche Bibelgesellschaft, 1990). The English translations in this study are mine; the text of the LXX is, when available, quoted from the available Göttingen's Septuagint, and otherwise from *Septuaginta: Id est Vetus Testamentum graece iuxta LXX interpretes*, ed. Alfred Rahlfs (Stuttgart: Deutsche Bibelgesellschaft, 1979).⁴ Also, what follows in this book will quote Greek translations of the OT and follow the versification of the LXX with the corresponding bracketed reference to the MT.

Rhetorical Context of Hebrews

Hebrews represents first century Jewish-Hellenistic synagogue homily, which was called "a word of exhortation" (Heb 13:22; Acts 13:15).⁵ In other words,

---

² Fernando L. Canale, "Philosophical Foundations and the Biblical Sanctuary," *AUSS* 36 (Autumn 1998): 202.

³ See George H. Guthrie, "Hebrews' Use of the Old Testament: Recent Trends in Research," *CBR* 1 (April 2003): 276.

⁴ The Göttingen critical edition of the LXX has not yet been published for every OT book but Exodus is available from *Exodus*, ed. John William Wevers, Septuaginta: Vetus Testamentum Graecum, ed. auctoritate Academiae Scientiarum Gottingensis, vol. 2 (Göttingen: Vandenhoeck & Ruprecht, 1991).

⁵ McCullough observes that there "is considerable agreement that the book [Hebrews] is a homily" (J. C. McCullough, "Hebrews in Recent Scholarship [Part 2]," *IBS* 16 [July 1994]: 112). Thyen even proposes that Hebrews is the only fully preserved homily we have from the period. Hartwig Thyen, *Der Stil der jüdisch-hellenistischen Homilie*, FRLANT, ed. Rudolf Bultmann, vol. 65 (Göttingen: Vandenhoeck & Ruprecht, 1955), 106. Swetnam accepts Hebrews as a homily by summarizing Thyen's work (James Swetnam, "On the Literary Genre of the 'Epistle' to the Hebrews," *NovT* 11 [October 1969]: 261). Gelardini is a recent supporter of Thyen's position. Gabriella Gelardini, "Hebrews, an Ancient Synagogue Homily for *Tisha be-Av*: Its Function, Its Basis, Its Theological Interpretation," in *Hebrews: Contemporary Methods—New Insights*, ed. Gabriella Gelardini, BIS, ed. R. Alan Culpepper and Ellen van Wolde, vol. 75 (Leiden: Brill, 2005), 108.

Auctor intended his message to be heard when Hebrews was read during a Christian worship service of the Sabbath gathering.[6]

Descriptive analysis of biblical texts necessitates the use of a certain reading strategy. How should we choose the right strategy for Hebrews? Since our understanding of *Auctor*'s rhetoric and argument depends heavily on our view about the identity of *Auctor*'s intended audience, I will adopt what Rabinowitz calls audience-oriented criticism for Hebrews.[7] Audience-oriented criticism stands within the broad spectrum of rhetorical analysis.[8] The strength of rhetorical criticism or analysis is that it highlights the oral or aural appeal of the discourse of Hebrews. The purpose here is to identify *Auctor*'s audience, to understand the nature and purpose of audience-oriented analysis, and to glean the authorial reading in light of Christ as Yahweh.

Identity of *Auctor*'s Audience

The goal here is not to reconstruct a community behind *Auctor*'s text but to establish a reading strategy treating Hebrews as addressed to a *specific* Christian audience (the authorial audience) rather than to a *general* Christian audience. Writing in 1970, Harvey states that the identity of the audience of Hebrews was "by no means certain."[9]

This study proposes the tool of audience-oriented criticism because a knowledge of these worshipers and their social and historical context is critical for understanding the significance of *Auctor*'s message to them.[10] A profile of the original audience will be drawn from internal details of the text instead of

---

[6] Some defenders of this perspective are: Arthur Hayes Williams Jr., "An Early Christology: A Systematic and Exegetical Investigation of the Traditions Contained in Hebrews, and of the Implications Contained in Their Later Neglect" (Th.D. diss., Johannes Gutenberg University of Mainz, 1971), 64-65; Harald Tomesch, "Genre and Outline: The Key to the Literary Structure of Hebrews" (Th.D. diss., Concordia Seminary, St. Louis, 1996), 17; Gelardini, "Hebrews as Homily," 115-16.

[7] See Peter J. Rabinowitz, "Whirl without End: Audience-Oriented Criticism," in *Contemporary Literary Theory*, ed. G. Douglas Atkins and Laura Morrow (Amherst: University of Massachusetts Press, 1989), 85.

[8] See Susan R. Suleiman, "Introduction: Varieties of Audience-Oriented Criticism," in *The Reader in the Text: Essays on Audience and Interpretation*, ed. Susan R. Suleiman and Inge Crosman (Princeton, NJ: Princeton University Press, 1980), 6.

[9] A. E. Harvey, *The New English Bible: Companion to the New Testament* (Oxford: Oxford University Press, 1970), 686.

[10] Stine argues that *Auctor*'s audience was worshipers. Donald Medford Stine, "The Finality of the Christian Faith: A Study of the Unfolding Argument of the Epistle to the Hebrews, Chapters 1-7" (Th.D. diss., Princeton Theological Seminary, 1964), 187-88.

any preconceived hypothesis about the *Sitz im Leben* of Hebrews.[11] Commenting on the *Sitz im Leben*, Thurén writes:

> ... in most cases we do not know much about the original circumstances of the author or the audience—and even if we knew, it is not certain that the author shared our knowledge ... it is useful to search for the type of the situation in which the text appears to be aimed to function as appeal or argument, that is, its *rhetorical situation*. This can be discovered by searching not only for explicit but also for implicit material in the text.[12]

My exegesis will not depend upon any preconceived *Sitz im Leben* of Hebrews, but any insights into the *Sitz im Leben* of Hebrews which the examination of its content suggests will, of course, be brought out for the rhetorical analysis.

According to MacLeod, the work of E. M. Roth in 1836 is the catalyst that changes the scholarly perspective about the identity of *Auctor*'s audience.[13] Prior to Roth, most scholars generally held that the intended audience was Jewish Christians (believers). After 1836, more scholars argued that *Auctor*'s audience was Gentile Christians. Were the audience Jews or Gentiles?[14]

The title of the Book, "to the Hebrews," was probably not part of the original document but was added at a very early date since the title appears in P^{46} (dated around AD 200) and a writing of Clement of Alexandria (dated around AD 180).[15] Guthrie admits that "there is nothing in the Book which demands a Jewish destination."[16] He continues:

> While admitting that the title may not be authentic, we ought not to dismiss it too lightly since there is no evidence that the epistle bore any other address.[17]

---

[11] Lategan says: "The *Sitz-im-Leben*, the famous concept developed by form criticism, presupposed a reconstruction of the audience and of the situation of reception." Bernard C. Lategan, "Introduction: Coming to Grips with the Reader," *Semeia* 48 (1989): 4.

[12] Lauri Thurén, *Argument and Theology in 1 Peter: The Origins of Christian Paraenesis*, JSNTSup, ed. Stanley E. Porter et al., vol. 114 (Sheffield: Sheffield Academic Press, 1995), 32.

[13] David John MacLeod, "The Theology of the Epistle to the Hebrews: Introduction, Prolegomena, and Doctrinal Center" (Th.D. diss., Dallas Theological Seminary, 1987), 63-64. Harnack followed Roth and it is Harnack's thesis being cited by many scholars until today (Adolf Harnack, "Probabilia über die Adresse und den Verfasser des Hebräerbriefs," *ZNW* 1 [1900]: 19). Laansma follows Harnack (Jon C. Laansma, "Hebrews, Book of," in *DTIB*, 280).

[14] Synge believes that the warnings in Hebrews were written to non-Christian Jews who were "on the verge of Christianity." See Francis Charles Synge, *Hebrews and the Scriptures* (London: S.P.C.K., 1959), 48, 51. This position is very weak. See Buist M. Fanning, "A Theology of Hebrews," in *A Biblical Theology of the New Testament*, ed. Roy B. Zuck and Darrell L. Bock (Chicago: Moody Press, 1994), 410.

[15] MacLeod, "Theology of Hebrews," 63-64.

[16] Donald Guthrie, *New Testament Introduction*, 4th ed. (Downers Grove, IL: InterVarsity Press, 1990), 686.

[17] Ibid., 683.

The most obvious support for Jewish audience is the wide appeal made to the Old Testament and *Auctor*'s assumption that the OT is authoritative to his readers. Also, there is the reference to "Abraham's descendants" (Heb 2:16), the argument that Jesus is superior to Moses (Heb 3:1-19) and the emphasis on "Sabbath rest" (Heb 4:1-11) which would only appeal to Jews. This argues strongly for the view that Hebrews is best understood as written to a Jewish audience.[18]

From the internal evidence, the purpose of Hebrews seems to convince its readers of the sufficiency and superiority of Christ (Heb 9:14), the danger of drifting away from Christ (Heb 2:3) and to exhort them to remain faithful (Heb 3:6). This internal evidence fits the context of Jewish Christian readers well because the Jewish Christians were especially vulnerable to have doubts about Christ and to ponder returning to the familiar rituals of their past in Judaism since many had been persecuted by their own countrymen (2 Cor 11:24-25; Acts 8:1-3; 14:2-7; 18:12-13; 21:27-28). Hence, Guthrie maintains that even though "no dogmatic conclusion can be reached on the grounds of internal evidence, yet a definite balance in favor of a Jewish Christian destination must be admitted."[19]

I have argued why *Auctor*'s intended audience is Jewish believers. But how should one understand the nature of their faith in relation to the warning passages? There are five major views of the warning passages in the contemporary literature. The five views are (1) loss-of-salvation (Arminian); (2) means-of-salvation, (3) hypothetical loss-of-salvation, (4) loss-of-rewards, and (5) test-of-genuineness.[20] Recently, Thomas has critically evaluated the five approaches to the warning passages and defends the test-of-genuineness view in his dissertation.[21] Since I agree with Thomas' position, it is not necessary to delineate the major interpretations of the warning passages but to offer a brief exposition of the test-of-genuineness view here. Supporters of the test-of-genuineness view take Heb 6:4-5 and other warnings passages as depicting the experience of those who had been exposed to the gospel, who had been associated with a

---

[18] This is the thesis of Sanford and Morrison. See Carlisle Junior Sanford, "The Addressees of Hebrews" (Th.D. diss., Dallas Theological Seminary, 1962), 231; Michael Duane Morrison, "Rhetorical Function of the Covenant Motif in the Argument of Hebrews" (Ph.D. diss., Fuller Theological Seminary, 2006), 30.

[19] Guthrie, *New Testament Introduction*, 687.

[20] Caneday and Schreiner provide a very helpful overview for these views (excluding the hypothetical-loss-of-salvation view) in a comparative chart. Ardel B. Caneday and Thomas R. Schreiner, *The Race Set before Us: A Biblical Theology of Perseverance & Assurance* (Downers Grove, IL: InterVarsity Press, 2001), 45. For a somewhat different listing identified with specific names of scholars, see Scot McKnight, "The Warning Passages of Hebrews: A Formal Analysis and Theological Conclusions," *TJ* 13 (Spring 1992): 23-25.

[21] C. Adrian Thomas, *A Case for Mixed-Audience with Reference to the Warning Passages in the Book of Hebrews* (New York: Peter Lang, 2008), 69-96.

Christian assembly, and who had made a profession of faith, but who eventually rejected what they knew about Christ or professed to accept. This rejection of Christ indicates that those professed Jewish Christians who "fall away" (παραπεσόντας) in Heb 6:6 were unbelievers and would suffer the consequence of eternal condemnation. Thomas explains why the test-of-genuineness view fits the rhetorical context for mixed audience in Hebrews as follows:

> What this [warning] suggests is that the audience to which this "word of exhortation" (13:22) was addressed consists of a mixture of true and false believers. In this setting, then, the warnings can be given their full force without in any way threatening the security of the believers, since those who are in danger of absolute apostasy from the gospel are not genuine believers, but false professors.[22]

It is commonly charged that "the test-of-genuineness view makes the warnings against apostasy applicable only to the false professors in the community, since genuine believer cannot apostatize."[23] Verbrugge bolsters this charge by positing that Heb 6:4-6 does not depict "the individual Christian but upon the church as a corporate body, as a covenant community."[24] Verbrugge suggests the use of Isa 5:1-7 as the background to interpret Heb 6:7-8 which depicts land that is completely blessed or cursed. Verbrugge argues that the significance of the illustration in Heb 6:7-8 lies in its ability to explain why it is impossible to renew the people to repentance. In short, *Auctor*'s warnings are addressed to the community as a whole and he would hardly make a distinction between false and genuine believers. This certainly is possible but I do not think it outweighs the explanation for the impossibility of repentance stated earlier in Heb 6:6. That is, the people "are crucifying the Son of God all over again and subjecting him to public disgrace" and so they cannot be renewed to repentance.

Also, Verbrugge's argument depends heavily upon seeing *Auctor* as addressing a community only and not individuals in it. The idea of "community," as Verbrugge proposes, is certainly found in the Scriptures.[25] But,

---

[22] Ibid., 91.

[23] Ibid., 95.

[24] V. D. Verbrugge, "Towards a New Interpretation of Hebrews 6:4-6," *CTJ* 15 (April 1980): 72.

[25] Powers argues for the corporate nature of salvation owing to the salvific perspective in the early church. See Daniel G. Powers, *Salvation through Participation: An Examination of the Notion of the Believers' Corporate Unity with Christ in Early Christian Soteriology*, CBET, ed. Tj. Baarda et al., vol. 29 (Leuven: Peeters, 2001), 17. Vanhoye also argues for the corporate nature of salvation in Hebrews in terms of believers' solidarity with Christ. See Albert Vanhoye, *Old Testament Priests and the New Priest: According to the New Testament*, trans. J. Bernard Orchard, Studies in Scripture, ed. Cyril Karam, Mary Clare Vincent, and Leonard Maluf (Petersham, MA: St. Bede's Publications, 1986), 104-105.

frequently in passages containing the communal concept the idea of the individual is also expressed. Fatal to Verbrugge's thesis, I believe, is the comparison of Heb 6:4–6 with Heb 3:12 and Heb 10:26 passages addressing individuals within the community in light of *Auctor*'s use of τινι "none of you" (Heb 3:12) and τις "anyone" (Heb 10:28). Also, the land imagery in Heb 6:7–8 is more suitable to describe individual believers and is incompatible with Verbrugge's concept of either corporate faithfulness with some apostates present or corporate apostasy with some faithful believers present. Hence, to see Heb 6:4–6 as referring only to the community is too limited. It is better to see both communal and individual aspects present in Hebrews. In summary, *Auctor* is addressing professed Jewish believers in general even though he is concerned that a specific group of those "believers" may be part of the non-elect (i.e., those who had professed faith in Christ but were in danger of leaving Christianity to lapse back into Judaism).[26]

Nature and Purpose of Audience-Oriented Criticism

After identifying the authorial audience, attention must be given to the nature and purpose of the audience-oriented analysis. The present study proposes that the authorial audience would have injected crucial elements related to their socio-cultural (i.e., Jewish) perspectives of reality (ontology) for interpreting *Auctor*'s message. The community orientation of *Auctor* and the audience of Hebrews toward the OT are undeniable, and one should try to engage in exegesis within their common tradition.

I will adhere more broadly to a historical-grammatical approach which appreciates the fundamental stability of the OT text within both its own canon and in its use in the NT texts. In using audience-oriented criticism, I will not discard rhetorical concerns but will make a shift in the focus of inquiry from the observed (i.e., *Auctor*) to the interaction between the observed and the observer (the authorial/ancient audience).[27]

Suleiman has argued that "any criticism that conceives of the text as a message to be decoded, and that seeks to study the means whereby authors attempt to communicate certain intended meanings or to produce certain intended effects, is both rhetorical and audience-oriented."[28] Audience-oriented criticism places more emphasis on the *shared* conventions of *Auctor* and authorial audience. In this approach, the design of *Auctor*'s rhetorical argument is based upon the assumptions that *Auctor* makes concerning his authorial audi-

---

[26] Shultz provides five purposes God had in the Atonement for the non-elect. Gary L. Shultz Jr., "God's Purposes in the Atonement for the Nonelect," *BSac* 165 (April-June 2008): 145-63.

[27] Suleiman, "Audience-Oriented Criticism," 4.

[28] Ibid., 10.

ence. No author can make any rhetorical decisions without relying on assumptions about the values, experiences, habits, and familiarity with interpretive conventions that the author's authorial audience will bring to the text.[29] Reading (by the audience) involves a process of decoding what has been encoded (by the author) within the text. The text is seen as a form of communication that includes the speaker, the hearer, and a message in which the author and the reader of a text are related to each other as the sender and the receiver of a message. Says Lefkovitz:

> To be understood, every act of communication requires someone who sends the message and someone who receives it, the message itself, knowledge of the context in which the message is conveyed (the same words mean different things in different contexts), knowledge of the code (the English language or the language of science, if the message is a medical prescription), and a method of contact (the words on the page, the telephone line).[30]

The focus of the audience-oriented criticism is in what the intended audience would do with it, since interpretive communities fulfill the process of decoding the cultural codes that have been encoded within the text.[31] Reading as the authorial audience, however, does recognize that *Auctor* allows certain constraints to be placed upon his choices in content, style, and rhetoric, based upon the assumptions made concerning his authorial audience (i.e., the interpretive community—the communal nature of reading the text).[32]

Motyer says, "It is essential that Hebrews actually mounts arguments that appeal to its readers."[33] Thus, to communicate successfully, *Auctor* must work within certain conventional constraints according to the expectations that his authorial audience possesses when they encounter a text. As a summary, Rabinowitz says:

> In short, authorial reading—in the sense of understanding the values of the authorial audience—has its own kind of validity, even if, in the end, actual readers share neither the experience nor the value presumed by the author.[34]

---

[29] Rabinowitz, *Before Reading*, 20-22.

[30] Lori H. Lefkovitz, "Creating the World: Structuralism and Semiotics," in *Contemporary Literary Theory*, ed. G. D. Atkins and L. Morrow (Amherst: University of Massachusetts Press, 1989), 65.

[31] Wolfgang Iser, *The Implied Reader: Patterns of Communication in Prose Fiction from Bunyan to Beckett* (Baltimore, MD: Johns Hopkins University Press, 1974), 284.

[32] Lategan, "Reader," 8.

[33] Stephen Motyer, "The Psalm Quotations of Hebrews 1: A Hermeneutic-Free Zone?" *TynBul* 50 (1999): 9.

[34] Rabinowitz, *Before Reading*, 36.

The next section will uncover this shared knowledge between *Auctor* and his *first* (authorial) readers: that is, the authorial reading in light of Christ as Yahweh.

Authorial Reading in Light of Christ as Yahweh

Since audience-oriented criticism examines both the text and the broader milieu in an effort to determine how an audience would understand the text, such an approach requires modern readers to seek to become part of the conversation between author and audience. Audience-oriented criticism recognizes that the writer and the authorial audience shared certain background knowledge (literary, historical, and cultural) that made communication possible. Both the content of information and the manner in which it was written were dependent upon such shared knowledge. Lincoln says:

> Clearly the Jewish Scriptures function in Hebrews as an authoritative and effective vehicle of communication for the writer's formulation of his word of exhortation.... Yet, for the writer, the more significant source of solidarity with his readers is, or should be, their common confession about Christ.[35]

In the same vein, Michel argues that "ὁμολογία of Hb. [Hebrews] is a firmly outlined, liturgically set tradition by which the community must abide."[36] What is the common confession about Christ by which the community must abide? I will argue that in Hebrews, the key shared knowledge is the confession of Christ as Yahweh. Hence, Witherington rightly says:

> What we are dealing with here [in Hebrews] is a group of people who had had profound religious experiences that they interpreted as encounters with the living God—that is, with Jesus the Christ.[37]

There are three reasons (theological, rhetorical, and covenantal) why the confession of Christ as Yahweh should be utilized as the universal premise whereby *Auctor* and his audience attempt to construct their Christology.

---

[35] Andrew T. Lincoln, "Hebrews and Biblical Theology," in *Out of Egypt: Biblical Theology and Biblical Interpretation*, ed. Craig Batholomew and Anthony Thiselton, SHS, ed. Craig G. Batholomew, vol. 5 (Grand Rapids: Zondervan Publishing House, 2004), 321.

[36] Otto Michel, "ὁμολογία," *TDNT*, 5:215.

[37] Ben Witherington III, "Jesus as the Alpha and Omega of New Testament Thought," in *Contours of Christology in the New Testament*, ed. Richard N. Longenecker, MNTS, ed. Stanley E. Porter (Grand Rapids: William B. Eerdmans Publishing Company, 2005), 44-45.

Theological Reason

From a theological perspective, the divine identity between Christ and Yahweh should be a universal premise presupposed by modern readers to read the Scriptures. In the NT, this presupposed Christology (i.e., the authorial reading of Christ as Yahweh) is very explicit in John's use of Isaiah 6:10 in John 12:39-41. When commenting on John 12:41, Brown says, "John supposes that it was the glory *of Jesus* that Isaiah saw."[38] Similarly, Bauckham demonstrates that *from the beginning* Christ shared the divine identity in all the crucial aspects: with regard to the divine "Name," in relation to all other things, and in relation to Israel.[39] Or, as Bauckham argues in his own terms:

> The earliest Christology was already the highest Christology. I call it a Christology of divine identity, proposing this as a way to move beyond the standard distinction between 'functional' and 'ontic' Christology, a distinction which does not correspond to early Jewish thinking about God and has therefore seriously distorted our understanding of New Testament Christology.[40]

Fee endorses Bauckham's paradigm shift for studies on the NT's Christology and says, "Writing particularly in response to the many recent studies by Hengel, Kim, Dunn, and others, who see a divine mediatorial figure in Second Temple Judaism as the way forward (Hengel) or backward (Dunn), Bauckham argues that these studies are working backwards by using a small amount of questionable data to the exclusion of the large amount of certain data."[41] Since Bauckham's study focuses on Christology, his methodology is especially relevant to Hebrews where *Auctor* arranges and coordinates the great *loci*, or themes, of Scripture with the doctrine of Christ as the center.[42]

It is important to read Hebrews in light of *Auctor's assumed* Christology, presumably shared with his audience. In this vein, Fee suggests the same strategy for reading the Pauline Epistles when he writes:

---

[38] Raymond E. Brown, *The Gospel according to John I-XII*, AB, ed. William Foxwell Albright and David Noel Freedman, vol. 29 (New York: Doubleday, 1966), 487.

[39] Richard Bauckham, *Jesus and the God of Israel: God Crucified and Other Studies on the New Testament's Christology of Divine Identity* (Grand Rapids: Eerdmans, 2008).

[40] Ibid., x.

[41] Gordon D. Fee, *Pauline Christology: An Exegetical-Theological Study* (Peabody, MA: Hendrickson Publishers, 2007), 14-15. Finding a model for *Auctor's* Christology in semi-divine intermediary figures in early Judaism is very common in the scholarship of Hebrews. McNicol adopts this model for his dissertation. See Allen James McNicol, "The Relationship of the Image of the Highest Angel to the High Priest Concept in Hebrews" (Ph.D. diss., Vanderbilt University, 1974), 188.

[42] David John MacLeod, "The Doctrinal Center of the Books of Hebrews," *BSac* 146 (July 1989): 291-300.

> Our christological task is to try to tease out what Paul himself understood *presuppositionally* about Christ, and to do so on the basis of his explicit and incidental references to Christ. . . . we are seldom reading Paul's *argued* Christology, but rather his *assumed* Christology, and in these letters a Christology that he also assumed on the part of his readers.[43]

For Hebrews, this precondition of *assumed* Christology shared by *Auctor* and his audience is the divine identity of Jesus Christ as Yahweh—God of Israel. Thus, says Kreeft:

> Religious Jews before Jesus had already learned from their own prophets . . . truths about God (though they did know that God had an eternal Son). . . . All Jesus did was to *show* what they already *knew*, to show it "up close and personal," to put God's face, "in their face." He did not show them a new God or teach a new concept of God or a new attribute of God, but He gave them a new *deed* of God, the greatest of all divine deeds, the Incarnation, and in it the redemption by His divine suffering, death, and resurrection.[44]

The greater the distance (i.e., geographical, cultural, and chronologically) between *Auctor* and his actual readers, the more of a challenge it is to read the text in light of this presupposed Christology possessed by the authorial (first) audience.

In short, the present study calls this interpretive strategy the authorial reading of Christ as Yahweh in Hebrews. This nomenclature serves to underscore Jewish ethnicity of *Auctor*'s readers and the confessional continuity with respect to the only God's personal name (Yahweh) revealed to Jews. Bauckham is the first to suggest the use of the theological precondition (the divine identity between Jesus and Yahweh) as a presupposition to read Scriptures and his method is practically identical to the present method.[45]

Rhetorical Reason

From a rhetorical perspective, it is reasonable to characterize the authorial audience by the theological precondition that reads Christ as Yahweh. This theological precondition is originated from the Christological conviction and

---

[43] See Fee, *Pauline Christology*, 3-4. Capes follows Fee. See David B Capes, "Pauline Exegesis and the Incarnate Christ," in *Israel's God and Rebecca's Children: Christology and Community in Early Judaism and Christianity, Essays in Honor of Larry W. Hurtado and Alan F. Segal*, ed. David B. Capes et al. (Waco, TX: Baylor University Press, 2007), 147.

[44] Peter Kreeft, *The Philosophy of Jesus* (South Bend, IN: St. Augustine's Press, 2007), 18-19.

[45] For example, see Bauckham's exegesis of 1 Cor 8:1-6. Richard Bauckham, "Biblical Theology and the Problems of Monotheism," in *Out of Egypt: Biblical Theology and Biblical Interpretation*, ed. Craig Batholomew and Anthony Thiselton, SHS, ed. Craig G. Batholomew, vol. 5 (Grand Rapids: Zondervan Publishing House, 2004), 222-23.

confession shared by both *Auctor* and his audience in the monotheistic Jewish community.[46] If one is to understand the text, one should read the text in light of the characteristics of the authorial audience.

One of the most central elements of such liturgical confession (ὁμολογία) is the divine identity of Christ as Yahweh. Though the content and nature of the audience's ὁμολογία (Heb 3:1; 4:14; 10:23) is debated, Mackie has cogently demonstrated that the content and nature of the confession is actually revealed in the phrase τῷ ὀνόματι αὐτοῦ (Heb 13:15).[47] Scholars generally acknowledge that αὐτοῦ refers to God's name but the difficulty for them is to determine the referent of ὄνομα.[48] Most scholars posit that the referent of ὄνομα is the new title υἱός given to Jesus in light of Heb 1:4-5.[49]

However, Vanhoye refutes this common view and identifies the new ὄνομα for Jesus as "Highpriest."[50] On the other hand, I agree with Gieschen and Bauckham because they both interpret the referent of ὄνομα as the proper name (Yahweh) given to Jesus in light of Heb 1:4 and Phil 2:9.[51] In light of

---

[46] Without interacting with Richard Bauckham, Ruffatto argues that "he [Moses] is allowed to share in God's divinity" (Kristine J. Ruffatto, "Polemics with Enochic Traditions in the *Exagoge* of Ezekiel the Tragedian," *Journal for the Study of the Pseudepigrapha* 15 [May 2006]: 197). Contra, Bauckham who offers a different interpretation for both Enoch and Moses traditions concerning deification. Bauckham argues that the inclusion of an exalted patriarch (Enoch or Moses) in the divine identity is only partial. Bauchham, *Jesus and the God of Israel*, 16; see also idem, "Biblical Theology," 218.

[47] Scott D. Mackie, "Confession of the Son of God in Hebrews," NTS 53 (January 2007): 125-26.

[48] See J. Harold Greenlee, *An Exegetical Summary of Hebrews* (Dallas, TX: Summer Institute of Linguistics, 1998), 597. Though Westcott does not specify what exactly the name of God in Heb 13:15 *Auctor* refers to, he argued that the name of God is revealed in Christ. Brooke Foss Westcott, *The Epistle to the Hebrews: The Greek Text with Notes and Essays*, 3rd ed. (London: Macmillan and Co., 1903), 446. On the other hand, Ellingworth shows that "Hebrews does not use ὄνομα of the name of Christ." Paul Ellingworth, *The Epistle to the Hebrews: A Commentary on the Greek Text*, NIGTC, ed. I. Howard Marshall and W. Ward Gasque (Grand Rapids: William B. Eerdmans Publishing Company, 1993), 721. Hence, though the term of ὄνομα is used four times in Hebrews (Heb 1:4; 2:12; 6:10; 13:15), this seems signals the impossibility to designate a specific name for God.

[49] Some of them are: J. W. Thompson, "The Structure and Purpose of the Catena in Heb 1:5-13," *CBQ* 38 (July 1976): 355; Mackie, "Confession," 126; Harald Hegermann, "Christologie im Hebräerbrief," in *Anfänge der Christologie: Festschrift für Ferdinand Hahn zum 65. Geburtstag*, ed. Cilliers Breytenbach and Henning Paulsen (Göttingen: Vandenhoeck & Ruprecht, 1991), 343; William R. G. Loader, *Sohn und Hoherpriester: Eine traditionsgeschichtliche Untersuchung zur Christologie des Hebräerbriefes*, WMANT, ed. Günther Bornkamm and Gerhard von Rad, vol. 53 (Neukirchen-Vluyn: Neukirchener Verlag, 1981), 251.

[50] Vanhoye, *New Priest*, 85.

[51] Richard Bauckham, "Monotheism and Christology in Hebrews 1," in *Early Jewish and Christian Monotheism*, ed. Loren T. Stuckenbruck and Wendy E. S. North, *Early Christianity in Context*, ed. John M. G. Barclay, JSNTSup, ed. Mark Goodacre, vol. 263 (London: T & T Clark International, 2004), 175; idem, *Jesus and the God of Israel*, 239; Charles A. Gieschen, "The Real

the liturgical context of Heb 1:4; 2:12; 13:15 and the identity of the authorial audience, it seems natural that *Auctor* refers to the Tetragrammaton as the proper name of God whom only Jews alone worship. Strictly speaking "Son" and "Highpriest" are not "proper names." Bauckham says:

> In our passage of Hebrews, the Son is the one who inherits the name from his Father, not what he inherits. What he inherits must be something that belongs to his Father, whereas 'Son' is uniquely the Son's title.[52]

Moreover, since the content and nature of the confession (profession) is revealed in the phrase τῷ ὀνόματι αὐτοῦ (Heb 13:15) and the referent of ὄνομα is the Tetragrammaton, it is not difficult to conclude that such liturgical confession (ὁμολογία) is the divine identity of Christ as Yahweh.

The confession of Christ as Yahweh in Hebrews is an argument from silence but it is a powerful argument from silence for three reasons. First, the silence of Yahweh in Hebrews is understandable. According to Freedman and O'Connor, "in the period of the Second Temple the name [Yahweh] had come to be regarded as unspeakably holy and therefore unsuitable for use in public reading, although it continued to be used privately"[53] Second, by using the "divine passive," Grenz declares, "the name 'Yahweh' was actually present, even in its unspoken absence, in the New Testament."[54] Reinhartz explains this use of divine passive as follows: "For many characters . . . the absence of the proper name does not consign them to narrative oblivion but simply requires that the readers interact with, analyze, or construct the unnamed character on a basis other than the proper name."[55] Third, *Auctor* holds the perspective of high Christology—Jesus is God. As a matter of fact, when *Auctor* quotes Ps 44:6-7 (MT Ps 45:7-8), he uses the term θεός to refer Christ in Heb 1:8-9.

Since *Auctor* exhorts his audience to hold fast the confession (Heb 3:1; 4:14; 10:23), it is very likely that such profession about Christ must be of utmost significance to the faith of the community. Laub argues that the exhortation to hold fast to the confession is the "paraenetic center of gravity for the

---

Presence of the Son before Christ: Revisiting an Old Approach to Old Testament Christology," *CTQ* 68 (April 2004): 120.

[52] Bauckham, *Jesus and the God of Israel*, 239.

[53] D. N. Freedman and M. P. O'Connor, "יהוה," *TDOT*, 5:500.

[54] Stanley J. Grenz, *The Named God and the Question of Being: A Trinitarian Theo-Ontology* (Louisville, KY: Westminster John Knox Press, 2005), 260.

[55] Adele Reinhartz, *Why Ask My Name? Anonymity and Identity in Biblical Narrative* (New York: Oxford University Press, 1998), 188.

letter."[56] *Auctor* chooses not to use the Trinitarian confession even though he demonstrates the doctrine of the Trinity through the many quotations in the work. Says Hübner:

> In the quotations of the Epistle to the Hebrews the speaking God is quoted. But also the Son of God speaks (Heb 2:12-14; 10:5-7), and so does the Holy Spirit (Heb 3:7-11; 10:15-17). One could almost talk about God as revealing in the Trinity.[57]

It is not difficult to understand that either the confession of Christ as Yahweh or the Trinitarian confession indicates a complete break from Judaism to Christianity. Also, both confessional stances would distinguish Jews from pagans in the conflict with Hellenism and could function as a significant benchmark for distinguishing elect from non-elect Jewish Christians. Why would *Auctor* exhort his audience to hold fast to the confession of Christ as Yahweh instead of the Trinitarian confession? This may due to the identity of the authorial audience as Jewish believers who have a special covenantal relation with the God of Israel—Yahweh. As a matter of fact, Yahweh is the only proper name of God for Jews. Wyschogrod explains why there is only one proper name for the God of Israel as follows:

> The God of Israel is not just a Thou. *The God of Israel has a proper name.* There is no fact in Jewish theology more significant than this. And the tradition always understood the significance of this fact.[58]

In the judgment of Bauckham, "That YHWH the God of Israel is the only God and that he alone may be worshiped were at the heart of Jewish religious self-understanding in the late Second Temple period."[59] Since Yahweh is the one God's proper name revealed to Jews, by audience-oriented criticism, it is natural that *Auctor* would stress the confessional continuity between the Hebrew Scriptures and the Christ event by exhorting his audience to hold fast to the confession of Christ as Yahweh when the exalted Son has inherited the

---

[56] Franz Laub, *Bekenntnis und Auslegung: Die paränetische Funktion der Christologie im Hebräerbrief*, BU, ed. Jost Eckett and Josef Hainz, vol. 15 (Regensburg: Verlag Friedrich Pustet, 1980), 234.

[57] Hans Hübner, "New Testament Interpretation of the Old Testament," in *From the Beginnings to the Middle Ages (until 1300)*, ed. Chris Brekelmans, Menahem Haran, and Magne Sæbø, *Hebrew Bible / Old Testament: The History of Its Interpretation*, ed. Magne Sæbø, vol. 1, pt. 1, *Antiquity* (Göttingen: Vandenhoeck & Ruprecht, 1996), 364.

[58] Michael Wyschogrod, *The Body of Faith: God and the People of Israel*, 2nd ed. [1st published as *The Body of Faith: Judaism as Corporeal Election*. New York: Seabury Press, 1983] (Northvale, NJ: Jason Aronson, 1996), 91.

[59] Richard Bauckham, "The Throne of God and the Worship of Jesus," in *The Jewish Roots of Christological Monotheism: Papers from the St. Andrews Conference on the Historical Origins of the Worship of Jesus*, ed. Carey C. Newman, James R. Davila, and Gladys S. Lewis, SupJSJ, ed. John J. Collins, vol. 63 (Leiden: Brill, 1999), 43.

proper name from the Father (Heb 1:4). Seitz calls the inheritance of the proper name by Christ as a personal "transfer."[60] Capes argues that the transfer indicates "a 'mutation' took effect with regard to Jewish monotheism."[61] In the same vein, Fee writes:

> . . . these transfers of biblical languages from Yahweh to Christ are a part of what Paul does regularly. None of this argued *for*, as though some kind of christological innovation was a point Paul wanted to make. To the contrary they are used in such a way that Paul assumes them to be common knowledge between him and his readers.[62]

Moreover, the intended audience must have experienced a real temptation to draw away from such a profession. If the first readers are Jewish Christians, it is understandable why *Auctor* needs to urge them to hold fast the confession that Christ is Yahweh. For those non-elect, professing Jewish-Christians, the social pressure to withdraw from Christian worship is strong. To support this perspective, Skarsaune argues that "Jewish believers in Jesus were perceived as *apostates* [by their Jewish relatives and friends] in a way Gentile believers were not."[63]

As a result, the personal temptation to denounce the confession of Jesus as Yahweh is also very strong for a professed Christian who acknowledges exclusively one Jewish God—Yahweh.[64] If God is one (Deut 6:4), how can Jesus also be God? By exhorting his community to affirm Christ as Yahweh, *Auctor* calls his fellow Christians to fidelity and obedience and seeks to prepare them for suffering.

Covenantal Reason

Since the continuity-renewal model is the correct model to interpret the revelatory relation between the Old and New Covenant in Hebrews, this means there is a "confessional continuity" between the two Covenants—that is, the

---

[60] Christopher R. Seitz, *Figured out: Typology and Providence in Christian Scripture* (Louisville, KY: Westminster John Knox Press, 2001), 143.

[61] David B. Capes, "YHWH Texts and Monotheism in Paul's Christology," in *Early Jewish and Christian Monotheism*, ed. Loren T. Stuckenbruck and Wendy E. S. North, *Early Christianity in Context*, ed. John M. G. Barclay, JSNTSup, ed. Mark Goodacre, vol. 263 (London: T & T Clark International, 2004), 133.

[62] Fee, *Pauline Christology*, 24-25.

[63] Oskar Skarsaune, "Jewish Believers in Jesus in Antiquity-Problems of Definition, Method, and Sources," in *Jewish Believers in Jesus: The Early Centuries*, ed. Oskar Skarsaune and Reidar Hvalvik (Peabody, MA: Hendrickson Publishers, 2007), 7.

[64] See Michael Mach, "Concepts of Jewish Monotheism During the Hellenistic Period," in *The Jewish Roots of Christological Monotheism: Papers from the St. Andrews Conference on the Historical Origins of the Worship of Jesus*, ed. Carey C. Newman, James R. Davila, and Gladys S. Lewis, SupJSJ, ed. John J. Collins, vol. 63 (Leiden: Brill, 1999), 25.

same God has entered into a covenant relationship with His people.[65] The continuity-renewal model will be defended as the correct model in chapter seven. The continuity-renewal model posits that the New Covenant is the Old Covenant renewed by the power of God in order to achieve a renewed relationship between God and his people.

Just as the Old Covenant people recall and make contemporary the Exodus as they celebrate the Passover,[66] the New Covenant people remember and relive the sacrifice of Jesus Christ in the celebration of the Lord's Supper. Exodus traditions and motifs function as a unified Testament of confessional continuity between the old and new generations of God's people.

Due to the concerns of *Auctor* and the needs of his community, he gives priority in preserving the confessional continuity and reestablishing the worship of Yahweh in the Person of Christ—the Son of God. After the coming of Jesus Christ, for both the Old and New Covenant generations (Heb 11:39-40), there is only one central event (Heb 12:2), or actually a complex of events (Christ's incarnation, death, resurrection, and exaltation). This pivotal event assimilates the Exodus traditions (e.g., the Sinai Covenant) and motifs (e.g., apostasy and covenant renewal in the golden calf narrative) into itself, generating a new covenant theology and eschatology. Each successive generation that valued these biblical traditions would keep them alive by believing they were God's revelation to that generation.[67]

The biblical traditions would then continue to address the communities and would serve a normative function for them, not as a record of past history, but as a blueprint for knowing how to live in confessional continuity with God. Within this continuity of divine revelation, *Auctor* also reveals escalations and antitypes in light of the Christ events. In other words, *Auctor* updates the Exodus traditions and motifs in relation to the person and work of Christ to speak to the Hebrews about their own need.

In summary, the theological precondition of reading Christ as Yahweh should be explicitly utilized as the universal premise to deduce the Christology in Hebrews. Reading the text through the lens of the authorial audience is controlled and dictated by the shared presupposition(s) about both author and intended audience.[68] This type of reading requires that the actual (modern) audience participate in the conventional and rule-governed activity of

---

[65] For an excellent explanation of such confessional continuity in the context of Hebrews, see Lincoln, "Hebrews and Biblical Theology," 320.

[66] See Harold Sahlin, "The New Exodus of Salvation according to St. Paul," in *The Root of the Vine*, ed. Anton Fredrichsen (New York: Philosophical Library, 1953), 81.

[67] See Trevor Hart, "Tradition, Authority, and a Christian Approach to the Bible as Scripture," in *Between Two Horizons: Spanning New Testament Studies and Systematic Theology*, ed. Joel B. Green and Max Turner (Grand Rapids: William B. Eerdmans Publishing Company, 2000), 192.

[68] Rabinowitz, *Before Reading*, 56.

reading that would have dictated how the intended audience understood and interpreted Hebrews. Hence, says Seitz:

> Sadly, it must be regarded as a particularly Christian temptation to underestimate the significance of God's giving to Jesus the "name which is above every name," because that name (YHWH) was not universally available but existed within the bosom of Israel and her faith.[69]

In any case, in light of the identity of *Auctor*'s audience and the rhetorical setting of Hebrews, it is indeed natural to understand that these Jewish Christians worshiped Jesus as Yahweh. By explicitly bringing out the transfer of the Tetragrammaton to Christ, Hebrews has thrown new light on the whole of Christology, especially when one examines *Auctor*'s use of Exodus. In this manner, the audience-oriented analysis highlights the continuity between the Old and New Covenant worship-systems and thereby gives a more precise and more profound understanding of the riches of Christ. The authorial reading of Christ as Yahweh invites modern readers to read Hebrews in light of the Mosaic-biblical ontology and epistemology that are shared by *Auctor* and the authorial audience. Though Canale's work is the first prescriptive study in Exodus,[70] this work appears to be the first prescriptive study in Hebrews to follow the reading strategy that understands Christ as Yahweh, and this strategy should yield a new synthesis and presentation of *Auctor*'s Christology.

Significance of Apostasy in Exodus 31:18–34:35 to Hebrews

The golden calf episode is significant in earliest Christianity for Stephen referred to it (Acts 7:39-41). The centrality of apostasy in Hebrews is an accepted fact.[71] Hence, before conducting a descriptive analysis significant Exodus citations and cultic vocabulary in Hebrews, I want to argue that the apostasy in Hebrews should be understood in light of the golden calf episode and so the motif of apostasy serves as a global contextual link between Exodus and Hebrews within the broader logic of *Auctor*'s argument. Put simply, Exod 31:18-34:35 is the controlling text to reveal his understanding of apostasy and

---

[69] Seitz, *Typology and Providence*, 217, n. 24.

[70] Fernando Luis Canale, *A Criticism of Theological Reason: Time and Timelessness as Primordial Presuppositions*, AUSDDS, vol. 10 (Berrien Springs, MI: Andrews University Press, 1987), 294, n. 2; 393.

[71] See G. R. Osborne, "A Classical Arminian View," in *Four Views on the Warning Passages in Hebrews*, ed. Herbert W. Bateman IV (Grand Rapids: Kregel Publications, 2007), 87. The centrality of apostasy in the structure of Hebrews is demonstrated by George E. Rice, "Apostasy as a Motif and Its Effect on the Structure of Hebrews," *AUSS* 23 (Spring 1985): 29-35.

covenant. The passage also provides a hermeneutical lens for interpreting the work and person of Yahweh as Christ in Hebrews. As a result, the text provides a framework for understanding what *Auctor*'s art of allusion generally entails. I demonstrate along the literary, theological, and hermeneutical significance of Exod 32:18-34:35 in relation to the authorial reading of Hebrews.

Literary Significance of Exodus 31:18-34:35 to Hebrews

Van Wijk-Bos says, "Torah is considered to be God's special and exclusive gift to the Jewish people and is thought of as the source of its life."[72] Scholars have already acknowledged the revelatory and historical significance of Exod 32-34 in the Book of Exodus and the rest of the Torah (i.e., the first five Books of Hebrews Scriptures).[73] To support this understanding, Sweeney states:

> Exodus 32-34 plays a key role in relation to the structure of the wilderness traditions in particular and that of the Pentateuch in general. . . . Exodus 32-34 constitutes a major transition in the Pentateuchal wilderness tradition in that the wilderness narratives focus on YHWH's aid in overcoming genuine needs of the people prior to the golden calf incident, but emphasize illegitimate rebellion against YHWH following the golden calf incident. . . . Exodus 32-34 appears at a crucial point in the general Pentateuchal narrative as well, immediately following YHWH's instructions concerning the building of the tabernacle in Exodus 25-31 and the compliance report in Exodus 35-40 which establishes the tabernacle as the holy center for YHWH's presence in the midst of the people.[74]

Gelardini has demonstrated the presence of an intertextual link between Exod 31:18-34:35 and Hebrews.[75] From a literary perspective, Young-Jae Lee shows that the unit Exod 31.18-34.35 is the center of the center of the Penta-

---

[72] Johanna W. H. van Wijk-Bos, *Making Wise the Simple: The Torah in Christian Faith and Practice* (Grand Rapids: William B. Eerdmans Publishing, 2005), 6.

[73] See Marc Vervenne, "Current Tendencies and Developments in the Study of the Book of Exodus," in *Studies in the Book of Exodus: Redaction, Reception, Interpretation*, ed. Marc Vervenne, BETL, vol. 126 (Leuven: Leuven University Press, 1996), 26, n. 20. The focus of the intertextuality is often within the Hebrew Bible. For example, van Seters and McKenzie have examined the narrative of the golden calf in connection with other part of the Hebrew Bible. John van Seters, *The Life of Moses: The Yahwist as Historian in Exodus-Numbers* (Louisville: Westminster/John Knox Press, 1994), 290-318; Tracy J. McKenzie, "An Analysis of the Innertextuality between Exodus 32:7-20 and Deuteronomy 9:12-21" (Ph.D. diss., Southeastern Baptist Theological Seminary, 2006), 1-2.

[74] Marvin A. Sweeney, "The Wilderness Traditions of the Pentateuch: A Reassessment of Their Function and Intent in Relation to Exodus 32-34," in *Society of Biblical Literature: 1989 Seminar Papers*, ed. David J. Lull, SBLSPS, ed. David J. Lull, no. 28 (Atlanta: Scholars Press, 1989), 292-93.

[75] See Gabriella Gelardini, "«Verhärtet eure Herzen nicht»: Der Hebräer, eine Synagogenhomilie zu *Tischa be-Aw*" (Ph.D. diss., University of Basel, 2004), 154-68.

teuch.[76] Lee's thesis is mutually reinforced by Timmer's thesis that Exod 31:18-34:35 has the Sabbath frame around the golden calf episode (Exod 31:12-17; 35:1-3).[77] The arguments of Lee and Timmer are especially relevant in Hebrews when the audience is understood to be Jewish Christians. If the golden calf episode is the center of the center of the Torah, it seems very likely that *Auctor*'s audience would understand the notion of apostasy and the person of God in light of Exod 31:18-34:35.

Theological Significance of Exodus 31:18-34:35 to Hebrews

Commenting on how to read Scripture as a coherent story, Bauckham says, "If Scripture does indeed tell the story of God's purpose for the world, then we should certainly expect to find unity and coherence in it."[78] In any case, Exodus 31:18-34:35 as the center of the center of Torah explains why the golden calf story is of central significance for the identification of the biblical-theological intertextuality between the biblical books within the canon. To support this understanding, McCann says, "Exodus 32:1-14, along with the larger narrative which it introduces (Exod. 32-34), is fundamental for understanding the Book of Exodus, the Pentateuch, the entire Old Testament, and indeed the New Testament and the whole history of God's dealing with humanity."[79]

Exodus 32-34 shows that the continuing existence of God's chosen people is because of divine grace (forgiveness) toward the unfaithful, grace paradoxically mediated by Moses.[80] It reveals that the grace of Yahweh cannot be destroyed by Israel's apostasy.[81] It emphasizes the faithful intercession and

---

[76] Young-Jae Lee, "A Study in the Composition of the Unit Exodus 31.18-34.35 as the Centre of the Centre of the Pentateuch: A Synchronic and Diachronic Reading of the Text" (Ph.D. diss., Aberdeen University, 2004).

[77] Daniel C. Timmer, "Creation, Tabernacle and Sabbath: The Function of the Sabbath Frame in Exodus 31:12-17; 35:1-3" (Ph.D. diss., Trinity Evangelical Divinity School, 2006), iv. This is published as *Creation, Tabernacle, and Sabbath: The Sabbath Frame of Exodus 31:12-17; 35:1-3 in Exegetical and Theological Perspective*, FRLANT, ed. Dietrick-Alex Koch et al. (Göttingen: Vandenhoeck & Ruprecht, 2009), 11. Lee and Timmer appear to be working independently since they do not interact with each other.

[78] Richard Bauckham, "Reading Scripture as a Coherent Story," in *The Art of Reading Scripture*, ed. Ellen F. Davis and Richard B. Hays (Grand Rapids: William B. Eerdmans Publishing Company, 2003), 38.

[79] J. Clinton McCann Jr., "Exodus 32:1-14," *Interpretation* 44 (July 1990): 277. Buerger reinforces McCann's thesis by expanding the background of Exodus 32-34 to the larger narrative of the wilderness narratives in Exodus-Numbers. See Martin A. Buerger, "Judgment and Grace in the Wilderness Narrative" (Ph.D. diss., Concordia Seminary, 1985), 270.

[80] See Hoyt C. Woodring Jr., "Grace under the Mosaic Covenant" (Th.D. diss., Dallas Theological Seminary, 1956), 160.

[81] See James Washington Watts, "The Meaning of Yahweh in Exodus" (Ph.D. diss., Southern Baptist Theological Seminary, 1933), 158.

centrality of Moses. Timmer says, "The fact that Yahweh responds by establishing the covenant indicates his granting of Moses' request."[82] The work Moses accomplished and the position in which he was placed anticipated the coming of a new Moses who would redeem and rule over God's covenant people.[83]

The golden calf would have represented a way of worshiping god (or God) on the people's terms, despite the fact that "Yahweh had made clear repeatedly that he would be received and worshipped only on *his* terms."[84] The people were not just asking for a deity, but were seeking continuity between their past experience and their present need for a deity's presence.[85] Moberly calls this "the paradigm for apostasy."[86] The people were practicing syncretism, for any type of syncretism (illegitimate worship of the one true God) is idolatry (Exod 20:2-6). The idolatry is a sin against God's holiness. Idolatry essentially is false worship or misrepresentation of the one true God—Yahweh. Yahweh's expectation was that his people should be holy. When those Jewish believers already in the unique position of worshiping Jesus as Yahweh in the heavenly sanctuary (Heb 12:22-24) align themselves with those who crucified Jesus and exposed him to public shame, they effectively put Jesus Christ out of their own lives and hold Him up to the contempt of others.[87] Their worship under the Old Covenant system is illegitimate and idolatrous in light of their personal knowledge about Christ as Yahweh.[88]

---

[82] Timmer, *Creation*, 136.

[83] For a brief discussion of the centrality of Moses as the only active counterpart to Yahweh within the structural framework of Exod 32-34, see Scott J. Hafemann, *Paul, Moses, and the History of Israel: The Letter/Spirit Contrast and the Argument from Scripture in 2 Corinthians 3*, Paternoster Biblical Monographs, ed. I. Howard Marshall and Richard J. Bauckham (Waynesboro, GA: Paternoster, 2005), 225-26; Raik Heckl, "Die Religionsgeschichte als Schlüssel für die Literargeschichte: Eine neu gefasste Überlieferungskritik vorgestellt am Beispiel von Ex 32," *TZ* 63, no. 3 (2007): 208-209. For a detailed exposition of how *Auctor* presents Christ as the new Moses in Hebrews, see William Henry Marty, "The New Moses" (Th.D. diss., Dallas Theological Seminary, 1984), 223-66.

[84] John I. Durham, *Exodus*, WBC, ed. David A. Hubbard and Glenn W. Barker, vol. 3 (Waco, TX: Word Books, 1987), 422.

[85] R. W. L. Moberly, *At the Mountain of God: Story and Theology in Exodus 32-34*, JSOTSup, ed. David J. A. Clines, Philip R. Davies, and David M. Gunn, vol. 22 (Sheffield: JSOT Press, 1983), 47.

[86] Ibid., 46.

[87] Charles Edwin Carlston, "Eschatology and Repentance in the Epistle to the Hebrews," *JBL* (1959): 300.

[88] See David Rancier Darnell, "Rebellion, Rest, and the Word of God (An Exegetical Study of Hebrews 3:1-4:13)" (Ph.D. diss., Duke University, 1973), 193.

Hermeneutical Significance of Exodus 31:18-34:35 to Hebrews

Exodus 31:18-34:45 is hermeneutically significant because it reveals the portrait and character of the OT God.[89] Whereas Lee and Timmer affirm that Exod 31:18-34:35 is the center of the center of the Torah, Harmon sharpens the focus to show that Exod 34:6-7 functions as the climax of the golden calf episode.[90] Furthermore, Spieckermann argues that Exod 34:6-7 may be the theological center of the OT.[91] In other words, Exodus 34:6-7 is very likely the apex of divine self-revelation in the OT.[92]

Morberly says, "Exod. 32-34 stresses his [God's] searching grace."[93] Likewise, Pigott argues that God's grace is more prominent than his judgment and justice in Exod 34:6-7.[94] The historical tension between law and grace is laid bare for the first time by the initial breach of the Mosaic Covenant (Exod 32). The net reaction of the heinous depravity of Israel upon God was not to evoke the fiery manifestation of wrath but to call forth a further revelation of the divine grace upon God's people. The profound meaning and prominence of God's grace is central to Israel's cult and history. It is God's compassionate grace triumphing over his judgment upon apostasy that prevents God from bringing an end to Israel as God's chosen people. Hence, the divine forgiveness revealed in the golden calf episode provides the ultimate basis for the renewal and re-institution of the Mosaic (Old) Covenant.

In light of the confessional continuity between the OT people and *Auctor*'s readers, it seems reasonable to assume that the portrait of the OT God is in harmony with the God in Hebrews. This means three things relevant for the present study. First, it seems possible that *Auctor* utilizes Exod 31:18-34:35 as the paradigmatic backdrop and basis for formulating the relationship between the Old and New Covenants.[95] Hafemann explains this point:

---

[89] See Billy O. Smith, "The Reconciliation of the Moral Attributes of Yahweh as Revealed in Exodus 34:6-7" (Th.D. diss., New Orleans Baptist Theological Seminary, 1953), 7-8.

[90] Jerry R. Harmon, "Exodus 34:6-7: A Hermeneutical Key in the Open Theism Debate" (Ph.D. diss., Mid-America Baptist Theological Seminary, 2005), 135. This is published as *Exodus 34:6-7: A Hermeneutical Key in the Openness Debate*, Studies in Biblical Literature, ed. Hemchand Gossai (New York: Peter Lang, 2008).

[91] Hermann Spieckermann, "Barmherzig und gnädig ist der Herr . . . ," ZAW 102, no.1 (1990): 18.

[92] Smith, "Exodus 34:6-7," 1.

[93] R. W. L. Moberly, "Exodus, Book of," in *DTIB*, 215. Contra, Harmon sees symmetry between God's love and his justice. See Harmon, "Exodus 34:6-7," 178.

[94] Susan Marie Pigott, "'God of Compassion and Mercy': An Analysis of the Background, Use, and Theological Significance of Exodus 34:6-7" (Ph.D. diss., Southwestern Baptist Theological Seminary, 1995), 210.

[95] See Hafemann, *2 Corinthians 3*, 446.

Moses was called to declare the saving will of God to the people without the accompanying life-giving work of the Spirit. As a result, the necessity of the veil in Exod. 34:29-35 announced the need for the ultimate replacement of the Sinai covenant. What Jeremiah and Ezekiel declared concerning the "problem" of the old covenant (cf. 2 Cor. 3:6), Exod. 34:29 ff. already demonstrates (2 Cor. 3:7-11): although the covenant was renewed, Israel's hearts remained "stiff-necked," so that the covenant could not be kept (cf. Deut. 29:2-4). From its very beginning, therefore, the old covenant of the Law without the Spirit implicitly looked forward to the time when the Law would encounter a people whose hearts had been changed and empowered to keep God's covenant.[96]

Second, it seems natural to assume that Exod 31:18-34:35 serves as the controlling grid or lens through which *Auctor* views the portrait of Yahweh. Since the apostasy is tied to one's view of covenantal relationship between Yahweh and His people, it is likely that *Auctor* understands apostasy in light of Exod 31:18-34:35. This perspective of understanding the intertextual link between Exodus and Hebrews will be reinforced by the thesis demonstrated in chapter seven: that is, the revelatory relation between the Old and New Covenant is best interpreted according to the continuity-renewal model.

Finally, God will never forsake his people—Jewish believers (Heb 13:5).[97] Newing says:

Yahweh is the God who both judges and forgives who punishes and relents (Exo. 34.6-7). He is present with his people in spite of his holiness and their sinfulness. This paradox within the nature of God himself is the only way we can make sense of the unconditional presence and the conditionality of the Deuteronomic [Mosaic] covenant.

He continues, "Whatever happens Yahweh will never abandon his people. There is always hope for renewal."[98] If the irreversible apostasy (Heb 6:6) means a fall from grace resulting in eternal loss from which there is an impossibility of recovery, this eternal loss of covenantal relationship between God and his people cannot apply to God's people.[99] The eternal security of the believer rests upon the perfect sacrifice of Christ inasmuch as it rests upon the *character* of Yahweh.[100] It is the salvation that depends on "the finality of the

---

[96] Ibid., 441-42.

[97] Edward George Newing, "A Rhetorical and Theological Analysis of the Hexateuch," *SEAJT* 32, no. 2 (1981): 14.

[98] Ibid.

[99] This is the thesis of Woodring, "Mosaic Covenant," 110. Ha follows Woodring's perspective. See John Ha, *Genesis 15: A Theological Compendium of Pentateuchal History*, BZAW, ed. Otto Kaiser, vol. 181 (Berlin: Walter de Gruyter, 1989), 163.

[100] See James A. Kitchens, "The Death of Jesus in the Epistle to the Hebrews" (Th.D. diss., New Orleans Baptist Theological Seminary, 1964), 86.

sacrifice of Christ and the consequent hopelessness of one who knowingly rejects that sacrifice."[101] If the apostasy at any time is dire enough, it is reasonable for *Auctor* to believe that the covenant people are reduced to the faithful remnant (i.e., genuine believers)—only some individuals (τις) in his community depart from Christ in rebellion.[102] Therefore, the warnings in Hebrews are best interpreted from the grid of the test-of-genuineness purpose with the lens of a mixed-audience. *Auctor* speaks of the irreversible apostasy resulting in eternal loss of salvation for false professors of Christian faith only.

Auctor's Use of Exodus 25:40 in Hebrews 8:5

Hebrews 8:5 is a clear quotation of Exod 25:40.[103] The verbal agreement is unmistakable:

ὅρα ποιήσεις κατὰ τὸν τύπον τὸν <u>δεδειγμένον</u> σοι ἐν τῷ ὄρει
(Exod) = [וראה ועשה בתבניתם אשר־אתה מראה בהר]
ὅρα γάρ φησιν ποιήσεις πάντα κατὰ τὸν τύπον τὸν <u>δειχθέντα</u> σοι ἐν τῷ ὄρει (Heb).

Lane says, "With the addition of πάντα, Exod 25:40 was adapted into an exegetical principle, according to which all the features of the cult become clues to the heavenly liturgy accomplished by Christ."[104] By using Exod 25:40, *Auc-*

---

[101] Buist M. Fanning, "A Classical Reformed View," in *Four Views on the Warning Passages in Hebrews*, ed. Herbert W. Bateman IV (Grand Rapids: Kregel Publications, 2007), 184-85.

[102] *Auctor* seems to adopt a remnant perspective because he uses the pronoun τις repeatedly to refer some individuals among his community, who may depart from their faith in Christ (Heb 3:12, 13, 16, 17, 18; 4:1, 6, 7, 11; 10:25, 27, 28; 12:7, 15, 16; 13:2).

[103] Exodus 25:40 is recognized as a quotation in Hebrews by Leon Morris, "Hebrews," in *EBC*, vol. 12 (Grand Rapids: Zondervan Publishing House, 1981), 76; Philip Edgcumbe Hughes, *A Commentary on the Epistle to the Hebrews* (Grand Rapids: William B. Eerdmans Publishing Company, 1977), 293; Harold W. Attridge, *The Epistle to the Hebrews: A Commentary on the Epistle to the Hebrews*, ed. Helmut Koester, Hermeneia, ed. Helmut Koester et al. (Philadelphia: Fortress Press, 1989), 219; F. F. Bruce, *The Epistle to the Hebrews: Revised*, rev. ed., NICNT, ed. Gordon D. Fee (Grand Rapids: William B. Eerdmans Publishing Company, 1990), 184; William L. Lane, *Hebrews 9-13*, WBC, ed. David A. Hubbard and Glenn W. Barker, vol. 47B (Dallas, TX: Word, 1991), 244; Ellingworth, *Hebrews*, 407; Craig R. Koester, *Hebrews*, AB, ed. William Foxwell Albright and David Noel Freedman, vol. 36 (New York: Doubleday, 2001), 378; David A. deSilva, *Perseverance in Gratitude: A Social-Rhetorical Commentary on the Epistle "to the Hebrews"* (Grand Rapids: William B. Eerdmans Publishing Company, 2000), 282; Luke Timothy Johnson, *Hebrews: A Commentary*, NTL, ed. C. Clifton Black and John T. Carroll (Louisville, KY: Westminster John Knox Press, 2006), 200; Alan C. Mitchell, *Hebrews*, SPS, ed. Daniel J. Harrington, vol. 13 (Collegeville, MN: Liturgical Press, 2007), 162.

[104] Lane, *Hebrews 1-8*, 207. The same view is expressed by Friedrich Schröger, *Der Verfasser des Hebräerbriefes als Schriftausleger*, BU, ed. Otto Kuss, vol. 4 (Regensburg: Verlag Friedrich Pustet, 1968), 160, n.3.

tor reminds his community that there is something above and beyond the material tabernacle which God revealed to Moses.

Since God has never requested the building of a temple but a tabernacle-sanctuary (Exod 25:8-9; cf. 2 Sam 7:6), it is reasonable that *Auctor* chooses to focus only on the Mosaic tabernacle in relation to the heavenly tabernacle. The concept of the Mosaic tabernacle-sanctuary is central in the biblical cultus for it is, in the words of Canale, "a God-building-human-beings structure."[105]

Canale creates the term "God-building-human-beings" to denote the whole thing—the things or entities belong together and are put together by the "dash."[106] God-building-human-beings structure means: God, is the One who creates the building and dwells in the building, and relates to the human-beings who come to the building to relate to God. Commenting on this structure, Canale writes:

> This structure brings into view the inner connection that exists between sanctuary and philosophical foundations. The connection takes place through the ideas of God and human nature which are essentially involved in the notion of sanctuary.[107]

When the "dash" connects each individual entity together, God-building-human-beings structure points to one ontological relational reality because the reality of sacred entities exists in relations. All these parts or entities are parts of the overall relationship—it is God who relates to human beings through the building. Hence, Son argues that Exodus 25:40 "reveals the author's hermeneutical principle which provides the intellectual basis of both his selection of the OT texts and also his theological view with which he interprets the OT texts in Hebrews."[108]

In short, Exodus 25:40 is very significant because it serves as an explanatory, theological, and hermeneutical marker in Hebrews. Since everything which was associated with the earthly tabernacle was a dim representation of something greater, something heavenly, *Auctor* activates Exod 25:40 to call his community to center their hopes on the true tabernacle and the true High Priest in heaven.

---

[105] Canale, "Biblical Sanctuary," 184.
[106] Ibid.
[107] Ibid.
[108] Kiwoong Son, *Zion Symbolism in Hebrews: Hebrews 12:18-24 as a Hermeneutical Key to the Epistle*, Paternoster Biblical Monographs, ed. I. Howard Marshall et al. (Waynesboro, GA: Paternoster Press, 2005), 244.

Auctor's Use of Exodus 3:14 in Hebrews 11:6

Hebrews 11:6 contains a clear allusion to Exod 3:14.[109] NA[27] lists eight Exodus allusions in Heb 11 and Exod 3:14 is the first of these eight allusions. Exodus 3:14 is pivotal because it serves as the ontological signpost to direct readers toward a proper understanding of the divine identity and activity of God in biblical history. Canale says, "Throughout the history of Christian thinking, Exod 3:14-15 has been recognized as the *locus classicus* where the being of God is brought into language."[110] Similarly, Neyrey states:

> Were we pursuing Jewish expressions of this, the targums on Exod 3:14 provide convincing evidence that "I am who am [sic]" was popularly interpreted as referring to God's activity in the past, the present, and the future.[111]

The verbal connection between Hebrews and LXX Exodus is conspicuous:

εἶπεν ὁ θεὸς πρὸς Μωυσῆν ἐγώ εἰμι ὁ ὤν (Exod) =
τὸν προσερχόμενον τῷ θεῷ ὅτι ἔστιν (Heb).

Conceptual as well as contextual parallels exist between Exod 3:14-15 and Heb 11:6. In both contexts, the passages speak of God's personal identity and "ontic presence."[112] As a matter of fact, the LXX translates יהוה in Exod 3:15 as κύριος and *Auctor* refers to Jesus Christ by the same title throughout Hebrews—κύριος (Heb 2:3; 7:14; 8:2; 13:20). When the God of Israel reveals His name to Moses in Exod 3:14, Canale says:

> Through the meaning of the "sound-name" as a pointer beyond itself to the reality to which it is open, the name introduces the interpretation and understanding of both God and His Being.[113]

---

[109] Apart from the editors of NA[27], there are at least seven other scholars who recognize the allusive use of Exod 3:14 in Heb 11:6. These are Lane, *Hebrews 9-13*, 338; Ellingworth, *Hebrews*, 577; Wilfried Eisele, *Ein unerschütterliches Reich: Die mittelplatonische Umformung des Parusiegedankens im Hebräerbrief*, BZNW, ed. James D. G. Dunn et al., vol. 116 (Berlin: Walter de Gruyter, 2003), 405; Erich Grässer, *Der Glaube im Hebräerbrief*, MTS, ed. Werner Georg Kümmel and Hans Graß, vol. 2 (Marburg: N. G. Elwert, 1965), 133, n. 402; Donald A. Hagner, *Hebrews*, New International Biblical Commentary, ed. W. Ward Gasque (Peabody, MA: Hendrickson Publishers, 1990), 185; Victor C. Pfitzner, *Hebrews*, Chi Rho Commentary, ed. Everard Leske (Street Adelaide, South Australia: Lutheran Publishing House, 1979), 170; Richard D. Phillips, *Hebrews*, Reformed Expository Commentary, ed. Richard D. Phillips and Philip Graham Ryken (Phillipsburg, NJ: P&R Publishing, 2006), 418.

[110] Canale, "Biblical Sanctuary," 202.

[111] Jerome H. Neyrey, "'Without Beginning of Days or End of Life' (Hebrews 7:3): Topos for a True Deity," *CBQ* 53 (July 1991): 454, n. 48.

[112] Canale, *A Criticism of Theological Reason*, 354.

[113] Ibid., 342-43.

In other words, Canale argues that Exod 3:14 brings "to light the revelation of God's being in his historical presence."[114] Similarly, Seitz writes:

> In the case of Exodus 3:14, we are not learning something about God's substance or essence but something about a personal identity and history he is about to make good on at Sea and Sinai.[115]

In short, it is clear that *Auctor* emphasizes the ontic presence of the covenant God and his activity throughout ancient Jewish history in Heb 11.[116] In this way, then, the view of Esler about *Auctor* holds true:

> By retelling the story of Israel's past, he was able to say important things about who they were. The identity of the group is installed in the selves of individual members as social identity.[117]

The point of all this is that if *Auctor*'s intended audience is a mixed group of the elect and the non-elect (or professed) Jewish Christians, *Auctor*'s call for commitment should foster solidarity between those genuine believers within the community of faith.[118] Continuing then to summarize his argument from Heb 11:6, *Auctor* declares that the faith necessary for every genuine believer includes two elements of confession, which Westcott lines out: "(α) that God is, and (β) that He is morally active; in other words it is a Faith in the existence and in the moral government of God."[119] By the authorial reading of Hebrews, this confession effectively means that Christ is Yahweh.

Christ as Yahweh involves Himself existentially (Heb 13:8) and personally (morally) in the lives of believers. This view of God denies Greek or Philonic ontology. For example, Sterling notes that for Philo, "God was unnameable."[120] To support this understanding, Sterling goes on to say:

---

[114] Canale, "Biblical Sanctuary," 203.

[115] Seitz, *Typology and Providence*, 140.

[116] See Pamela Eisenbaum, "Heroes and History in Hebrews 11," in *Early Christian Interpretation of the Scriptures of Israel: Investigations and Proposals*, ed. Craig A. Evans and James A. Sanders, Studies in Scripture in Early Judaism and Christianity, ed. Craig A. Evans and James A. Sanders, vol. 5, JSNTSup, ed. Stanley E. Porter, vol. 148 (Sheffield: Sheffield Academic Press, 1997), 394.

[117] See Philip Francis Esler, "Collective Memory and Hebrews 11: Outlining a New Investigative Framework," in *Memory, Tradition, and Text: Uses of the Past in Early Christianity*, ed. Tom Thatcher and Alan Kirk, Society of Biblical Literature: Semeia Studies, ed. Gale A. Yee, no. 52 (Atlanta, GA: Society of Biblical Literature, 2005), 161-62.

[118] See Walter G. Übelacker, *Der Hebräerbrief als Appell: Untersuchungen zu Exordium, Narratio und Postscriptum (Hebr 1-2 und 13,22-25)*, ConBNT, vol. 21 (Stockholm: Almqvist and Wiksell International, 1989), 216.

[119] Westcott, *Hebrews*, 358.

[120] Gregory E. Sterling, "The First Theologian: The Originality of Philo of Alexandria," in *Renewing Tradition: Studies in Texts and Contexts in Honor of James W. Thompson*, ed. Thomas H.

If Philo acknowledged a name for God, he would by necessity include predication (e.g., the good God = God is good) which would entail plurality since it requires a relationship with something else (e.g., God is good with respect to something else [analogous sense: father vs. son]). Philo understood what was at stake. He therefore rejected any name because he rejected predication and by extension plurality with respect to God. . . .

. . . The only time that Philo wavers from this assertion is in *On Abraham* where he says that "Being" (ὁ ὤν) is God's "proper name" (κύριον ὄνομα) [Abr. 121].[121]

Philo may include "Being" (ὁ ὤν) as one of the names for God but his idea of "Being" as a name is not ontologically *personal* in the biblical sense. On the other hand, according to Exod 3:14 of the LXX, God reveals His name to Moses as "Being" (ὁ ὤν) personally. In other words, Philo believes in an impersonal God even though his *Vorlage* is the LXX. Siegert explains how Philo comes to this view of ontology from Exod 3:14 of LXX as follows:

Philo finds the true name of God in Exod 3:14 (LXX): ἐγώ εἰμι ὁ Ὤν. God "is" (*Opif.* 170), he is "the Being One" and "being" (τὸ ὄν) [neuter] at once. The fusion of LXX language with Platonic concepts become evident. Both qualifications, the masculine (= personal) [ὁ] one of the Bible and the neuter [τὸ] one of philosophy, occur with equal frequency. . . .

This does not mean that Philo's God is beyond gender: He is "male" in the sense of "active," "creative"; matter . . . is female and passive. Thus the whole system of cross-references between the world of ideas and material cosmos, which is the basis of Philo's allegorical interpretations, relies on naturalistic pre-conceptions of an extreme kind.[122]

Hence, *Auctor's* use of Exod 3:14 in the argumentative context of Hebrews demonstrates the presence of biblical (Mosaic) ontology rather than Greek ontology.[123]

Auctor's Use of Cultic Vocabulary from Exodus

If Exodus was an important source for *Auctor's* thought, then a comparative study of the cultic vocabularies of the two books should reveal significant

---

Olbricht, Mark W. Hamilton, and Jeffrey Peterson, Princeton Theological Monograph Series, ed. K. C. Hanson, vol. 65 (Eugene, OR: Pickwick Publications, 2007), 152.

[121] Ibid., 153.

[122] Folker Siegert, "Early Jewish Interpretation in a Hellenistic Style," in *From the Beginnings to the Middle Ages (until 1300)*, ed. Chris Brekelmans, Menahem Haran, and Magne Sæbø, *Hebrew Bible / Old Testament: The History of Its Interpretation*, ed. Magne Sæbø, vol. 1, pt. 1, Antiquity (Göttingen: Vandenhoeck & Ruprecht, 1996), 168.

[123] Dennis J. McCarthy, "Exod 3:14: History, Philosophy and Theology," *CBQ* 40 (July 1978): 318.

connections. If the vocabularies have only slight connections, the case for an intertextual relationship is severely compromised. The purpose of this section is to demonstrate the rhetorical significance of Exodus by establishing such intertextual link and confessional continuity in terms of significant cultic vocabulary shared by Exodus and Hebrews.

A comprehensive study of the cultic vocabularies of Exodus and Hebrews lies beyond the scope of this study. What is critical to support the thesis of this study is to show that key words in *Auctor*'s vocabulary can be discovered in Exodus and that they have close affinities in meaning. Words, like manuscripts in textual criticism, are to be weighed, not counted. It is not enough to have a large number of the same words used by both writers; the words themselves must be significant and also be used with a similar significance in order to establish an intertextual link and confessional continuity.

According to Fiorenza, the key cultic terms in the NT are temple, priest, and sacrifice.[124] This writer will build on Fiorenza's work by examining sanctuary, tabernacle, priest, and sacrifice, because there is no temple in Exodus and Hebrews. There are two steps: (1) an analysis of sanctuary and tabernacle in Exodus and their significance to Hebrews; (2) an analysis of priests and sacrifices in Exodus and their significance to Hebrews.

Auctor's Use of Sanctuary and Tabernacle from Exodus

Within the LXX Pentateuch, Exodus is the first book that mentions "sanctuary"—derived from ἁγίασμα (מִקְדָּשׁ) or τὸ ἅγιον (הַקֹּדֶשׁ).[125] Since the word "sanctuary" is derived from ἅγιος (קֹדֶשׁ), Procksch argues that it "is very closely linked with the cultic. Anything related to the cultus, whether God, man things, space or time, can be brought under the term קֹדֶשׁ."[126] It is important to note that the first occurrence of sanctuary (Exod 15:17) refers to "the heavenly sanctuary." Ninow acknowledges that מִקְדָּשׁ in Exod 15:17 can refer to the promised land or the earthly sanctuary (the tent of meeting) in the desert. But he argues that מִקְדָּשׁ in Exod 15:17 should refer to the heavenly sanctuary because מִקְדָּשׁ occurs in parallelism with מָכוֹן in only two passages: in Exod 15:17 and Dan 8:11, where these words appear in the context of the heavenly sanctuary.[127]

---

[124] Elisabeth S. Fiorenza, "Cultic Language in Qumran and in the NT," *CBQ* 38 (January 1976): 168.

[125] Exodus uses ἁγίασμα to refer sanctuary only twice (Exod 15:17; 25:8) whereas τὸ ἅγιον is used to refer sanctuary as a place at least 18 times (Exod 26:33, 34; 28:29, 30, 35, 43; 29:30, 31; 31:11; 35:19, 35; 36:1, 3, 4, 6; 39:1, 12, 18). The holy of holies is mentioned twice in Exodus (Exod 26:33, 34).

[126] Otto Procksch, "ἅγιος," in *TDNT*, 1:89.

[127] Friedbert Ninow, *Indicators of Typology within the Old Testament: The Exodus Motif*, Friedensauer Schriftenreihe, ed. Wolfgang Kabus et al., vol. 4 (Frankfurt am Main: Peter Lang,

Its second occurrence immediately points to the earthly sanctuary (מִשְׁכָּן) in the form of the tabernacle "σκηνή" (Exod 25:8-9).[128] It is in this passage that Yahweh requests the construction of the Israelite sanctuary. Then Yahweh commands Moses to construct the tabernacle according to the τύπος (תַּבְנִית) shown to him on the mountain (Exod 25:40). In this context, it seems reasonable to understand that תַּבְנִית is a miniature model of the heavenly sanctuary and so functions as a model for the construction of the earthly sanctuary.

In any case, the repeated mention of the fact that Moses built the tabernacle according to the pattern (τύπος) shown to him must be taken seriously.[129] Auctor seems to recognize this significance by linking the heavenly sanctuary "τῶν ἁγίων" with the true (heavenly) tabernacle (τῆς σκηνῆς τῆς ἀληθινῆς) in Heb 8:2.[130] Also, he immediately quotes Exod 25:40 (in Heb 8:5) after the first appearance of the heavenly sanctuary (Heb 8:2).[131] Hübner rightly asserts that Auctor actually intends to "honor" the Old Covenant cult with the citation (Exod 25:40) though the OT cult was only temporary for him (Heb 8:13).[132] He chooses the tabernacle as the locus of the cultic worship because it has the prestige of the divine origin behind it. No Jew of the day could fail to acknowledge the legitimacy of the tabernacle. It was, so to speak, a getting back to the first theological foundation for Auctor and his community.

Auctor's Use of Priests and Sacrifices from Exodus

Duke argues that the "priestly activities, symbolized in rituals involving sight, smell and sound, time, space, and status, taught the healthy fear of being confronted with the presence of the holy God."[133] According to Exodus, a priest "ἱερεύς" (כֹּהֵן) is consecrated to provide its cult when a tabernacle is found-

---

2001), 135-36. DeSouza's view is the same as Friedbert Ninow. See Elias Brasil deSouza, "The Heavenly Sanctuary/Temple Motif in the Hebrew Bible: Function and Relationship to the Earthly Counterparts" (Ph.D. diss., Andrews University, 2005), 148.

[128] The LXX translates both מִשְׁכָּן and אֹהֶל as σκηνή. See Ralph E. Hendrix, "מִשְׁכָּן and מוֹעֵד אֹהֶל: Etymology, Lexical Definitions, and Extra-Biblical Usage," AUSS 29 (Autumn 1991): 4.

[129] The word תַּבְנִית occurs 3 times in Exodus (Exod 25:9 [twice], 40).

[130] Σκηνή occurs 10 times in Hebrews to indicate four different things: (1) the earthly sanctuary or tabernacle (Heb 8:5; 9:2, 6, 8, 21; 13:10); (2) the holy of holies (Heb 9:3); (3) the heavenly sanctuary or tabernacle (Heb 8:2; 9:11); (4) the patriarch's tent (Heb 11:9).

[131] Though ἁγίασμα is not used in the NT, τὰ ἅγια (and its variants) occurs 10 times in the NT, all of them in Hebrews (Heb 8:2; 9:1, 2, 3, 8, 12, 24, 25; 10:19; 13:11). See Alwyn P. Salom, "Ta Hagia in the Epistle to the Hebrews," Issues in the Book of Hebrews, ed. Frank B. Holbrook, DRCS, vol. 4 (Silver Spring, MD: Biblical Research Institute, 1989), 219. I will demonstrate that "τῶν ἁγίων" should be translated as "the two holy places" in chapter seven.

[132] Hübner, "NT Interpretation of the OT," 365.

[133] R. K. Duke, "Priests, Priesthood," in DOTP, 654.

ed.¹³⁴ Vanhoye correctly proposes that the "role of the priest is to open to the people the possibility of communion with God and the communion with all humanity, since the one necessarily involves the other."¹³⁵ In order to meet this need of humanity, the priest must be able to usher people (sinners) to God who manifests his presence in the sanctuary. Thus, says Vanhoye:

> The *central element* is the favorable acceptance obtained before God. The priest is primarily the man of sanctuary.¹³⁶

Nevertheless, this priestly role has never been actually accomplished by the OT priesthood.¹³⁷ Says Schrenk:

> Levitical priesthood cannot really deal with sin. It does not set it aside, and therefore it does not bring fellowship with God or τελείωσις.¹³⁸

But Jesus Christ has accomplished the goal of perfection for believers. Hence, *Auctor* calls Jesus both great high priest "ἀρχιερέα μέγαν" (Heb 4:14) and great priest "ἱερέα μέγαν" (Heb 10:21).¹³⁹

In the sanctuary the priests performs cultic ceremonies, the most important of which is sacrifice. The goal here is to demonstrate that the sacrificial vocabulary of Exodus is important to *Auctor* from three perspectives—epistemological, canonical, and rhetorical.

From an epistemological perspective, Thiele has argued that the most important sources for understanding the concept of sacrifice in Pentateuch "are the Cultic Decalogue (Exod. 34), the Book of the Covenant (Exod. 20:22-23:33), Deut. 12-26."¹⁴⁰ The significance of Exod 34 is obvious because we have seen that Exod. 32-34 is the controlling revelation in Hebrews.

---

¹³⁴ The LXX translates כֹּהֵן as either ἱερεύς or ἱεράτευμα in Exodus: (1) ἱερεύς occurs nine times (Exod 2:16; 3:1; 18:1; 19:22, 24; 29:30; 35:19; 36:8; 37:19); (2) ἱεράτευμα occurs fourteen times and its variants) (Exod 19:6; 28:1, 3, 4, 41; 29:1, 44; 30:30; 31:10; 35:19; 39:41; 40:13, 15 [twice]).

¹³⁵ Vanhoye, *New Priest*, 31.

¹³⁶ Ibid., 30.

¹³⁷ Ibid., 219.

¹³⁸ Gottlob Schrenk, "ἀρχιερεύς," in *TDNT*, 3:278.

¹³⁹ *Auctor* uses ἱερεύς to refer four types of person: (1) Christ (Heb 8:4; 10:21); (2) Melchizedek (Heb 7:1, 3); (3) the Melchizedekian priest according to Psalm 109:4 [MT 110:4] (Heb 5:6; 7:15, 17, 21); (4) the Levitical priests (Heb 7:14, 20, 23, 9:6, 10:11). The LXX translates כֹּהֵן as ἀρχιερεύς only once in the Pentateuch. *Auctor* uses ἀρχιερεύς seventeen times: (1) ten times for Christ (Heb 2:17; 3:1; 4:14, 15; 5:5, 10; 6:20; 7:26; 8:1; 9:11); (2) seven times for Aaronic high priest (Heb 5:1; 7:27, 28; 8:3; 9:7, 25; 13:11).

¹⁴⁰ F. Thiele, "θύω," in *NIDNTT*, 3:418. Thiele's observation is made according to his analysis of the following six terms for sacrifices: (1) θύω "to sacrifice, slaughter" (e.g., Exod 8:4; 24:5; 1 Cor 5:7); (2) θυσία "sacrifice, offering, act of offering" (e.g., Exod 24:5; 29:34; Heb 5:1); (3) θυσιαστήριον "altar" (e.g., Exod 40:29; Heb 13:10); (4) προσφορά "offering, act of offering, the

The rhetorical significance of the Sinai Covenant is also unmistakable in light of *Auctor*'s repeated mention of the pivotal event: (1) a quotation (Exod 24:8 in Heb 9:20); (2) a paraphrase (Exod 24:3-8 in Heb 9:19). In Deut 12-26, Moses states the covenantal principle that if this relationship is to continue, Israel must be loyal to Yahweh and obey His commands. The passage is a review of the previous covenantal stipulations in the Sinai Covenant before the covenant renewal has taken place at Moab (Deut 27-30).[141] Hence, Deut 12-26 is significant because it is related to Exod 20-23.[142]

When we focus on the epistemological significance of Exodus, it is necessary to bear in mind that the issue of epistemology is especially important for cultic texts. Bergman, Lang, and Ringgren say:

> Sacrifice refuses to allow for a simple analysis, because the conservative ritual embodies differences of place and time in the understanding of sacrifice, and also because each specific occasion contributes to the meaning of the sacrifice.[143]

Hence, in any case, Thiele's observation is important because it basically points to Exodus as the *primary* epistemological source for interpreting cultic texts.[144] This suggests that it is reasonable to interpret *Auctor*'s understanding of cultic vocabulary mainly in light of the cultic texts in Exodus. However, such an interpretive approach would not be feasible if *Auctor* had not employed the same cultic terminology for depicting sacrifices. Hence, a comprehensive word search in both books is necessary to ascertain the extent of the shared sacrificial vocabulary.

There are three key terms for depicting sacrifices/offerings in Exodus: (1) חַטָּאת (sin offering brought for sin or impurity);[145] (2) עֹלָה (burnt offering);[146] (3)

---

offering that is brought" (e.g., Ps 39:7; Heb 10:5); (5) εἰδωλόθυτον "a thing sacrificed to idols" (e.g., 1 Cor 8:1); (6) ὁλοκαύτωμα "whole burnt offering" (e.g., Exod 10:25; 24:5; Heb 10:6).

[141] Merrill argues for Deut 29-30 as a covenant affirmation or renewal of Sinaitic Covenant. Eugene H. Merrill, *Deuteronomy*, NAC, ed. E. Ray Clendenen, vol. 4 (Nashville, TN: Broadman & Holman Publishers, 1994), 379.

[142] Cotton posits that the Exod 20-23, Lev 17-27 and Deut 12-26 are interrelated rhetorically and thematically in the Torah. Roger D. Cotton, "An Exegetical Analysis of the Torah Collection of the Pentateuch (Exodus 20-23; Leviticus 17-27; Deuteronomy 12-26): A Description of Their Expressions of Theological Ideas Based on an Analysis of Their Principles of Rhetorical and Thematic Organization" (Th.D. diss., Concordia Seminary, 1983).

[143] J. Bergman, B. Lang, and H. Ringgren, "זבח," in *TDOT*, 4:25.

[144] Though there are many ritual texts in the Pentateuch, Thiele's observation provides readers with an epistemological reason to focus on Exodus primarily. Thiele, "θύω," 3:417-38.

[145] Richard E. Averbeck, "חטאה," in *NIDOTTE*, 2:93. The LXX translates חטאה as ἁμαρτία (Exod 29:14).

[146] Richard E. Averbeck, "עלה," in *NIDOTTE*, 3:405. In the LXX, עלה is translated as three different words: (1) ὁλοκαύτωμα (Exod 24:5); (2) θυσία (Exod 10:25); (3) κάρπωμα (Exod 30:9).

זֶבַח (slaughter, slaughter for communion sacrifice).[147] Apart from the first word, these Hebrew words are translated by a variety of Greek terms in the LXX to depict various kinds of sacrifices and offerings. Despite the diversity of the Greek translations for these cultic terms, it is significant to note that *Auctor* actually employs three Greek words best reflecting their canonical and rhetorical significance in their original context.

In Hebrews, these three sacrificial words are ἁμαρτία (חַטָּאת), θυσία (עֹלָה or זֶבַח) and ὁλοκαύτωμα (עֹלָה).[148] *Auctor's* choice of these Greek terms points to the same epistemological source of cultic terminology in Exodus since they are linked to all three Hebrew words (חַטָּאת, עֹלָה, and זֶבַח) linguistically. These three Hebrew words encapsulate the key aspects of the sacrificial system in the Torah. They reflect various liturgical/sacrificial concepts normative for the community's worship in Israel.[149]

The word ἁμαρτία (חַטָּאת), according to Stählin et al., means "an individual act" or an "expression for the whole sinful nature of man."[150] Koch argues that the "root חטא belongs to the language of the cult and has its *Sitz im Leben* in specific ceremonies."[151] Says Averbeck:

> Canonically, the *first* reference to the sin offering is in regard to the consecration of the priests (Exod 29:14; cf. Lev 8:2, 14).[152]

Hence, *Auctor* seems to adopt this sense of sin-offering as a marker pointing to the priestly consecration in the LXX.[153] The purpose of this sin-offering is to

---

[147] Richard E. Averbeck, "זבח," in *NIDOTTE*, 1:1066. The LXX translates זֶבַח in four different ways: (1) ὁ θυσιάζων (Exod 22:19); (2) θῦμα (Exod 29:28); (3) θυσίασμα (Exod 23:18); (4) θυσία (Exod 18:12).

[148] Gustav Stählin et al., "ἁμαρτάνω," in *TDNT*, 1:295 Johannes Behm, "θύω," in *TDNT*, 3:181; Thiele, "θύω," 3:434.

[149] See Donald L. Williams, "The Israelite Cult and Christian Worship," in *The Use of the Old Testament in the New and Other Essays: Studies in Honor of William Franklin Stinespring*, ed. James M. Efird (Durham, NC: Duke University Press, 1972), 112.

[150] Stählin et al., "ἁμαρτάνω," 1:295-96.

[151] K. Koch, "חטא," in *TDOT*, 4:313.

[152] Averbeck, "חטאת," 2:93, emphasis added.

[153] Vanhoye defends this view. Vanhoye, *New Priest*, 133. For scholars defending the same view, see Olaf Moe, "Der Gedanke des allgemeinen Priestertums in Hebräerbrief," *TZ* 5 (March-June 1949): 167-68. The texts regulating the ceremonies of priestly consecration are Exod 29:22, 26, 27, 31, 34; Lev 7:37; 8:22, 26, 28, 29, 31, 33 (see Gerhard Delling, "τέλος," in *TDNT*, 8:80-81). The word ἁμαρτία and its variants occur twenty-five times in Hebrews (1:3; 2:17; 3:13; 4:15; 5:1, 3; 7:27; 8:12; 9:26 (twice); 10:2, 3, 4, 6, 8, 11, 12, 17, 18, 26; 11:25; 12:1, 4; 13:11). All these passages speak of ἁμαρτία as sin per se except the three verses—Hebrews 10:6, 8; 13:11. Hebrews 6-8 is a quotation from Psalm 39:7-9 where ἁμαρτία is translated from חַטָּאת twice to mean "sin-offering." *Auctor* quotes Psalm 39 in connection with the language of τελειόω (Heb 10:1, 14). The verb τελειόω carries the sense of "to consecrate" in the context of priestly consecration. See Daniel E. Buck, "The Rhetorical Arrangement and Func-

Descriptive Analysis

put someone in the position in which he can come, or stand, before God. This sin-offering is no longer necessary because Christ has consecrated (ἁγιάζω) believers by his blood (Heb 13:12).

In light of this cultic background, it seems safe to posit that Auctor uses τελειόω to communicate the fact that believers are brought to a state of priestly consecration (Heb 10:14). This signifies the consummation of the sacrificial sequence and consecration ceremony. This state of priestly consecration enables believers to have access to God to worship and serve Him. Johnsson says,

> Thus, "perfection" in Hebrews (in terms of the people of God) signifies *the benefits of the new cultus*. It does not indicate a growth in character or a goal for Christians to strive toward.[154]

The sacrificial system is a sacrament of forgiveness and deliverance. It is a ritual method ordained and provided by God, whereby sinners may be reconciled to him. Williams writes:

> The cult sustains, creates, and recreates a relationship—not magically, but sacramentally—a relationship initiated, sustained, and continually renewed by God himself.[155]

God himself has prescribed this veritable means of grace.[156] In order to achieve the state of priestly consecration, a cultic sacrifice is necessary to bring forth this transformation under the Old Covenant system. A cultic offering usually refers to any prescribed sacrifice under the constitution of the Old Covenant. However, Auctor also wants to focus on the role of the high priest as the person who makes the cultic offering in relation to atonement. Stählin et al. point out:

> In Hebrews the question of sin is treated from the twofold standpoint of the high-priestly ministry and sacrifice, and consequently of the institution set up under the *old covenant* to make atonement for sin.[157]

Despite the frequent use of ἁμαρτία in the LXX of Exodus and its significance in relation to one's understanding of τελειόω, Auctor employs ἁμαρτίας

---

tion of OT Citations in the Book of Hebrews: Uncovering Their Role in the Paraenetic Discourse of Access" (Ph.D. diss., Dallas Theological Seminary, 2002), 249. Similarly, according to Westcott, ἁμαρτία of Heb 13:11 speaks of OT "sin-offering" in connection with the animal blood carried into the inner compartment of the sanctuary by the high priest (see Westcott, *Hebrews*, 442).

[154] William G. Johnsson, "Defilement/Purification and Hebrews 9:23," *Issues in the Book of Hebrews*, ed. Frank B. Holbrook, DRCS, vol. 4 (Silver Spring, MD: Biblical Research Institute, 1989), 102.

[155] Williams, "Cult and Worship," 112.

[156] See K. Koch, "חטא," in *TDOT*, 4:313.

[157] Stählin et al., "ἁμαρτάνω," 1:313, emphasis added.

only once (Heb 13:11) to denote a cultic sacrifice in the context of the Old Covenant worship.¹⁵⁸ Even this use of ἁμαρτία as cultic sacrifice functions primarily to direct readers' attention toward the superior sanctifying work of Christ through his blood under the New Covenant (Heb 13:12). By suppressing the use of ἁμαρτία as cultic sacrifice, *Auctor* actually brings out the inadequacy of the first covenant and the complete adequacy of the new. In Hebrews, it is only the sacrifice of Christ that can bring believers to this perfect goal. The rare use of ἁμαρτία as a cultic sacrifice in Hebrews indicates that θυσία and ὁλοκαύτωμα are given preference for the same purpose by *Auctor*. A word search in Hebrews does indicate that *Auctor* employs primarily only two *Pentateuchal* Greek terms in the LXX to depict cultic sacrifice—θυσία and ὁλοκαύτωμα.¹⁵⁹ This is unusual because *Auctor* has chosen not to utilize at least four other similar terms for cultic sacrifice (in the sense of deriving from the same Hebrew terms— זֶבַח and עֹלָה).¹⁶⁰

What is the possible reason for preferring θυσία and ὁλοκαύτωμα as cultic sacrifice in Hebrews? I suggest that *Auctor*'s choice is primarily due to the fact that θυσία (זֶבַח) and ὁλοκαύτωμα (עֹלָה) are the inaugural sacrifices or offerings for the Old Covenant in Exod 24:3-8.¹⁶¹ From the canonical perspective, this particular act of the cultic offering (θυσία and ὁλοκαύτωμα) is a fulfillment of what Moses has told Pharaoh before the plague of darkness: will you also provide us with burnt offerings (ὁλοκαυτώματα) and sacrifices (θυσίας) that we may present them to Yahweh our God? (Exod 10:25). This is the pivotal event

---

¹⁵⁸ The use of ἁμαρτία in Heb 10:6, 8 also refers to a cultic sin-offering. But the passages are actually quoted from Ps 39 and they have already carried the sense of cultic sin-offering (חַטָּאָה) in its OT context. *Auctor* simply uses it in relation to Christ's incarnation (Heb 10:9).

¹⁵⁹ D. Kellermann, "עֹלָה," in *TDOT*, 11:111-12; Behm, "θύω," 3:181-82. According to Thiele, *Auctor* uses three Greek terms related to sacrifices/offering: (1) θυσία (Heb 5:1; 7:27; 8:3; 9:9, 23, 26; 10:1, 5, 8, 11, 12, 26; 11:4; 13:15, 16); (2) προσφορά (Heb 10:5, 8, 11, 14, 18); (3) ὁλοκαύτωμα (Heb 10:6, 8). Thiele, "θύω," 3:417. The word προσφορά is not found in LXX Pentateuch. Apart from the quotation of Ps 39:7-9 in Heb 10:5-8, *Auctor* only employs προσφορά to denote the sacrifice in connection with Christ's "self-offering." See Stählin et al., "ἁμαρτάνω," 1:314.

¹⁶⁰ The words חַטָּאָה, זֶבַח, and עֹלָה are the key terms used to denote a cultic offering in the Pentateuch. The word חַטָּאָה "sin-offering" (Exod 10:17; 29:14, 36; 30:10; 32:21) occurs less frequently than the other two words in Exodus: (1) זֶבַח "sacrifice/slaughter" (Exod 3:18; 5:3, 8, 17; 8:4, 21, 22, 23, 24, 25; 10:25; 12:27; 13:15; 18:12; 20:24; 22:19; 23:18; 24:5; 29:28; 32:8; 34:15, 25); (2) עֹלָה "burnt offering or sacrifice" (Exod 10:25; 18:12; 20:24, 26; 24:5; 29:18, 25, 42; 30:6, 28; 32:6, 30; 40:29). The LXX translates זֶבַח in four different ways: (1) ὁ θυσιάζων (Exod 22:19); (2) θῦμα (e.g., Exod 29:28; 34:15, 25); (3) θυσίασμα (Exod 23:18); (4) θυσία (Exod 12:27; 18:12; 24:5). On the other hand, עֹלָה is translated as three different words: (1) ὁλοκαύτωμα (Exod 10:25; 18:12; 20:24; 24:5; 29:18; 30:28; 32:6); (2) θυσία (Exod 10:25; 29:42); (3) κάρπωμα (Exod 30:9; 40:6, 10, 29).

¹⁶¹ See Herbert Wolf, "זֶבַח," *TWOT*, 1:234.

Descriptive Analysis

in the biblical history of sacrificial priesthood because there is no sacrificial priesthood prior to the institution of the Aaronic or Levitical priesthood on the basis of the Mosaic Covenant.

Also, θυσία and ὁλοκαύτωμα are offered together only twice as an act of corporate worship and yet with different functions: (1) to offer praise and thanksgiving for the redemption of Israel (Exod 18:10-12);[162] (2) to celebrate the enactment of the Old Covenant with Israel (Exod 24:3-8).[163] These two functions of the sacrifices are coherent with the argument of Hebrews in terms of corporate worship, covenant sacrifice, and ratification. This is not surprising because Heb 7-10 as a unit focuses on the relationship between the Old and New Covenant systems of worship.[164]

When the present analysis is compared with the theme of Exod 19-24, it is not difficult to find many thematic parallels in terms of cultic vocabulary for worship, especially covenant and sacrifices.[165] Throughout Hebrews, *Auctor* utilizes θυσία and ὁλοκαύτωμα as the paradigmatic cultic sacrifice for rendering corporate praise to God in light of his redemptive work, his promise and enactment of covenantal relationship to believers. *Auctor* even climatically "fuses" θυσία and ὁλοκαύτωμα with προσφορά (the key word denoting the sacrifice in connection with Christ's self-offering) in Heb 10:8 by the phrase "θυσίας καὶ προσφορὰς καὶ ὁλοκαυτώματα."[166] The lion's share of these three terms occurs in Heb 7-10.[167] In Hebrews, *Auctor* portrays the sacrificial worship operating the Old and New Covenant dispensations. Furthermore, it is obvious that the sanctuary/tabernacle is closely linked to covenant and sacri-

---

[162] The phrase ὁλοκαυτώματα καὶ θυσίας occurs only three times in the LXX Pentateuch (Exod 10:25; 18:12; Lev 23:37). Leviticus 23:37 speaks of the sacrifices or offerings required for the Day of Atonement and so suggests the redemptive nature of the sacrifices/offerings. Prior to the giving of the Sinai Covenant (Exod 19-24), Exodus 18:12 records Jethro's offering of ὁλοκαυτώματα καὶ θυσίας to praise God for His great redemptive work for the Israelites (Exod 18:10-11).

[163] Hilber argues that "Exodus 24 holds a prominent place for understanding worship." John W. Hilber, "Theology of Worship in Exodus 24," *JETS* 39 (June 1996): 177.

[164] For example, Vanhoye has proposed a structural outline for this unit (Heb 7-10) to highlight the theme of worship in relation to priesthood and covenant. Note that Vanhoye expounds the structure of Hebrews in six chapters, his full outline of Heb 7-10 must be derived from two structural outlines (Vanhoye, *New Priest*, 94, 176) and his two specific comments about his structural outlines: (1) the "'capital point' of his sermon" (8:1-2) (ibid., 173); (2) he distinguishes two levels of worship in his outline (ibid., 176) and clarifies his meaning—"earthly and figurative [level of worship] on one side (A) [8:3-6], it is heavenly and authentic [level of worship], and consequently definitive, on the other (A') [9:24-28]" (ibid., 177).

[165] Hilber, "Worship," 177.

[166] See Stählin et al., "ἁμαρτάνω," 1:314.

[167] That is 18 out of 22 occurrences (82%): (a) 13 out of 17 occurrences—θυσία (Heb 5:1; 7:27; 8:3; 9:9, 23, 26; 10:1, 5, 8, 11, 12, 26; 11:4; 13:15, 16) and ὁλοκαύτωμα (Heb 10:6, 8); (b) the word προσφορά occurs 5 times only in Heb 10 (Heb 10:5, 8, 11, 14, 18).

fices theologically and ritually. From this perspective, Vanhoye notes the cultic and explanatory significance of Exod 25:40 in Heb 8:5. He proposes that *Auctor* uses Exod 25:40 "to guarantee the validity of [the] Israelite cult, by affirming that the sanctuary set up by Moses corresponded to a model revealed by God himself."[168]

Indeed, Exodus 25:40 must be a significant cultic text for activating the whole sacrificial system in the Torah because there seems to be no other Pentateuchal cultic text quoted in Heb 7-10. This observation is based on the citation references listed in NA[27]. Hence, Vanhoye's observation is valid but he does not explain the rhetorical significance of how the text (Exod 25:40) serves as the "guarantee." In order to answer this question, one needs to understand how cultic texts communicate information to believers in relation to the ritual or sacramental activity during worship. Gane declares:

> A *religious ritual* is ritual that involves belief in a deity. The ancient Israelite sanctuary rituals . . . obviously belong to this type.[169]

He argues that even though "all ritual has some kind of meaning or it is not ritual,"[170] ritual actions "have no inherent meaning."[171] Also, ritual actions may convey concepts or information through symbolic activity but they "are essentially transfers of value rather than information."[172] Hence, it is the worshiper who values his or her religious ritual who will attach meaning to the cultic texts.[173] This dynamic of ritual worship can be understood as follows:

Figure 1. Dynamic of Ritual Worship

When each worshiper attaches meaning to cultic texts, these cultic texts become "ritualized" as the ritual texts for the purpose of worship expressed by the ritual/sacramental ceremonies or activities. Gorman says, "Because rituals and their texts were not universally valid expressions of religion, they could not provide access to Truth."[174] In other words, the choice of an appropriate

---

[168] Vanhoye, *New Priest*, 180.

[169] Roy E. Gane, *Cult and Character: Purification Offerings, Day of Atonement, and Theodicy* (Winona Lake, IN: Eisenbrauns, 2005), 16.

[170] Ibid., 7.

[171] Ibid., 6.

[172] Roy E. Gane, *Ritual Dynamic Structure*, GDR, vol. 14 (Piscataway, NJ: Gorgias Press, 2004), 67.

[173] See F. H. Gorman Jr., "Ritual Studies and Biblical Studies: Assessment of the Past; Prospects for the Future," *Semeia* 67 (1994): 21-22.

[174] Ibid., 20.

OT cultic text is crucial to the rhetorical argument of Hebrews since *Auctor* intends to present a new and authentic form of worship available through the death of Christ to the Jewish readers. Williams explains why the choice of cultic text is critical when one is dealing with the relationship between the ancient Israelite or Christian worship:

> If we are to take the Israelite cult seriously, then we are confronted with the demand to *reactivate* the purpose of re-presentation by historical recital, to view creedal affirmations not as tests of theological soundness, but as a means of existential identification with the past, as a means of bridging the time and space gap, as a means of re-creating the original event and existentially participating in those events which have accomplished our salvation. . . . The loss of historical identification undercuts the dynamism of the Christian faith; Israel's cultic pattern has pointed the way to a recovery of that historical involvement in Christian worship.[175]

By reactivating the pivotal cultic texts and using them as the ancient creedal affirmation (Exod 24:3-8, 25:40), *Auctor* can expect that his creative presentation of Christian worship in terms of the heavenly liturgy of Christ will be accepted and recognized universally by the *Auctor's* community.[176] However, the presence of these intertextual links and confessional continuities do not suggest that the sacraments of Christian worship (e.g., Eucharist, prayer, or praise) present themselves as ceremonies/rituals that have value in themselves. When Vanhoye comments on the value of Christian sacraments, he correctly writes:

> Their value comes solely from the existential offering of Christ, whose effective presence they serve only. Thus they gave the faithful the opportunity of adhering fully, with body and soul, to this offering and of allowing themselves to be transformed by it.[177]

From a rhetorical perspective, the pattern of θυσία and ὁλοκαύτωμα as corporate sacrifice in Exodus functions only as the backdrop to portray the New Covenant cultus in Hebrews.[178] Hence, Willi-Plein argues that the OT worship "revealed the limits and the imperfections of the earthly worship, which could not go straight to the divine realities."[179]

---

[175] Williams, "Cult and Worship," 118, emphasis added.

[176] Arland J. Hultgren, "Liturgy and Literature: The Liturgical Factor in Matthew's Literary and Communicative Art," in *Texts and Contexts: Biblical Texts in Their Textual and Situational Contexts*, ed. T. Fornberg and D. Hellholm (Oslo: Scandinavian University Press, 1995), 669.

[177] Vanhoye, *New Priest*, 229.

[178] See Ina Willi-Plein, "Some Remarks on Hebrews from the Viewpoint of Old Testament Exegesis," in *Hebrews: Contemporary Methods–New Insights*, ed. Gabriella Gelardini, BIS, ed. R. Alan Culpepper and Ellen van Wolde, vol. 75 (Leiden: Brill, 2005), 25.

[179] Ibid.

Since θυσία and ὁλοκαύτωμα belong to the worship under the Old Covenant,[180] this form of cultic offering must undergo the process of "transference."[181] This transference is effected through Christ's perfect offering. In other words, Christ's sacrifice has decisively shifted the "ritual meaning" of the Old Covenant cultus to the "language meaning" of the New Covenant cultus.[182] Says Gane:

> The difference between "language meaning" and "ritual meaning" is that in language, meaning is information, transferred through symbols or combinations thereof that *represent/refer to* certain referents . . . but in ritual, meaning involves interpretation of activity as *interacting with* certain inaccessible entities. In a formulaic prayer, language meaning occurs within a ritual framework. What makes such a prayer a ritual is not the fact that it is language, but the fact that it is formulaic and it interacts with an ordinarily inaccessible party on a cognitive task level.[183]

Hence, the New Covenant form of worship is no longer ritual.[184] The great chasm between the Holy God and sinners is practically and existentially bridged under a new form of worship.[185] This transference removes the ambiguity and subjectivity of those who interpret the cultic texts for the purpose of worship. These significant changes are expected because the New Covenant operates under a different order of priesthood. In sum, *Auctor* attaches real meaning to the New Covenant sacramental worship by depicting the perfect existential offering of Christ. This new form of worship will not consist in ritual sacrifices of the kind prescribed in the Old Testament. The New Covenant cultus becomes a sacramental worship corresponding to reality via the death of Christ.

Summary

I have demonstrated that the influence of Exodus upon *Auctor* is evident in light of his use of quotation, allusions, and cultic vocabulary. The most important allusion is Exod 3:14 (Heb 11:6) because it serves as the ontological marker to indicate the divine identity and activity of God in biblical history. The rhetorical analysis of this allusion in Heb 11:6 shows that *Auctor*'s ontology does not reflect Platonic or Philonic philosophy but is derived from Exodus.

---

[180] See Stählin et al., "ἁμαρτάνω," in *TDNT*, 1:313; Vanhoye, *New Priest*, 233.
[181] Fiorenza, "Cultic Language," 161.
[182] Gane, *Ritual Dynamic*, 67.
[183] Ibid., 67.
[184] Ibid., 66.
[185] See Edmund Leach, *Culture and Communication: The Logic by Which Symbols Are Connected*, Themes in the Social Sciences, ed. Jack Goody and Geoffrey Hawthorn (Cambridge: Cambridge University Press, 1976), 38-39. See also Williams, "Cult and Worship," 117.

Descriptive Analysis

The most important quotation is Exod 25:40 (Heb 8:5) for it serves as an explanatory, theological, and hermeneutical marker in Hebrews. Exodus 25:40 reveals *Auctor*'s ontology because it directs readers towards the first principles of metaphysics.[186] *Auctor* forcefully announces that the climax of his argument has now been reached when he reveals the cultic ministry of Christ in the heavenly Tabernacle (Heb 8:1–5).

A comprehensive word search and examination of the cultic vocabulary (tabernacle, sanctuary, priests, and sacrifices) within the context of Exodus and Hebrews has been provided for both books. A comparative analysis between the cultic terminology for Old and New Covenant worship reveals significant conceptual parallels and verbal links. The analysis shows that the inaugural corporate sacrificial worship in Exod 24:3-8 and the pattern of Mosaic tabernacle (Exod 25:40) serve as an objective and valid paradigmatic pattern of the ancient ritual worship in Hebrews. The identification of Exod 24:3-8 in Heb 9:19 as a paraphrase amplifies the significance of the Sinai Covenant as the possible epistemological source of cultic vocabulary. Exodus 24:3-8 and 25:40 provide a significant source for liturgical worship forms deemed normative for the ancient cult. *Auctor* strategically activates these ancient cultic texts to ensure that his Jewish readers will value the new form of Christian liturgy actualized by the death of Christ.

---

[186] Canale, "Biblical Sanctuary," 186.

Part Two: Prescriptive Use of Exodus in Hebrews

• CHAPTER THREE •

Presuppositions of a Prescriptive Analysis in Hebrews

Choosing an appropriate reading strategy is the key to any descriptive analysis of Hebrews. I have argued that audience-oriented criticism should be adopted to understand the descriptive or rhetorical function of Exodus in Hebrews in terms of *Auctor*'s significant citations and cultic vocabulary. The reasons discussed are theological, rhetorical, and covenantal. Now, we must move beyond the level of descriptive analysis to a prescriptive one. This means that we must explain why audience-oriented criticism is preferred from an ontological perspective.

Since prescriptive analysis involves a criticism of theological reason, the crucial question is: which structure of reason should we adopt for understanding Hebrews? The answer to this question provides the rationale for understanding why audience-oriented criticism is preferred ontologically for understanding *Auctor*'s use of citations and cultic vocabulary from Exodus. Here I will explain why the theo-onto-logical structure of reason is adopted as the methodological presupposition for the present work.

Theo-Onto-Logical Structure of Reason

In order to proceed with any intellectual enterprise, there are theological, philosophical, and methodological assumptions or presuppositions. Since these three aspects are inseparable for any biblical study, a discussion of methodological presupposition will suffice.[1] According to Erickson, the methodological presuppositions "pertain to the use of logic, inference, induction and deduction, and the like."[2] In light of the work done by Canale, I choose the "theo-onto-logia" (i.e., the theo-onto-logical structure of reason) as

---

[1] Canale illustrates how the three aspects are inseparable hermeneutically. Fernando L. Canale, "Deconstructing Evangelical Theology?" *AUSS* 44 (Spring 2006): 102-104.

[2] Millard J. Erickson, "Presuppositions of Non-Evangelical Hermeneutics," in *Hermeneutics, Inerrancy, and the Bible*, ed. Earl D. Radmacher and Robert D. Preus (Grand Rapids: Academie Books, 1984), 594.

the methodological presupposition for the present study.³ Canale argues that this methodological presupposition is a type of macro-hermeneutical principle encompassing one's assumption "about reality, including understanding about Being (general ontology), God (theology proper), human nature (anthropology), world (cosmology), and reality as a whole (metaphysics), and principles about human knowledge, including understanding about hermeneutics, revelation-inspiration, and theological method."⁴ That said, Erickson's perspective grants us a clear and proper understanding for beginning to use a prescriptive analysis:

> We are not, by the use of terms such as "presupposition" or "preunderstanding," suggesting that these hermeneutical methodologies assume the conclusions, i.e., the meaning of given passages, in advance of the actual work of attempting to interpret it. To do so would be quite unfair . . . Rather we contend that because these elements presupposed are inseparable from the method utilized, they inevitably *influence* the outcome. Thus, to some extent at least, the conclusion may be implicit within the methodology.⁵

In other words, exegesis of Scripture without presuppositions is impossible in actual practice but such presuppositions should not determine or control the outcome of the exegesis. The scriptural text contains truth which the skilled reader discerns and must extract more or less intact, all the while being careful not to impose upon it.⁶ Also, one should anticipate that the Scripture would correct his presupposition(s). Hence, the process of critical reading and exegesis remains essentially open even when one presupposes and employs the ontological and epistemological paradigm of the theo-onto-logical structure of reason during the process of criticism.

Comparison of Two Ontological Grounds

I will compare and contrast two major ontological presuppositions: "theo-onto-logia" and "onto-theo-logia." Both "theo-onto-logia" and "onto-theo-logia" are ontological terms used by philosophers and theologians to represent

---

³ Fernando Luis Canale, *A Criticism of Theological Reason: Time and Timelessness as Primordial Presuppositions*, AUSDDS, vol. 10 (Berrien Springs, MI: Andrews University Press, 1987). This is based on Canale's "Toward a Criticism of Theological Reason: Time and Timelessness as Primordial Presuppositions" (Ph.D. diss., Andrews University, 1983).
⁴ Canale, "Evangelical Theology," 104.
⁵ Erickson, "Non-Evangelical Hermeneutics," 594, emphasis added.
⁶ Rosalind M. Selby, *The Comical Doctrine: An Epistemology of New Testament Hermeneutics*, Paternoster Biblical Monographs, ed. I. Howard Marshall et al. (Waynesboro, GA: Paternoster, 2006), 4.

two different presuppositions that ground their construction of theology.[7] Both terms describe one's view of reality (*ontos*) in relation to his view of God (*theos*) and his methodology (*logia*). Commenting on *logia*, Canale says: "*Logia* as a constitutive element of theology is . . . known as reason."[8] I will explain how the theo-onto-logia serves as the ontological ground (presupposition) for the four types of methodology in relation to the alternative—the onto-theo-logia (see Table 2).

Table 2. Comparision of Two Ontological Presuppositions

Types of Methodology	ONTOLOGICAL PRESUPPOSITIONS (GROUNDS)	
	THEO-ONTO-LOGIA	ONTO-THEO-LOGIA
A: Audience-Oriented Criticism	*Possibility* of Using a Theological Norm (*theos*) for Reading Scripture	Priority of Using Natural Theology (*ontos*) for Reading Scripture (*theos*)
B: General Method of Inquiry	Priority of Scripture (*theos*) over Methodology (*logia*)	Priority of Natural Theology (*ontos*) over Methodology (*logia*)
C: Hermeneutical and Theological Approach	Priority of Scripture (*theos*) over Natural Theology (*ontos*)	Priority of Natural Theology (*ontos*) over Scripture (*theos*)
D: Intertextual Approach (Revelatory Sources for Intertextual Borrowing)	Autopistic Use of Revelatory Source = Scripture (Special Revelation)	Axiopistic Use of Revelatory Sources=Scriptures + Extra-biblical Writings + Natural Revelation
(Pedagogical Role of General Revelation as a Constitutive Element of Theology) ➡	General Revelation ≠ Natural Theology	(a) General Revelation = Natural Theology (b) Natural Theology = Philosophy

Since one's methodology of doing theology is tied to the types of reason he presupposes, I will discuss how various types of hermeneutical methodology construe reason differently for the construction of one's doctrinal system in chapter 8. Though both *logia* and *logos* mean "reason" as a constitutive element of theology, *logos* refers specifically to the Platonic or classical reason whereas *logia* can be used to indicate any types of reason.[9] The term onto-theo-logia means that the notion of reality or being (*ontos*) determines the concepts of God (*theos*) and the methodology (*logia*). The reality (*ontos*) in the context of onto-theo-logia is derived from natural theology and general revelation equals natural theology as in human philosophy. When commenting on the relation-

---

[7] For an excellent recent discussion about the meaning of the two ontological terms, see Stanley J. Grenz, *The Named God and the Question of Being: A Trinitarian Theo-Ontology* (Louisville, KY: Westminster John Knox Press, 2005), 90-130; Iain D. Thomson, *Heidegger on Ontotheology: Technology and the Politics of Education* (Cambridge: Cambridge University Press, 2005), 7-43; Ilia Delio, "Theology, Metaphysics, and the Centrality of Christ," TS 68 (June 2007): 266.

[8] Canale, *Theological Reason*, 1.

[9] Ibid., 88.

ship between natural theology and general revelation in the context of onto-theo-logia, Canale writes:

> Christian theology has traditionally identified general revelation as natural theology. However, general revelation is a revelatory act of God, while natural theology is a cognitive act of human beings. Natural theology is synonymous with human philosophy, and in Christian theology is the philosophical approach to the knowledge of God.[10]

In other words, the general revelation is given a higher revelatory priority in comparison to the Scripture and extra-biblical literature. It is impossible to posit a theological norm for reading the Scripture due to the priority or precondition of using natural theology for understanding the Scripture.

On the other hand, the term theo-onto-logia signifies that the concept of God (*theos*) determines or grounds the concepts of being or reality (*ontos*) and the methodology (*logia*). Since the concept of God in the context of the theo-onto-logia is derived only from the Scripture, it is possible to posit a specific theological and hermeneutical position (e.g., the premillennial dispensational hermeneutic) as a precondition to understanding the ultimate reality (*ontos*). Also, one can use a universal premise (e.g., Christ is Yahweh) as a theological precondition to read the Scripture whereas such precondition is impossible to operate under the rubric of onto-theo-logia.

There are two reasons why theo-onto-logia is better for this work. First, I will defend the thesis that *Auctor*'s ontology reflects the theo-onto-logia point of view by examining his philosophy of history and his reception of the history of the interpretive influence of Exod 3:14 in chapter 6. Second, by deriving the biblical ontology from Exod 3:14, Canale has already defended why theo-onto-logia is better than onto-theo-logia.[11] Hence, theo-onto-logia is better for Christian thinkers because it uses *biblical* "ontological insights as macro-hermeneutical presuppositions from which to build their theologies."[12]

Canale argues that the theo-onto-logia avoids doing theology "from the hermeneutical basis of Greek ontology (*ontos*) that defined the meaning of God's being (*theos*), and from it the interpretation of Christian doctrines as *logia*."[13] In other words, the theological criticism of theological reason, free from extra-theological philosophical conditioning, is possible. In his dissertation, Canale also demonstrates the significance of Exod 3:14 for biblical ontology and metaphysics. As a result, Canale's dissertation brings a significant paradigm shift in NT studies. To support this perspective, McKnight writes:

---

[10] Fernando L. Canale, *The Cognitive Principle of Christian Theology* (Berrien Springs, MI: Andrews University Lithotech, 2005), 39.
[11] Canale, *Theological Reason*, 285-387.
[12] Canale, "Evangelical Theology," 108.
[13] Ibid.

New Testament interpretation today is influenced decisively by different presuppositions concerning what is real (ontology), how the real is known (epistemology), and the relationship between the two.[14]

However, it is not easy for bible students to understand and capitalize on the contribution of Canale's dissertation for biblical interpretation. For example, Canale told me that Parry misunderstood his 2001 book, *Back to Revelation-Inspiration: Searching for the Cognitive Foundation of Christian Theology in a Postmodern World*.[15] This book is not easy to read because it is built upon the foundational work of Canale's 1983 dissertation. Parry does not understand how Canale's work has brought a significant and paradigm shift in theological studies when he says:

> I am not convinced that the Classical Model with its timeless God *necessarily* falls foul of his objections and I suspect that a CR-I [Classical revelation-inspiration] model could accommodate more of Canale's insights than he is willing to allow. I am also not convinced that he does manage to stretch every inch of the Bible nor that it matters whether it does for inspiration can take up the slack.[16]

In contrast, both Glanz and Gulley rightly recognize the significant contribution of Canale's work.[17] For example, Gulley says, "In the light of his [Canale's] penetrating analysis of presuppositional structures for the classical and liberal models of revelation-inspiration, he has effectively exposed the limitations of these models in the context of a timeless God."[18] Gulley continues:

> Canale has presented a new model for revelation-inspiration that is far superior to the classical and liberal models because it is a scientific analysis that does justice to what Scripture says about itself and the phenomena which it presents. Therefore, instead of jettisoning foundationalism, his method makes Scripture the foundation of a system

---

[14] Edgar V. McKnight, "Presuppositions in New Testament Study," in *Hearing the New Testament: Strategies for Interpretation*, ed. Joel B. Green (Grand Rapids: William B. Eerdmans Publishing Company, 1995), 278.

[15] Robin Parry, review of *Back to Revelation-Inspiration: Searching for the Cognitive Foundation of Christian Theology in a Postmodern World*, by Fernando L. Canale, *EvQ* 76 (April 2004): 186-89.

[16] Ibid., 188.

[17] See Oliver Glanz, "Time, Reason, and Religious Belief: A Limited Comparison, Critical Assessment, and Further Development of Herman Dooyeweerd's Structural Analysis of Theoretical Thought and Fernando Canale's Phenomenological Analysis of the Structure of Reason and Its Biblical Interpretation" (M.A. thesis, Vrije Universiteit Amsterdam, 2006), 49-80; idem, "Who Is Speaking? Who Is Addressed? A Critical Study into the Conditions of Exegetical Method and Its Consequences for the Interpretation of Participant Reference-Shifts in the Book of Jeremiah" (Ph.D. diss., Vrije Universiteit Amsterdam, 2010), 32-42; Norman R. Gulley, *Prolegomena*, vol. 1 of *Systematic Theology* (Berrien Springs, MI: Andrews University Press, 2003), 116-27, 133-36, 373-74.

[18] Ibid., 126-27.

that sees in Scripture God's cognitive revelation written down as divine thoughts given through human thoughts, language, and logic.[19]

Canale's dissertation concludes that Christian theology for the last two thousand years was constructed according to onto-theo-logia.[20] Biblical scholars should not be surprised by this sweeping conclusion because Canale only reinforces the same thesis previously argued by Heidegger.[21] However, unlike Heidegger, Canale goes on to construct Christian theology that is free from extra-theological philosophical conditioning. One of his 2005's books has already become a pioneer example of constructing the systematic theology according to theo-onto-logia.[22]

Onto-theo-logia is an extra theologico-philosophical speculation of Greek ontology and epistemology derived from the philosophy of Parmenides (born c. 515 BC). Canale argues that Parmenides is "the first philosopher to give expression to the foundational relationship that exists between epistemological and ontological frameworks."[23] This Parmenidean tradition has been decisively adopted as the philosophical foundation for formulating the classical or traditional Christian theology since the early church.[24] It is well-known that main stream evangelical seminaries advocate the multiplicity of sources as the foundation of theology (see Figure 2).

Figure 2. Foundation of Classical Theology

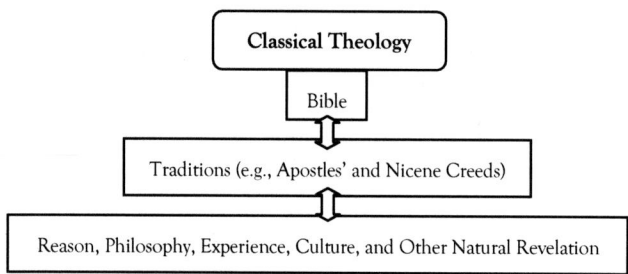

---

[19] Ibid., 127.

[20] Canale, *Theological Reason*, 390; idem, "Evangelical Theology," 112.

[21] Martin Heidegger, "The Onto-Theo-Logical Constitution of Metaphysics," in *Identity and Difference*, trans. Joan Stambaugh, Martin Heidegger Works, ed. J. Glenn Gray (New York: Harper & Row, 1969), 59.

[22] Fernando Canale, *Basic Elements of Christian Theology: Scripture Replacing Tradition* (Berrien Springs, MI: Andrews University Lithotech, 2005). Check the bibliography of this book to find out the other two books published by Canale in 2005.

[23] Canale, *Theological Reason*, 76.

[24] Canale, "Evangelical Theology," 108-109.

Though main stream evangelical seminaries emphasize the authority and inerrancy of Scriptures, these seminary teachers and students have to utilize various extra-biblical sources (extra-biblical writings and natural revelation) to construct their theology. Let me briefly explain the pedagogy of these traditional theological schools. Since the Scriptures are inspired by God and are inerrant, they must be the starting point of theological reflection. This means that though extra-biblical sources are utilized in the formation of doctrinal system, their suitability must be critically judged in light of the Scriptures.

The Bible acts like the master of the house which represents a theological system. All extra-biblical players are like servants in the same house but they must be submitted to the master so that the house can be kept in harmony, especially in an ontological sense. Theoretically, bible students are able to reject those sources which are ontologically inconsistent with the master—the Scriptures. In practice, this remains an idealistic vision. Why? Put simply, the Scripture is the intended starting point but it has never been accorded the actual role as the master in the formation of traditional theology so that one can determine which extra-biblical sources are ontologically consistent or inconsistent with the Scripture itself. Very often, bible students are "instructed" to construct doctrines in light of the creeds of church councils lest they be branded heretics or are unable to graduate with their theological degrees. This fear is common despite the fact that these creeds cannot be inerrant.

After Martin Heidegger examined the foundation of classical theology from the ontological perspective, he argues that the epistemology for classical theology is "onto-theo-logic."[25] "Onto-theo-logy" is the way in which Heidegger refers to the metaphysical ground upon which all Christian theologies (classical, evangelical and modern) stand. He demonstrates that this metaphysical perspective "appears, most early and most authentically in Western thought . . . [from] Parmenides."[26]

In other words, Heidegger demonstrates that the Bible functions only as a servant in the construction of theology. This should not be surprising since Scriptures have never been accorded the foundational role in Christian reflection about God. As a result, believers are incapable of resolving their crisis of faith simply by utilizing the advances of modernity and postmodernity because their starting point for theologizing is fatally flawed.

This epistemological impasse explains why there are of various competing models for understanding *Auctor*'s theology of revelation and his reception of the history of the interpretive influence of Exodus (cf. chapter 6). From the ontological perspective, Martin rightly calls this phenomenon the "crisis of

---

[25] Heidegger, "Onto-Theo-Logical Constitution," 59.

[26] Martin Heidegger, "The Principle of Identity," in *Identity and Difference*, trans. Joan Stambaugh, Martin Heidegger Works, ed. J. Glenn Gray (New York: Harper & Row, 1969), 27.

faith."[27] The root of this crisis is due to the use of onto-theo-logia as the ontological presupposition for constructing the traditional (classical) Christian theology. Humanistic epistemological conventions change. Consequently, onto-theo-logical based Christian doctrine inevitably changes with the latest philosophical fashion; it ends up being incoherent and inconsistent since the onto-theo-logical matrix is derived from extra-biblical speculation drawn originally from ancient Greek ontology.[28] However, after Canale uncovered biblical ontology from Exodus in his 1983 dissertation, he has provided bible students with biblico-ontological ground to resolve the crisis of faith. Briefly stated, he has demonstrated that biblical ontology is theo-onto-logical. Despite the enormous significance of Canale's dissertation, his work is noticeably missing in subsequent biblical scholarship.[29] This is also the main reason why scholarship in Hebrews remains at the descriptive stage.

In sum, the theo-onto-logical framework is Bible-centered and it also represents *Auctor's* theological construct (cf. chapter 6). It provides *the* biblical way for bible students to replace extra-biblical traditions with Scriptural ones when constructing a systematic theology.

Methods

Four kinds of methods (tools) are relevant in this study. These are audience-oriented criticism, the general method of inquiry, the hermeneutical and theological approach, and the intertextual approach. I have discussed audience-oriented criticism in chapter two. Here I want to explain why the other three methods are used in this study.

General Method of Inquiry

From the perspective of descriptive analysis, there are three possible levels of understanding *Auctor's* use of Exodus in Hebrews: (1) situation-oriented exposition (i.e., to what extent a citation itself and *Auctor's* exegesis of it contribute to an understanding of the Christ event for the original audience); (2) text-oriented exegesis (i.e., to identify the features/contexts of the citations by an inter-textual and grammatical analysis); (3) method-oriented exegesis (i.e., to what extent *Auctor's* hermeneutic corresponds to a given definition of the prophecy-fulfillment scheme or of some other Jewish exegetical methods). Chapter two of the present study reflects situation-oriented exposition and

---

[27] Robert K. Martin, *The Incarnate Ground of Christian Faith: Towards a Christian Theological Epistemology for the Educational Ministry of the Church* (Lanham, MD: University Press of America, 1998), 10.

[28] Canale, "Evangelical Theology," 127.

[29] For a recent review of Canale's work, see Gulley, *Prolegomena*, 116-27, 133-36, 373-74.

text-oriented exegesis because both approaches can be subsumed under the broad spectrum of rhetorical criticism.

Audience-oriented criticism is a type of situation-oriented exposition. Since it is important to read Hebrews in light of *Auctor*'s assumed Christology, I have argued for the use of a theological norm (*theos*) for reading the Scriptures. That is the authorial reading of Christ as Yahweh (*theos*). This deductive reading of Scriptures is possible only under the theo-onto-logical structure of reason. On the other hand, under the onto-theo-logia, it is impossible to read Scriptures with a theological norm because readers have interpreted the biblical texts inductively via natural theology (*ontos*).

Since methodology reflects the reason (*logia*) utilized for constructing one's theology, I have excluded method-oriented exegesis in the descriptive analysis in chapter two because my preferred structure of reason is theo-ontologia. Method-oriented exegesis will be conducted after the ontological (prescriptive) analysis in Hebrews has been done. In other words, my approach reflects the priority of scripture (*theos*) over methodology (*logia*).

The prescriptive study (chapters 5 and 7) serves as a theological "bridge" between text-oriented and method-oriented exegeses. This interpretive bridge is essential in light of the paradox of *Auctor*'s two-fold attitude towards the OT Scriptures. Hughes describes this paradox as follows:

> ... how in one context can the scriptures of the Old Testament function so immediately as a vehicle for the Word of God while in other contexts the covenant which those same scriptures enshrine is unceremoniously dismissed as outmoded?[30]

Hughes posits, rightly, that while most studies of Hebrews have been descriptive of *Auctor*'s use of the OT, this is inadequate, since so many other contemporary literatures use the *same methods*.[31] In the same vein, France writes:

> ... what we find in Hebrews is *not* typical synagogue preaching, but the new approach to Scripture which was inevitable for a Jew who had come to follow Jesus, and for whom Jesus himself was now the interpretative key. A non-Christian synagogue hearer would no doubt have felt at home with the *style* of much of Hebrews' use of the Old

---

[30] Graham Hughes, *Hebrews and Hermeneutics: The Epistle to the Hebrews as a New Testament Example of Biblical Interpretation*, SNTSMS, ed. R. McL. Wilson and M. E. Thrall, vol. 36 (Cambridge: Cambridge University Press, 1979), 35.

[31] For a similar insight, see Christopher D. Stanley, "The Rhetoric of Quotations: An Essay on Method," in *Early Christian Interpretation of the Scriptures of Israel: Investigations and Proposals*, ed. Craig A. Evans and James A. Sanders, Studies in Scripture in Early Judaism and Christianity, ed. Craig A. Evans and James A. Sanders, vol. 5, JSNTSup, ed. Stanley E. Porter, vol. 148 (Sheffield: Sheffield Academic Press, 1997), 58.

Testament, but would have been bewildered by the theological context in which it was set.[32]

Briefly stated, it is *Auctor's theology* of revelation that is crucial. Hence, prior to method-oriented exegesis in chapter eight, the prescriptive analysis functions as an interpretive grid for understanding how to interpret *Auctor's* use of Exodus and how he integrates teachings in the Old and New Testament concerning similar motifs in light of the Christ event/Person. This general approach of inquiry recognizes not only the primary significance of *Auctor's* theology but also the function of the theology of the underlying Exodus citation upon his argument.[33] This general method of inquiry is a type of criticism of theological reason and is consistent with the methodological presupposition of the theo-onto-logical structure of reason. By following this general method of inquiry, one can move beyond the descriptive stage of many previous studies in Hebrews to a prescriptive stage.

Hermeneutical and Theological Approach

The New Covenant in Hebrews is variously interpreted in the immediate context, in its application within different theological systems of eschatology, and different hermeneutical principles adopted to explain biblical prophecy. For example, Master interprets the New Covenant from a dispensational perspective while Rayburn understands the New Covenant from the perspective of covenant theology.[34] Hence, in order to investigate *Auctor's* view of the analogical relationship between the Old and New Covenant by focusing on the use of Exodus in Hebrews, it is necessary to establish a proper hermeneutical and theological approach for this study.

In light of Romans 11 and the progressive nature of biblical revelation, I suggest a premillennial, dispensational hermeneutic.[35] However, this herme-

---

[32] R. T. France, "The Writer of Hebrews as a Biblical Expositor," *TynBul* 47 (November 1996): 275.

[33] See David H. Wenkel, "*Gezerah Shawah* as Analogy in the Epistle to the Hebrews," *BTB* 37 (Summer 2007): 67.

[34] See John R. Master, "The New Covenant," in *Issues in Dispensationalism*, ed. Wesley R. Willis and John R. Master (Chicago: Moody Press, 1994), 93-94; Robert Stout Rayburn, "The Contrast between the Old and New Covenants in the New Testament" (Ph.D. diss., Aberdeen University, 1978), 189-91.

[35] A brief defense for premillennial hermeneutics is provided by Elliott E. Johnson, "Premillennialism Introduced: Hermeneutics," in *The Coming Millennial Kingdom: A Case for Premillennial Interpretation*, ed. Donald K. Campbell and Jeffrey L. Townsend (Grand Rapids: Kregel Publications, 1997); John F. Walvoord, "The Theologoical Context of Premillennialism," *BSac* 150 (October-December 1993): 388. An introduction to the debate between dispensational and non-dispensational (covenant) theology is provided by Richard P. Belcher, *A Comparison of Dispensationalism and Covenant Theology* (Southbridge, MA: Crowne Publications, 1986); Robert

neutic as a type of *logia* must be applied *after Auctor*'s theology of revelation between the Old and New Covenant is uncovered as the ontological ground for understanding the relationship between Israel and Church. Otherwise, the use of any hermeneutical grid (dispensational or covenant theology) from which to work when dealing with biblical texts may seem artificial.

The strength of dispensational position is that this approach, by a consistent grammatical-historical interpretation, according to Bateman, "stresses the uniqueness of the church and confidence that a future exists for national Israel—[and it] is derived from the Bible."[36] In other words, the nation of Israel has not lost her identity in the Church. To be sure, there is only one New Covenant, for if the New Covenant which is operative today belongs to the church and is distinct from Israel's New Covenant, it certainly could not provide for the salvation of Israelites under the Mosaic dispensation. Hebrews 12:22-24 reveals that all redeemed saints are accorded a place in eternity in virtue of Christ's work as the Mediator of the New Covenant. This appears to argue against a two-new-covenant theory for if there were two New Covenants, one for Israel and one for the Church, one would expect them to be differentiated in this passage.

Also, in light of Heb 9:15-17, the New Covenant belongs to Israel (instead of the church), but under it a redemptive provision has also been made available for both Jewish and Gentile believers in the present dispensation (cf. Matt 26:28).[37] In other words, church believers are beneficiaries of blessings resulting from the New Covenant enacted by the death of Christ.

The premillennial perspective of the New Covenant envisions that there is a future for Israel as an ethnic nation in the millennium with a millennial temple. During the millennium, there will be a consummated fulfillment of the New Covenant with Israel on earth, and Yahweh will once again take up residence among His people (Ezek 40-48).[38]

L. Saucy, *The Case for Progressive Dispensationalism: The Interface between Dispensational & Non-Dispensational Theology* (Grand Rapids: Zondervan Publishing House, 1993).

[36] Herbert W. Bateman IV, "Dispensationalism Tomorrow," in *TCICD* (Grand Rapids: Kregel Publications, 1999), 316.

[37] See John F. McGahey, "An Exposition of the New Covenant" (Th.D. diss., Dallas Theological Seminary, 1957), 227-28, 243. Contra, James Henry Luther Jr., "The Use of the Old Testament by the Author of Hebrews" (Ph.D. diss., Bob Jones University, 1977), 215.

[38] The spiritual approach interprets the majority of Ezek 40-48 symbolically as fulfilled by the church. This view has won much popularity because it exempts itself from explaining the reestablishment of Mosaic legislation, specifically the reinstitution of certain animal sacrifices. For a defense of the literal approach, see J. M. Hullinger, "A Proposed Solution to the Problem of Animal Sacrifices in Ezekiel 40-48" (Th.D. diss., Dallas Theological Seminary, 1993).

Intertextual Approach

Hebrews incorporates extensive OT language, imagery, and concepts. This is evident as one examines the marginal listing of numerous LXX texts of NA²⁷.[39] This suggests that in studying Hebrews it is imperative to identify the sources of citations. Does *Auctor* use extra-biblical sources and natural (general) revelation to formulate his doctrinal center?

Though both the themes of Christ's sonship and priesthood are significant in Hebrews, scholars have already demonstrated decisively that *Auctor*'s doctrinal center is the priesthood of Christ.[40] The question is: does *Auctor* use extra-biblical sources and natural (general) revelation to construct his doctrinal center? In other words, can one ascertain whether *Auctor*'s hermeneutic is autopistic or axiopistic?

"Autopistic" is derived from the Greek word "αὐτοπιστος" and means "self-attested." This means that the subject (e.g., the priesthood of Christ) is authenticated from the Scriptures only. On the other hand, "axiopistic" means the use of the Scriptures and extra-biblical sources including natural (general) revelation to derive the knowledge of the subject.[41]

I will argue that *Auctor*'s hermeneutic is autopistic in chapter 8 after the ontological (prescriptive) analysis of his use of Exodus has been done in chapters five to seven. Prior to the present study, since there is no other prescriptive analysis of Exodus in Hebrews, *Auctor*'s hermeneutic is undefined. This means that scholars are free to adopt any ontological ground as the starting point for studying how NT authors use OT texts. In other words, they have consciously or unconsciously presupposed either onto-theo-logia or theo-onto-logia for understanding *Auctor*'s theology in light of the interpreted intertextual connection between the Old and New Testaments.

My choice of theo-onto-logia primarily reflects my commitment to the use of Scripture alone for formulating theology. This commitment does not automatically imply that the same ontological ground is shared by *Auctor*. However, since the burden of the present study is to move beyond a descriptive stage to a prescriptive level of analysis, it is important to prescribe a method of

---

[39] *Novum Testamentum Graece*, ed. Barbara and Kurt Aland, Johannes Karavidopoulos, Carlo M. Martini, and Bruce M. Metzger, 27th rev. ed. (Stuttgart: Deutsche Bibelgesellschaft, 1993).

[40] For examples, this is the thesis of Tetley and MacLeod. Joy D. Tetley, "The Priesthood of Christ as the Controlling Theme of the Epistle to the Hebrews" (Ph.D. diss., University of Durham, 1987), 1; David John MacLeod, "The Theology of the Epistle to the Hebrews: Introduction, Prolegomena, and Doctrinal Center" (Th.D. diss., Dallas Theological Seminary, 1987), 260.

[41] See A. T. B. McGowan, *The Divine Spiration of Scripture: Challenging Evangelical Perspectives* (Nottingham, England: Apollos, 2007), 31; W. Gary Phillips, "Apologetics and Inerrancy: An Analysis of Select Axiopistic Models" (Th.D. diss., Grace Theological Seminary, 1985), 5.

intertextuality coherent to the methodological presupposition of this study. To illustrate this prescriptive influence, let me provide an example here.

In 1989, Richard Hays proposed a new method of intertextuality.[42] His proposal is so influential that many scholars have subsequently adopted his methodology in understanding the intertextual relation between the Old and New Testaments.[43] I reject the proposal of Hays because his ontological presupposition is onto-theo-logical.

On the other hand, there are still a few scholars advocating a method of intertextuality coherent to the theo-onto-logical structure of reason even though these scholars have not interacted with Hays. That is, they do not explain why their method is better than the proposal of Hays. For example, both Dale Brueggemann and Jeffrey Rankin simply assume the theo-onto-logia as the starting point in their doctoral work about intertextuality.[44] In other words, they presuppose the Scriptures as the only epistemological sources for biblical writers' intertextual borrowing. There are at least two reasons why the method of Brueggemann and Rankin excels Hays's. First, from a practical point of view, Hays' seven criteria are difficult to apply precisely. Stockhausen observes:

> Hays says that his "account of Paul's interpretative activity has discovered no systematic procedures at work in his reading of Scripture" and . . . Some would not agree, arguing that there is ample evidence that Paul worked with a consistent set of rudimentary procedures. It has not been Hays's goal to discover these. He has not analyzed Paul's texts carefully to find them.[45]

Similarly, Porter says: "Terms such as echo, allusion, and paraphrase . . . are poorly defined within Hays' own work."[46]

---

[42] Richard B. Hays, *Echoes of Scripture in the Letters of Paul* (New Haven: Yale University Press, 1989).

[43] For example, Fowler simply adopts Hays' criteria for evaluating evidence of intertextuality between Ezekiel and the Fourth Gospel uncritically. William G. Fowler, "The Influence of Ezekiel in the Fourth Gospel: Intertextuality and Interpretation" (Ph.D. diss., Golden Gate Baptist Theological Seminary, 1995), 209-22. After Fowler, Russell and Allen also use Hays' methodology uncritically. See Brian Douglas Russell, "The Song of the Sea: The Date and Theological Significance of Exodus 15:1-21" (Ph.D. diss., Union Theological Seminary and Presbyterian School of Christian Education, 2002), 194-96; David M. Allen, *Deuteronomy and Exhortation in Hebrew: A Study in Narrative Re-presentation*, WUNT, ed. Jörg Frey et al., vol. 238 (Tübingen: Mohr Siebeck, 2008), 17.

[44] See Jeffrey Jay Rankin, "An Intertextual Reading of the Inclusio around the יהוה מלך Psalms" (Ph.D. diss., New Orleans Baptist Theological Seminary, 2006), 36-37; Dale A. Brueggemann, "The Use of the Psalter in John's Apocalypse" (Ph.D. diss., Westminister Theological Seminary, 1995), 34.

[45] Carol L. Stockhausen, review of *Echoes of Scripture in the Letters of Paul*, by Richard B. Hays, *JBL* 111 (Spring 1992): 157.

[46] Stanley E. Porter, "Further Comments on the Use of the Old Testament in the New Testament," in *The Intertextuality of the Epistles: Explorations of Theory and Practice*, ed. Thomas L.

Second, from the epistemological perspective, since Hays does not presuppose theo-onto-logical structure of reason, the Scripture is not the only starting point. Hays focuses his analysis on Pauline Epistles and proposes that the epistemological framework for intertextuality should be *both* literary (either biblical or extra-biblical texts) and historical. Says Hays:

> The primary mode of reflection in this study is literary, but historical knowledge both informs and constrains my readings. Likewise, there are historical implications to the readings that I propose—especially for shaping our understanding of the relation between Jewish and Gentile Christians during Paul's lifetime, before the Jewish War of 66–70 C.E.[47]

Similarly, Koptak rightly observes that "Hays' approach points to a radical newness in relation to existing texts, a newness that continues and does not supersede the earlier work."[48] As a result, according to Stockhausen:

> At his most honest and possibly his best, he [Hays] gives to Paul a canonical voice of Scripture which transcends his [Paul's] own (unreachable to us) intended meaning and becomes the voice of Scripture speaking from Scripture to Scripture, as it were, the word of God generating new speech into the ears of readers in new ages without the specific restriction of authorial intent, or beyond it. . . . Paul has in fact been transformed [by Hays] from a first-century Jewish Pharisee become Christian into a twentieth-century hermeneut and a useful, if dehistoricized, model for contemporary communities and scholars.[49]

While Hays moves toward what the modern reader understands, readers adhering to the theo-onto-logia moves toward what the biblical author intended his first audience to apprehend.[50] This is why the authorial reading of Christ as Yahweh is coherent with the theo-onto-logia. Hays uses the notion of a late twentieth-century reader reading, while my approach is similar to the methodology of Stanley. Stanley approaches citations from the standpoint of Paul's apparent assumptions about his audience, rather than trying to reconstruct their actual assumptions. Stanley states nine assumptions and the first one refers to the starting point of Stanley's epistemological framework. Says Stanley:

Brodie, Dennis R. MacDonald, and Stanley E. Porter, NTM, ed. Stanley E. Porter, vol. 16 (Sheffield: Sheffield Phoenix Press, 2006), 99. Gieschen is less critical in his assessment. See Charles A. Gieschen, "Listening to Intertextual Relationships in Paul's Epistles with Richard Hays," *CTQ* 70 (January 2006): 17, n. 2.

[47] Hays, *Echoes*, 28.
[48] Paul E. Koptak, "Intertextuality," in *DTIB*, 333.
[49] Stockhausen, "Review of Hays," 156.
[50] See Brueggemann, "Psalter in Apocalypse," 30; Rankin, "An Intertextual Reading," 63.

Paul's audiences acknowledged the authority of the Jewish Scriptures as a source of truth and a guide for Christian conduct. From the way Paul refers to the Jewish Scriptures in his letters, it seems clear that he not only accepted the sacred text as authoritative for his own life but also expected a similar response from his audiences.[51]

Hence, when I know my epistemology is theo-onto-logical, this provides a benchmark for me to examine scholars' methods of intertextuality. This enables me to judge which method is coherent with the ontological ground by which I intend to adopt and proceed with the investigation.

Summary

In order to conduct a prescriptive analysis in Hebrews, one must find an ontological ground as the starting point to proceed with such an intellectual enterprise. Previous studies in Hebrews have not gone beyond the descriptive analysis because these studies have not critically selected and prescribed a structure of reason to examine *Auctor*'s use of the Hebrew Scriptures. The goal of subsequent prescriptive analysis is to demonstrate that *Auctor*'s structure of reason is indeed theo-onto-logical in light of his use of Exodus.

---

[51] Christopher D. Stanley, *Arguing with Scripture: The Rhetoric of Quotations in the Letters of Paul* (New York: T & T Clark International, 2004), 40.

• CHAPTER FOUR •

Prelude to Prescriptive Analysis in Hebrews

Due to the complexity of prescriptive analysis, the purpose of this chapter is to outline the basics of prescriptive analysis which will be dealt with in details in the rest of this book. The goal is to show readers how the prescriptive significance of Exodus in the theology of Hebrews has been utilized by *Auctor* to construct his doctrinal system. In other words, bible students are incapable of doing the prescriptive analysis in Hebrews unless the ontological significance of Exodus in Hebrews is recognized.

Goal of Prescriptive Analysis in Hebrews

In order to demonstrate the prescriptive significance of Exodus in the theology of Hebrews, I will defend the central thesis that *Auctor* uses the Book of Exodus to develop the ontological grounds for his systematic construction of the doctrinal system. This section provides readers with an overall picture of how the rest of this book is organized to achieve this goal.

The fundamental issue in the scholarship of Hebrews is that there are various metaphysical (ontological) models proposed for understanding *Auctor*'s use of symbolism or religious language.[1] A prescriptive analysis focuses on the quest for the biblical ontological grounds for the construction and formulation of *Auctor*'s beliefs and theology.[2] When the ontological grounds for the doctrinal systems of various theologians are unveiled, according to Hartmann, their "doctrinal systems can be classified as founded or unfounded ones, regardless of their respective points of view or doctrinal tendencies."[3] In other words, by using the Book of Exodus, *Auctor* formulates his biblical ontology whereby he understands the interrelation of living beings with God as the

---

[1] See Robert Masson, "Analogy and Metaphoric Process," *TS* 62 (September 2001): 572.
[2] Fernando L. Canale, "The Quest for the Biblical Ontological Ground of Christian Theology," *JATS* 16 (Spring 2005): 5.
[3] Nicolai Hartmann, *New Ways of Ontology*, trans. Reinhard C. Kuhn (Chicago: Henry Regnery Co., 1953), 5.

center of life. The focus here is not to present *Auctor*'s theology according to the various categories of systematic theology (e.g., Christology, eschatology, soteriology) per se because such an approach is descriptive and has been done before.[4] Instead, using the terms of Canale, "we will turn our attention to the ontological nature of systematic theology."[5]

Overall Process of Prescriptive Analysis

The central thesis is that the state of indeterminacy created by descriptive analysis in Hebrews can only be overcome by a prescriptive analysis of *Auctor*'s pedagogy (reason) and the function of Exodus in the theology of Hebrews (see chapter 1). Since the process of prescriptive analysis involves a criticism of *Auctor*'s theological reason and an attempt to understand how *Auctor* derives the ontological grounds for constructing his doctrinal system, it is important to note that there are two categories of epistemological sources for building his ontology: (1) theophanies, dreams, visions, and principles of interpretation; (2) history, nature, interpreted events, data, and information.[6] The former serves as the grounding source of revelation for building ontology whereas the latter plays a subordinate role. The grounding sources are more cognitive specific than the subordinate ones. The degree of cognitive specificity determines the role played by the sources of revelation. Canale writes:

> Sources with higher cognitive specificity (theophanies, Jesus Christ, visions, and prophecies) play grounding roles. Sources with lower levels of cognitive specificity (history and nature) play subordinate roles. . . . Because revelation always must be interpreted based on the biblical writer's presuppositions, only sources with a high level of cognitive specificity can provide those presuppositions. Thus, biblical writers always interpreted new information based on presuppositions from earlier revelations with the higher levels of cognitive specificity.[7]

---

[4] A comprehensive descriptive presentation of theology of Hebrews would take us far beyond the limits of our present subject. Many excellent studies focus on the theology of Hebrews. For examples, David John MacLeod, "The Theology of the Epistle to the Hebrews: Introduction, Prolegomena, and Doctrinal Center" (Th.D. diss., Dallas Theological Seminary, 1987); Barnabas Lindars, *The Theology of the Letter to the Hebrews* (Cambridge: Cambridge University Press, 1991); Mathias Rissi, *Die Theologie des Hebräerbriefs*, WUNT, ed. Joachim Jeremias et al., vol. 41 (Tübingen: Mohr Siebeck, 1987).

[5] Fernando L. Canale, "From Vision to System: Finishing the Task of Adventist Biblical and Systematic Theologies—Part II," *JATS* 16 (Spring 2005): 136.

[6] Fernando L. Canale, *The Cognitive Principle of Christian Theology* (Berrien Springs, MI: Andrews University Lithotech, 2005), 315.

[7] Ibid., 316.

Since there are two epistemological sources for *Auctor*, I will defend the central thesis by demonstrating how Exodus plays a significant dual role (subordinate and grounding) for constructing the ontology within *Auctor*'s doctrinal system. The overall analysis from chapters five to eight will progress from the less cognitive epistemological revelatory sources to the more cognitive ones (see Figure 3).

Figure 3. Cognitive Epistemological Revelatory Sources from Exodus in Hebrews

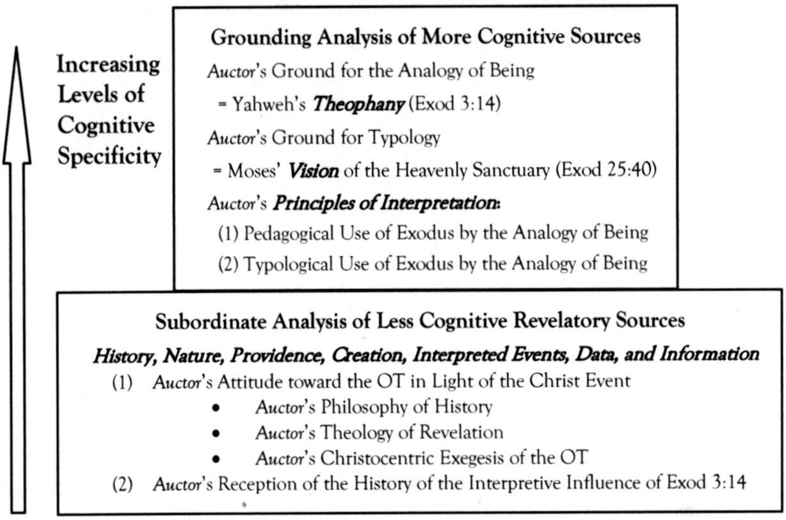

Increasing Levels of Cognitive Specificity →

Grounding Analysis of More Cognitive Sources
Auctor's Ground for the Analogy of Being
= Yahweh's ***Theophany*** (Exod 3:14)
Auctor's Ground for Typology
= Moses' ***Vision*** of the Heavenly Sanctuary (Exod 25:40)
Auctor's ***Principles of Interpretation***:
(1) Pedagogical Use of Exodus by the Analogy of Being
(2) Typological Use of Exodus by the Analogy of Being

Subordinate Analysis of Less Cognitive Revelatory Sources
History, Nature, Providence, Creation, Interpreted Events, Data, and Information
(1) *Auctor*'s Attitude toward the OT in Light of the Christ Event
 • *Auctor*'s Philosophy of History
 • *Auctor*'s Theology of Revelation
 • *Auctor*'s Christocentric Exegesis of the OT
(2) *Auctor*'s Reception of the History of the Interpretive Influence of Exod 3:14

From the perspective of the subordinate sources, the prescriptive significance of Exodus will be demonstrated by a twofold analysis of (1) *Auctor*'s attitude toward the OT in light of the Christ event, and (2) *Auctor*'s reception of the history of the interpretive influence of Exodus. In addition, from the perspective of the grounding sources, the prescriptive significance of Exodus will be demonstrated by a twofold analysis of (1) *Auctor*'s pedagogical use of Exodus in light of the Christ event, and (2) *Auctor*'s typological use of Exodus in light of the Christ event. Chapters five to eight will conduct the twofold subordinate and grounding analyses in details.

In summary, the goal of the remaining chapters is to demonstrate the central thesis (supra) so that one can safely assert that *Auctor*'s doctrinal system is founded or grounded biblically by using the ontological framework derived from Exodus.

Ontological Context of *Auctor*

Auctor's use of Exodus is both descriptive and prescriptive. The intertextual study is descriptive because it explains how *Auctor* activates citations from Exodus to support his theological argumentation. Hübner says:

> The *function* of quotations is particularly clear in the *Epistles* of the New Testament. There they support *theological argumentation*.[8]

Hübner also argues that *Auctor* "has a *christological* intention when he quotes God speaking."[9] From an intertextual perspective, we have seen the descriptive significance of Exodus citations in light of the rhetorical context of *Auctor*'s argument. The descriptive function of Exodus citation in Hebrews is primarily apologetical instead of constructive.[10] That is, *Auctor* has to presuppose a certain ontological ground for constructing his theology before he actually posits the exegetical or apologetical meaning of the biblical texts as well as his understanding of biblical theology in light of the interpreted intertextual connection between the Old and New Testaments.[11]

Similarly, modern readers must presuppose a certain ontological ground for interpreting the biblical texts in order to propose a certain description of theology about divine reality and divine activities. Since readers come to the Scriptures with various ontological grounds to formulate their doctrinal systems, each individual's ontological ground in fact functions as the context by which each reader knows the meaning of texts in relation to reality. Spiegelberg says:

> *Reality* means here the "standing-on-its-own account" (in and of itself) of any object; as such it is independent of any observer and of his observation. Accordingly, everything real occupies a definite place of its own in the tissue of the real world.[12]

One view's of reality is independent because it axiomatically determines not only how he knows God but also how he relates to God and other created beings. Since I have uncovered two ontological grounds in chapter three, this

---

[8] Hans Hübner, "New Testament Interpretation of the Old Testament," in *From the Beginnings to the Middle Ages (until 1300)*, ed. Chris Brekelmans, Menahem Haran, and Magne Sæbø, *Hebrew Bible / Old Testament: The History of Its Interpretation*, ed. Magne Sæbø, vol. 1, pt. 1, *Antiquity* (Göttingen: Vandenhoeck & Ruprecht, 1996), 335.

[9] Ibid., 364.

[10] See Canale, "Ontological Ground," 5.

[11] See Canale, "Systematic Theologies," 136.

[12] Herbert Spiegelberg, "The 'Reality-Phenomenon' and Reality," in *Philosophical Essays: In Memory of Edmund Husserl*, ed. Marvin Farber (New York: Greenwood Press, 1968), 86.

indicates that there are at least two types of doctrinal systems in the history of interpretation if we assume that there is no mixed ontology derived from both grounds. Figure 4 depicts axiopistic system in the context of onto-theo-logia whereas Figure 5 depicts autopistic system in the context of theo-onto-logia.

Figure 4. Context of Axiopistic System before the Contribution of Immanuel Kant

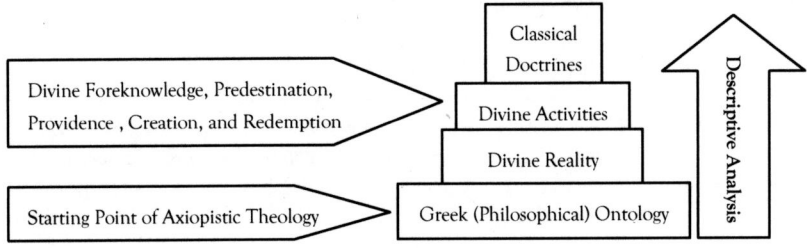

Figure 5. Context of Autopistic System after the Contribution of Fernando Canale

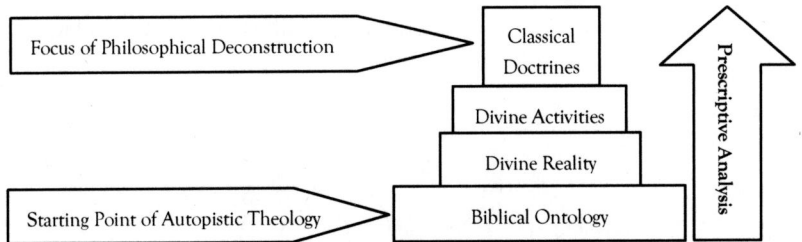

In addition to axiopistic and autopistic systems, there is another theological system constructed via modern or Kantian ontology. Since modern ontology was developed by Immanuel Kant (born c. 1724), there would not be any interpretive influence upon *Auctor*. It is impossible for *Auctor* to have adopted such ontology to construct his doctrinal system. Hence, I do not discuss modern ontology in chapter three. In other words, after Canale, the ontological context for *biblical authors* is either Greek ontology or biblical ontology or both. I will demonstrate that *Auctor*'s ontology is indeed coherent with biblical ontology in chapter six.

Ontological Context of Modern Readers

Now, as readers coming to interpret Hebrews, we must appreciate the full ontological context within which we conduct prescriptive analysis. Speaking in a less technical way, theologians often call such ontological context as received pedagogies or traditions.[13] Here I want to describe the received pedagogies (traditions) reflected in the pre-understanding of *modern readers*. Then, the biblical pedagogy shared by *Auctor* and his first readers will be discussed.

There are two received traditions for *modern readers*: (1) classical pedagogy (reason) and (2) modern pedagogy (reason).[14] Each received tradition functions as a pedagogical device.[15] According to Canale, these two pedagogical devices are representatives of their time and subsequently have influenced thinkers for many years:

> We have mentioned Aristotle as standing for the classical age, Immanuel Kant similarly represents the modern age. These two became icons of philosophy because of how they interpreted reason, which resulted in paradigm shifts during their respective periods. Moreover, their views still present Christian theology with a choice in methodologies, resulting in divided schools of theological thought and Christian denominations.[16]

These two devices are the presupposed interpretive paradigms which modern readers utilize to make sense of their view of God and ultimate reality. The devices belong to the grounding sources of revelation because they are principles of interpretation.[17] Canale visualizes the differences and similarities between the two pedagogical models as follows:[18]

Figure 6. Modern Pedagogy   **Figure 7. Classical Pedagogy**

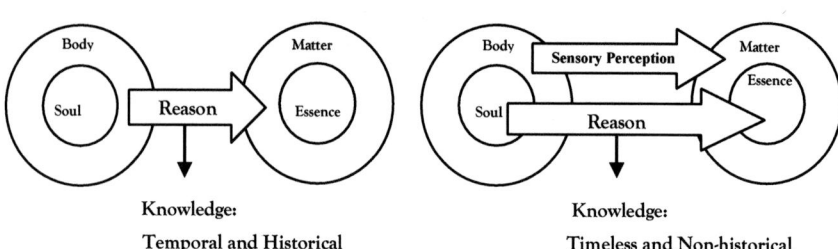

The two figures are reprinted by permission of the publisher. All rights reserved.

---

[13] Fernando L. Canale, *Back to Revelation-Inspiration: Searching for the Cognitive Foundation of Christian Theology in a Postmodern World* (Lanham, MD: University Press of America, 2001), vill.

[14] Canale, *Cognitive Principle*, 111-224.

[15] Fernando Luis Canale, *A Criticism of Theological Reason: Time and Timelessness as Primordial Presuppositions*, AUSDDS, vol. 10 (Berrien Springs, MI: Andrews University Press, 1987), 199.

[16] Canale, *Cognitive Principle*, 142.

[17] Ibid, 316.

[18] Ibid., 143, 146.

Classical pedagogy is derived from Greek ontology and it has five major characteristics: (1) a human has a spatiotemporal body and a timeless soul; (2) human reason resides in the body and soul of the human (i.e., reason is able to reach the timeless reality—soul, and yet it is also bound to time in the body); (3) an inanimate object has a spatiotemporal matter/form and a timeless essence; (4) since only human reason is timeless, it is able to understand and reach the essence of an inanimate object; (5) the matter/form of an inanimate object can be understood by human sensory perception.[19] The only actual or real knowledge is timeless and nonhistorical knowledge derived from human reasoning.

According to Plato, the knowledge derived from sensory perception is only an illusion because it is changing and transient. Commenting on Plato's epistemology, Canale writes:

> What is transient cannot be a basis for permanent truth and knowledge; it is mere opinion.[20]

The strength of classical pedagogy is that it focuses on the question: what can we know? To answer this question, the pedagogical device begins by interpreting reality as a whole, and from there it attempts to understand reason and other epistemological issues.

It was Kant who made a significant change to classical model. According to Canale, "Kant's view of reason is not entirely historicized, but because he claimed that reason works within the limits of space and time, he set the stage for that historicization, which has come to fruition in postmodernity."[21] As a result, modern pedagogy was born. Under both Figures 6 and 7, the two circles on the left represent a human subject whereas the two circles on the right represent the known inanimate object. The outer circle is spatiotemporal but the inner circle is timeless. The arrow represents human reason whereby the different realms are bridged to derive a certain type of knowledge about the reality of nature.

According to modern pedagogy, it is impossible for human reason to understand or reach timeless reality (i.e., the soul of human and the essence/nature of inanimate object) because reason is bound spatiotemporally. According to Canale, this means that the real knowledge derived from classical pedagogy/reason "is built on an illusion—the notion that human reason can somehow contact timeless reality beyond space and history."[22] The strength of modern pedagogy is that it focuses on the question: how do we

---

[19] Ibid., 142-44.
[20] Ibid., 143.
[21] Ibid., 145.
[22] Ibid., 146.

76   Chapter Four

know what we know? To answer this question, the pedagogical device begins by interpreting the human subject and its cognitive capabilities.

We have seen that the two models of pedagogy or reason generate two different views of ultimate reality. It is not difficult to see that they also generate different knowledge about God (see Figures 8 and 9).[23]

Figure 8. Modern View of Nature and Supernature

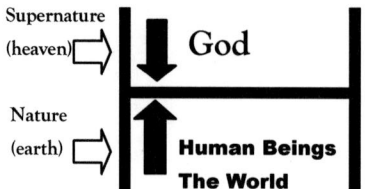

Figure 9. Classical View of Nature and Supernature

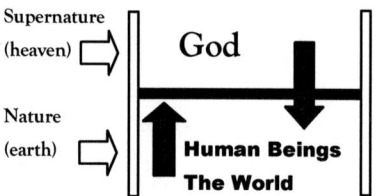

The two figures are reprinted by permission of the publisher. All rights reserved.

Canale uses the letter "H" to depict the realms of nature and supernature. The vertical arrows, "one in each world, symbolize the attempts of God and human beings to communicate with each other."[24] Since the knowledge about God is reachable by classical pedagogy, the vertical downward arrow originating from the supernatural realm is able to reach the natural realm of human beings and the world. This vertical arrow represents human reason existing in both timeless (soul) and spatiotemporal (body) realms. Even though "God's cognitive communication can only take place within the realm of timelessness,"[25] temporal human beings can still derive knowledge about God by the analogy of being. Reason in classical pedagogy becomes the ontological ground whereby the doctrine of the analogy of being can be formulated.[26]

Contrary to classical pedagogy, human reason is bound entirely in realm of the nature in modern pedagogy. Canale says:

> Because human knowledge cannot reach [timeless] God in this [modern] view, natural theology cannot exist.[27]

---

[23] Ibid., 95, 98.
[24] Ibid., 98.
[25] Ibid.
[26] Both Lee and Lyttkens derive the analogy of being via classical pedagogy. See Patrick Lee, "Language about God and the Theory of Analogy," NS 58 (Winter 1984): 40; Hampus Lyttkens, *The Analogy between God and the World: An Investigation of Its Background and Interpretation of Its Use by Thomas of Aquino* (Uppsala: Almqvist and Wiksells Boktryckeri, 1952), 477.
[27] Canale, *Cognitive Principle*, 98.

It is impossible to formulate natural theology by the doctrine of the analogy of being because there is an absolute and unbridgeable gap (represented by the thick and shaded boundary line in the figure above) between nature and supernature. Reason cannot function as the ground for constructing the doctrine of analogy. Hence, according to Canale, "the analogy of being between nature and supernature begins to lose its philosophical foundation."[28] After Kant, the classical doctrine of analogy can no longer be the *only* answer or ground to provide a basis for human beings to express their religious languages about God.[29]

Ontological Context of *Auctor*'s Intended Audience

We have seen that the classical doctrine of analogy has lost its philosophical ground since Kant. Since Kant, scholars have been able to *prescribe* their views of *Auctor*'s theology cogently according to his "personal conviction."[30]

This explains why there are various crises of belief in contemporary biblical interpretations. These crises are inevitable because biblical commentators have consciously or unknowingly used extra-biblical pedagogies or philosophical traditions to interpret the Scriptures. Canale writes:

> Motivated by the practical desire to defend and share their faith, early Christian thinkers began to use philosophical sources—a momentous methodological decision. Initially, they intended not to modify the faith by philosophy but to use philosophy as a missionary tool. But after several centuries, what had begun as a missionary tool became a series of theological presuppositions determining classical hermeneutics. For example, when we read Augustine, we discover that his teaching [pedagogy] is based on hermeneutical principles drawn from Greek philosophical sources, especially Platonism and Neoplatonism.[31]

In order to understand the *prescribed* theology of a biblical writer, one should first ask whether there is a biblical pedagogy—a pedagogical doctrine of analogy grounded on the structure of reason revealed by biblical ontology. If there is no biblical pedagogy, it seems impossible for the first recipients of Hebrews to understand the prescribed theology of *Auctor*. Biblical ontology (pedagogy)

---

[28] Ibid., 146.
[29] This view is in conflict with Geisler because his pedagogical reasoning is classical. See Norman L. Geisler, "Analogy: The Only Answer to the Problem of Religious Language," *JETS* 16 (Summer 1973): 167.
[30] Canale, *Cognitive Principle*, 146.
[31] Ibid., 147-48. Canale's understanding of Augustine is shared by Frederick Sontag, *How Philosophy Shapes Theology: Problems in the Philosophy of Religion* (New York: Harper & Row, Publishers, 1971), 142-56.

does exist and it was born in 1983.³² By using Exod 3:14, Canale has already derived biblical ontology (pedagogy).³³ Prior to 1983, Canale's insight is found in its embryonic form in the work of Cullmann, McCarthy and Moltmann.³⁴

In chapter six, I will show that biblical pedagogy is the ontological context shared by *Auctor* and his audience. The remainder of the present chapter conveys an understanding of biblical pedagogy by (1) a comparative analysis of classical, and modern pedagogies in relation to biblical pedagogy, and (2) a description of biblical pedagogy.

Comparative Analysis

Biblical pedagogy differs from other pedagogical devices—both classical and modern. Classical and modern pedagogies are built upon the onto-theo-logical and the onto-logical structures of reason respectively. Comparing these two pedagogical systems serves to illustrate the need of a deconstruction of classical analogy of being via biblical pedagogy.

According to modern pedagogy, reality (*ontos*) grounds the understanding of reason and method (*logia* or *logos*)—the structure of onto-logia.³⁵ Hence, modern pedagogy does not involve God (*theos*) as one of the grounding sources of revelation. This does not mean that the adherents of modern pedagogy deny the existence of God. Canale says:

> While Kant did not deny the existence of the soul and of God, he did maintain that since they are timeless, we cannot know them.³⁶

In other words, though God exists, according to Kant, one cannot know divine reality (*theos*) through reason and method (*logos*). For example, Marion adopts modern reason to argue that classical pedagogy teaches the false god

---

³² Fernando Luis Canale, "Exodus 3:14: Toward a Biblical Ontology" (unpublished report presented for [course] OTST850 Theology of Pentateuch and [course] OTST890 Directed Reading in Old Testament Studies, Andrews University, April 1981). A summarized version of the doctoral report is now included in the chapter three of his published dissertation. Canale, *Theological Reason*, 285-387.

³³ Canale, *Theological Reason*; idem, "Exodus 3:14."

³⁴ Oscar Cullmann, *Christ and Time: The Primitive Christian Conception of Time and History*, trans. Floyd V. Filson (Philadelphia: Westminster Press, 1949), 62; Jürgen Moltmann, *Theology of Hope: On the Ground and the Implications of a Christian Eschatology*, trans. James W. Leitch (New York: Harper & Row, 1967), 15-58. Dennis J. McCarthy, "Exod 3:14: History, Philosophy and Theology," *CBQ* 40 (July 1978): 311-12.

³⁵ Anthony J. Godzieba, "Ontotheology to Excess: Imagining God without Being," *TS* 56 (March 1995): 7.

³⁶ Canale, *Cognitive Principle*, 146.

because the true God is not knowable and so He "can never serve as an object [of our rationality], especially not for theology."[37]

Hence, the adherents of modern pedagogy create the word G⨯d (the "o" crossed by the X) to designate the true God in distinction from the false god taught by classical pedagogy.[38] Since God does not have a relationship with *logos*, Marion argues that theological language is "most certainly a human *logos*."[39]

Marion summarizes how modern pedagogy teaches theology as follows: "To do theology is not to speak the language of gods or of 'G⨯d,' but to let the Word speak us (or make us speak) in the way that it speaks of and to God."[40]

On the other hand, classical pedagogy includes God (*theos*) as one of the subordinate sources of revelation. Classical pedagogy follows the onto-theological structure of reason. In other words, the notion of reality (*ontos*) determines the concept of God (*theos*) as well as the understanding of reason and method (*logos*). The classical doctrine of analogy allows one to speak about God. Analogy always flows from God to human beings, never the reverse. Use of analogy involves judgment, and such judgment is part of our everyday discourse. God remains always God, and human beings are related to Him, though never He to them.[41] It is obvious that both the classical and modern pedagogical devices do not reflect the evidence of the biblical data.

Since modern pedagogy renders the doctrine of analogy useless, such pedagogy should be rejected. As a matter of fact, human beings are able to know God via the Incarnation and the revelation of the Scriptures. The Scriptures reveal what God does on our level of history. The doctrine of analogy should not be rejected since God made human beings "in His own image and likeness" (Gen 1:26-27). Moreover, creation itself reveals the knowledge of God— i.e., general revelation as described in Romans 1. In this biblical sense, classical pedagogy is better than the modern one. However, in chapter six, I will show that the classical analogy of being actually follows a mixed model of ontology derived in the context of two conflicting views of metanarratives— Mosaic-biblical and philosophical-Parmenidean. In other words, classical pedagogy is grounded on a mixed model of ontology in need of deconstruction and reconstruction according to the Mosaic-biblical metanarrative.

---

[37] Jean-Luc Marion, *God without Being: Hors-Texte*, trans. Thomas A. Carlson, Religion and Postmodernism, ed. Mark C. Taylor (Chicago: University of Chicago Press, 1991), 139.

[38] Ibid., 76.

[39] Ibid., 143.

[40] Ibid.

[41] Roger White, "Notes on Analogical Predication and Speaking about God," in *The Philosophical Frontiers of Christian Theology: Essays Presented to D. M. MacKinnon*, ed. Brian Hebblethwaite and Stewart Sutherland (Cambridge: Cambridge University Press, 1982), 224.

Description of Biblical Pedagogy

Since biblical pedagogy forms the basis for teaching about God and Scripture, it is necessary to construct pedagogy according to the Mosaic-biblical metanarrative. In other words, biblical pedagogy is derived according to the theo-onto-logical structure of reason because theo-onto-logia is the only ontological paradigm that really gives primacy to the Trinitarian God revealed in the Bible.[42] I have already argued why the presupposition of this study follows the theo-onto-logical structure of reason (see chapter 3). Now, another important reason emerges. Since this study is focused on the subject matter of God and Scripture, it should follow biblical pedagogy to communicate its findings or teaching about God and Scripture. By choosing the theo-onto-logia, I actually reject the other alternate pedagogies.

Since "the Bible has been given to mankind for practical purposes," Canale argues, "it is mainly concerned with *pedagogical* temporal exemplifications of timeless truth."[43] Biblical pedagogy and its corresponding view of nature and supernature can be visualized:[44]

Figure 10. Biblical View of Nature and Supernature

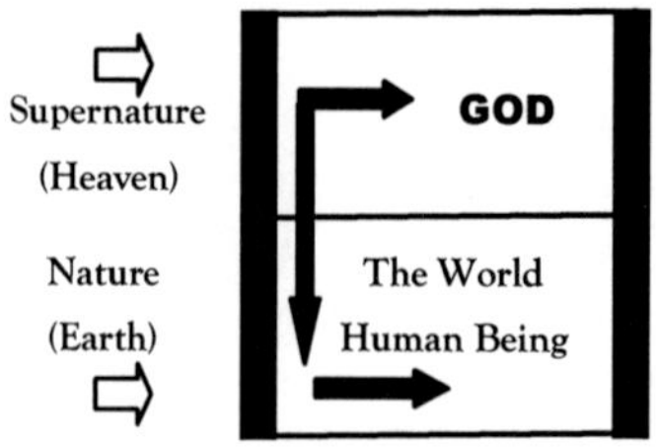

Figure 11. Biblical Pedagogy

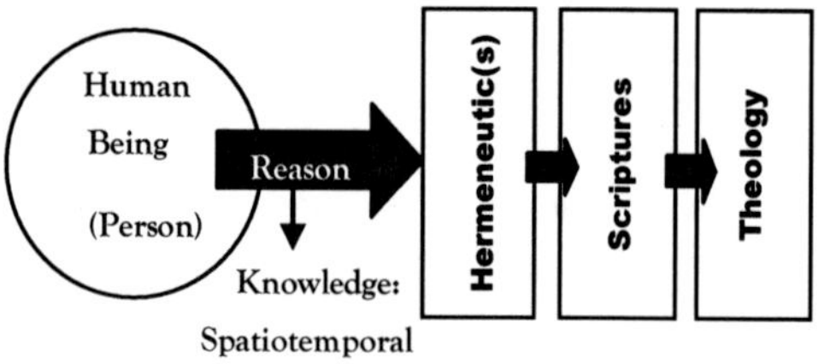

According to the biblical view of nature, there is no gap between supernature and nature. Though the two realms are different (i.e., heaven and earth), the two shaded vertical legs of "H" emphasize that both realms are of the *same* nature—"both share the same characteristics of time, history, and life."[45] Canale describes Figure 10 as follows:

> The heavenly and earthly realms experience this commonality [time, history, and life] each according to the specificity of its respective reality. The Creator experiences the sequence of time and history in the eternity of His infinite being, while creatures ex-

---

[42] For a detailed explanation, see supra (51-55) and infra (153-56).
[43] Canale, *Theological Reason*, 207, emphasis added.
[44] Canale only draws Figure 10—the biblical view of nature and supernature (Canale, *Cognitive Principle*, 105). Figure 10 is reprinted by permission of the publisher. All right reserved.
[45] Ibid., 105.

perience time and history in a finite and limited manner. The horizontal arrows indicate the historicity of God's activity from within eternal time in supernature and in the limited, created time of nature. The vertical arrow indicates that God can act in human history from within the flow of created time, but also from within his own uncreated, eternal time.[46]

In Scripture, Muilenburg argues, "biblical time is *concrete time*."[47] He continues to say, "Biblical faith moves in the world of time."[48] Similarly, Lategan says, "Time and space act as basic coordinates for the configuration of what we understand to be reality, history and narrative."[49] Hence, like the shaded horizontal arrows in Figure 11, the shaded arrows in Figure 10 indicate the spatiotemporal knowledge derived from sensory reception (e.g., vision and theophany) and reason in distinction from the classical and modern knowledge.[50]

Biblical pedagogy rejects dualistic view of human being though there seems to be a biblical distinction between the soul (spirit) and body. The Scripture actually emphasizes the unity of man—a *person*.[51] Wyschogrod says, "Man is a unity of spirit and body and it is for this reason that death is real."[52] Similarly, Canale says:

> In Scripture, then, "soul" means human person, a living operating human body possessing the full use of all its capabilities.[53]

This unity of man is reflected by a circle without an inner circle in Figure 11. Green reaches this holistic view of human beings after examining the nature of humanity in the Bible.[54] Cullmann asserts the unity of man as follows:

---

[46] Ibid.

[47] James Muilenburg, "The Biblical View of Time," HTR 54 (October 1961): 236.

[48] Ibid., 243.

[49] Bernard C. Lategan, "History, Historiography and Hermeneutics," *Philosophical Hermeneutics and Biblical Exegesis*, ed. Petr Pokorný and Jan Roskovec, WUNT, ed. Jörg Frey, Martin Hengel, and Otfried Hofius, vol. 153 (Tübingen: Mohr Siebeck, 2002), 205.

[50] See Nota, *Phenomenology and History*, 99.

[51] For a similar view, see Stanley Winter Theron, "Paraenesis in the Epistle to the Hebrews (D.Div. diss., University of Pretoria, 1984), 284. Contra, Kenneth L. Schenck, *Cosmology and Eschatology in Hebrews*, SNTSMS, ed. John M. Court, vol. 143 (Cambridge: Cambridge University Press, 2007), 143.

[52] Michael Wyschogrod, *The Body of Faith: God and the People of Israel*, 2nd ed. [1st published as *The Body of Faith: Judaism as Corporeal Election*. New York: Seabury Press, 1983] (Northvale, NJ: Jason Aronson, 1996), 177.

[53] Fernando Canale, *Basic Elements of Christian Theology: Scripture Replacing Tradition* (Berrien Springs, MI: Andrews University Lithotech, 2005), 213.

[54] Joel B. Green, *Body, Soul, and Human Life: The Nature of Humanity in the Bible* (Grand Rapids: Paternoster/Baker Academic, 2008), 179.

> The contrast, for the Christian, is not between the body and the soul, not between outward form and Idea, but rather between the creation delivered over to death by sin and new creation; between the corruptible, fleshly body and the incorruptible resurrection body.[55]

This means that the classical doctrine of the immortality of soul should be rejected.[56] Classical theologians would have difficulty to reach this conclusion because they would argue that general revelation does give Christian thinkers warrant to build the doctrine of the immortality of soul. However, according to biblical pedagogy, the doctrine of the immortality is supported by natural theology instead of general revelation. Canale says:

> We should distinguish carefully between general revelation and natural theology. According to the Bible, general revelation is a means other than Scripture used by the Holy Spirit to reach all human beings with the possibility of salvation. Natural theology is another name for human philosophy, which seeks to unveil God through the interpretation of nature and history.[57]

Biblical pedagogy does not deny the epistemological significance of general revelation because man receives general revelation from the world through nature and history. Moreover, since man is a personal being, he receives personal knowledge by interacting with God, angels, and, other human beings. However, this general revelation and personal knowledge function only as the subordinate sources of revelation for biblical pedagogy. In other words, biblical pedagogy rejects classical pedagogy which follows the onto-theo-logical structure of reason. The grounding instead of subordinate source of revelation should be one's hermeneutics in relation to Scriptures.

Biblical pedagogy builds its teachings of theology on special revelation derived from the Bible-centered hermeneutics—the theo-onto-logical structure of reason according to the Mosaic-biblical metanarrative. The subject of biblical pedagogy is the human being and its object is Scripture.

However, Figure 11 above indicates that *hermeneutic(s)* is actually ontologically (and epistemologically) prior to Scripture. Here, it is important to note that *hermeneutic(s)* means hermeneutical methodology which refers to *hermeneutics and hermeneutic* (see Table 5 in chapter 8). Hermeneutics concerns the

---

[55] Oscar Cullmann, *Immortality of the Soul or Resurrection of the Dead? The Witness of the New Testament* (London: Epworth Press, 1958; reprint, New York: Macmillan, 1964), 31. Similarly, Galenieks defends the unity of man from the OT. See Ēriks Galenieks, "The Nature, Function, and Purpose of the Term שְׁאוֹל in the Torah, Prophets, and Writings" (Ph.D. diss., Andrews University, 2005), 618. Contra, Schenck, *Cosmology*, 136.

[56] This is the thesis of Galenieks and Cullmann. See Galenieks, "Term שְׁאוֹל," 618; Cullmann, *Immortality*, 25.

[57] Canale, *Cognitive Principle*, 40.

rules of interpretation while hermeneutic refers to the process of understanding a text.

Why is hermeneutical methodology ontologically prior to Scripture? This is because, one's hermeneutical methodology includes "assumptions on ontology, epistemology, and metaphysics [articulation]."[58] Martin rightly describes these assumptions as a pair of spectacles fitted for our mind and rationality.[59]

Biblical Analogy of Being

Auctor does use the concept of analogy (Heb 9:23). Measell has already examined the development of the concept of analogy in philosophy up to 1850. He notes that both Plato and Aristotle recognized the value of analogy as an epistemological instrument.[60] Selby says:

> Analogy is to be used first as a tool to understand something new and secondly to let the *core* of similarity show where similarity ends.[61]

Travers declares, "Thinking is essentially analogical."[62] The classical analogy is in need of being reconstructed because it is built upon natural theology. When natural theology is replaced by bible-centered hermeneutics as the ontological ground for constructing theological teachings to edify the church, a paradigm of biblical pedagogy emerges. Biblical pedagogy provides theologians a new paradigm to teach the divine and ultimate via a biblical analogy of being. The Biblical doctrine of analogy works on the basis of the spatiotemporal knowledge derived in the context of biblical pedagogy. I will describe biblical analogy of being within two contexts: (1) the ontological context; (2) the theological context.

Analogy of Being in Ontological Context

All revelation is educational or pedagogical, since it involves communication of new knowledge built upon prior knowledge. This principle underlies the

---

[58] Canale, "Sanctuary and Hermeneutics," 42.

[59] Robert K. Martin, *The Incarnate Ground of Christian Faith: Towards a Christian Theological Epistemology for the Educational Ministry of the Church* (Lanham, MD: University Press of America, 1998), 10.

[60] See J. S. Measell, "Development of the Concept of Analogy in Philosophy, Logic, and Rhetoric to 1850" (Ph.D. diss., University of Illinois at Urbana-Champaign, 1970), 25.

[61] Rosalind M. Selby, *The Comical Doctrine: An Epistemology of New Testament Hermeneutics*, Paternoster Biblical Monographs, ed. I. Howard Marshall et al. (Waynesboro, GA: Paternoster, 2006), 57.

[62] Michael E. Travers, "The Use of Figures of Speech in the Bible," *BSac* 164 (July-September 2007): 6.

progressive nature of biblical revelation just as it underlies the progressive nature of intellectual growth. Brown pointedly declares:

> Now if intellectual truths require intellectual preparation, far more do divine truths require divine preparation. Things beyond our experience can be explained to us only by analogies.[63]

The Biblical doctrine of analogy is ontologically significant because it determines one's hermeneutic(s) and his view of God and ultimate reality.

> The problem of analogy is in principle prior to every particular revelation. For the revelation has to be thought to be received, and can be thought about only by the aids of words or finite images; and these cannot signify of God unless the appropriate "mode of signification" functions in our minds.[64]

The doctrine of analogy is a fundamental and indispensable hermeneutical principle in Christian theology because biblical commentators assume it to be prior to the actual reading of the special revelation from the Scriptures.[65]

Since each type of pedagogy corresponds to a unique doctrine of analogy, variations in understanding the pedagogy have direct and momentous repercussions in the church's life and teachings. Chapter six below shows that the classical doctrine of analogy works on the basis of timeless and nonhistorical knowledge in the context of classical pedagogy to produce an extra-biblical ontology. The classical doctrine of analogy is constructed within the context of the axiopistic system and so it should be redefined by biblical pedagogy.

Analogy of Being in Theological Context

Analogy is an important tool in the process of biblical interpretation. Since the biblical doctrine of analogy is grounded in the Bible-centered hermeneutics, one is able to claim independence from classical pedagogy to reconstruct the whole enterprise of systematic theology. In the past, systematic theology was constructed from classical pedagogy in the context of the axiopistic system. The denial of classical *analogia entis* does not deny the value of analogy but simply calls for a redefinition and reconstruction.

According to biblical ontology, the analogy in the relation of God and creation is found within time. When this biblical approach was born in

---

[63] Stephen J. M. Brown, *The World of Imagery: Metaphor and Kindred Imagery* (London: Kegan Paul, Trench, Trubner & Co., 1927; reprint, New York: Russell and Russell, 1966), 255.

[64] Austin Farrer, *Finite and Infinite: A Philosophical Essay*, 2nd ed., Seabury Library of Contemporary Theology (London: Dacre Press; New York: Seabury Press, 1979), 2.

[65] See E. L. Mascall, *Existence and Analogy: A Sequel to "He Who Is"* (London: Longmans, Green, and Co., 1949), 95.

1983,[66] it became necessary to reconstruct the whole enterprise of systematic theology in light of this new approach. Canale surmises, "The move from a timeless to a temporal understanding of divine reality entails the major hermeneutical paradigm shift in the history of Christian theology."[67]

It is beyond the scope of this work to present a reconstruction of the whole of Christian systematic theology within the context of the autopistic system.[68] However, in order to highlight the theological significance of the new *analogia entis*, it is necessary to illustrate how the new approach is able to formulate various aspects of autopistic Christian theology. Canale has already illustrated how the use of the temporal *analogia entis* is able to reconstruct the eight basic elements of autopistic Christian theology. These are, (1) the basic characteristic of God's reality and acts, (2) God's Trinitarian nature (divine entity and life), (3) divine foreknowledge (cognition), (4) predestination (will), and (5) creation (design and power); the origin and nature of (6) the angels, (7) human beings, and (8) the world.[69]

Summary

Canale declares that the process of this theological reconstruction of an autopistic Christian system involves both an opportunity and a risk.[70] Despite the risk, I am very encouraged to find that some scholars have already capitalized on the opportunity by starting the process of a systematic reconstruction of Christian theology.[71] I follow in the path of these scholars to taking advantage of the opportunity to see God's activity within the spatiotemporal framework. This new journey may sound risky because it is an unfamiliar and adventurous path. But, I believe this journey is not risky at all because one can now rest assured that he steps on the immovable rock of the Scriptures without resorting

---

[66] Canale, *Theological Reason*.

[67] Canale, "Sanctuary and Hermeneutics," 50.

[68] For a very concise overview of how to reconstruct the whole doctrine of God according to the new doctrine of analogy, see Fernando L. Canale, "Doctrine of God," in *Handbook of Seventh-day Adventist Theology*, ed. Raoul Dederen, CRS, ed. George W. Reid, vol. 12 (Washington, DC: Review and Herald Publishing Association, 2000), 105-59.

[69] See Canale, *Scripture Replacing Tradition*, 234-35.

[70] See Canale, *Theological Reason*, 308-309.

[71] For example, see Norman R. Gulley, *Prolegomena*, vol. 1 of *Systematic Theology* (Berrien Springs, MI: Andrews University Press, 2003), 127; Oliver Glanz, "Time, Reason, and Religious Belief: A Limited Comparison, Critical Assessment, and Further Development of Herman Dooyeweerd's Structural Analysis of Theoretical Thought and Fernando Canale's Phenomenological Analysis of the Structure of Reason and Its Biblical Interpretation" (M.A. thesis, Vrije Universiteit Amsterdam, 2006), 149; Duane Howard Larson, "The Temporality of the Trinity: A Christian Theological Concept of Time and Eternity in View of Contemporary Physical Theory" (Ph.D. diss., Graduate Theological Union, 1993), 14.

to the shifting sands of extra-biblical sources to ground an autopistic rendering of theology.

• CHAPTER FIVE •

Auctor's Attitude toward the Old Testament in Light of the Christ Event

I have explained in chapter four that the goal of the twofold subordinate analysis is to defend the dual thesis that *Auctor*'s subordinate ontological framework is derived from (1) the OT and (2) especially the Book of Exodus. This chapter focuses on the first part of the dual thesis.

Introduction

It is obvious that *Auctor* has a special esteem for the Scripture of the OT. This is supported by the facts that *Auctor* identifies the source of the OT citations as God (Heb 1; 4:3; 7:21; 8:5, 8; 10:30), the Holy Spirit (Heb 3:7; 9:8; 10:15), and Christ (Heb 2:12; 5:5-6; 10:5).[1] *Auctor* also presupposes in his argument that the religion of Israel is the only pre-Christian religion.[2] In order to show that *Auctor*'s ontological framework is grounded in the OT, this section will demonstrate that his attitude toward the OT in light of the Christ event is consistently biblically-centered in terms of his concept of history and nature (providence and creation) as well as his understanding of events and information (e.g., the life of Christ, and the wilderness and pilgrimage experience of Israel during Exodus).

---

[1] Erich Grässer, "Der Hebräerbrief 1938-1963," *TRu* 36 (October 1964): 206-7.
[2] See Heinrich Zimmermann, *Die Hohepriester-Christologie des Hebräerbriefes: Vortrag beim Antritt des Rektorats und zur Eröffnung des Studienjahres 1963/64 der Philosphisch-Theologischen Akademie zu Paderborn, gehalten am 22. Oktober 1963* (Paderborn: Ferdinand Schöningh, 1964), 24; Graham Hughes, *Hebrews and Hermeneutics: The Epistle to the Hebrews as a New Testament Example of Biblical Interpretation*, SNTSMS, ed. R. McL. Wilson and M. E. Thrall, vol. 36 (Cambridge: Cambridge University Press, 1979), 70.

To reveal *Auctor*'s attitude toward the OT, the researcher needs to investigate the belief or ideology that *Auctor* "brought to Scripture."[3] Hence, this study pursues three sub-analyses corresponding to three major aspects of *Auctor*'s ideology. These three aspects are: (1) *Auctor*'s philosophy of history, (2) *Auctor*'s theology of revelation, and (3) *Auctor*'s Christological exegesis of the OT. This trio appears to serve as a reasonable benchmark to reflect *Auctor*'s attitude toward the OT in light of the Christ event. Also, the first two parts of the trio appear to be extensive enough to capture a sufficient ontological influence exerted by the subordinate sources in *Auctor*'s thought. For example, *Auctor*'s philosophy of history reflects his understanding of history and nature. It also reveals how *Auctor* interprets God's providence, divine creation, and human events. *Auctor*'s theology of revelation indicates how he interprets the relation of the revelation of the OT to historical events and especially the Christ event.[4]

This descriptive analysis is conducted within the classical (traditional) and modern (Kantian) framework of evangelical Christian theology.[5] Using the terminology of Canale, the purpose here is to illustrate the need of "the philosophical deconstruction of the ontology on which Christian theology was constructed."[6]

Finally, the third part of the trio about *Auctor*'s Christocentric exegesis of the OT attempts to explain how the Christ event serves as a bridge to integrate *Auctor*'s philosophy of history and theology of revelation. This part is a bridge to link the other two parts because Christocentric exegesis plays the grounding role to integrate *Auctor*'s philosophy of history and theology of revelation ontologically. The Incarnation plays a grounding role for formulating *Auctor*'s ontology because the Incarnation is a theophany. This is because, in Scripture, theophanies are the spatiotemporal appearance of God. Using Exod 3:14, Canale demonstrates that there is no difference between God's Being and His appearance because the two belong together.[7]

Let me explain briefly how Canale's dissertation has significantly renewed our understanding of theophany and Incarnation. On the one hand, in the

---

[3] John E. Goldingay, *Approaches to Old Testament Interpretation* (Downers Grove, IL: InterVarsity Press, 1981), 153.

[4] See Fernando L. Canale, *The Cognitive Principle of Christian Theology* (Berrien Springs, MI: Andrews University Lithotech, 2005), 319.

[5] The descriptive analysis in the context of the biblical (historical-cognitive) framework is not possible unless the prescriptive significance of Exodus in Hebrews is recognized via the twofold grounding analysis (see chapter 7).

[6] Fernando L. Canale, "Deconstructing Evangelical Theology?" *AUSS* 44 (Spring 2006): 96.

[7] Fernando Luis Canale, *A Criticism of Theological Reason: Time and Timelessness as Primordial Presuppositions*, AUSDDS, vol. 10 (Berrien Springs, MI: Andrews University Press, 1987), 352-64.

OT, it is true that God does not become the form through which He *manifests* His spatiotemporal presence in the world. On the other hand, if theophanies can only happen as they did in the OT, it follows that if the Incarnation is a theophany, Jesus Christ does not identify with the external form through which He manifested His divinity. As a result, the Incarnation is to be understood as a new form of theophany in which God identifies Himself forever with the form that reveals His being and presence. Stated briefly, the Incarnation redefines and deepens our understanding of theophany, the showing of God via the divine accommodation of His Being within the limitations of His creation. This perspective allows Bible scholars to understand that the divine life can experience a new thing in the future-present-past flux of time whereas divine reality (ontology) remains unchanged.

However, in contradistinction to Canale's perspective, the appearance of God is mere appearance and not real Being according to the classical and modern ontology: there is an ontological dichotomy between God's Being and His appearance when Being is considered to be timeless instead of temporal. In short, both classical and modern ontology presuppose that a theophany is the showing of God in His own transcendent Being instead of the spatiotemporal presence of God in the future-present-past flux of time. Both classical and modern theologians presuppose that both divine reality and life cannot experience anything new spatiotemporally. Hence, scholars propose various speculative theories to understand ontological (immanent) Trinity in relation to the Incarnation.

Furthermore, *Auctor*'s Christocentric exegesis as a principle of interpretation also belongs to the grounding analysis of ontology. In light of the first two perspectives (philosophy of history and theology of revelation), this third sub-analysis of his Christocentric exegesis actually functions as a transition "zone" to unite the epistemological realms of subordinate sources with the grounding ones. If there were no Christ event, one could not find any historical divine reality to bridge the transcendental or ontological gap between the natural and special sources of revelations. In this vein, Harrisville writes:

> For this reason, entry into the [heavenly] holy place (10:19) [in Hebrews] does not occur by way of departure from the earthly reality but by way of the historical event, "the blood of Jesus."[8]

The Christ event provides *the* indispensable ontological link to bridge the natural and supernatural realms of theology. Says Holladay:

---

[8] Roy A. Harrisville, *Fracture: The Cross as Irreconcilable in the Language and Thought of the Biblical Writers* (Grand Rapids: William B. Eerdmans Publishing Company, 2006), 245.

> It [the Christ event] not only establishes the hermeneutical principles for our author [*Auctor*], it *is* his hermeneutical principle. It shapes his understanding of past, present, and future, and consequently gives him a Christ-defined sense of time. Since he cannot think of heaven and earth apart from Christ, this conviction also defines his sense of space.[9]

It is in this sense that the authorial reading of Christ as Yahweh in Hebrews recommends itself as the most apt methodology for the analysis of the descriptive function of Exodus in *Auctor*'s theology. The authorial reading of Christ as Yahweh explicitly integrates a conscious religious commitment of *Auctor* with his experience of faith during the present prescriptive analysis of his theology. Rice says:

> The most important variable affecting the relation of rational inquiry to the experience of faith is the presence or absence of conscious religious commitment.[10]

Whether or not a contemporary or authorial reader has undergone the same conversion will make a big difference in the way that person understands *Auctor*'s theology.

Auctor's Philosophy of History

According to Nash, "The first Christian philosopher is the author of the New Testament book known as the Epistle to the Hebrews."[11] As a philosopher and theologian, *Auctor* would have decided on a certain ontological ground to support and formulate his understanding of divine reality in relation to history. Roughly speaking, this understanding may be called *Auctor*'s philosophy of history. Richard writes:

> A "philosophy of history" refers to the way one views the totality of world events of the past and present, and the futuristic direction, if any, toward which those events are moving.[12]

In other words, without a philosophy of history, *Auctor* is unable to integrate both world and biblical events to support his philosophically based theological system.

---

[9] Carl R. Holladay, *A Critical Introduction to the New Testament: Interpreting the Message and Meaning of Jesus Christ* (Nashville, TN: Abingdon Press, 2005), 451.

[10] Richard Rice, *Reason and the Contours of Faith* (Riverside, CA: La Sierra University Press, 1991), 248.

[11] Ronald H. Nash, *The Meaning of History* (Nashville, TN: Broadman & Holman Publishers, 1998), 44.

[12] Ramesh P. Richard, "Premillennialism as a Philosophy of History: Part 1, Non-Christian Interpretations of History," *BSac* 138 (January–March 1981): 13.

The goal here is to defend the thesis that *Auctor*'s philosophy of history is consistent with the theo-onto-logical constitution of metaphysics. In other words, a corollary thesis is that his philosophy of history is derived from the OT. This will be demonstrated by distinguishing *Auctor*'s position from other views of history—views reflecting philosophy that is "onto-theo-logic."[13] The onto-theo-logical philosophy uses natural theology to derive the ontology (*ontos*) which provides the framework to construct a doctrine of God (*theos*) and to formulate its methods of interpretation (*logia*).

According to Dray, there are three views of history: (a) classical; (b) modern Western; and (c) Christian.[14] He argues that the classical view finds the intelligibility or meaning of history "only to the extent to which the historical process reflects or exemplifies certain timeless, rational forms."[15] Richard observes that this approach is adopted by "the Greek and Hindu cyclical views, and the skeptic's chaotic view."[16] This philosophy of history is also followed by the allegorical method of Alexanderia.[17] Dray also says:

> At the opposite end of the scale is the modern Western view. This finds historical significance *entirely* in the unique effects of human freedom and in the linear, developmental pattern of events which results.[18]

Briefly stated, the modern Western view of history excludes the presence of God in the world and so God Himself.[19] Grelot describes how the Christian philosophy of history can be distinguished from the modern Western view as follows:

> History in the Bible, whether it is directly in view, as in the narrative books, or whether it is contained in books with a different aim, such as those of the prophets, is always seen from the perspective of its religious significance, through faith in the God uniquely revealed to Israel. The fabric of this history is composed, on its surface, of the events that take place, the people who experience them or make them happen, and the varying fortunes of the nations. However, all of these things are depicted from a particular angle, because the story is truly woven together from the unfolding of

---

[13] See Martin Heidegger, "The Onto-Theo-Logical Constitution of Metaphysics," in *Identity and Difference*, trans. Joan Stambaugh, Martin Heidegger Works, ed. J. Glenn Gray (New York: Harper & Row, 1969), 59.

[14] William H. Dray, *Philosophy of History*, Foundations of Philosophy Series, ed. Monroe Beardsley and Elizabeth Beardsley (Englewood Cliffs, NJ: Prentice-Hall, 1964), 98-112.

[15] Ibid., 99.

[16] Ramesh P. Richard, "Premillennialism as a Philosophy of History: Part 2, Elements of a Biblical Philosophy of History," *BSac* 138 (April–June 1981): 109.

[17] James Graydon Dukes, "Eschatology in the Epistle to the Hebrews" (Th.D. diss., Southern Baptist Theological Seminary, 1956), 33-34.

[18] Dray, *Philosophy of History*, 99.

[19] See Jeffrey Jay Rankin, "An Intertextual Reading of the Inclusio around the יהוה מלך Psalms" (Ph.D. diss., New Orleans Baptist Theological Seminary, 2006), 41.

God's plan, which is what really underlies the events, characters, and successes and failures of the tiny nation that is looking back at its past. It follows from this that not everything recorded in the Bible will have equal value for us as "history" in the modern sense.[20]

It is not difficult to argue that *Auctor* holds neither the modern Western nor classical positions. *Auctor* does not reflect the philosophy of the modern Western view because such position leaves no room for the presence of the supernatural, transcendental aspect or significance in history. Nash argues that "Yahweh controls the entire process of history; God's plan infuses history with meaning."[21]

Hebrews deals with the issue of the relation between a historical event—the history of Jesus, and an occurrence transcending history—the heavenly deeds of Christ.[22] Says Nota:

> Mankind does not return to God in whom it preexisted but finds its completion through Christ in its Creator, to whom it owes the newness and uniqueness of its existence.[23]

By the authorial reading of Hebrews, it is the God of Israel (Yahweh) who provides the covenantal redemption and the eternal inheritance to His people (Heb 9:12-15). Yahweh, in the person of Jesus, mediates the eschatological covenant blessings of inheritance in the heavenly order.

Neusner describes the Hebraic idea of history as being congruent to "nature's time."[24] Hence, the fact that *Auctor*'s audience is Jewish argues strongly that *Auctor* assumes a divine ontology reflecting the Hebraic (Jewish) notion of historical time.[25] Similarly, Canale says, "Many recognize that Christianity is a historical religion because it claims God became a historical being in Christ."[26]

---

[20] Pierre Grelot, *The Language of Symbolism: Biblical Theology, Semantics, and Exegesis*, trans. Christopher R. Smith (Peabody, MA: Hendrickson Publishers, 2006), 104-105.

[21] Nash, *History*, 42.

[22] This is the thesis of Erwin W. Lutzer, "A Response to Homiletics and Hermeneutics," in *Hermeneutics, Inerrancy, and the Bible*, ed. Earl D. Radmacher and Robert D. Preus (Grand Rapids: Academie Books, 1984), 192.

[23] John H. Nota, *Phenomenology and History*, trans. Louis Grooten and John H. Nota (Chicago, IL: Loyola University Press, 1967), 50.

[24] Jacob Neusner, "The Idea of History in Rabbinic Judaism: What Kinds of Questions Did the Ancient Rabbis Answer?" in *Historical Knowledge in Biblical Antiquity*, ed. Jacob Neusner, Bruce D. Chilton, and William Scott Green (Blandford Forum, UK: Deo Publishing, 2007), 174.

[25] See Richard, "Philosophy of History: Part 2," 109.

[26] Fernando Canale, *Basic Elements of Christian Theology: Scripture Replacing Tradition* (Berrien Springs, MI: Andrews University Lithotech, 2005), 239.

If so, why does the classical Christian tradition conceive divine ontology as timeless and interpret salvation as a spiritual non-historical event according to Greek ontology? Similarly, why does the modern (liberal) Christian tradition presuppose divine ontology as both timeless and temporal instead of a spatio-temporal series of historical events according to Scripture?[27] Canale provides an answer to these two perplexing questions:

> Scripture carefully frames its understanding of God's revelation in Jesus Christ from a historical understanding of the theological matrix. Old Testament authors carefully uncovered and articulated the historical matrix New Testament authors assumed when they testified about God's revelation and acts in Jesus Christ.
>
> Unfortunately, Christian tradition replaced the Old Testament understanding of the basic elements of Christian theology and the matrix they generate with a philosophical/scientific understanding of them. This early paradigm shift in the interpretation of biblical theology is at the basis of Christian tradition as we know it today. By rejecting Old Testament thinking about the basic elements of theology and its matrix, Christian tradition has not yet been able to properly understand God's plan and its ongoing historical fulfillment through Jesus Christ.[28]

According to Canale, the basic elements of theology and its matrix are derived from the divine ontology that God acts historically in human time and space.[29] In the same vein, Wyschogrod notes that OT thinking about divine ontology is contrary to classical ontology because "classical ontology has always found it necessary to exclude time from the realm of being."[30]

By the authorial reading of Christ as Yahweh, it is difficult to imagine that *Auctor* would replace the OT understanding of the basic elements of Christian theology with a classical (Parmenidean) understanding of them.[31] In other words, Hebrews does not reflect the philosophy of the classical view.[32] Classical ontology is contrary to *Auctor*'s ontology for he is convinced of the reality of history and its significance for eternity. Commenting on *Auctor*, Laansma says, "His approach to the OT takes seriously its historical nature but insists that it speaks directly to the Christian context."[33] Since *Auctor* is a believer de-

---

[27] Ibid. Dukes also notes a similar paradox in the scholarship of Hebrews. See Dukes, "Eschatology," 26.

[28] Canale, *Scripture Replacing Tradition*, 239-40.

[29] Ibid., 56-73.

[30] Michael Wyschogrod, *The Body of Faith: God and the People of Israel*, 2nd ed. [1st published as *The Body of Faith: Judaism as Corporeal Election*. New York: Seabury Press, 1983] (Northvale, NJ: Jason Aronson, 1996), 133.

[31] Ibid., 132.

[32] Nash, *History*, 53. Oscar Cullmann, *Christ and Time: The Primitive Christian Conception of Time and History*, trans. Floyd V. Filson, rev. ed. (Philadelphia: Westminster Press, 1962), 53.

[33] Jon C. Laansma, "Hebrews, Book of," in *DTIB*, 280. Contra, Luz posits that *Auctor* "dehistoricizes" the OT so that it emcompasses past and present, and can only be understood fully

claring "it is impossible for God to lie" (Heb 6:18), it is not difficult to conclude that he derives his Christian philosophy of history from the OT. Richard rightly says:

> . . . Christians recognize all philosophies to be theologies of history, they are not ashamed to postulate their own to be at least as valid and objective as the others. Thus the revelation of God in the Scriptures becomes the cornerstone of their interpretation of history. Christians hold that God's Word is objective and valid in its "reading" of history.[34]

In sum, *Auctor*'s methodological presupposition of constructing his ontology for theology or philosophy is by way of a theo-onto-logical constitution of metaphysics.

Auctor's Theology of Revelation

Canale explains the inseparable connection between one's ontology (logic of reality) and theology of revelation as follows:

> The readers should bear in mind that the search for the meaning of revelation follows the logic of reality. The way we interpret God's reality sets logical limitations on the way we can conceive His activities without contradicting ourselves.[35]

We have seen that *Auctor*'s philosophy of history follows the theo-onto-logical model. In light of his theo-onto-logical philosophy of history, one may correctly deduce that *Auctor*'s theology of revelation reflects the ontological framework of the theo-onto-logical model. Hebrews scholarship, however, has not always correctly identified this logical deduction. This is yet another example of the "crisis of belief" like the one illustrated in chapter one.

Auctor's theology of revelation has been variously interpreted within different ontological frameworks whose orientations are consistent with either the theo-onto-logical or onto-theo-logical models. This crisis of belief is due to the fact that previous scholarship of Hebrews has not yet moved beyond the descriptive analysis of *Auctor*'s theology to the prescriptive one. Previous scholarship of Hebrews' theology of revelation needs to be deconstructed philosophically and then reconstructed within *Auctor*'s theo-onto-logical philosophy of history.[36] To achieve this objective, I will demonstrate the need for philosophical deconstruction as well as the prescriptive significance of Exodus

---

in light of Christ event. Ulrich Luz, "Der Alte und der Neue Bund bei Paulus und im Hebräerbrief," *EvT* 27 (1967): 333.

[34] Richard, "Philosophy of History: Part 2," 109.
[35] Canale, *Scripture Replacing Tradition*, 46.
[36] Canale, "Evangelical Theology," 96.

for the philosophical reconstruction of the ontology from which *Auctor* understands God's being and actions.

Need for Philosophical Deconstruction

No one willingly deconstructs his own doctrinal system, although a crisis of belief might compel someone to reconsider his doctrine. However, the need of deconstruction is validated or confirmed only when one discovers that his doctrinal system is groundless or unfounded ontologically.[37] In any case, this exercise is only effective for those open-minded believers, with humble spirits, willing to admit that their theologies can be wrong during the process of criticism. As far as I am concerned, my commitment behind this exercise is to allow the Scripture to correct my presuppositions.

Several "theo-onto-logical" theologians like Canale and Norman Gulley have already recently confirmed that the classical (traditional) ontological paradigm for constructing Christian theologies is indeed groundless. I have argued in chapter three that since the times of Parmenides, the classical (traditional) Christian theology has been onto-theo-logical: in practical terms, this means the use of multiple sources for doing theological projects: such epistemological ground is almost universally presupposed by the early church fathers as well as Protestant and Roman Catholic theologians.[38] Hence, McCormack rightly asserts:

> The consequence of this methodological decision is that the way taken to knowledge of God controls and determines the kind of God-concept one is able to generate; thus, epistemology controls and determines divine ontology.[39]

In the same vein, Canale writes:

> The leading projects of Christian theology use tradition as the "light" from which to continue interpreting Scripture and constructing Christian doctrines.[40]

Like Canale, McCormack appears to hold the same ontological valuation of the classical and modern (liberal) theological projects.[41] Later in chapter six, I

---

[37] Nicolai Hartmann, *New Ways of Ontology*, trans. Reinhard C. Kuhn (Chicago: Henry Regnery Co., 1953), 5.

[38] See Canale, *Scripture Replacing Tradition*, 21-22; Bruce L. McCormack, "The Actuality of God: Karl Barth in Conversation with Open Theism," in *Engaging the Doctrine of God: Contemporary Protestant Perspectives*, ed. Bruce L. McCormack (Grand Rapids: Baker Academic, 2008), 211; idem, "What's at Stake in Current Debates over Justification? The Crisis of Protestantism in the West," in *Justification: What's at Stake in the Current Debates*, ed. Mark Husbands and Daniel J. Treier (Downers Grove, IL: InterVarsity Press, 2004), 106.

[39] McCormack, "Actuality of God," 187.

[40] Canale, *Scripture Replacing Tradition*, 22.

[41] McCormack, "Actuality of God," 185-242.

will show that onto-theology is groundless because of the classical ontology on which Christian theology was constructed.[42] In other words, philosophy has been the master whereas theology or Scripture has been the servant. Canale writes:

> They [Most theologians] allow some form of philosophy to decide the actual content of the hermeneutical principle thereby allowing that form of philosophy to condition the actual limits, shape, procedures, and rules of theological methodology.[43]

Elsewhere Canale writes:

> It may be said that Greek philosophical ideas tended very much to displace OT thought from its proper role in Christian theology.[44]

Hence, Sontag has argued that "we propose that philosophy shapes theology according to the kind of philosophic theory employed."[45] As a result, there is no need to argue for deconstructing the various theological systems that are at odds with the theo-onto-logical model. Instead, it will do simply to state that there is a crisis of belief when one comes to understand *Auctor*'s theology of revelation. Also, I intend to provide a picture of various theological models through which one can understand how *Auctor*'s theology of revelation relates to his use of cultic vocabulary activated by the Exodus citations.

Auctor's theology of revelation constitutes an indissoluble link with his valuation of the relation of the Old and New Covenant as the theme of covenant (διαθήκη) pervades Hebrews. Hughes demonstrates that διαθήκη is consistently used in the LXX to mean "covenant."[46]

Current Hebrews scholarship illustrates the need for prescriptive analysis by singling out the question of how the theology of revelation relates to the Old and New Covenants in Hebrews. There are at least three reasons to justify this choice. First, it is obvious that the issue of the relationship between the Old and New Covenants is central for understanding the argument of Hebrews.[47] Second, MacLeod's dissertation has already addressed *Auctor*'s theol-

---

[42] Canale, "Evangelical Theology," 96.

[43] Fernando Canale, "Interdisciplinary Method in Christian Theology?" *NZSTR* 43, no. 3 (2001): 377.

[44] Fernando L. Canale, *Back to Revelation-Inspiration: Searching for the Cognitive Foundation of Christian Theology in a Postmodern World* (Lanham, MD: University Press of America, 2001), 37.

[45] Frederick Sontag, *How Philosophy Shapes Theology: Problems in the Philosophy of Religion* (New York: Harper & Row, Publishers, 1971), 169.

[46] John J. Hughes, "Hebrews 9:15ff and Galatians 3:15ff: A Study in Covenant Practice and Procedure," *NovT* 21 (January 1979): 29-32.

[47] See Donald Gordon Manuel, "The Religious Identity of the Recipients of the Epistle to the Hebrews" (Th.D. diss., New Orleans Baptist Theological Seminary, 1965), 131. Like Manuel, Grässer also argues for the centrality of "Bundes-Theologie" in Hebrews. Erich Grässer,

ogy of divine revelation at a general level.[48] This work expands MacLeod's work by focusing on the relation between the two Covenants in the context of *Auctor*'s theology of revelation. Finally, since the key cultic vocabulary utilized for the grounding analysis is the heavenly sanctuary and the sanctuary is intimately connected within "the sanctuary-covenant relational structure,"[49] the present analysis of the revelatory relation between the Old and New Covenants provides the context within which the heavenly sanctuary in Hebrews can be properly interpreted ontologically. This sanctuary-covenant structure reveals history and prophecy in such a way that it will help us to unveil the metanarrative in Hebrews. *Auctor*'s cosmology is also reflected by his metanarrative which is the grand story whereby it encompasses "all overarching stores that explain and give meaning to life."[50]

When the present *illustrative* descriptive analysis of Hebrews is coupled with the *already* validated descriptive analysis of various theological systems, one can safely posit that the need of the subsequent twofold grounding analysis for Hebrews is validated. In other words, the twofold grounding analysis is imperative because the present descriptive *theologies* of Hebrews are formulated or interpreted according to the structure of classical reason.[51]

Since the classical structure of reason (i.e., the onto-theo-logical model) is groundless and so in need of being deconstructed, the need to deconstruct immediately points to the need of reconstruction. The process of reconstruction will be demonstrated by the twofold grounding analysis within the context of the theo-onto-logical model reflected by *Auctor*'s philosophy of history. Before the reconstruction, one needs to demonstrate the crisis of belief by surveying various theological models proposed for interpreting *Auctor*'s valuation of the relationship between the Old and New Covenants in the light of the Christ event.

Theological Models

A theological model, explains Dulles, "is a relatively simple, artificially constructed case which is found to be useful and illuminating for dealing with re-

---

Der Alte Bund im Neuen, WUNT, ed. Joachim Jeremias et al., vol. 35 (Tübingen: J. C. B. Mohr [Paul Siebeck], 1985, 95.

[48] See David John MacLeod, "The Theology of the Epistle to the Hebrews: Introduction, Prolegomena, and Doctrinal Center" (Th.D. diss., Dallas Theological Seminary, 1987), 163-78.

[49] Fernando L. Canale, "From Vision to System: Finishing the Task of Adventist Theology—Part III: Sanctuary and Hermeneutics," *JATS* 17 (Autumn 2006): 61-62.

[50] Mark L. Y. Chan, "Following Jesus as the Truth: Postmodernity and Challenges of Relativism," *EvRT* 31 (October 2007): 307. Canale also provides a very helpful comparison and contrast between metaphysics and metanarrative (see Canale, "Sanctuary and Hermeneutics," 57).

[51] See Canale, *Theological Reason*, 200-201.

alities that are more complex."⁵² In other words, theological models are constructed from certain ontological presupposition about reality so that they can provide some "ideal, simplified, and schematic accounts of a much more complex reality."⁵³

Current scholarship remains indeterminate concerning *Auctor*'s theology, and one finds a variety of models that present *Auctor*'s valuation of the Old and New Covenants in light of the new revelation of the Christ event. The thesis here is that such an impasse in the scholarship of Hebrews can only be resolved when the prescriptive power of Exodus in the theology of Hebrews is recognized. A prescriptive analysis for identifying *the* correct theological perspective to understand the cultic language in Hebrews will be offered after demonstrating the significance of Exodus citations for understanding *Auctor*'s use of analogy theologically.

Hebrews scholars agree that (1) the theme of covenant is of great significance to *Auctor*'s argument and (2) *Auctor* is interested in the relation of the Old Covenant to the New Covenant.⁵⁴ However, they disagree in their individual models about *Auctor*'s valuation of the Old Covenant in light of the new revelation in the Christ event.

An analysis of various scholars' descriptions about *Auctor*'s assessment of the relation between the Old and New Covenants is not necessary for three reasons. First, the thesis here is to show that the ambiguous position of descriptive analysis in scholarship still continues despite the fact that there are some important studies recognizing the significance of Exodus in Hebrews. Second, Beavis has already done a definitive analysis in light of scholarship covering from 1938 to 1980.⁵⁵ The work of Beavis is a master's thesis with the caliber of a doctoral dissertation because the thesis includes an extensive evaluation of related French and German works. Therefore, my study focuses on the work of Beavis and relevant works after 1980. Third, despite the significant contribution of Beavis, her work remains at the descriptive stage because she has not moved her analysis to the prescriptive stage. Beavis' study has not recognized the ontological significance of the Exodus citations in *Auctor*'s ar-

---

⁵² Avery Dulles, *Models of Revelation*, 2nd ed. (Maryknoll, NY: Orbis Books, 1992), 30.

⁵³ Canale, *Revelation-Inspiration*, 76.

⁵⁴ See Hilary Arthur Nixon, "Typology of the Mosaic Tabernacle and Its Articles as Interpreted by Authors of the Nineteenth and Twentieth Centuries" (Ph.D. diss., Drew University, 1984), 458; Michael Duane Morrison, "Rhetorical Function of the Covenant Motif in the Argument of Hebrews" (Ph.D. diss., Fuller Theological Seminary, 2006), 177.

⁵⁵ Mary A. L. Beavis, "A Study of the Relation of the Old and New Covenants in the Epistle to the Hebrews, in the Light of Scholarship 1938-1980" (M.A. thesis, University of Manitoba, 1981). To my knowledge, Beavis's thesis is still one of the most comprehensive treatments of the relation between the two covenants in *Hebrews* (about 178 pages, Beavis, "Hebrews," 13-190) and yet her work is noticeably missing in subsequent scholarship including the recent doctoral work by Morrison. Morrison, "Covenant Motif."

gument. As a result, she is unable to activate the prescriptive power of the Exodus citations (Exod 3:14 and Exod 25:40) in Hebrews in order to identify the correct valuation of *Auctor*'s theology of the Old and New Covenants. Hence, what remains to be demonstrated is that the descriptive mode of Hebrews' scholarship continues after 1980. In other words, the purpose is to show the current deadlock in the scholarship on Hebrews when *Auctor*'s prescriptive use of Exodus is not given its due emphasis.

Auctor's theology of revelation is present in the very first two verses of Hebrews (Heb 1:1-2). Most scholars recognize elements of both continuity and discontinuity/contrast in *Auctor*'s valuation of the Old Covenant in relation to the new revelation. However, Smillie says, "Most commentators after Chrysostom and right up to the present either argue for a strong contrast or else reflexively assume it."[56] Hence, there are two major models of *Auctor*'s valuation of the Old Covenant in light of the new revelation in the contemporary literature: (1) the discontinuity model; (2) the continuity model.[57]

Survey of Relevant Studies

There are two major theological models whereby scholars attempt to understand *Auctor*'s theology of revelation in terms of the relation between the Old and New Covenant. This study shows that the ambiguous position in scholarship continues despite some important studies recognizing the significance of Exodus in Hebrews. The thesis is defended by a survey of their individual assessments of *Auctor*'s valuation of the Old Covenant in the light of the new revelation.[58] The question concerns whether these recent studies have recog-

---

[56] Gene R. Smillie, "Contrast or Continuity in Hebrews 1.1-2?" *NTS* 51 (October 2005): 545.

[57] Ibid., 543.

[58] In the context of the present study, the following relevant studies have been identified as significant enough for this dissertation in Chapter One: Streeter Stanley Stuart Jr., "The Exodus Tradition in Late Jewish and Early Christian Literature: A General Survey of the Literature and a Particular Analysis of the Wisdom of Solomon, II Esdras and the Epistle to the Hebrews" (Ph.D. diss., Vanderbilt University, 1973); James E. Reynolds, "A Comparative Study of the Exodus Motif in the Epistle to the Hebrews" (Th.D. diss., Southwestern Baptist Theological Seminary, 1976); Martin Emmrich, "Pneumatological Concepts in Hebrews" (Ph.D. diss., Westminster Theological Seminary, 2001); Russell E. Miller Jr., "The Doctrine of Rest in Hebrews 3-4 and Its Implications for Liberation Theology's Use of the Exodus" (Ph.D. diss., Bob Jones University, 2004); Kiwoong Son, "Sinai and Zion Symbolism and the Hermeneutics of Hebrews: Heb. 12:18-24 as an Interpretative Key to the Epistle" (Ph.D. diss., Brunel University, 2004); Gabriella Gelardini, "«Verhärtet eure Herzen nicht» Der Hebräer, eine Synagogenhomilie zu *Tischa be-Aw*" (Ph.D. diss., University of Basel, 2004). Though two of the above studies are prior to 1981, Beavis does not interact with them in her thesis. At least four of these studies have been published. These are: Martin Emmrich, *Pneumatological Concepts in the Epistle to the Hebrews: Amtscharisma, Prophet, & Guide of the Eschatological Exodus* (Lanham, Maryland: University Press of America, 2003); Kiwoong Son, *Zion Symbolism in Hebrews: Hebrews 12:18-24 as a*

nized the ontological significance of the two Exodus citations (Exod 3:14 and 25:40) employed by *Auctor*. The result of my survey can be summarized by Table 3 below.

Table 3 indicates that all the relevant studies have not recognized the prescriptive and descriptive significance of Exod 3:14 in Hebrews. Also, though three of the studies have recognized the descriptive significance of Exod 25:40 in Hebrews, all have not recognized its prescriptive significance. This is very unusual because all of them have recognized the implication of covenant and priesthood in Hebrews, yet they do not recognize the significance of sanctuary. This points out that scholars generally do not perceive that covenant and priesthood are inseparable from sanctuary, theologically and philosophically.

Also, using the definitive work done by Beavis, the positions of all these studies can be classified as either following the continuity or discontinuity model. Since all these relevant studies remain at the descriptive stage, only their significant descriptive contribution will be mentioned.

Table 3. Summary of Relevant Studies[59]

Scholars	Model for Interpreting the Relation between Old and New Covenants	Analysis of *Auctor*'s Use of Exodus 3:14	Analysis of *Auctor*'s Use of Exodus 25:40
Streeter Stanley Stuart	Continuity	None	Descriptive
James E. Reynolds	Continuity	None	None
Martin Emmrich	Continuity	None	None
Russell E. Miller Jr.	Continuity	None	None
Kiwoong Son	Discontinuity	None	Descriptive
Gabriella Gelardini	Continuity	None	Descriptive

Though both Stuart and Reynolds focus on *Auctor*'s use of Exodus, they do not advance the work of Beavis from the descriptive perspective. Emmrich recognizes the significance of Käsemann's work.[60] By adopting Käsemann's

---

Hermeneutical Key to the Epistle, Paternoster Biblical Monographs, ed. I. Howard Marshall et al. (Waynesboro, GA: Paternoster Press, 2005); Gabriella Gelardini, *Verhärtet eure Herzen nicht: Der Hebräer, eine Synagogenhomilie zu Tischa be-Aw*, BIS, ed. Ellen van Wolde, and R. Alan Culpepper (Leiden: Brill, 2007); Ted Miller, *Refuting Liberation Theology's Use of the Exodus with Hebrews 3-4* (Greenville, SC: Bob Jones University Press, 2009).

[59] See Stuart, "Exodus Tradition," 103, 151, 156, 163; Reynolds, "Exodus Motif," 78, 119; Emmrich, "Pneumatological Concepts," 32; idem, *Eschatological Exodus*, 53-54, Miller, "Hebrews 3-4," 148-49; Son, "Sinai and Zion," 121, 221; idem, *Zion Symbolism*, 97; Gelardini, "Synagogenhomilie," 154-68, 267-68.

[60] Emmrich, "Pneumatological Concepts," 16. Both Beavis and Grässer acknowledge the appearance of Käsemann's *Des wandernde Gottesvolk* as a turning point in the scholarship on Hebrews. Ernst Käsemann, *Das wandernde Gottesvolk* (Göttingen: Vandenhoeck & Ruprecht, 1938); Beavis, "Hebrews," 18; Grässer, "Hebräerbrief," 144. Note that Beavis interacted only

thesis, Emmrich maintains that the Old and New Covenant liturgies are related ontologically in Hebrews.[61] Emmrich continues his argument that *Auctor's* theology of revelation must be understood from his "eschatological framework."[62] Emmrich emphasizes the significance of the Exodus motif within the eschatological framework and approaches Hebrews from a non-dispensational (covenant) theology.[63] Within this eschatological, framework, he posits that *Auctor* follows a dialectical relation of the Old and New Covenants in terms of the horizontal typology.[64] Emmrich argues that "the author operates in the firm conviction that history belongs to God and that he had brought about the nation's birth in the event of the exodus as a typological intervention anticipating subsequent redemptive acts."[65]

Emmrich's perspective of continuity is very unique because he emphasizes the Holy Spirit's involvement in both the OT (during Israel's Exodus) and Christ's priestly ministry.[66] It is not Yahweh as Christ,[67] but Yahweh is primarily in the Person of the Holy Spirit, who involves himself ontologically and eschatologically in the cultic activities of God's people.[68]

Miller adopts the developmental perspective to understand *Auctor's* theology of revelation.[69] He argues that "the author [of Hebrews] presents the Old Testament as finding its fulfillment in Jesus Christ."[70] Miller posits that *Auctor* "demonstrates an organic link between the old and new; he does not wish to denigrate the old, but merely to establish the superiority of the new."[71]

Gelaridini proposes the renewal perspective to interpret the relation between the Old and New Covenants in Hebrews.[72] She suggests that Hebrews is

---

with the German version of Käsemann's book because the English version was not available until 1984 (three years after Beavis' work).

[61] Emmrich, *Eschatological Exodus*, 60 ; idem, Emmrich, "Pneumatological Concepts," 20. Käsemann adopts the continuity model whereby the Old and New Covenants related ontologically. Käsemann, *Wandering People*, 33. The underlying principle of Käsemann's work is that both the Sinai generation and the Christian community are united in the continuity of the whole revelation and as the bearer of revelation in Hebrews (ibid., 63).

[62] Emmrich, *Eschatological Exodus*, 55; idem, "Pneumatological Concepts," 5.

[63] Emmrich, "Pneumatological Concepts," 139.

[64] Ibid., 153.

[65] Emmrich, *Eschatological Exodus*, 53-54 ; idem, "Pneumatological Concepts," 32.

[66] Emmrich, *Eschatological Exodus*, 88-89; idem, "Pneumatological Concepts," 3.

[67] See A. T. Hanson, "Hebrews," in *It Is Written: Scripture Citing Scripture, Essays in Honour of Barnabas Lindars, SSF*, ed. D. A. Carson and H. G. M. Williamson (Cambridge: Cambridge University Press, 1988), 301; idem, "The Gospel in the Old Testament according to Hebrews," *Theology* 52 (July 1949): 248.

[68] Emmrich, *Eschatological Exodus*, 63 ; idem, "Pneumatological Concepts," 104.

[69] Miller, "Hebrews 3-4," 149.

[70] Ibid.

[71] Ibid., 148.

[72] Gelaridini, "Synagogenhomilie," 268.

a synagogue homily preached on *Tisha be-Av*. She argues that Hebrews is intertextually linked to Exod 31:18-32:35 (the *sidrah*) whereby *Auctor* teaches his audience that they have broken the Old Covenant.[73] Since the audience is capable of covenant renewal like the people of Israel at Mount Sinai, *Auctor* appeals to Jer 31:31-34 (the *haphtarah*) as the basis of the covenant renewal for his audience.[74] She proposes the reading of the *sidrah* and the *haphtarah* as "the hermeneutical key to this homily."[75]

According to Son, the relation of the two covenants is to be understood in the context of Sinai and Zion symbolism.[76] Put simply, "Zion symbolizes the new covenant in the NT."[77] Son rejects the renewal perspective for relating the Old and New Covenants in Hebrews.[78] Instead, he posits the literary-motif perspective to understand *Auctor*'s theology of revelation in light of the metaphysical or ontological assumption of Jewish apocalyptic literature.[79] In this interpretation, the religious language of the New Covenant in Hebrews seems to have no ontological and cultic significance because the heavenly cultus serves primarily as the ideational context to understand the superiority of the death and sacrifice of Jesus in relation to the earthly cultus.[80] Son argues that the "conceptual background of the antithesis between the superior heavenly temple and its earthly counterpart is derived neither from Platonic metaphysical dualism nor from the architectural language of a sketch plan on the basis of a temporal eschatology."[81]

Son's thesis is apparently "inconsistent" because the Jewish apocalyptic literature assumes the renewal perspective—the continuity camp,[82] and yet Son appeals extensively to the Jewish apocalyptic literature to defend the literary-

---

[73] Gabriella Gelardini, "Hebrews, an Ancient Synagogue Homily for *Tisha be-Av*: Its Function, Its Basis, Its Theological Interpretation," in *Hebrews: Contemporary Methods–New Insights*, ed. Gabriella Gelardini, BIS, ed. R. Alan Culpepper and Ellen van Wolde, vol. 75 (Leiden: Brill, 2005), 119; idem, "Synagogenhomilie," 154-168;

[74] See David Noel Freedman and David Miano, "People of the New Covenant," in *The Concept of the Covenant in the Second Temple Period*, ed. Stanley E. Porter and Jacqueline C. R. de Roo, SupJSJ, ed. John J. Collins, vol. 71 (Leiden: Brill, 2003), 25.

[75] Gelardini, "Hebrews as Homily," 120.

[76] Son, *Zion Symbolism*, 97; idem, "Sinai and Zion," 121.

[77] Son, *Zion Symbolism*, 96.

[78] Ibid., 97.

[79] Ibid., 103.

[80] Ibid., 111, n. 36.

[81] Ibid., 184.

[82] See Freedman and Miano, "New Covenant," 25; Gelardini, "Hebrews as Homily," 117. Dupont-Sommer writes: "Everything in the Jewish New Covenant heralds and prepares the way for the Christian New Covenant." A. Dupont-Sommer, *The Dead Sea Scrolls: A Preliminary Survey*, trans. E. Margaret Rowley (Oxford: Basil Blackwell, 1952), 99.

motif perspective—the discontinuity camp.[83] Prior to Son's work, Beavis has already noted that the presence of such inconsistency is pervasive among the scholars she examined.[84] The fact that Beavis's study excludes the relevant studies focusing on *Auctor*'s use of Exodus does not weaken Beavis's verdict. Indeed, her observation is reinforced by Son's dissertation—Son cannot avoid the trap of inconsistency even when he focuses on the *Auctor*'s use of Exodus in terms of the antithesis between Sinai and Zion.[85] Son's work demonstrates once again that it is easy for scholars to disassociate *Auctor*'s theology of revelation from his metaphysical assumption especially when the onto-theo-logical structure of reason is adopted for Hebrews.

It would be unreasonable to attempt in a few lines to pass a comprehensive judgment on the above recent works. That said, what kind of theological contribution can be made by these recent works whose focuses are on *Auctor*'s use of Exodus? The answer indicates that the models of these relevant works reflect at best a descriptive analysis. These scholars are capable of devising their own respective theological lenses to understand *Auctor*'s valuation of the Old Covenant in light of the new revelation.[86] As a result, one is left with the option of various sophisticated theological models from which to choose to understand the pedagogical and typological function of Exodus in *Auctor*'s theological argumentation. In other words, one *can* interpret *Auctor*'s use of pedagogy and typology in the context of any conceptual/theological presupposition because there seems to be no definitive clue provided in the sermon to direct his audience to understand the pedagogical and typological language in a proper theological context. This indeterminacy in the sermon obviously disengages *Auctor*'s audience theologically. Would an effective orator like *Auctor*, communicate his sermon with such a state of indeterminacy? I will demonstrate that *Auctor* prescribes *his* theological lens via *his* use of Exodus citations in Hebrews. A two-fold grounding analysis will be given later to examine two important citations in Hebrews—Exod 3:14 (in Heb 11:6) and Exod 24:50 (in Heb 8:5).[87]

---

[83] For an extensive list of Jewish apocalyptic literature used by Son, see Son, *Zion Symbolism*, 56-57.

[84] Beavis, "Hebrews," 125.

[85] Son, *Zion Symbolism*, 16. "Sinai and Zion are not only presented as the sites of the two different covenants but their symbolism expresses the different quality of the two covenants" (ibid., 95).

[86] According to Canale, from the perspective of ontology, the difference "boils down to a different 'index of reality.'" Fernando Canale, *Creation, Evolution, and Theology: The Role of Method in Theological Accommodation* (Berrien Springs, MI: Andrews University Lithotech, 2005), 74.

[87] Recent monographs in Hebrews continue to miss the prescriptive theological significance of Exod 25:40 and Exod 3:14. See Gerd Schunack, *Der Hebräerbrief*, Zürcher Bibelkommentare, ed. Hans Heinrich Schmid and Hans Weder, vol. 14 (Zürich: Theologischer Verlag, 2002), 224; Georg Gäbel, *Die Kulttheologie des Hebräerbriefes: Eine exegetisch-*

Auctor's Christocentric Exegesis of the Old Testament

By the authorial reading in light of Christ as Yahweh in Hebrews, one can easily posit that the Christ of the NT is the incarnate God of the OT. This is *the* important link between the Old and New Testaments.[88] It is the same God who reveals and inaugurates the Old and New Covenants in both Testaments. The authorial reading in light of Christ as Yahweh does not prove the thesis that *Auctor*'s exegesis of the OT *is* Christocentric. Also, the authorial reading in light of Christ as Yahweh in Hebrews does not indicate how the Christ of the NT appears Himself to the people of God under the Old Covenant.[89] Hence, the twofold thesis of this section is that *Auctor*'s exegesis of the OT is Christocentric and he believes in the Christophany—the theophany of Christ in human form.[90]

Auctor's Exegesis Is Christocentric

To support the first part of the twofold thesis, the argument proceeds from three perspectives—literary, pedagogical, and hermeneutical.

First, from a literary perspective, it is evident that *Auctor* makes the link between OT citations and the meaning of the citations with respect to Christ.[91] In other words, *Auctor* establishes or explains the link between the

---

religionsgeschichtliche Studie, WUNT, ed. Jörg Frey et al., vol. 212 (Tübingen: Mohr Siebeck, 2006), 555; Lloyd Kim, *Polemic in the Book of Hebrews*, Princeton Theological Monograph Series, ed. K. C. Hanson, vol. 64 (Eugene, OR: Pickwick Publications, 2006), 123-24; Sebastian Fuhrmann, *Vergeben und Vergessen: Christologie und Neuer Bund im Hebräerbrief*, WMANT, ed. Günther Bornkamm and Gerhard von Rad, vol. 113 (Neukirchen-Vluyn: Neukirchener Verlag, 2007), 276; Guido Telscher, *Opfer aus Barmherzigkeit: Hebr 9, 11-28 im Kontext biblischer Sühnetheologie*, FB, ed. Rudolf Schnackenburg and Josef Schreiner, vol. 112 (Würzburg, Germany: Echter Verlag, 2007), 134-37; Martin Karrer, *Der Brief an die Hebräer. Kapitel 5,11-13,25*, OTNT, ed. Rudolf Hoppe and Michael Wolter, vol. 20 (Gütersloher: Gütersloher Verlagshaus, 2008), 108-112; Susan E. Docherty, *The Use of the Old Testament in Hebrews: A Case Study in Early Jewish Bible Interpretation*, WUNT, ed. Jörg Frey et al., vol. 260 (Tübingen: Mohr Siebeck, 2009), 219.

[88] See Gwilym George Lloyd, "The Treatment of the Mosaic Law in the Epistle to the Hebrews with Some Comparison of the Pauline Attitude" (Ph.D. diss., University of Edinburgh, 1944), 92.

[89] *Auctor* explicitly states that Christ appears as God's Son to the people under the New Covenant (Heb 1:1-3).

[90] The thesis is important for the twofold grounding analysis.

[91] See Otfried Hofius, "Biblische Theologie im Lichte des Hebräerbriefes," in *New Directions in Biblical Theology: Papers of the Aarhus Conference, 16-19 September 1992*, ed. Sigfred Pedersen, NovTSup, ed. C. K. Barrett et al., vol. 76 (Leiden: E. J. Brill, 1994), 114; George H. Guth-Guthrie, "Hebrews' Use of the Old Testament: Recent Trends in Research," *CBR* 1 (April

text and Christ on the basis that the OT is God's unfolding plan of salvation which culminates in Christ (Heb 1:1-2).

Second, *Auctor*'s pedagogy is Christocentric. Grelot argues for NT authors' use of pedagogy as follows:

> Christ Jesus, considered within the total unfolding of his mystery, becomes the key to interpreting all of the texts that preceded him, announced his coming, and prepared the way for it, and that served as a "pedagogy of faith" for the people who received the word of God through the intermediaries that he sent: prophets, sages, psalmists, and all of the other sacred writers.[92]

It is indeed natural that *Auctor*'s exegesis of the OT is Christocentric (cf. Luke 24:44) because Hebrews is a sermon written for a pedagogical purpose—teaching and preaching.[93] Greenhaw says, "Preaching is to name God in consciousness."[94] Similarly, Clowney claims, "He who would preach the Word must preach Christ."[95] The authorial reading of Christ as Yahweh means to name Christ in *consciousness* and in *preaching*.

Finally, from a hermeneutical perspective, Davidson has already demonstrated that "the typology found in Hebrews is similar to the typology found elsewhere in Scripture."[96] Bird adds that *Auctor*'s hermeneutics "is aided by Christological typology."[97] As a result, one can safely conclude that *Auctor*'s exegesis is Christocentric because the Christ event (the life, death, and resur-

---

2003): 290; Andrew T. Lincoln, "Hebrews and Biblical Theology," in *Out of Egypt: Biblical Theology and Biblical Interpretation*, ed. Craig Batholomew and Anthony Thiselton, Scripture and Hermeneutics Series, ed. Craig G. Batholomew, vol. 5 (Grand Rapids: Zondervan Publishing House, 2004), 322.

[92] Grelot, *Symbolism*, 205.

[93] See Craig A. Evans, "The Old Testament in the New," in *The Face of New Testament Studies: A Survey of Recent Research*, ed. Scot McKnight and Grant R. Osborne (Grand Rapids: Baker Academic, 2004), 145; David M. Greenhaw, "The Formation of Consciousness," in *Preaching as a Theological Task: World, Gospel, Scripture in Honor of David Buttrick*, ed. Thomas G. Long and Edward Farley (Louisville, KY: Westminster John Knox Press, 1996), 11.

[94] Ibid., 7.

[95] Edmund P. Clowney, *Preaching and Biblical Theology* (Grand Rapids: William B. Eerdmans Publishing Company, 1961), 74.

[96] Richard M. Davidson, "Typology in the Book of Hebrews," *Issues in the Book of Hebrews*, ed. Frank B. Holbrook, DRCS, vol. 4 (Silver Spring, MD: Biblical Research Institute, 1989), 135. Davidson also affirms that *Auctor*'s typological exegesis is theo-onto-logical because the typology in Hebrews "finds its roots not in pagan thought, but in Israel's Scriptures" (ibid.). Ninow reinforces Davidson's thesis by showing that *Auctor*'s typology is established on the basis of his careful exegesis of the Old Testament. See Friedbert Ninow, "The Indicators of Typology within the Old Testament: The Exodus Motif" (Ph.D. diss., Andrews University, 1999), 303.

[97] Chad L. Bird, "Typological Interpretation within the Old Testament: Melchizedekian Typology," *Concordia Journal* 26 (January 2000): 52.

rection of Jesus) becomes the hermeneutical key for his typological interpretation and application of the Jewish Scriptures.[98]

Auctor's Belief in Christophany

We have seen that *Auctor's* exegesis of the OT is Christocentric. This fact does not reveal his belief in the Christophany—i.e., the appearance of Christ in human form in the OT. *Auctor's* Christocentric exegesis of the OT suggests that his belief in Christophany is probable—this belief is likely to be true or real. However, there are at least two reasons (epistemological and theological) to indicate that *Auctor* does believe the Christophany.

First, from an epistemological perspective, we have seen that *Auctor's* philosophy of history reflects the theo-onto-logical model. This means that *Auctor's* epistemological source for his Christocentric exegesis is *only* the OT. This fact is important because *Auctor's* epistemology is implicitly linked to his presupposed ontological framework upon which he grounds his hermeneutics. Haight says:

> Hermeneutical theory applies not only to interpreting texts but also to interpreting any symbol, since implicitly it is an epistemology or an historically conscious ontology of understanding itself.[99]

In light of this insoluble connection between ontology and epistemology, even though modern readers are unable to determine how *Auctor* interprets the ontological reality of the theophanies of Christ in the OT, they can investigate how *anyone* would understand the divine reality of theophanies revealed within the same epistemological source (i.e., the OT) utilized by *Auctor* for his exegesis. Borland has already done this investigation in his dissertation and concludes that the Christophany in the OT history *is* an actual ontological divine reality revealed in history (i.e., within time and space).[100] Yahweh's Christophany in the OT and the Incarnation of Christ in the NT are different but in some sense the same ontological reality—in terms of being the same God revealed in space and time.[101] As a result, in light of Borland's thesis, it is reasonable to posit that *Auctor* believes in the Christophany—the theophany of Christ in human form in the OT. Furthermore, since any principle of interpretation has to be operated from a presupposed ontological viewpoint, one

---

[98] Evans, "OT in the New," 145.
[99] Roger Haight, "Jesus and Salvation: An Essay in Interpretation," *TS* 55 (June 1994): 235.
[100] James Allen Borland, "Christophanies: Old Testament Appearances of Christ in Human Form" (Th.D. diss., Grace Theological Seminary, 1976), 1.
[101] See Hanson, "Hebrews," 301; Carl Michalson, "The Real Presence of the Hidden God," in *Faith and Ethics: The Theology of H. Richard Niebuhr*, ed. Paul Ramsey (New York: Harper & Brothers, 1957), 265.

can say that *Auctor* adopts the Christocentric approach to the OT *because* he is convinced of the historical reality of the Christophany. This reality about Christ (i.e., His presence in time and space) in the OT history serves as the indispensable ontological ground for Hebrews as well as other NT writers who adopt the Christocentric exegesis of the Scripture.

Second, *Auctor*'s Christocentric exegesis of the OT reflects his theological conviction about the actual presence of Christ in OT history.[102] When commenting on *Auctor*'s approach to the OT, Ellingworth says:

> Christ, by whom God has now spoken his final word (1:1f.), was alive and active in Creation (1:2) and throughout Israel's history. . . . Indeed, since Christ was already at work in OT times, even an OT text without a future reference (such as Ps. 40:6-8 = Heb. 10:5-7) may be applied to Christ.[103]

Though *Auctor* is convinced of the pre-existence of Christ in the OT, this fact is *not* sufficient to reflect or determine that he believes in the real presence of Christ in the OT.[104] From the perspective of classical theology (i.e., the onto-theo-logical framework), the pre-existence or theophany of Christ in the OT is not real because it is understood as a timeless divine reality. This classical theology, Canale argues, "completely prevents God from performing new actions in created time and relating to temporal creatures historically within the flow of created time."[105]

In other words, according to this classical ontology, the pre-existence or theophany of Christ in the OT is not a real presence "in the future-present-past flux of time."[106] Though this view completely contradicts *Auctor*'s philosophy of history, it is nevertheless a theological view consistent within the ontological framework of the classical Christian theology. Canale says:

> Due to this fateful theological error in early Christian theology, Christianity rejected its theological and social roots in the Old Testament and Israel.[107]

---

[102] Hanson defends the real presence of Christ in the OT and calls this ontological assumption "the most important clue to the understanding of the NT exegesis of the OT." Anthony Tyrell Hanson, *Jesus Christ in the Old Testament* (London: SPCK, 1965), 7. Gieschen supports Hanson's thesis from a theological perspective. Charles A. Gieschen, "The Real Presence of the Son before Christ: Revisiting an Old Approach to Old Testament Christology," *CTQ* 68 (April 2004): 108.

[103] Paul Ellingworth, *The Epistle to the Hebrews: A Commentary on the Greek Text*, NIGTC, ed. I. Howard Marshall and W. Ward Gasque (Grand Rapids: William B. Eerdmans Publishing Company, 1993), 41-42.

[104] For an opposing view, see Paul Ellingworth, "The Old Testament in Hebrews: Exegesis, Method and Hermeneutics" (Ph.D. diss., Aberdeen University, 1977), 398.

[105] Canale, *Scripture Replacing Tradition*, 52.

[106] Ibid.

[107] Ibid.

This theological error occurs when theologians utilize a subordinate source of revelation (i.e., theological conviction about the pre-existence of Christ in the OT) to determine or interpret the nature of a grounding source (theophany). In other words, classical theologians unknowingly, Canale argues, "invert the order of interpretation" formulated by the theo-onto-logical cognitive model.[108]

However, since *Auctor*'s exegesis of the OT is Christocentric, this fact is sufficient for modern readers to determine that he believes in the real or actual presence of Christ in the OT history. There are two reasons. First, Gieschen has defended the thesis: "*the christocentricity of the Old Testament should also be expressed by emphasizing the real presence of the Son in the B.C. events of the Scriptures.*"[109] In light of Gieschen's thesis, one can safely assert that *Auctor*'s Christocentric exegesis of the OT is hermeneutically linked to the theological conviction about the real presence of Christ in the OT. The Christocentricity of *Auctor*'s exegesis actually brings out the theological significance of the real presence of Christ in the OT history. One cannot avoid asking how does a biblical author interpret the theophany of Christ in the OT when that author demonstrably understands certain OT texts Christocentrically.

Second, since *Auctor*'s exegesis belongs to a grounding source of revelation, modern readers are able to utilize the grounding source to investigate how *Auctor* interprets the nature of the theophanies of Christ in the OT history via a logical synthesis of the facts and theses. On the one hand, a theophany (grounding source of revelation) occurred in the realms of nature and history (subordinate sources of revelation), this indicates that the most consistent and natural exegesis of the Scripture is the Christocentric exegesis of OT history in accordance with the ontological framework reflected by *Auctor*'s philosophy of history. On the other hand, when this observation is understood in light of Gieschen's work and the fact that *Auctor*'s philosophy of history reflects the theo-onto-logical framework of ontology, one can safely posit that *Auctor* interprets the theophanies of Christ in the OT history as *actual* appearances of Christ in space and time. According to Gieschen, the actual or real presence or appearance of Christ means His appearance with "a tangible and local presence."[110] Hence, under this matrix of process and relation, it is impossible for modern readers to interpret *Auctor*'s understanding about the nature of Christ's theophany as the timeless (unreal) presence of Christ in accordance with classical Christian theology. In short, since any real or actual presence of

---

[108] Canale, *Cognitive Principle*, 315.
[109] Gieschen, "Real Presence of the Son before Christ," 108.
[110] Ibid.

Christ in the OT is Christophany,[111] modern readers are led to conclude that *Acutor* believes in Christophany.

Summary

From an ontological and epistemological perspective, we have seen that *Auctor* adopts the Christocentric approach to the OT *because* he is convinced of the historical reality of the Christophany. From a theological perspective, we have also reached the same conclusion by looking at the other side of the same coin: that is, *Auctor's* conviction about the historical reality of Christophany is derived from his Christocentric exegesis of the OT history in light of his philosophy of history. The consistency of the present analysis is a reflection of the consistency of the divine reality—Christophany. Any further analysis should only reveal the same understanding of *one* divine reality.

Some modern readers may accuse this type of exegesis of being anachronistic: to use the words of Gieschen, it is "spiritual eisegesis that reads Christ *into* the Old Testament with uncritical lenses ground and colored by the study of Jesus in the New Testament."[112] However, this way of reading had been shared by many biblical interpreters prior to the rise of the historical-critical analysis of Scriptures.[113] Moreover, it is important to note that what appears to be anachronistic eisegesis to modern readers is actually the theological precondition for the NT authors. Says Hübner:

> It was their [NT authors'] conviction that the christological understanding of the holy Scripture would supply it with the indisputable and indispensible eschatological-messianic meaning, which, in pointing toward the Christ event, already was the original meaning. Furthermore, the messianic interpretation of the Old Testament is reconfirmed by God through the event of Easter. Thus the identity of God who speaks in Israel's holy Scripture with the God who accomplished salvation in Christ for all humankind, is the *theological* precondition for the *hermeneutical* basic conviction of the New Testament authors.[114]

---

[111] This is the thesis of Sam Whittemore Fowler, "The Visual Anthropomorphic Revelation of God" (Th.D. diss., Dallas Theological Seminary, 1978), 2.

[112] Gieschen, "Real Presence of the Son before Christ," 106.

[113] See Stanley J. Grenz, *The Named God and the Question of Being: A Trinitarian Theo-Ontology* (Louisville, KY: Westminster John Knox Press, 2005), 174. Grenz provides a quotation from the early church father Ambrose who declared that "It was not the Father who spake to Moses in the bush, or in the desert, but the Son" (ibid.).

[114] Hans Hübner," "New Testament Interpretation of the Old Testament," in *From the Beginnings to the Middle Ages (until 1300)*, ed. Chris Brekelmans, Menahem Haran, and Magne Sæbø, *Hebrew Bible / Old Testament: The History of Its Interpretation*, ed. Magne Sæbø, vol. 1, pt. 1, *Antiquity* (Göttingen: Vandenhoeck & Ruprecht, 1996), 334.

Like Hübner, Hegermann, Walter, and Gäbel argue that *Auctor* accepts the confessed Christology and reinterprets this theological precondition in light of the New Covenant cultus theologically.[115] Hartog prefers to call this theological precondition "the hermeneutical norm." Hartog says:

> Christ is the hermeneutical center, theme, and climax to Scripture. He is the prism through which the illuminating rays of Scripture must pass in order to reveal their full colors.... The confession of Jesus Christ as Lord is the hermeneutical key that opens the treasures of the Scriptures.[116]

I agree with Hartog's terminology because the term theological precondition can be misconstrued as a subordinate source of revelation whereas the hermeneutical norm clearly presents itself to play a grounding role for formulating the doctrinal system of the NT writers.[117]

In sum, before investigating the prescriptive significance of Exodus, it is necessary to derive *Auctor*'s ontological framework by examining his attitude toward the OT in light of the Christ event in terms of (1) his philosophy of history, (2) his theology of revelation, and (3) his Christocentric exegesis of the OT. This investigation establishes that *Auctor*'s ontological framework is grounded by the Mosaic-biblical metanarrative.

---

[115] See Harald Hegermann, "Christologie im Hebräerbrief," in *Anfänge der Christologie: Festschrift für Ferdinand Hahn zum 65. Geburtstag*, ed. C. Breytenbach and H. Paulsen (Göttingen: Vandenhoeck & Ruprecht, 1991), 343-45; Nikolaus Walter, *Praeparatio Evangelica: Studien zur Umwelt, Exegese und Hermeneutik des Neuen Testaments*, WUNT, ed. W. Kraus and F. Wilk, vol. 98 (Tübingen: J. C. B. Mohr [Paul Siebeck], 1997), 154-55; Gäbel, *Kulttheologie*, 240-41.

[116] Paul Hartog, "The 'Rule of Faith' and Patristic Biblical Exegesis," *TJ* 28 (Spring 2007): 75.

[117] The theological precondition/matrix plays a grounding role in biblical hermeneutics. See Canale, *Scripture Replacing Tradition*, 239.

• CHAPTER SIX •

History of the Interpretive Influence of Exodus in Hebrews

One's reception of *Wirkungsgeschichte* (i.e., history of the interpretive influence) of Exodus affects or shapes his pre-understanding of Exodus in relation to the reality of history, nature, and interpreted events.[1] Hence, an investigation of *Auctor*'s reception of the history of the interpretive influence of Exodus indicates how the subordinate source of revelation shapes his ontological framework. We have demonstrated that the most important citation from Exodus, which gives *Auctor* the most interpretive control for constructing his view of ontology, is Exod 3:14. The goal here is to defend the thesis that *Auctor*'s ontological framework is *not* grounded by his reception of the history of the interpretive influence of Exod 3:14. In other words, *Auctor*'s ontology is derived solely from his exegesis of Exod 3:14 in the context of the biblical metanarrative despite his conscious reception of other ontological frameworks.

To achieve the objective, I argue here that another crisis of belief surfaces, equal to that encountered with *Auctor*'s theology of revelation (a subordinate source of revelation). The crisis recurs when one utilizes the history of the interpretive influence of Exodus (a subordinate source of revelation) to ground *Auctor*'s ontological framework. Since *Auctor*'s reception of the history of the interpretive influence of Exodus is variously interpreted by commentators, this section will illustrate the need for the prescriptive analysis of Exodus by revealing the ontological continuity (similarity) and discontinuity (dissimilarity) between *Auctor*'s ontology and scholars' ontological valuations of the history of the interpretive influence of Exodus.

From a rhetorical perspective, we have seen that Exod 3:14 has contributed significantly to Hebrews' ontology. Now, from the perspective of the history of interpretation prior to or contemporary with *Auctor*, this section

---

[1] The term *Wirkungsgeschichte* is from Hans-Georg Gadamer, *Truth and Method*, trans. Joel Weinsheimer, and Donald G. Marshall, 2d rev. ed. (N. p.: Sheed and Ward, 1975; reprint, New York: Continuum Publishing Co., 1989), 300-307.

evaluates the extent of the ontological influence derived from his reception of the history of the interpretive influence of Exod 3:14 in Hebrews. This analysis consists of four parts: (1) *Auctor*'s ontology (i.e., view of God and ultimate reality); (2) an analysis of the history of the interpretive influence of Exod 3:14; (3) a comparative analysis between *Auctor*'s ontology and his reception of the history of the interpretive influence of Exod 3:14; (4) toward a prescriptive analysis of Exodus in Hebrews.

Auctor's Ontology

One cannot directly measure *Auctor*'s reception of the history of the interpretive influence of Exodus but it is possible to assess the extent of ontological pre-understanding (reception) contributed by the history of the interpretive influence of Exodus in the thought of *Auctor*. This assessment can be done via a benchmark of *Auctor*'s ontology whereby a comparative analysis can be provided to reveal the ontological similarity and dissimilarity between *Auctor*'s ontology and scholars' ontological valuation of the history of the interpretive influence of Exod 3:14.

Since it is impossible for *biblical* authors to maintain two conflicting views of God and ultimate reality, *Auctor*'s ontology derived from the subordinate sources must be consistent or coherent with his ontology derived from the grounding sources.[2] Indeed, we have demonstrated that *Auctor* maintains a consistent view of reality: both his philosophy of history (a subordinate source) and his Christocentric exegesis of the Old Testament (a grounding source) reflect the same ontological orientation (index of reality)—the theo-onto-logical model (see Figure 12).[3]

Figure 12. *Auctor*'s Overall Index of Reality

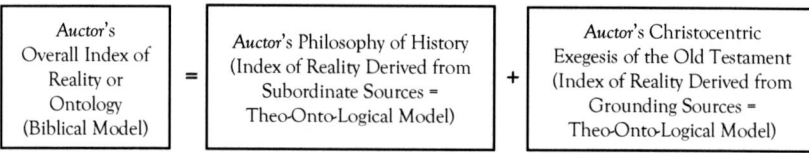

There is an ontological consistency when both *Auctor*'s view and scholars' valuation of the history of the interpretive influence of Exodus agree with the

---

[2] This is the thesis of Gene Smillie, "Living and Active: The Word of God in the Book of Hebrews" (Ph.D. diss., Trinity Evangelical Divinity School, 2000), 260.

[3] Canale argues that the ontological difference between various revelatory sources "boils down to a different 'index of reality.'" Fernando Canale, *Creation, Evolution, and Theology: The Role of Method in Theological Accommodation* (Berrien Springs, MI: Andrews University Lithotech, 2005), 74

theo-onto-logical model—that is, "reality is spatiotemporal."[4] If this were not the case, there would be an ontological inconsistency such as when scholars' valuation of the history of the interpretive influence agrees with the onto-theo-logical model—picking up on Greek ontology where "reality is timeless."[5] Here I want to reveal this ontological inconsistency because it supports the thesis that *Auctor*'s ontology is not grounded by his reception or pre-understanding of the history of the interpretive influence of Exodus.

History of the Interpretive Influence of Exodus 3:14

The thesis here is that scholars' ontological valuations of the history of the interpretive influence of Exod 3:14 reveal that it is variously interpreted by commentators following the theo-onto-logical model, the onto-theo-logical model, or both. I am indebted to Canale's groundbreaking dissertation which has demonstrated the present thesis in an embryonic form.[6] Hence, Canale's dissertation will be updated here with relevant studies.[7]

Canale does not examine the ontology in Hebrews but he has decidedly differentiated biblical ontology derived from Exod 3:14 (i.e., theo-onto-logical model) and Greek ontology derived from the philosophical interpretation of Exod 3:14 (onto-theo-logical model). After an in-depth analysis of the history of the interpretive influence of Exod 3:14, Canale says:

> The analysis of the Biblical context, as represented in the original reflection on the Ground of Being that Exodus 3:14 expresses, shows that Biblical rationality does address itself to foundational ontology as it explicitly puts Being into words. Thus, Exod 3:14 seems to provide the necessary ground, even the intellectual justification, for a Biblical philosophy that can stand independently from the Greek traditions of

---

[4] Ibid., 63.

[5] Ibid.

[6] Fernando Luis Canale, *A Criticism of Theological Reason: Time and Timelessness as Primordial Presuppositions*, AUSDDS, vol. 10 (Berrien Springs, MI: Andrews University Press, 1987), 285-387.

[7] After Canale's groundbreaking work on the history of the interpretive influence of Exod 3:14, there seems to be only three relevant studies for the present purpose: John Osemeikhian Akao, "The Burning Bush: An Investigation of Form and Meaning in Exodus 3 and 4" (Ph.D. diss., University of Glasgow, 1985); Sean M. McDonough, *YHWH at Patmos: Rev. 1:4 in Its Hellenistic and Early Jewish Setting*, WUNT, ed. Martin Hengel and Otfried Hofius, vol. 107 (Tübingen: Mohr Siebeck, 1999); Graham I. Davies, "The Exegesis of the Divine Name in Exodus," in *The God of Israel*, ed. Robert P. Gordon, University of Cambridge Oriental Publications, vol. 64 (Cambridge: Cambridge University Press, 2007), 139-56. Canale's dissertation was done in 1983. All three scholars do not interact with Canale's work. Akao's work is important because he investigates the history of the interpretive influence of the Exodus 3-4. On the other hand, both McDonough and Davies focus on the history of the interpretive influence of Exod 3:14.

philosophy. In other words, it seems that we could speak of two different philosophical traditions—namely the Parmenidean and the Mosaic-Biblical traditions.

... In short, it seems that theology, in following the Parmenidean philosophical interpretation of reason's structure was not only disregarding its own rational structure but was following an interpretation of reason which is incompatible with the one used as its original reflection and concepts were constituted and communicated in the Bible.[8]

Hence, Canale demonstrates that the ontological valuation of Exod 3:14, which is derived from classical Christian theology, rejects or conflicts with the Mosaic-Biblical tradition derived from a spatiotemporal understanding of Exod 3:14. Canale argues that the temporal understanding of God's Being suggested in Exod 3:14 sets the stage or ground for divine ontology on God's historical appearances and activities within the sequence of our created time which He experiences also as sequences within His own infinite analogical time.[9] In other words, God experiences in His life (not his Being) real sequences and knows and does new things not only for us but also for Himself (e.g., the Incarnation is a new thing that God did and also did not exist from eternity). Hence, we will reach the knowledge or meaning of God's Being only as we gather together to our mind the "tension distension" of divine activities throughout human history.

The language of "tension distension" is taken from Heidegger. The distension is ontological, which is "meaning" spread out through salvation history via the spatiotemporal acts of God. The tension is epistemological, which is the work of reason reaching outside itself from its present to the past and the future (prophecy) as well as bringing together all the meanings revealed in the ontological divine distension of the history of salvation. So the ontological distension takes place in God's infinite analogous time as it relates and adapts to our created time. The tension takes place in our limited time and historical reason and experiences. Hence, the ontological valuation of Exod 3:14 rejects the classical doctrine of the analogy of being on which the system of the Christian theology has been built so far.

Davies also recognizes the ontological inconsistency of various interpretive traditions in terms of the timeless (onto-theo-logical framework) or spatiotemporal (theo-onto-logical framework) presence of Yahweh in Exod 3:14.[10] In the final analysis, he argues for the latter perspective when he writes:

---

[8] Canale, *Theological Reason*, 393-94.
[9] Ibid., 358, 376 n. 2, 384, 403.
[10] Davies, "Divine Name in Exodus," 151.

The attention drawn by this exegesis to Yahweh's [spatiotemporal] presence also fits in well with, and provides a foundation for, the rich development of this theme in the later chapters of Exodus.[11]

In the same vein, by an exegesis of Exod 3-4, Akao reinforces Davies' position because Akao observes that Yahweh's presence in the burning bush is spatiotemporal.[12] In summary, one can safely posit that Exod 3:14 is variously interpreted by commentators following either biblical ontology (theo-onto-logical model) or classical (Greek) ontology (onto-theo-logical model).

Comparative Analysis

Auctor's ontological framework is not grounded by his reception of the history of the interpretive influence of Exod 3:14. We have seen that there is a conflicting ontological valuation of Exod 3:14 in the history of interpretation. Hence, to achieve the present objective, I will defend a twofold thesis (1) *Auctor* is definitively susceptible to the conflicting ontological valuation present in his reception of the history of the interpretive influence of Exod 3:14; and (2) *Auctor*'s ontology is not grounded by his reception of the history of the interpretive influence of Exod 3:14 because his ontology does not reflect a conflicting ontological valuation of Exod 3:14. Since we have already demonstrated that *Auctor*'s ontology is consistent, what remains here is to defend the first part of the twofold thesis.

To defend this thesis, one must ask when the historical paradigm shift from a theo-onto-logical lens to a mixed (i.e., both theo-onto-logical and onto-theo-logical) understanding of Exod 3:14 happened. If Hebrews was written after the historical turning point *and* a close contemporary with *Auctor* can be identified to adopt a mixed ontology definitively, one can argue that *Auctor* is definitively susceptible to a mixed and conflicting ontological valuation of Exod 3:14. To locate this historical turning point, one must first find out why and how someone can rationally accommodate a conflicting view of ontology.

Canale explains that someone can continue to maintain a conflicting view of ontology when he utilizes two incompatible metanarratives (grand stories) "to explain the entire history of reality."[13] He continues, "One [type of metanarrative], of philosophical origin, understands God and ultimate reality as timeless/spiritual; another, of biblical origin, understands God and ultimate reality as historical."[14] The former one came much later through the decisive influence of Parmenides (born c. 515 B.C.). Says Marías:

---

[11] Ibid.
[12] See Akao, "Burning Bush," 297.
[13] Canale, *Role of Method*, 154.
[14] Ibid.

> In Parmenides' thinking we see already beginning the division between the two worlds, the world of truth and the world of appearances (opinion or *dóxa*); the latter world is false when it is taken as true reality. This division comes to be decisive in Greek thought.[15]

Similarly, Wyschogrod observes that the philosophical metanarrative "was *first* proclaimed by Parmenides."[16] On the other hand, the biblical (theo-onto-logical) one is derived from the Mosaic-biblical tradition (i.e., the Torah).[17] Also, the philosophical one is centered on thought whereas the biblical one focuses on the personal relationship between God and human beings on the basis of faith.

Wyschogrod provides an excellent comparative analysis between the onto-theo-logical (Parmenidean) and theo-onto-logical (Mosaic-biblical) models of ontology. He summarizes the differences as follows:

> Relationship to God requires faith, whereas being is grasped by thought. . . . Being does not require faith. It is the object of thought. Being must, of course, not be confused with particular beings that are ontic and not ontological entities.[18]

One can maintain a mixed view of ontology by theological accommodation: that is, through a reinterpretation of God's reality (see Figure 11). When explaining how one can hold such a mixed ontology, Canale writes:

> In this hermeneutical context, a literal interpretation of scripture is impossible because it involves an inner contradiction. God cannot be temporal and timeless at the same time. To solve this problem, they [classical theologians] interpret scripture "theologically" or "spiritually." For them, scripture is symbolic, metaphorical, or mythical language indirectly referring to God's spiritual, non-historical reality. In technical jargon, scripture speaks about "ultimate" reality.[19]

The mixed model is presupposed by the both classical and modern (liberal) Christian doctrinal systems.[20] Though the mixed model consists of two conflicting views of reality, this inner contradiction does not necessarily render such belief irrational as long as such a philosophical position can be *believed*

---

[15] Julián Marías, *History of Philosophy*, trans. Stanley Appelbaum and Clarence C. Strowbridge (New York: Dover Publications, 1967), 23.

[16] Michael Wyschogrod, *The Body of Faith: God and the People of Israel*, 2nd ed. [1st published as *The Body of Faith: Judaism as Corporeal Election*. New York: Seabury Press, 1983] (Northvale, NJ: Jason Aronson, 1996), 132, emphasis added.

[17] Canale, *Theological Reason*, 393.

[18] Wyschogrod, *Israel*, 143.

[19] Fernando L. Canale, "From Vision to System: Finishing the Task of Adventist Theology—Part III: Sanctuary and Hermeneutics," *JATS* 17 (Autumn 2006): 56.

[20] Norman R. Gulley, *Prolegomena*, vol. 1 of *Systematic Theology* (Berrien Springs, MI: Andrews University Press, 2003), 127.

dogmatically. Hence, Mintek has demonstrated that rational belief can be built on an untrue premise:[21] that is, some rational beliefs can be shown to be groundless and unfounded. This is not difficult to understand when one realizes how powerful human imagination can be at uniting thoughts that are not necessarily deductively justified or mutually coherent.

**Figure 13. Index of Reality for
Classical Christian Doctrinal System**

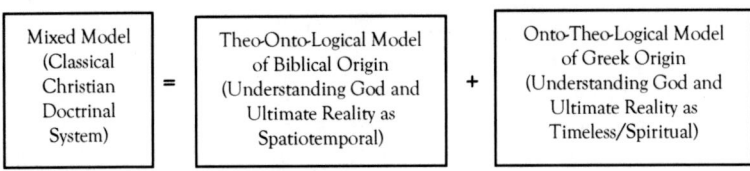

The union of the philosophical and biblical metanarratives allows someone to reach a mixed metanarrative whereby one can understand God and ultimate reality from both timeless/spiritual and spatiotemporal perspectives. When Canale describes how this inconsistent model can be logical, he writes:

> In the end, the inner logic of accommodation will lead to a spiritualized panentheistic view of God's reality.[22]

In other words, the two metanarratives are considered to be mutually enriched by each other to understand ultimate reality. After investigating the root cause of why and how someone maintains a mixed (and conflicting) view of reality, one actually simultaneously discovers that Parmenides is the originator of such a mixed view in the history of philosophy.

Now it seems that Parmenidean ontology has a positive contribution to *Auctor*'s reception or pre-understanding of the history of the interpretive influence of Exod 3:14. It is still necessary, however, to ascertain whether *Auctor* is susceptible to the conflicting ontological valuation present in his reception of the history of the interpretive influence of Exod 3:14. After Parmenidean (classical) ontology was born in the course of the history of philosophy, it seems impossible for modern readers to determine when exactly his ontology began to influence the exegesis of Scripture. However, according to McDonough, a controlling or definitive influence of Parmenidean ontology has become evident since the time of the LXX translation. He argues that the formulation of God as ὁ ὤν in Exod 3:14 by the LXX was "a radical innovation."[23] Commenting on this textual innovation, McDonough writes:

---

[21] See Shawn J. Mintek, "Rationality and Absolute Presuppositions" (Ph.D. diss., University of Washington, 1977), 13.

[22] Canale, *Role of Method*, 154.

[23] McDonough, *YHWH at Patmos*, 137.

It would constitute the first evidence we possess for an identification of God and Being (or God as *the* Being).[24]

McDonough notes that even though previous scholarship has generally argued for "little or no influence from Greek popular philosophy" in the LXX, "Ex. 3:14 would be the exception, not the rule."[25] In the same vein, Seitz aptly summarizes the ontological influence of this innovative translation of the LXX in the New Testament:

> ... [T]he rendering of the Hebrew behind "I am who I am" was picked up differently in the LXX, as a statement involving God's being. ... It was this nuance, arguably different than the narrative direction of Exodus, that in turn influenced certain New Testament and subsequent theological statements, focused on being, rather than personality. It is a very small leap to see how *ousia* dominated the options for trinitarian confession.[26]

Hence, in light of the fact that the *Vorlage* for *Auctor* is the LXX, it seems safe to conclude tentatively that *Auctor* is susceptible to the conflicting ontological valuation present in his reception of the history of the interpretive influence of Exod 3:14. This conclusion is tentative but can be affirmative if one can show that there is a close contemporary of *Auctor*—who exhibits such a definitive pre-understanding of Exod 3:14. I will show that there is a definitive example in Judaism during the NT time.

It is generally agreed that the classical or Greek ontological valuation of Exod 3:14 has made its way into Judaism via Platonism.[27] In contrast, Jewish exegesis reflects the original or Mosaic-biblical ontology that is found in Exodus 3:14. In fact, after studying Jewish or rabbinic ontological valuation of Exod 3:14, Canale concludes:

> Thus, whatever ontological meaning the rabbinic renderings may involve, they cannot be understood as expressing the Thomistic [classical] interpretation of Being, but rather as expressing an understanding of the original ontological meaning that is found in Exod 3:14, 15 on which both the rabbinic and the New Testament renderings find their ground and source.[28]

When Jewish exegetes intermingled the Mosaic-biblical metanarrative with the philosophical one to interpret God and ultimate reality, a mixed ontological

---

[24] Ibid., 134.

[25] Ibid.

[26] Christopher R. Seitz, *Figured out: Typology and Providence in Christian Scripture* (Louisville, KY: Westminster John Knox Press, 2001), 140.

[27] See Gregory E. Sterling, "'The Jewish Philosophy': The Presence of Hellenistic Philosophy in Jewish Exegesis in the Second Temple Period," in *Ancient Judaism in Its Hellenistic Context*, ed. Carol Bakhos, SupJSJ, ed. John J. Collins, vol. 95 (Leiden: Brill, 2005), 139.

[28] Canale, *Theological Reason*, 300.

valuation of Exod 3:14 was born in the course of the history of Jewish interpretation. Hence, Himmelfarb says:

> I have shown that possession of the Torah permits Philo of Alexandria and Josephus to adapt Greek ideas and values in the service of a new understanding of Jewish tradition, which is, nonetheless, distinctively Jewish.[29]

Sterling has demonstrated that Philo, a close contemporary with *Auctor*, is one of the clearest examples of an exegete adopting this mixed model of ontology in Judaism. Sterling says:

> The Torah exegete [Philo] did not believe that Platonism and Judaism were antagonistic systems; rather, he held that Moses and Plato understood the same realities.[30]

Hence, in the final analysis, one can now assert that *Auctor* is definitively susceptible to the conflicting ontological valuation present in his reception of the history of the interpretive of Exod 3:14.[31] Moreover, despite his definitive or conscious reception of a mixed ontology, *Auctor* continues to maintain an original (pure) form of ontology derived from Exod 3:14 in the context of the biblical metanarrative. Not a few readers of the Hebrew Scriptures are like Philo as it is very easy to introduce Greek ontology into the original ontology revealed in Exodus. When warning of the danger of this ontological eisegesis, DeVaux writes:

> One must take care not to introduce into it [Exod 3:14] the [classical] metaphysical notion of Being . . . as elaborated by Greek philosophy. . . . Such a notion is foreign to the biblical mentality.[32]

In sum, by his conscious rejection of Greek ontology which is present in his reception of the history of the interpretive influence of Exod 3:14, *Auctor* actually brings out his determination to ground his ontology by the Mosaic-biblical metanarrative.

---

[29] Martha Himmelfarb, "The Torah between Athens and Jerusalem: Jewish Difference in Antiquity," in *Ancient Judaism in Its Hellenistic Context*, ed. Carol Bakhos, SupJSJ, ed. John J. Collins, vol. 95 (Leiden: Brill, 2005), 128.

[30] Gregory E. Sterling, "'Philo Has Not Been Used Half Enough': The Significance of Philo of Alexandria for the Study of the New Testament," *PRS* 30 (Fall 2003): 254.

[31] This perspective is defended by Sterling, "Jewish Philosophy," 139.

[32] Roland deVaux, "The Revelation of the Divine Name YHWH," in *Proclamation and Presence: Old Testament Essays in Honour of Gwynne Henton Davies*, ed. John I. Durham and J. R. Porter (Richmond, VA: John Knox Press, 1970), 70.

Toward a Prescriptive Analysis of Exodus in Hebrews

In order to highlight the prescriptive significance of Exodus in Hebrews, this study proceeds to discuss two important corollaries derived from the thesis demonstrated above, which affirms that *Auctor*'s ontology is not grounded by his reception of the history of the interpretive influence of Exod 3:14. This section states the two corollaries and presents a case study to illustrate how one can utilize the prescriptive power of Exodus to identify *the* correct valuation of *Auctor*'s use of Exodus citations among various options proposed by scholars.

Two Important Corollaries

Given that *Auctor*'s ontology is not grounded by his reception of the history of the interpretive influence of Exod 3:14. The first corollary is that *Auctor* actually prescribes or reveals his ontology (theo-onto-logical view) by rejecting the other alternatives (the pure onto-theo-logical view or a mixed model) consciously. This corollary directly supports the overall thesis of this book because an analysis of *Auctor*'s use of Exodus does reveal the prescriptive significance of Exodus in Hebrews. The second corollary is that *Auctor*'s reception of the history of the interpretive influence of *any* Exodus citation may reflect his preunderstanding of other views of reality, but his view of ontology remains unchanged and should be understood from the theo-onto-logical point of view.[33]

Use of the Prescriptive Power of Exodus in Hebrews

By using the second corollary above, the purpose here is to illustrate how one can use the prescriptive power of Exod 3:14 to determine the correct valuation of *Auctor*'s ontological use of Exodus citations among the various options presented in the history of interpretation.

We have already identified Exod 3:14 and Exod 25:40 as the most significant Exodus citations in Hebrews. This section will illustrate the prescriptive significance of Exod 3:14 by showing how its prescriptive power can resolve the well-known debate surrounding the ontological valuation of Exod 25:40. Now, in order to appreciate the prescriptive power, this study will first present a brief summary of scholars' valuation of *Auctor*'s reception of the history of the interpretive influence of Exod 25:40.

---

[33] This corollary is obvious because biblical authors do not maintain a conflicting view of God and ultimate reality (see supra, 104-5).

The prescriptive power of Exod 3:14 in Hebrews is effective in resolving the crisis of belief about *Auctor*'s ontology. To demonstrate this prescriptive power, it is necessary to introduce an ongoing and unresolved debate in the scholarship of Hebrews. The existence of such debate is a crisis of belief. One of the ongoing and well-known debates in the scholarship is the valuation of *Auctor*'s reception of the interpretive influence of Exod 25:40 in Heb 8:5. As a matter of fact, each scholar's valuation of *Auctor*'s ontology points to a certain interpretation of the heavenly tabernacle. Commenting on the debate, Schenck says that "it is dangerous ground on which to build any particular understanding of the heavenly tabernacle."[34] Schenck's judgment is only correct if one does not recognize the prescriptive power of Exod 3:14 in Hebrews. Nevertheless, his observation does validate the present crisis of faith resulting from a descriptive analysis regarding the use of Exod 25:40 in Heb 8:5.

Table 4. Scholars' Valuations of *Auctor*'s Ontology Reflected by Descriptive Analysis of His Use of Exod 25:40 in Heb 8:5[35]

Representative Scholars	Scholars' Valuations of *Auctor*'s Ontology
Lyle Osborne Bristol; A. Berkeley Mickelsen; August Strobel; Ronald R. Cox	Mixed Ontology
Gregory E. Sterling	Greek Ontology
Ronald Williamson	Mosaic-biblical Ontology

To illustrate this crisis, I have found that there are three models in terms of scholars' valuation of *Auctor*'s reception of the history of the interpretive influence of Exod 25:40: (1) a mixed model (Greek ontology and biblical ontology); (2) the onto-theo-logical model (Greek ontology); (3) the theo-onto-

---

[34] Kenneth L. Schenck, *Cosmology and Eschatology in Hebrews*, SNTSMS, ed. John M. Court, vol. 143 (Cambridge: Cambridge University Press, 2007), 157.

[35] See Lyle Osborne Bristol, "The Logos Doctrine of Philo Judaeus and the Epistle to the Hebrews" (Th.D. diss., Victoria University, Toronto, 1947), 4; A. Berkeley Mickelsen, "Methods of Interpretation in the Epistle to the Hebrews" (Ph.D. diss., University of Chicago, 1950), 154; August Strobel, *Der Brief an die Hebräer*, Das Neue Testament Deutsch: Neues Göttinger Bibelwerk, ed. Hans Conzelmann et al., vol. 13 (Göttingen: Vandenhoeck & Ruprecht, 1991), 94; Ronald R. Cox, "By the Same Word: The Intersection of Cosmology and Soteriology in Hellenistic Judaism, Early Christianity and 'Gnosticism' in the Light of Middle Platonic Intermediary Doctrine" (Ph.D. diss., University of Notre Dame, 2005), 224; Gregory E. Sterling, "Hellenistic Philosophy and the New Testament," in *Handbook to Exegesis of the New Testament*, ed. Stanley E. Porter, NTTS, ed. Bruce M. Metzger and Bart D. Ehrman, vol. 25 (Leiden: Brill, 1997), 332; Ronald Williamson, *Philo and the Epistle to the Hebrews*, ALGHJ, ed. K. H. Rengstorf, vol. 4 (Leiden: E. J. Brill, 1970), 567.

logical model (biblical ontology). Table 4 summarizes the positions of some representative scholars.

For mixed ontology, I have included several scholars in Table 4 to illustrate the fact that there are various combinations of Greek and Mosaic-biblical ontological contribution in the various mixed models. For example, even though both Mickelsen and Bristol have argued for a mixed ontology in *Auctor*'s reception after a study of *Auctor*'s reception of the history of the interpretive influence of Exod 25:40 in Heb 8:5, their ontological valuation of *Auctor*'s mixed model is different. Hence, one should not say *the* mixed ontology because there are various kinds of mixed ontology proposed by scholars. In the final analysis, Mickelsen only concedes a little Greek ontology in his mixed model of ontology because he detects that only certain passages reveal the presence of Greek ontology in Hebrews.[36] On the other hand, Bristol is willing to allow Greek ontology to intermingle fully with biblical metanarrative because he documents the presence of Greek ontology throughout Hebrews at a grammatical level.[37]

Contrary to Mickelsen and Bristol, Sterling argues that *only* Greek ontology is present in *Auctor*'s reception of the interpretive influence of Exod 25:40:

> Although some have challenged the Platonism of this statement in recent years, several factors lead me to conclude it is present: the use of the Platonic image ('shadow'), the earthly/heavenly contrast, and the citation of Exod. 25:40 as a textual basis for the distinction. . . . What is surprising is that the reality ('image') is situated temporally rather than ontologically. I suggest that the audience and author both accept the Platonic distinction, but that the author *adds* the eschatological twist in keeping with his christological understanding of history.[38]

For Sterling, *Auctor*'s reception of the interpretive influence of Exod 25:40 reflects only the presence of Greek ontology, and yet *Auctor* decides to modify his reception by intermingling with biblical ontology (the theo-onto-logia) in light of the Christ event.

Finally, according to Williamson's analysis of *Auctor*'s reception of the history of the interpretive influence of Exod 25:40, the philosophical metanarrative of "Platonic Idealism does not extend into the Writer's way of looking at life as a whole."[39] In other words, *Auctor* does not use Greek ontology in an unquestioning manner because (1) only the intellect could enter the philosophical ideal world which is not a real heaven, and (2) Hebrews stresses that

---

[36] See Mickelsen, "Hebrews," 154.

[37] See Bristol, "Hebrews," 4. Bristol's dissertation is massive (491 pages excluding the bibliography). Grässer follows Bristol's position (Erich Grässer, *Der Glaube im Hebräerbrief*, MTS, ed. Werner Georg Kümmel and Hans Graß, vol. 2 [Marburg: N. G. Elwert, 1965], 174).

[38] Sterling, "Hellenistic Philosophy," 332, emphasis added.

[39] Williamson, *Philo and Hebrews*, 567.

Jesus entered the heavenly tabernacle in history when He completed His work on the Cross.[40]

We have seen that there is a crisis of belief in terms of the three models to value *Auctor*'s reception of the history of the interpretive influence of Exod 25:40. How can one determine which way is correct? One can ascertain the correct valuation by activating the prescriptive power of Exod 3:14 in Hebrews. To achieve this goal, one needs to employ the second corollary. Put simply, since biblical authors maintain the same (consistent) index of reality (i.e., theo-onto-logia),[41] one can deduce that *Auctor*'s ontological valuation of Exod 3:14 is the same as his ontological valuation of Exod 25:40, irrespective of his reception of the history of the interpretive influence of Exodus. As a result, one should reject the views that show the presence of either Greek ontology (e.g., Sterling), or a mixed ontology (e.g., Mickelsen) in *Auctor*'s reception of the history of the interpretive influence of Exod 25:40. One should only accept the view (e.g., Williamson) which values the presence of biblical ontology in *Auctor*'s reception of the history of the interpretive influence of Exod 25:40.

Auctor's Pedagogical Use of Exodus 3:14

We have seen how the biblical view of nature and supernature can be prescribed pedagogically by the temporal analogy of being drawn from Exod 3:14. In order to teach the theology of God, *Auctor* has to engage his audience pedagogically (didactically). Evans says:

> Hebrews is didactic throughout, and the argument is punctuated by passages of urgent exhortation which carry the main weight (2:1ff.; 3:1ff.; 4:1ff.; 5:11-6:20; 10:19-39; 12:3-13).[42]

Theologians can didactically prescribe various views of nature and supernature according to their presupposed models of pedagogy or reason.

The present purpose is to demonstrate the prescriptive power of Exod 3:14 in terms of its pedagogical power to reflect *Auctor*'s view of nature and supernature—*Auctor*'s pedagogical use of Exod 3:14 in Hebrews actually reveals

---

[40] Ronald Williamson, "Platonism and Hebrews," *SJT* 16 (March 1963): 419. Both Dukes and Schenck follow Williamson's position. See Schenck, *Cosmology*, 180; James Graydon Dukes, "Eschatology in the Epistle to the Hebrews" (Th.D. diss., Southern Baptist Theological Seminary, 1956), 320.

[41] See supra, 106, Figure 12.

[42] C. F. Evans, "The New Testament in the Making," in *From the Beginning to Jerome*, ed. C. F. Evans and P. R. Ackroyd, *Cambridge History of the Bible*, ed. C. F. Evans et al., vol. 1 (Cambridge: Cambridge University Press, 1970), 263.

his view of nature and supernature. For this reason, I argue that *Auctor* utilizes Exod 3:14 pedagogically in light of the Christ event. To support this thesis, I will demonstrate that *Auctor*'s pedagogy reflects the characteristics of biblical pedagogy. If *Auctor*'s pedagogy does reflect the characteristics of biblical pedagogy, one can safely posit that *Auctor* does utilize Exod 3:14 pedagogically. This deduction is derived from a union of two proven facts: (1) biblical pedagogy is built upon biblical ontology derived from Exod 3:14; (2) *Auctor* uses Exod 3:14 to *engage* his audience theologically or rhetorically in Heb 11:6.

To determine whether one's pedagogy reflects biblical pedagogy, it is necessary to examine the following three aspects of thoughts: (1) philosophy of history; (2) Christocentric exegesis of the Old Testament; (3) reception of the history of the interpretive influence of Exod 3:14. One's pedagogy reflects biblical pedagogy or reason when all three aspects of thought are consistent with the theo-onto-logical structure of reason. For a biblical writer, his pedagogy reflects biblical pedagogy when the first two aspects of his thoughts are consistent with the theo-onto-logical structure of reason and there is textual (epistemological) evidence to support the fact that he uses Exod 3:14 rhetorically or theologically. Since we have seen that all three aspects are reflected in the thoughts of *Auctor*, it is safe to posit that *Auctor*'s pedagogy is consistent with biblical pedagogy and so he uses Exod 3:14 pedagogically (didactically) in Heb 11:6.[43]

The prescriptive significance of Exod 3:14 comes from its pedagogical power to reveal *Auctor*'s view of nature and supernature. Since Exod 3:14 reveals biblical ontology, *Auctor*'s pedagogical use of Exod 3:14 means that he prescribes his *biblical* view or structure of nature and supernature because ontology is universal. To support this understanding, Wolterstorff says:

> Ontology . . . is a description of the most general structure of what there is. It is a description of a structure so general that every other discipline will deal with some details of the structure.[44]

The universal nature of biblical ontology means that the biblical view of God (*theos*) and His relation to reality (*ontos*) revealed in Exod 3:14 remains the same in the progress of revelation. If the Being of God (*theos*) and His relation to reality (*ontos*) are revealed in Exod 3:14, the Being of God and divine relation to reality are not to be changed (Heb 11:6). Hence, one can say that *Auctor*'s pedagogy reflects the biblical view of nature and supernature because he uses Exod 3:14 pedagogically in Heb 11:6.

---

[43] See Stanley Winter Theron, "Paraenesis in the Epistle to the Hebrews (D.Div. diss., University of Pretoria, 1984), 168.

[44] Nicholas Wolterstorff, *On Universals: An Essay on Ontology* (Chicago: University of Chicago Press, 1970), xii.

I have already defended the use of the authorial reading of Christ as Yahweh from the perspective of the audience-oriented criticism. Now, there is another reason to support this reading strategy. Since ontology is universal and *Auctor*'s exegesis of the Old Testament is Christocentric, one can posit that *Auctor* understands Exod 3:14 in the following manner: Yahweh was revealed in the burning bush to Moses (Exod 3:14), and Christ was there too.[45] Hence, D'Angelo rightly argues that "the glory of God which Moses saw, the divine Word by which were created heaven and earth, this is the son of God, Jesus."[46] The authorial reading of Christ as Yahweh effectively points to this same understanding of Exod 3:14 in Heb 11:6. This understanding of Heb 11:6 obviously raises a problem to the non-elect Jewish professed Christians in light of the mixed audience.

Summary

This section highlights the prescriptive significance of Exod 3:14 in Hebrews. The prescriptive power of Exod 3:14 in Hebrews is threefold. First, *Auctor* actually prescribes his ontological framework by rejecting the other two alternatives—the mixed (biblical-Greek) and Greek models, when he chooses consciously not to fuse or blend his ontology with Greek ontology present in his reception of the history of the interpretive influence of Exod 3:14. *Auctor* continues to maintain his ontological framework derived from the Mosaic-biblical metanarrative in spite of the alternative ontological understanding of Exod 3:14 in the history of interpretation.

Auctor's conscious rejection of the mixed and Greek models points to the second prescriptive power of Exod 3:14. That is, *Auctor* prescribes that his ontological understanding of other citations from Exodus should be interpreted according to the Mosaic-biblical metanarrative. This prescriptive function is significant in light of the various valuations of *Auctor*'s reception of the history of the interpretive influence of Exod 25:40. Put simply, *Auctor*'s ontological use of Exod 3:14 prescribes that Exod 25:40 should be understood in the context of the Mosaic-biblical metanarrative. This means scholars' valuation of *Auctor*'s use of Exod 25:40, in light of a mixed or Greek ontology, is not warranted. Third, *Auctor* also prescribes that his pedagogy (didactic approach) accords with biblical pedagogy because he utilizes Exod 3:14 pedagogically in

---

[45] Both D'Angelo and Manson argue for the same understanding. See William Manson, *The Epistle to the Hebrews: A Historical and Theological Reconsideration, the Baird Lecture, 1949* (London: Hodder and Stoughton, 1951), 80; Mary Rose D'Angelo, *Moses in the Letter to the Hebrews*, SBLDS, ed. Howard C. Kee and Douglas A. Knight, vol. 42 (Missoula, MT: Scholars Press, 1979), 177.

[46] Ibid.

light of the Christ event in Heb 11:6. This means that one should adopt biblical pedagogy to construct *Auctor*'s doctrine instead of classical or modern pedagogies.

• CHAPTER SEVEN •

Auctor's Typological Use of Exodus in Light of the Christ Event

This chapter is the second part of the twofold prescriptive analysis concerning *Auctor*'s pedagogical and typological uses of Exodus in light of the Christ event. The purpose here is to demonstrate the prescriptive power of Exod 25:40 in Hebrews. To achieve this objective, I will defend the thesis that the prescriptive power of Exod 25:40 comes from the prefigurative or prophetic power of Exod 25:40 to reveal *Auctor*'s metanarrative (i.e., the grand story) via his Christocentric-typological use of Exod 25:40. Hence, there are two parts: (1) *Auctor*'s Christocentric-typological use of Exod 25:40; (2) the prescriptive significance of *Auctor*'s metanarrative.

Auctor's Christocentric-Typological Use of Exodus 25:40

We have seen that *Auctor* interprets Exod 25:40 according to biblical ontology. The thesis here is that Exod 25:40 has the analogical and the prophetic power to reveal the spatiotemporal relationships between the heavenly and earthly tabernacle or sanctuary in Hebrews. The section is divided into two parts: (1) the grammatical significance of τῶν ἁγίων in Heb 8:2; (2) the typological use (significance) of Exod 25:40 in Heb 8:5.

Grammatical Significance of *Ton Hagion* in Hebrews 8:2

Since *Auctor*'s use of Exod 25:40 occurs after the *first* occurrence of τῶν ἁγίων in Heb 8:2, it necessary to examine the significance of τῶν ἁγίων before examining the prophetic typology of Exod 25:40 in Heb 8:5. The phrase τῶν ἁγίων (and its variants) occurs ten times in Hebrews and their translations are debated.¹ Since the debate among various commentators has been examined exegetically by Salom and Shea, the goal here is to present the fruit of their research in a summary manner.²

First, we observe the strength of Salom's analysis is his extensive survey of at least ten translations for the phrase τῶν ἁγίων (and its variants). However, Salom's personal translations of the phrase are vague because he refuses to identify the referent (the holy place or the most holy place) in light of the rhetorical contexts. For example, Salom suggests a translation of τῶν ἁγίων in Heb 10:19 as follows: "it is recommended that the translation of τῶν ἁγίων be left as 'sanctuary,' allowing the reader or commentator, on the basis of the literary and theological context, to draw his conclusions as to what part of the sanctuary is particularly in the mind of the author."³

Second, though Shea does not attempt to document a survey of various interpretations of the phrase τῶν ἁγίων (and its variants), he is able to identify the referent of the phrase in light of the rhetorical context. For example, he asserts that τῶν ἁγίων (Heb 8:2) should be interpreted as "a true genitive plural."⁴ As a result, he argues that the three occurrences of the phrase τῶν ἁγίων (Heb 8:2; 9:8; 10:19) should be translated as "the two holy places": "the holy place and the Most Holy Place taken together and subsumed under this true plural."⁵ After defending the translation grammatically, Shea writes:

> The first comparison in Heb 9 found in verse 1 where the singular form τὸ ἅγιον is used. Since it is evident from this occurrence that the writer knew the singular form well, it is also clear that this plural form in 8:2 is no accident. Beyond that there is an even more distinct parallel in 9:3 where the word ἁγίων is used in the compound phrase "holy of holies." ...
>
> ... In Lev 16 the word for "holy place" is found in the singular and it refers to only one place, i.e., the Most Holy Place. In Heb 8:2, in direct contrast within the context of the same word pair, the genitive plural is used. This emphasizes all the more that the true plural was intended and is significant and should be translated as a true plural.⁶

---

¹ Alwyn P. Salom, "Ta Hagia in the Epistle to the Hebrews," *Issues in the Book of Hebrews*, ed. Frank B. Holbrook, DRCS, vol. 4 (Silver Spring, MD: Biblical Research Institute, 1989), 219.

² Ibid. 220; William H. Shea, "The Significance and Function of Ton Hagion in Hebrews 8-10" (Unpublished Paper Collected by the Center for Adventist Research, 1989), 1. All quotations from the article in this book are reprinted by permission of the author. All rights reserved.

³ Salom, "Ta Hagia," 227.

⁴ Shea, "Hebrews 8-10," 1.

⁵ Ibid. Among all commentators surveyed by Salom, there is only one scholar (Wuest) who translates τῶν ἁγίων in Heb 8:2 as "holy places." Salom, "Ta Hagia," 227. However, Wuest's position is still very general and inconsistent because he translates τῶν ἁγίων in Heb 9:8 and Heb 10:19 as "Holiest" and "Holy of Holies" respectively (ibid.).

⁶ Shea, "Hebrews 8-10," 1.

By interpreting τῶν ἁγίων as "the two holy places,"[7] this means that the καί in the phase τῶν ἁγίων λειτουργὸς καὶ τῆς σκηνῆς (Heb 8:2) is not epexegetical because "epexegetical *kai* cannot be present when it joins a plural and a singular."[8] This perspective is supported by the sequential intrusion of λεῖτουργός. Shea also explains why the use of ἔπηξεν supports the same point:

> This tent was "was set up, erected by" the Lord. One can set up a tent but one does not set up a holy place. It is the presence of the Lord that makes that place holy. The verb applies to the tent but it does not apply to the holy places. Thus the picture is that of the two holy places enclosed by the overarching tent. . . .
>
> The functional conclusion of this matter is simply that Christ, as our high priest, has a ministry in both the holy place and the Most Holy Place of the heavenly sanctuary. He is not limited to the throne which is mentioned in Heb 8:1 but was free to move about the heavenly sanctuary to function in the various types of ministries represented by both of those holy places that are referred to in Heb 8:2.[9]

Hence, Hebrews 8:2 spells out the bipartite nature of the heavenly sanctuary (cf. Heb 9:8; 10:19).[10]

But how does *Auctor* describe the heavenly veil (καταπετάσματος) whereby the heavenly sanctuary becomes bipartite? Though *Auctor* uses καταπετάσματος three times (Heb 6:19; 9:3; 10:20),[11] only Heb 10:20 refers to the veil in connection with the "two holy places" in heaven (10:19).[12] Shea describes the heavenly veil:

> To interpret this [heavenly] veil in 10:20 as the veil between the holy place and the Most Holy Place breaks up the preceding reference to the "entrance into the holy places" which includes both of those holies. Thus the veil must be the veil into the

---

[7] Salom identifies eight commentators translating τῶν ἁγίων in Heb 8:2 as "sanctuary." Salom, "Ta Hagia," 220. Salom argues for a similar singular translation: "the heavenly sanctuary as a whole" (ibid., 224).

[8] Shea, "Hebrews 8-10," 2. Hofius defends the same view. Otfried Hofius, *Der Vorhang vor dem Thron Gottes: Eine exegetisch-religionsgeschichtliche Untersuchung zu Hebräer 6,19f. und 10,19f*, WUNT, ed. J. Jeremias and O. Michel, vol. 14 (Tübingen: J. C. B. Mohr [Paul Siebeck], 1972), 59-60. Contra, Otto Michel, *Der Brief an Die Hebräer*, KEK, ed. H. A. W. Meyer and F. Hahn, vol. 14 (Göttingen: Vandenhoeck & Ruprecht, 1984), 287-88.

[9] Shea, "Hebrews 8-10," 2.

[10] Hofius argues for the bipartite nature of the heavenly sanctuary. Otfried Hofius, *Katapausis. Die Vorstellung vom endzeitlichen Ruheort im Hebräerbrief*, WUNT, vol. 11 (Tübingen: J. C. B. Mohr [Paul Siebeck], 1970), 54. Contra, Leithart who sees an undivided heavenly sanctuary. Peter J. Leithart, "Womb of the World: Baptism and the Priesthood of the New Covenant in Hebrews 10.19-22," *JSNT* 78 (June 2000): 62.

[11] Rice argues that καταπετάσματος in Heb 6:19 could refer to three veils: to the courtyard, to the holy place, and to the Most Holy Place. George E. Rice, "Hebrews 6:19: Analysis of Some Assumptions Concerning *Katapetasma*," *Issues in the Book of Hebrews*, ed. Frank B. Holbrook, DRCS, vol. 4 (Silver Spring, MD: Biblical Research Institute, 1989), 234.

[12] Shea, "Hebrews 8-10," 2.

holy place which was the veil into both of the holies, it was the entrance, the entryway into the interior of the sanctuary. That is the same thing that the reference in 6:19. That text does not say that its καταπέτασμα was entryway into the holy place or the Most Holy Place. It simply says that it was the entryway into what lay behind it.[13]

By linking *Auctor*'s use of καταπέτασμα in the two texts (Heb 6:19; 10:20), it is possible to argue that readers are rhetorically led through the veil of the heavenly sanctuary and then they "pass out through that same veil because the discussion of the [heavenly] sanctuary is ended."[14] The two occurrences of the heavenly veil form an envelope construction around *Auctor*'s κεφάλαιον—the analogy between earthly and heavenly tabernacles (Heb 8:1-5). The doctrinal topics enclosed within the framework are better priest, better sanctuary, better covenant, and better blood.

Typological Use of Exodus 25:40 in Hebrews 8:5

The goal here is to examine why and how Exod 25:40 is important for revealing *Auctor*'s metanarrative. To achieve this objective, it is necessary to demonstrate the threefold problems: (1) why *Auctor*'s sanctuary typology derived from Exod 25:40 is analogical and prophetic/prefigurative; (2) why *Auctor*'s sanctuary typology reflects his metanarrative; (3) how *Auctor*'s typological use of Exod 25:40 reveals the spatial and temporal dimensions of his metanarrative. Since the first part of the threefold thesis has already been defended by others,[15] I will deal with the latter two parts only.

We have seen how Exodus significantly influences *Auctor*'s cultic vocabulary—sanctuary, tabernacle, priests, and sacrifices. Since *Auctor*'s argument is

---

[13] Ibid., 8.

[14] Ibid.

[15] In order to defend the first part of the threefold thesis, it is necessary to validate the following two propositions: (1) *Auctor*'s typological exegesis of the sanctuary typology of Exod 25:40 reflects the typological structure of the Old Testament; (2) the sanctuary/tabernacle typology of Exod 25:40 is prophetic. The first proposition is validated by Davidson. See Richard M. Davidson, "Typology in the Book of Hebrews," *Issues in the Book of Hebrews*, ed. Frank B. Holbrook, DRCS, vol. 4 (Silver Spring, MD: Biblical Research Institute, 1989), 186. This work on the typology in Hebrews is built on his dissertation (idem, *Typology in Scripture: A Study of Hermeneutical τύπος Structure*, AUSDDS, vol. 2 [Berrien Springs, MI: Andrews University Press, 1981]). The second proposition is validated by Nixon. See Hilary Arthur Nixon, "Typology of the Mosaic Tabernacle and Its Articles as Interpreted by Authors of the Nineteenth and Twentieth Centuries" (Ph.D. diss., Drew University, 1984), 55. Nixon acknowledges that his definition of type is taken from Douglas W. Friederichsen, "Hermeneutics of Typology" (Th.D. diss., Dallas Theological Seminary, 1970), 329. It is not necessary to demonstrate that sanctuary or tabernacle typology is analogical because prophetic or prefigurative typology includes analogical function. See Philip Edwards Powers, "Prefigurement and the Hermeneutics of Prophetic Typology" (Ph.D. diss., Dallas Theological Seminary, 1995), 185.

cultus-centered,[16] it is reasonable to assert that his metanarrative is sanctuary-oriented; it is a story about God's pilgrim community on the move toward the heavenly sanctuary.[17]

However, *Auctor*'s metanarrative is also a story of how God's people should worship Him when they enter the heavenly sanctuary. In fact, it is important to note that *Auctor* focuses on the Mosaic Law not as moral but as a system of worship.[18] This is why *Auctor*'s metanarrative is pedagogy about worship. We have seen that the grounding source of *Auctor*'s pedagogy is not philosophical metaphysics but Mosaic-biblical metanarrative.[19] Also, the privilege of access to and worship in the sanctuary is built upon the covenant relationship between God and His community.[20] Hence, Leithart rightly declares, "Covenant and sanctuary are inseparable."[21] In the same vein, Canale says:

> The covenant is the living historical relationship between God and human beings that requires the sanctuary setting to articulate the living historical relations of God with his people.[22]

The covenant had been enacted upon the promise that access to God would be possible to those who fulfilled the conditions laid down in the covenant. The worship of God by Israel in the earthly sanctuary is conceived in the Old Testament as based upon the Old Covenant. On the basis of the superiority of Christ's priestly service in the heavenly sanctuary, the New Covenant has been mediated between God and men. In other words, *Auctor*'s metanarrative reflects the sanctuary-covenant structure. Canale summarizes, "God brings his eternal plan of salvation to operation through a historical sequence of redemptive acts centered in the sanctuary-covenant structure."[23] Sanctuary typology is the spatiaotemporal expression of how God relates to His people on the basis of the promises revealed in the biblical covenants. Hence, Canale rightly declares, "The covenant without the sanctuary is blind."[24] Put simply,

---

[16] This is the thesis of Johnsson's dissertation. See William G. Johnsson, "Defilement and Purgation in the Book of Hebrews" (Ph.D. diss., Vanderbilt University, 1973), 428.

[17] William G. Johnsson, "The Pilgrimage Motif in the Book of Hebrews," *JBL* 87 (June 1978): 249.

[18] This is the thesis of Lloyd's dissertation. See Gwilym George Lloyd, "The Treatment of the Mosaic Law in the Epistle to the Hebrews with Some Comparison of the Pauline Attitude" (Ph.D. diss., University of Edinburgh, 1944), 381.

[19] See Fernando L. Canale, "From Vision to System: Finishing the Task of Adventist Theology—Part III: Sanctuary and Hermeneutics," *JATS* 17 (Autumn 2006): 57.

[20] Michael Duane Morrison, "Rhetorical Function of the Covenant Motif in the Argument of Hebrews" (Ph.D. diss., Fuller Theological Seminary, 2006), 177.

[21] Leithart, "Baptism and the Priesthood," 62-63.

[22] Canale, "Sanctuary and Hermeneutics," 61.

[23] Ibid., 60.

[24] Ibid., 61.

Auctor's sanctuary typology reflects his metanarrative by way of the sanctuary-covenant structure.[25]

By explaining why *Auctor*'s sanctuary typology reflects his metanarrative, I actually demonstrate how *Auctor*'s typological use of Exod 25:40 reveals the spatial and temporal dimensions of his matanarrative. Exod 25:40 is important for revealing *Auctor*'s metanarrative because sanctuary typology is both analogical and prophetic: the analogical aspect reveals the spatial dimension whereas the prophetic aspect reveals the temporal dimension of the metanarrative.

Since *Auctor*'s ontology follows biblical pedagogy derived from Exod 3:14, his pedagogical use of Exod 25:40 in Heb 8:5 indicates that the heavenly sanctuary is spatiotemporal. In other words, the pedagogical use of Exod 25:40 reveals the ontological reality of the *heavenly* sanctuary. This fact is so crucial that Ha and Treiyer utilize it as one of the presuppositions in their dissertations.[26] Both scholars unknowingly show *Auctor*'s pedagogical use of Exod 3:14. Both simply acknowledge the necessity to recognize the reality of the heavenly sanctuary as one of the axioms for them to construct their dissertation.[27]

This pedagogical use of Exod 25:40 is significant because it reveals the ontological ground whereby *Auctor* activates the analogical and prophetic roles of the heavenly sanctuary to construct his metanarrative. Without this knowledge about *Auctor*'s pedagogical use of Exod 25:40, one can still deduce logically that the heavenly sanctuary or tabernacle exists because sanctuary typology is analogical *and* prophetic (or prefigurative).[28] Davidson explains why sanctuary typology is unique in the Scriptures:

> We commonly refer to the OT person, event, or institution as the "type" (τύπος) and its respective NT fulfillment as the "antitype" (ἀντίτυπος). However, in Hebrews this terminology is reversed. The heavenly sanctuary is referred to as the "type" and the

---

[25] Ibid., 60.

[26] See Hong Pal Ha, *Heb 1:2-3: The Threefold Characterization of the Person of Christ as Prerequisite for the Fulfillment of a Complete Atonement*, KSUM, vol. 4 (Seoul, Korea: Institute for Theological Research, 1996), 14; Alberto R. Treiyer, "Le Jour des Expiations et la Purification du Sanctuaire" (Ph.D. diss., University of Strasbourg, 1982), 137.

[27] Treiyer assumes the spatiotemporal existence of the heavenly sanctuary when he discusses the notion of purification in relation to Heb 9:23 (ibid., 137, 250-51, 280, n.16).

[28] This is the thesis of Nixon, "Typology of the Mosaic Tabernacle," 480 It is important to note that Nixon does not demonstrate why the heavenly sanctuary is material or spatial from the perspective of biblical ontology. He simply defends the logical necessity of the existence of the material heavenly sanctuary in light of the analogical and prophetic abilities of the earthly sanctuary (tabernacle) to construct the temporal dimension of the biblical metanarrative. On the contrary, Löhr sees no analogical and prefigurative relation between the earthly and heavenly sanctuaries. Hermut Löhr, "›Umriß‹ und ›Schatten‹ Bemerkungen zur Zitierung von Ex 25,40 in Hebr 8," ZNW 84, no. 3/4 (1993): 222, n. 22.

earthly sanctuary as the "antitype." This appears to be due to the fact that the heavenly sanctuary *existed prior* to the OT sanctuary and was the basis for the origin of the latter. Hence, the apostolic author designates the heavenly reality as the τύπος (8:5) and the earthly sanctuary as the ἀντίτυπος (9:24)—"that which corresponds to"—the heavenly. However, since the *functional* movement of the typology in Hebrews is from OT reality to NT fulfillment, it is convenient and consistent to speak of the earthly as "type" and the heavenly sanctuary as its "antitype."[29]

We have seen that the view of ultimate reality depends on scholars' valuation of *Auctor's* ontology. Davidson's ontological valuation of the heavenly sanctuary in Hebrews appears spatiotemporal because he argues for the intersection between heaven and earth within the historical flux of time: "The earth/heaven axis intersects the horizontal time-continuum."[30]

Though it is difficult to verify what is the actual form (תַּבְנִית) of the heavenly sanctuary which Moses saw in his vision (Exod 25:9, 40), the Old Testament testifies to its "existence." The "existence" of the heavenly sanctuary can be understood in the sense of spatiotemporal (literal or physical) existence, or timeless pre-existence, or figurative existence.[31] Sanctuary or tabernacle typology is unique because the "existence" of the heavenly sanctuary empowers the earthly sanctuary *spiritually* with the prophetic or prefigurative power to foreshadow divine redemptive patterns.[32]

This heavenly "existence" serves as the *spiritual* ground to construct the temporal-*earthly* and spatial-*earthly* dimensions of *Auctor's* metanarrative via the *earthly* sanctuary. The "existence" is spiritual because it is derived from the analogous sense of eternal patterns existing between the heavenly tabernacle and the earthly tabernacle. The spiritual ground also serves as the analogous reason to explain why the heavenly tabernacle or sanctuary *should be* real. Johnsson says:

> His [*Auctor's*] concern throughout the sermon is to ground Christian confidence in objective *facts*, as we have seen. *Real* deity, *real* humanity, *real* priesthood—and we may add, a *real* ministry in a *real* sanctuary.[33]

However, the recognition of such analogous "existence" is not sufficient to serve as the *ontological* ground to construct the temporal-heavenly and spatial-

---

[29] Davidson, "Typology in Hebrews," 135.

[30] Ibid.; see also idem, *Typology in Scripture*, 342.

[31] William G. Johnsson, "The Heavenly Sanctuary: Figurative or Real?" *Issues in the Book of Hebrews*, ed. Frank B. Holbrook, DRCS, vol. 4 (Silver Spring, MD: Biblical Research Institute, 1989), 35.

[32] See Nixon, "Typology of the Mosaic Tabernacle," 473.

[33] William G. Johnsson, *In Absolute Confidence: The Book of Hebrews Speaks to Our Day*, Anvil Biblical Studies, ed. Gerald Wheeler (Nashville, TN: Southern Publishing Association, 1979), 91.

heavenly dimensions of *Auctor*'s metanarrative because the actual form of the heavenly sanctuary remains ontologically undefined.

Since the actual form of the heavenly sanctuary is consistent with *Auctor*'s biblical pedagogy, one can confidently posit that the heavenly sanctuary *is* real and exists as spatiotemporal reality in heaven. Allen says:

> Hebrews acknowledges the existence of some form of heavenly sanctuary that is the archetype of the Mosaic earthly σκην, both temporally and spatially (8:2; 9:23-24), the true tent already pitched by the Lord (8:2).[34]

As a result, one is able to utilize this spatiotemporal existence of the heavenly sanctuary as the *ontological* ground to construct the temporal-*heavenly* and spatial-*heavenly* dimensions of *Auctor*'s metanarrative via sanctuary typology. From this ontological perspective, one seems to be able to unlock the mysterious riddle that *Auctor* designates the heavenly reality as the τύπος (8:5) *and* the earthly holy place (ἄγια) as ἀντίτυπος (Heb 9:24).[35] In contradistinction to Davidson's perspective above,[36] I suggest that *Auctor* purposely designates the heavenly reality as the τύπος (8:5) *because* he understands the existence of the heavenly sanctuary as spatiotemporal (see Figure 14).

Figure 14. Mosaic-Biblical Metanarrative of *Auctor*

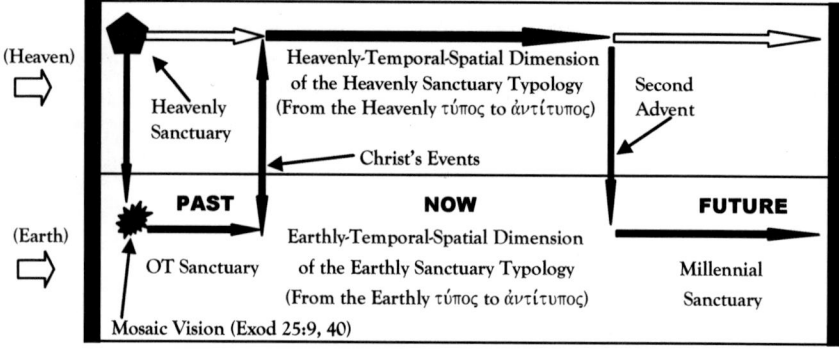

---

[34] David M. Allen, *Deuteronomy and Exhortation in Hebrews: A Study in Narrative Re-Presentation*, WUNT, ed. Jörg Frey et al., vol. 238 (Tübingen: Mohr Siebeck, 2008), 219; idem, "'Deuteronomic Re-Presentation in a Word of Exhortation': An Assessment of the Paraenetic Function of Deuteronomy in the Letter to the Hebrews" (Ph.D. diss., University of Edinburgh, 2007), 240.

[35] Shea demonstrates that τῶν ἁγίων λειτουργός, καὶ τῆς σκηνῆς τῆς ἀληθινῆς (Heb 8:2) is parallel to γὰρ εἰς χειροποίητα εἰσῆλθεν ἅγια Χριστός, ἀντίτυπα τῶν ἀληθινῶν (Heb 9:24). See Shea, "Hebrews 8-10," 7.

[36] Davidson, "Typology in Hebrews," 135.

In other words, in light of this ontological ground, *Auctor*'s intends to activate sanctuary typology as the pedagogical device from the perspective of the *heavenly* sanctuary to construct his metanarrative along the temporal-*heavenly* and spatial-*heavenly* dimensions. Similarly, *Auctor* correctly designates the earthly holy place (ἅγια) as ἀντίτυπος (Heb 9:24) because this earthly sanctuary is now construed as the NT functional and proleptic fulfillment of sanctuary typology along the temporal-*earthly* and spatial-*earthly* dimensions of his metanarrative in light of the Christ event.[37]

The vertical shaded arrow pointing downward and upward indicates the Incarnation and the Ascension of Christ respectively. After the Ascension of Christ, the earthy holy place is no longer functional because its analogical and prefigurative functions have been taken over by the heavenly holy place. In other words, *Auctor* designates the heavenly reality as the τύπος (8:5) to indicate that the new typological role of the heavenly sanctuary has been activated in the biblical history since the Christ event. This newly activated function of the heavenly sanctuary is expected by readers because *Auctor* has already made his main point explicit during his first mention of the heavenly sanctuary in the sermon: the heavenly sanctuary is spatiotemporally analogous to the earthly sanctuary because both sanctuaries have their respective tabernacles to pitch over the two holy places "τῶν ἁγίων" (Heb 8:2).[38] This ontological truth becomes the ground whereby *Auctor* utilizes the *heavenly* sanctuary typology as the pedagogical device to depict the ongoing heavenly ministry of Christ in the metanarrative of Hebrews. Treiyer says:

> Hebrews teaches that there is a heavenly sanctuary—wherein Jesus ministers in behalf of His people, which corresponded with the earthly sanctuary both in its arrangement and in his ministry.[39]

---

[37] Jelinek has already investigated the relationship between the heavenly sanctuary and the heavenly New Jerusalem in the entire Bible. See John Anthony Jelinek, "The Contribution of the City Metaphor toward an Understanding of the New Jerusalem" (Th.D. diss., Grace Theological Seminary, 1992), 260. Jelinek's approach to Hebrews is descriptive because he does not recognize the prescriptive significance of Exod 25:40 for revealing *Auctor*'s sanctuary-centered metanarrative. According to Jelinek, the heavenly city and sanctuary may be revealed in the eternal state or the millennium (ibid., 184, 260). However, I suggest that the heavenly sanctuary will continue to exist in the heavens during the millennium because Christ will re-institute pure worship in the *new* earthly sanctuary in the new earthly Jerusalem with the new torah (Ezek 40-48) from the perspective of premillennial dispensational hermeneutic (cf. the methods of chapter 3).

[38] We have already seen that τῶν ἁγίων in Heb 8:2 demonstrates that the earthly sanctuary is indeed analogous to the heavenly sanctuary. Shea provides a graphic representation of each τῶν ἁγίων (and its variants) in Hebrews. Shea, "Hebrews 8-10," 11.

[39] Alberto R. Treiyer, *The Day of Atonement and the Heavenly Judgment: From the Pentateuch to Revelation* (Siloam Springs, AR: Creation Enterprises International, 1992), 446.

The spatiotemporal heavenly sanctuary is indicated by the shaded pentagon in *Auctor*'s metanarrative and Moses saw it in his vision (Exod 25:9, 40). The unshaded horizontal arrow indicates its spatiotemporal existence without the presence of the incarnate Christ.

After the Second Coming of Christ, there will be reinstitution of sacrifices in the millennial sanctuary.[40] However, prior to the coming of the millennial sanctuary, Christ continues to serve as the high priest in the heavenly sanctuary. Hence, Ha says:

> If the atonement worked out by Christ was completed on the cross [John 19:30], for what purpose did Christ enter into the heavenly sanctuary? The symbolism of the OT sanctuary suggests that it was on the cross where the blood of the atonement was shed, an indispensable requirement for the inauguration of His intercessory ministry in the heavenly sanctuary. Thus, the Epistle to the Hebrews seems to point to something indispensable beyond the cross, but not without the cross, for the assurance of the man's salvation.[41]

Hence, *Auctor* correctly designates the earthly holy place (ἅγια) in the Old Testament as ἀντίτυπος (Heb 9:24) because its NT fulfillment from the perspective of the earthly dimension is proleptically realized in the cultic community of God in light of the Christ's ministry in the heavenly sanctuary.[42] Though the full manifestation of the earthly fulfillment will not be seen until the arrival of the millennial sanctuary, the earthly sanctuary typology still functions as a pedagogical device by *Auctor*, in the terms of Scholer, "to identify the readers as priests already during their *earthly* existence."[43] Scholer continues:

> In Heb. it is precisely this access to God, extended to earthly believers, which characterizes all Christians as 'proleptic priests'. Their priesthood is 'proleptic' and 'penul-

---

[40] Both Hoehner and McNickle argue for the reinstitution of sacrifices in the millennial sanctuary. Harold W. Hoehner, "The Reinstitution of Sacrifices in the Millennium" (Th.M. thesis, Dallas Theological Seminary, 1962); Alan A. McNickle, "The New Jerusalem in Amillennial Theology" (Th.D. diss., Dallas Theological Seminary, 1984).

[41] Ha, *Heb 1:2-3*, 12. Ha argues that "the position of 'sat down' [Heb 1:3] is to be understood as 'a formal acknowledgement of the right to exercise an activity'" (ibid., 264).

[42] Both Treiyer and Heppenstall examine the presence and use of *heavenly* sanctuary typology from the perspective of the biblical theology and systematic theology respectively. Treiyer, *The Day of Atonement and the Heavenly Judgment*; Edward Heppenstall, *Our High Priest: Jesus Christ in the Heavenly Sanctuary* (Washington, DC: Review and Herald Publishing Association, 1972). On the other hand, Nixon studies the analogical and prophetic significance of the *earthly* sanctuary typology. As a result, Nixon demonstrates how the prophetic power of the earthly sanctuary typology prefigures the new earthly sanctuary in the millennium. See Nixon, "Typology of the Mosaic Tabernacle," 481.

[43] John M. Scholer, *Proleptic Priests: Priesthood in the Epistle to the Hebrews*, JSNTSup, ed. David E. Orton, vol. 49 (Sheffield: JSOT Press, 1991), 207, emphasis added.

timate', because their entry into God's very presence [in the heavenly sanctuary] is achieved only in the Holy Spirit.[44]

The reality of Christ's ministry in the heavenly sanctuary is the ontological ground of believers' proleptic priesthood on the earth. The vision of the heavenly sanctuary has already inspired Moses and the Old Testament people to worship and serve Yahweh (Exod 25:9, 40). In light of the danger of apostasy, it is necessary for *Auctor* to activate the same beatific vision to motivate his audience to continue their confession of Christ as Yahweh. He capitalizes on the Mosaic vision and exhorts his audience not to drift away from Christ by demonstrating systematically why and how Jesus has already activated the new priestly ministry in the same pre-existing heavenly sanctuary (Heb 8:1-5). Put simply, his pedagogy is, in the terms of Canale, "from vision to system."[45]

Auctor is the master of the sanctuary and its typology. On the one hand, *Auctor* utilizes sanctuary typology to construct his metanarrative because the cognitive information (*logia*) derived from the vision of the *heavenly* sanctuary (Exod 25:9, 40) belongs to a grounding source of revelation. On the other hand, the vision of the heavenly sanctuary is also a theophany because the reality (*ontos*) of the sanctuary includes the dwelling of God (*theos*). A building of sanctuary without the dwelling of God is not a sanctuary. The building only becomes a sanctuary when God comes and dwells. *Auctor* uses sanctuary typology to construct his metanarrative because the reality (*ontos*) of the sanctuary (either earthly or heavenly one) reflects the divine reality—the supernature of God (*theos*), within the sanctuary-covenant structure. "In short," Rodríguez writes, "for the Israelites the sanctuary was the source of their life as a nation, representing the fulfillment of the covenant promise that God would dwell among the people of Israel and would be their God ([Exod] 29:45)."[46]

Prescriptive Significance of *Auctor*'s Metanarrative

Auctor's metanarrative reflects his doctrinal system. We have seen the crisis of belief in terms of various scholars' valuations of *Auctor*'s theology of how the revelation of the Old Covenant is related to the New Covenant. We have also identified *Auctor*'s metanarrative. The goal here is to resolve the theological crisis by prescribing the model(s) that is (are) most consistent with *Auctor*'s metanarrative—the benchmark of his doctrinal system. The thesis here is that

---

[44] Ibid.
[45] See Canale, "Sanctuary and Hermeneutics," 36.
[46] Angel Manuel Rodríguez, "Sanctuary Theology in the Book of Exodus," *AUSS* 24 (Summer 1986): 138.

Auctor's metanarrative reflects the most ontological consistency with the continuity model understood from the renewal perspective—the continuity-renewal model. This section will proceed in two parts: (1) support for the continuity model; (2) comparative-prescriptive analysis; (3) prescriptive-descriptive analysis.

Support for the Continuity Model

To demonstrate the continuity model, I begin by explaining why the discontinuity model should be rejected. The literary-motif perspective of Kiwoong Son should be rejected because this perspective does not value the ontological reality of the Mosaic cultus whereas *Auctor*'s utilizes the ontological reality of the heavenly sanctuary as the ground for formulating his metanarrative. Since *Auctor* regards the Mosaic cultus as an indispensable background to construct his metanarrative, the discontinuity model understanding the Mosaic cultus as either negative, neutral, or anti-Mosaic should be also rejected. For example, Cody holds to the discontinuity model with a neutral understanding of Mosaic cultus whereas Luz argues for a negative understanding of this cult.[47] The anti-Judaistic perspective assumes that Hebrews is a document bitterly opposed to Judaism; the Old and New Covenants are presented as having nothing (or very little) in common. In general, the history of interpretation does show some very anti-Jewish tendencies.[48]

The continuity model can be interpreted from three perspectives—dialectical, developmental, and renewal. Which perspective of the continuity model is correct? Though all three perspectives under the continuity model have some features consistent with *Auctor*'s metanarrative, the thesis here is that the renewal perspective is the correct valuation of *Auctor*'s theology of revelation. To defend the thesis, there are two parts: (1) a comparative-prescriptive analysis for each perspective to demonstrate that the continuity-renewal model reveals the least ontological inconsistency with *Auctor*'s metanarrative, and (2) a prescriptive-descriptive analysis for the continuity-renewal perspective to assert that it is the correct option.

Comparative-Prescriptive Analysis

A comparative analysis per se cannot be prescriptive unless a benchmark is available to make such judgment. The present analysis is comparative-

---

[47] See Aelred Cody, *Heavenly Sanctuary and Liturgy in the Epistle to the Hebrews: The Achievement of Salvation in the Epistle's Perspective* (St. Meinrad, IN: Grail Publications, 1960), 95; Ulrich Luz, "Der Alte und der Neue Bund bei Paulus und im Hebräerbrief," *EvT* 27 (1967): 332.

[48] See Wolfgang Kraus, "Neuere Ansätze in der Exegese des Hebräerbriefs," *VF* 48, no. 2 (2003): 78.

prescriptive because *Auctor*'s metanarrative can function as the benchmark of his doctrinal system. The present analysis is conducted by using the benchmark whereby the inconsistent ontological characteristics of developmental, dialectical, and renewal perspectives can be exposed. The goal is to demonstrate that the continuity-renewal model reveals the least ontological inconsistency with *Auctor*'s doctrinal system.

Hughes is the major proponent of the continuity model with the developmental perspective.[49] The developmental perspective regards the Old and New Covenants as being points on a continuum of revelation whose endpoint is the new covenant. The New Covenant is conceived as discontinuous with the Old Covenant *only* in that it is the perfect culmination of a linear process of development. This perspective sees Heb 1:1-4 as the key to understand *Auctor*'s theology of revelation. The "continuity-discontinuity dialectic" is reflected by the alternation between the theological exposition and paraenesis. In sum, according to Hughes, the developmental perspective conceives "the various moments of the revelation history [as] a recognizable continuity which allows them, in spite of their discontinuity, to be construed as parts of a single process."[50]

The developmental perspective is ontologically inconsistent with *Auctor*'s metanarrative for at least two reasons. First, the developmental perspective utilizes the unity of the progressive revelation of God in history to explain the ontological continuity of the revelation of the Old Covenant in relation to the New Covenant. However, *Auctor* utilizes the particular type of divine revelation (the Mosaic vision of the heavenly sanctuary) to explain the continuity *and* discontinuity between the Old and New Covenant. Second, the developmental perspective articulates the discontinuity between the two Covenants by a dialectical relationship between the realized and futurist eschatology. Again this is obviously contradictory to *Auctor*'s doctrinal system.

Ernst Käsemann is the major proponent of the continuity model with the dialectical perspective. The dialectical perspective presupposes that the Old Covenant points to the New Covenant and is in turn surpassed by it.[51] When the dialectical perspective is conceived eschatologically, the whole OT is understood as a book of promise, which comes to fulfillment only in Christ.[52] By means of this eschatological tension, Käsemann argues that *Auctor* explains

---

[49] Graham Hughes, *Hebrews and Hermeneutics: The Epistle to the Hebrews as a New Testament Example of Biblical Interpretation*, SNTSMS, ed. R. McL. Wilson and M. E. Thrall, vol. 36 (Cambridge: Cambridge University Press, 1979), 6. Dukes also argues for the continuity model with developmental perspective. See James Graydon Dukes, "Eschatology in the Epistle to the Hebrews" (Th.D. diss., Southern Baptist Theological Seminary, 1956), 36.

[50] Hughes, *Hebrews and Hermeneutics*, 6.

[51] Erich Grässer, "Der Hebräerbrief 1938-1963," *TRu* 36 (October 1964): 213.

[52] Francis Charles Synge, *Hebrews and the Scriptures* (London: S.P.C.K., 1959), 61.

"why the attitude of faith can only be described as wandering, and finally, in the heavenly world and its Jerusalem, has concretely revealed the ultimate goal of such wandering and the final consummation."[53]

For the continuity model, it is also possible to conceive the dialectical relation between the two covenants in terms of a "double" typology—one antithetical and one complementary. The overall perspective of double typology is the continuity between the two covenants because double typology is grounded in the unconditional binding word of God (Heb 6:17). The antithetical typology describes how an earthly phenomenon is contrasted with its heavenly or eschatological counterpart. According to Zimmermann, the point of the antithesis is that Christ terminates the sacrifices of the Old Covenant in order to place His obedience to the will of God in power.[54] The complementary typology explains how an earthly phenomenon is depicted as having some degree of continuity with those of the heavenly or eschatological realities.

There are at least two reasons why the dialectical perspective is ontologically inconsistent with *Auctor*'s metanarrative. First, the dialectical perspective grounds the continuity between the Old and New Covenant ontologically via the revelation of the Word of God whereas *Auctor* grounds the continuity between the two Covenants on the spatiotemporal reality of the heavenly sanctuary. Second, the dialectical perspective articulates the dialectic relation in terms of "double typology" (i.e., one antithetical and one complementary), whereas *Auctor*'s metanarrative does not reflect such "double typology." The articulation of "double typology" involves the fusion of the horizons of the antithetical phrase (antithesis) and the complementary phrase (i.e., thesis and synthesis).[55]

For *Auctor*, there is no dialectical fusion of the two theological traditions (or visions) between the Old and New Covenants. In fact, there is no fusion of the theological visions between the Old and New Covenants in Hebrews— both covenants remain distinct historically and functionally. In Hebrews, the ontological continuity between the Old and New Covenant is built upon by the ontology of the heavenly sanctuary. In other words, since the ontology of

---

[53] Ernst Käsemann, *The Wandering People of God: An Investigation of the Letter to the Hebrews*, trans. Roy A. Harrisville and Irving L. Sandberg (Minneapolis, MN: Augsburg Publishing House, 1984), 37.

[54] Zimmermann writes: "Christus hebt die Opfer des Alten Bundes auf, um an deren Stelle seinen vollkommenen Gehorsam dem Willen Gottes gegenüber in Kraft zu setzen." Heinrich Zimmermann, *Die Hohepriester-Christologie des Hebräerbriefes: Vortrag beim Antritt des Rektorats und zur Eröffnung des Studienjahres 1963/64 der Philosphisch-Theologischen Akademie zu Paderborn, gehalten am 22. Oktober 1963* (Paderborn: Ferdinand Schöningh, 1964), 24.

[55] For a graphic representation of the process of understanding in terms of thesis, synthesis, and antithesis in Hebrews, see Paul Ellingworth, "The Old Testament in Hebrews: Exegesis, Method and Hermeneutics" (Ph.D. diss., Aberdeen University, 1977), 456. He provides a concise evaluation of the dialectic understanding in Hebrews in relation to typology (ibid., 457-65).

the heavenly sanctuary remains the same historically, there is no dialectical progress in the work of God from the Old Covenant to the New Covenant. The ontological status of a believer is the same under the two covenants according to *Auctor*'s pedagogy. The reception of a new disposition (e.g., by the internalizing of Torah or regeneration) under the New Covenant by a believer does not transform him ontologically or metaphysically.[56] On the other hand, Olbricht rightly says:

> Typology posits a world in which that which comes afterward brings to fruition what is declared earlier. Such interpretation has a time line; it is horizontal. For Philo there was more of a vertical sense of allegorization.... The allegorization pointed upward (that is, beyond sense experience) and downward (that is, probing the foundational bedrock [of mysteries and symbols of the text]).[57]

Hence, the historical discontinuity between the Old and New Covenants is articulated by the historical movement of sanctuary typology: there is only a horizontal "typology" from the functional perspective for there is always *a* spatiotemporal sanctuary operating in history (see Figure 15).

Figure 15. Spatiotemporal Sanctuary
Operating in the Past, Now, and Future

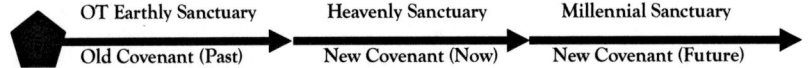

OT Earthly Sanctuary	Heavenly Sanctuary	Millennial Sanctuary
Old Covenant (Past)	New Covenant (Now)	New Covenant (Future)

According to classical pedagogy, "double typology" is necessary to account for the metaphysical or ontological gap between the nature (earth) and the supernature (heaven). In other words, due to the existence of the ontological gap in classical pedagogy, the typological relationship between the heavenly and earthly tabernacles is not ontological but figurative. However, *Auctor*'s biblical pedagogy reveals that there is no ontological gap between the nature (earth) and the supernature (heaven). In the Bible, the inaccessible gap preventing the intercourse between human (nature) and God (supernature) is not ontological but moral—it is sin. Sin creates a cultic gap between God and His people but it can be removed by blood (Heb 9:22) which signifies the death of Christ for the sins of men. Under the Mosaic sanctuary, the access to God is partial be-

---

[56] This is the thesis of Showers. See Renald E. Showers, "The New Nature" (Th.D. diss., Grace Theological Seminary, 1975), 26.

[57] Thomas H. Olbricht, "Analogy and Allegory in Classical Rhetoric," in *Early Christianity and Classical Culture: Comparative Studies in Honor of Abraham J. Malherbe*, ed. Thomas H. Olbricht, John T. Fitzgerald, and L. Michael White, SupNovT, ed. C. K. Barrett et al., vol. 110 (Leiden: Brill, 2003), 387.

cause only the high priest is allowed to enter the Holy of Holies once a year by the blood of sacrifice, both for himself and for the people. After the Ascension of Christ as the High Priest, a complete access to the presence of God in the heavenly sanctuary is now available for all humanity by faith in Christ.

This heavenly access to God is ontologically and objectively grounded in the blood of Jesus (Heb 10:19; 12:24) and it is Jesus' continuing life as High Priest in the heavenly sanctuary which is *the sine qua non* of the faith which is the means of access to that same sanctuary. The access is ontologically grounded because the blood of Jesus is ontologically present in the heavenly sanctuary (Heb 12:24). However, the access is also objectively grounded because it assumes something of the objective sense of authorization.[58] In sum, both the earthly and heavenly sanctuaries provide their respective structure and precision to the Old and New Covenant relationship between God and His community.[59]

The continuity-renewal model reveals the least inconsistency because there is no apparent ontological inconsistency between the renewal perspective and *Auctor*'s metanarrative. This renewal perspective will be *validated* by a prescriptive-descriptive analysis. Now, my goal is to argue why the continuity-renewal model is the correct valuation of *Auctor*'s theology of revelation.

According to the renewal perspective, the promises of the Old and New Covenants are identical except that the promises under the New Covenant are in the process of being realized by the power of God in order to achieve a renewed relationship between God and His people.[60] Put simply, *Auctor*'s metanarrative indicates that the Old Covenant is continuous with the New Covenant except that the latter is endowed with a unique and better promise to secure a continual-renewal of relationship between God and His people (Heb 8:8). The promise is unique because it is now activated and actualized by a *heavenly human* priest ministering in the heavenly spatiotemporal tabernacle (Heb 8:1). The promise under the New Covenant is better because believers under the present dispensation have complete access to God in the heavenly realm. This access is secured by the Incarnate Son of God with his unblemished blood for the benefit of believers. The actualized promise can never be annulled because it operates on the basis of the power of an indestructible life (Heb 7:16).

On the other hand, this same promise in the Old Covenant is "the Gospel" preached to the Exodus generation (Heb 4:2). Buchanan says:

---

[58] See Ceslas Spicq, *L'Épître aux Hébreux*, 3d ed., Etudes bibliques, ed. Th. Camelot, P. J. de Menasce, and V. Ducatillon, 2 vols. (Paris: J. Gabalda, 1952–1953), 2:315.

[59] Canale, "Sanctuary and Hermeneutics," 61.

[60] For an excellent description of sanctification from the perspective of continuity-renewal model, see William R. Eichhorst, "Man in the Image of God: Created and Renewed" (Th.D. diss., Grace Theological Seminary, 1973), 258.

The author [Hebrews] said that "the gospel" had "been preached to" him and his contemporary Christians just as it had been to the exodus generation. There is no indication that he was comparing two different gospels related to different promises.[61]

In Hebrews, Hanson asserts, "There are parts of the O.T. where it [the Gospel] is not just prefigured or symbolized, but actually set forth."[62] Westcott notes that the perfect participle (εὐηγγελισμένοι) of Heb 4:2 "marks the *present continuance* of the [same gospel] message, which was not simply one past announcement."[63] Hence, under the Old and New Covenants, the Gospel is the same. Treiyer says:

> As a matter of fact, "the good news" of Jesus Christ was preached in both dispensations: that of the Old Testament and that of the New (Heb 2:1-4; 4:2). There were not two antithetical gospels, because the message was the same in both epochs. Whereas ancient Israel received the gospel through the ministry established by Moses in the earthly sanctuary, "for a testimony of those things which were to be spoken after" (Heb 3:5 = KJ), Christians receive it "today" (Heb 4:7) in direct connection with the very reality in heaven.[64]

Prescriptive-Descriptive Analysis

The thesis here is that the renewal perspective is the correct way to understand *Auctor*'s theology of revelation revealed by the relation between the Old and New Covenants. To defend this thesis, it is necessary to activate the descriptive and prescriptive roles of Exodus in Hebrews to identify the correct option among all the available proposals. By activating the prescriptive role of Exodus in Hebrews, one can construct *Auctor*'s metanarrative. Since *Auctor*'s metanarrative is the benchmark of his doctrinal system, it enables readers to identify the theological model revealing the least ontological inconsistency with *Auctor*'s doctrinal system. The result of such analysis shows that the renewal perspective reveals no apparent ontological inconsistency with *Auctor*'s metanarrative.

On the other hand, by activating the descriptive role of Exodus in Hebrews, one can discover how *Auctor* utilizes the Exodus citations to engage his audience rhetorically. Though this descriptive function of Exodus in Hebrews cannot prescribe a specific theological model ontologically, it has explanatory

---

[61] George Wesley Buchanan, *To the Hebrews: Translation, Comment, and Conclusions*, AB, ed. William Foxwell Albright and David Noel Freedman, vol. 36 (New York: Doubleday, 1972), 20.

[62] A. T. Hanson, "The Gospel in the Old Testament according to Hebrews," *Theology* 52 (July 1949): 248.

[63] Brooke Foss Westcott, *The Epistle to the Hebrews: The Greek Text with Notes and Essays*, 3rd ed. (London: Macmillan and Co., 1903), 94, emphasis added.

[64] Treiyer, *The Day of Atonement and the Heavenly Judgment*, 418.

power. Canale calls this power, "a posteriori verification,"[65] which is to say it describes why a specific model is correct rhetorically—in the sense that the model fits *Auctor*'s argument. Since a rhetorically correct model can be ontologically inconsistent with *Auctor*'s pedagogy, it is necessary to conduct the prescriptive analysis first to identify the most ontologically consistent model. Only then can the descriptive analysis verify the prescribed model as the correct model. The order of analysis is significant here. The comparative-prescriptive analysis has already identified the renewal perspective as the most ontologically consistent model among the various options in light of *Auctor*'s pedagogy. The remaining task is to explain why the renewal perspective fits *Auctor*'s argument rhetorically.

When commenting on *Auctor*'s use of the term "reformation" in Heb 9:10, Fisher writes, "The term 'reformation' used here implies reconstruction or renewal, as opposed to building a new structure. It means 'making straight,' the idea of making stable."[66] The renewal view fits *Auctor*'s argument rhetorically because the notion of renewal is intimately connected with the apostasy and the breaking of covenant in Exodus.[67] The renewal view also fits contextually in Hebrews when the apostasy in Hebrews is understood in light of the golden calf episode.[68] This means one should understand *Auctor*'s concept of the New Covenant on the basis of the apostasy and renewal revealed under the Old or Mosaic Covenant from Exodus 31:18–34:35.

In other words, when there is apostasy, the curses of the Old Covenant are realized but God preserves for Himself a remnant by a covenant renewal.[69] This remnant is known as His people with whom Mosaic Covenant is renewed.[70] The covenant is broken and is in need of renewal when Jewish professed Christians have committed either the apostasy (for non-elect ones) or

---

[65] Fernando L. Canale, *Back to Revelation-Inspiration: Searching for the Cognitive Foundation of Christian Theology in a Postmodern World* (Lanham, MD: University Press of America, 2001), 51.

[66] John Fisher, "Covenant Fulfillment and Judaism in Hebrews," in *The Enduring Paradox: Exploratory Essays in Messianic Judaism*, ed. John Fisher (Baltimore, MD: Lederer/Messianic Jewish Publishers, 2000), 55-56.

[67] See James Hardy Sexton, "The Knowledge of Yahweh Motif in the Book of Exodus" (Ph.D. diss., New Orleans Baptist Theological Seminary, 1999), 120.

[68] Dunnill, Gelardini, and Blanton follow the renewal perspective. See Thomas R. Blanton IV, "Constructing a New Covenant: Discursive Strategies in the Damascus Document and Second Corinthians" (Ph.D. diss., University of Chicago, 2006), 245; John Dunnill, *Covenant and Sacrifice in the Letter to the Hebrews*, SNTSMS, ed. Margaret E. Thrall, vol. 75 (Cambridge: Cambridge University Press, 1992), 261; Gabriella Gelardini, "«Verhärtet eure Herzen nicht» Der Hebräer, eine Synagogenhomilie zu *Tischa be-Aw*" (Ph.D. diss., University of Basel, 2004), 154.

[69] See Alexander R. Gonzales, "The Divine Proclamation Formula as the Basis for Renewal of the Sinaitic Covenant: A Literary Exposition of Exodus 34:6-7" (S.T.M. thesis, Dallas Theological Seminary, 2005), 92.

[70] See Fisher, "Hebrews," 54.

idolatry (for elect ones) in Hebrews. When arguing how the continuity-renewal model fits *Auctor*'s argument, Hahn rightly says:

> Israel under the Levitical law appeared to receive a suspended sentence, but to adapt the legal metaphor, the divine court was temporarily adjourned so that the execution of the covenant curses could be delayed and deferred until someone could bear the curses–vicariously and redemptively–and so release the covenant blessings.
>
> Christ thus fulfills the Old Covenant by bearing the curse of death as a faithful firstborn son of God and royal high priest, thereby performing the vocation that Israel first accepted (Exod 19–24) and then spurned with the golden calf (Exod 32). The author thus presents the New Covenant as the only true and perfect renewal of the old. God establishes one covenant, which is broken but mercifully renewed and faithfully fulfilled in Christ. In order to do so, however, Christ had to realize–as high priest of the New Covenant–what the high priest of the Old Covenant only acted out on the Day of Atonement: a curse-bearing sacrifice that truly renews and fulfills the covenant.[71]

This deferral of curses under the Old Covenant continues until the time of a final, perfecting renewal arrives in the Christ event. By holding firm to the confession that Jesus is Yahweh—God of Israel, the broken covenant can be renewed internally in the hearts of professed Christians.[72] Also, by the perfect blood of Christ, the curses under the Old Covenant were removed, and the promise of New Covenant is actualized in the present dispensation (see Figure 16). Since the covenant and sanctuary are inseparable, the Old Covenant and the Mosaic tabernacle (sanctuary) have been done away from the time of Christ's inauguration of the New Covenant's cultus in the heavenly tabernacle.

Figure 16. Spatiotemporal Sanctuary Operating in the Mosaic, Extended, and New Exodus

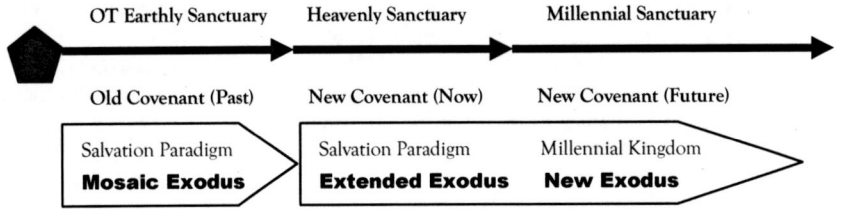

---

[71] Scott Hahn, *Kinship by Covenant: A Canonical Approach to the Fulfillment of God's Saving Promises*, Anchor Yale Bible Reference Library, ed. John J. Collins (New Haven: Yale University Press, 2009), 319.

[72] See David Stanley Gotaas, "The Old Testament in the Epistle to the Hebrews, the Epistle of James, and the Epistle of Peter" (Th.D. diss., Northern Baptist Theological Seminary, 1958), 167.

After Mosaic Exodus, the prophet Jeremiah has already envisioned the New Covenant on the basis of the "Exodus paradigm."[73] It is important to note that Jeremiah's vision of the "salvation paradigm" ("New Exodus") is millennial and earthly.[74] However, *Auctor*'s salvation paradigm is proleptic and millennial—it has already appeared "today" and it will be fully manifested in the new Exodus. The new Exodus prophesied in the OT is still futuristic according to *Auctor*'s salvation paradigm. To support this position, Thiessen says, "Hebrews renarrates Israel's history as an extended exodus."[75]

Thiessen's thesis is significant because he refutes the majority view that the salvation paradigm in Hebrews reflects the spiritual realization of new or second Exodus revealed in the OT.[76] During the extended (continuing) Exodus, that is "today," the eschatological salvation is available due to the inauguration of the New Covenant by the blood of Christ.[77] When commenting on *Auctor*'s notion of "today," Lombard says, "He declares that it is this 'today' which presents itself as a new offer in the place of the salvation which the desert-generation failed to obtain."[78]

Since "today" is still within the extended Exodus, this historical setting fits the renewal perspective whereby *Auctor* views the New Covenant as a renewed covenant, one that returns to the Old Covenant.[79] The arrival of the once-for-all renewed covenant (the New Covenant) makes the Old Covenant obsolete (Heb 8:13). However, the aging of the Mosaic (Old) Covenant is proleptic because a complete fulfillment of the New Covenant will be revealed via the earthly sanctuary during the millennium.

Joslin describes the renewal process as a Christological transformation.[80] The Old Covenant is transformed Christologically "today" so that God can

---

[73] See Emmanuel Yun-wing Hung, "Relationship and Rebirth: A Literary Study of the Exodus Motif in Jeremiah" (Ph.D. diss., Westminister Theological Seminary, 2001), 212. Hung's perspective is similar to Emmrich and Gleason. See Martin Emmrich, *Pneumatological Concepts in the Epistle to the Hebrews: Amtscharisma, Prophet, & Guide of the Eschatological Exodus* (Lanham, Maryland: University Press of America, 2003), 56-57; Nicholas J. Ellis, "Hebrews 6:4-6 and Divine Repentance" (M.A. thesis, Trinity Western University, 2006), 112; Randall C. Gleason, "A Moderate Reformed View," in *Four Views on the Warning Passages in Hebrews*, ed. Herbert W. Bateman IV (Grand Rapids: Kregel Publications, 2007), 342.

[74] See Powers, "Prophetic Typology," 253-88.

[75] Matthew Thiessen, "Hebrews and the End of the Exodus," *NovT* 49, no. 4 (2007): 353.

[76] Ibid., 355, n. 7.

[77] Ibid., 362, 367, n. 56.

[78] H. A. Lombard, "Κατάπαυσις in the Letter to the Hebrews," *Neot* 5 (1971): 66.

[79] Michael Wyschogrod, *The Body of Faith: God and the People of Israel*, 2nd ed. [1st published as *The Body of Faith: Judaism as Corporeal Election*. New York: Seabury Press, 1983] (Northvale, NJ: Jason Aronson, 1996), 231.

[80] Barry Clyde Joslin, "The Theology of the Mosaic Law in Hebrews 7:1-10:18" (Ph.D. diss., Southern Baptist Theological Seminary, 2005), 2. This work is published as *Hebrews, Chr-*

dispense the blessings promised in the New Covenant to the elect *Jewish* professed believers as a remnant of the nation.[81] Parts of the blessings under this renewed covenant (the New Covenant) are forever available "today," whereas the rest will be realized eschatologically in the millennial kingdom.[82]

Summary

The prescriptive power of Exod 25:40 in Hebrews is twofold. First, *Auctor*'s Christocentric-typological use of Exod 25:40 prescribes his metanarrative in terms of spatial and temporal dimensions in the realms of nature (earth) and supernature (heaven). This prescriptive power is significant because *Auctor*'s metanarrative is a miniature of his world-view. According to Canale, metanarrative allows us to articulate the ontological or "philosophical problem of the one and the many, the whole and the parts."[83] This leads to the second prescriptive power of Exod 25:40 in Hebrews, which is the use of *Auctor*'s metanarrative to prescribe the correct valuation of *Auctor*'s theology of revelation in the context of the relation between the Old and New Covenants: the continuity-renewal model has been identified as the correct one because it reveals the least ontological inconsistency with *Auctor*'s metanarrative and it fits the argument in Hebrews contextually. Hence, Exodus affects the entire structure of *Auctor*'s systematic theology.

---

ist, and the Law: The Theology of Mosaic Law in Hebrews 7:1–10:18, Paternoster Biblical Monographs, ed. Howard Marshall et al. (Colorado Springs, CO: Paternoster Press, 2008).

[81] See Wyschogrod, *Israel*, 223.

[82] For a summary of present and eschatological blessings, see David John MacLeod, "The Theology of the Epistle to the Hebrews: Introduction, Prolegomena, and Doctrinal Center" (Th.D. diss., Dallas Theological Seminary, 1987), 532.

[83] Canale, "Sanctuary and Hermeneutics," 57.

• CHAPTER EIGHT •

Hermeneutical Methodology Employed in the Use of Exodus by *Auctor*

A study of *Auctor*'s hermeneutical methodology is not easy because this concerns his hermeneutics and *hermeneutic*.[1] Hermeneutics concerns the rules of interpretation while *hermeneutic* refers to the process of understanding a text. Both hermeneutics and hermeneutic can be understood from various perspectives. I suggest that they be studied using text-oriented, pedagogy-oriented, and methodology-oriented levels of analysis. Though each level is singled out as a mini-thesis to be investigated and validated by various chapters of this study, it is obvious that all three levels are closely related to one another. By defending the first two mini-theses, I have already demonstrated the hermeneutical significance of Exodus in Hebrews from the explanatory (text-oriented analysis) and theological (pedagogy-oriented analysis) levels. This general order of inquiry is important because this chapter will continue to investigate the hermeneutical significance of Exodus in Hebrews from the methodology-oriented level via the mini-theses grounded by the text-oriented and the pedagogy-oriented analyses (see Table 5).

Auctor's hermeneutical methodology should be adjusted to the explanatory and theological nature of ground uncovered in the preceding chapters. The text-oriented and the pedagogy-oriented analyses have revealed the characteristics of *Auctor*'s hermeneutical methodology from the perspectives of hermeneutics and *hermeneutic*. The text-oriented exegesis indicates that: (1) his hermeneutic (the process of understanding the text) reflects the use of Exod 32–34 as the controlling revelation to understand the work and person of Yahweh as Christ; (2) Exodus 3:14 and 25:40 serve as the significant ontological and hermeneutical markers for *Auctor*'s hermeneutics (the rule of interpretation). The pedagogy-oriented analysis indicates that *Auctor*'s hermeneutics is

---

[1] The phrase "hermeneutical methodology" is taken from Fernando L. Canale, *Back to Revelation-Inspiration: Searching for the Cognitive Foundation of Christian Theology in a Postmodern World* (Lanham, MD: University Press of America, 2001), 49.

Christocentric-typological biblical pedagogy whereas his hermeneutic is theo-onto-logical.

Table 5. *Auctor*'s Hermeneutical Methodology in Light of His Use of Exodus

Perspective	Hermeneutics ⬇	Hermeneutic ⬇
Text-Oriented Study (Chapter 2)	Exod 3:14 = Ontological Marker Exod 25:40 = Hermeneutical Marker	Golden Calf Episode (Exod 32–34) = Controlling Revelation
Pedagogy-Oriented Study (Chapters 3 to 7)	Christocentric-Typological Biblical Pedagogy	Theo-Onto-Logical Structure of Reason
Methodology-Oriented Study (Chapter 8)	Goal of Constructing Christology Ontologically (Immanently) and Functionally (Economically) by Deductive Hermeneutics (Inductive Study Plus a Presupposition about Divine Ontology)	Goal of Constructing Doctrinal Center (Christology) Autopistically

The thesis of this chapter is that *Auctor*'s use of Exodus in the hermeneutical methodology enables him to construct his doctrinal center autopistically (instead of axiopistically), functionally (economically), and ontologically (immanently).[2] This study will defend the thesis by two comparative analyses: (1) a comparative analysis of *Auctor*'s hermeneutic from the perspective of two selected schools of hermeneutics; (2) a comparative analysis of *Auctor*'s methodology for portraying Christ in light of his use of Exodus. The former explains how *Auctor*'s hermeneutical use of Exodus indicates that he constructs his doctrinal center autopistically instead of axiopistically. The latter explains why *only* the Christocentric-typological use of Exod 25:40 can enable *Auctor* to construct his doctrinal center ontologically and functionally by deductive hermeneutics (inductive hermeneutics plus the authorial reading of Christ as Yahweh).

Comparative Analysis of *Auctor*'s Hermeneutic

Auctor constructs his doctrinal center autopistically instead of axiopistically. In other words, *Auctor*'s use of Exodus indicates that he appeals to evidence or criteria of credibility within (i.e., internal instead of external to) the epistemological realm of investigation for formulating his doctrinal center. Defending this thesis involves three steps: (1) an analysis of *Auctor*'s doctrinal center in relation to its ground; (2) to identify the differences between the autopistic

---

[2] I have defined the meaning of autopisty and axiopisty in terms of the scope of the use of revelatory sources to construct systematic theology in Table 2 of chapter three. For an excellent discussion of the two terms, see W. Gary Phillips, "Apologetics and Inerrancy: An Analysis of Select Axiopistic Models" (Th.D. diss., Grace Theological Seminary, 1985), 5.

and axiopistic hermeneutics; (3) an analysis of *Auctor*'s hermeneutic by investigating *Auctor*'s epistemological realm for formulating doctrine as well as his epistemological realm revealed by his use of Exodus.

Auctor's Doctrinal Center in Relation to Its Ground

Though both the themes of Christ's sonship and priesthood are significant in Hebrews, Tetley and MacLeod have already demonstrated decisively that *Auctor*'s doctrinal center is the priesthood of Christ.[3] Since I have argued in chapter seven that *Auctor* utilizes Exod 25:40 to reveal his doctrinal ground in Heb 8:5, it is necessary here to explain (1) why *Auctor* waits until half way through his material to present his doctrinal ground for Christological priesthood in Heb 8, and (2) why *Auctor* introduces the topic of priesthood in Heb 5 and yet waits until Heb 8 to reveal the doctrinal ground. In order to address the two questions, this study will first defend a structure for Hebrews and then use it to explain *Auctor*'s development of his doctrinal center and ground. Though scholars have proposed various structures for Hebrews, one should develop a structure for Hebrews in light of *Auctor*'s theology of the revelatory relation between the Old and New Covenants—the continuity-renewal model.

Clary has recently defended a structure for Hebrews using the continuity-renewal perspective. He writes:

> The generic structure of Hebrews can be outlined as a covenant document; Hebrews can be read as a covenant. Hebrews is a written sermon that exhibits characteristics consistent with OT covenant formulations.[4]

Clary proposes the following structural outline (see Figure 17) to reflect the flow of *Auctor*'s argument taken as a covenant. He defends the structure by interpreting Hebrews as a covenant document in the context of the continuity-renewal perspective after demonstrating generic (literary) continuity between the two covenants as well as between Deuteronomy and Hebrews. He concludes, "A claim for generic or literary continuity between the old and new covenants in general, and a connection specifically between Deuteronomy and Hebrews, is justified."[5]

Clary's thesis should not be considered as an exception to the rule because his thesis is independently validated by Allen's work done in the same year.

---

[3] This is the thesis of Tetley and MacLeod. Joy D. Tetley, "The Priesthood of Christ as the Controlling Theme of the Epistle to the Hebrews" (Ph.D. diss., University of Durham, 1987), 1; David John MacLeod, "The Theology of the Epistle to the Hebrews: Introduction, Prolegomena, and Doctrinal Center" (Th.D. diss., Dallas Theological Seminary, 1987), 260.

[4] Henry Walter Clary, "Hebrews as a Covenant Document: A New Proposal" (Ph.D. diss., Southwestern Baptist Theological Seminary, 2007), 243. All the quotations in this work are reprinted by permission of the author. All rights reserved.

[5] Ibid., 246.

Allen demonstrates that Hebrews is written with the OT covenant forms in mind to show the continuity between God's activity in former and present times via Deuteronomic re-representation.[6]

Figure 17. Structural Outline of Hebrews

I. 1:1-4—Preamble, giving titles and parties to the covenant: God, Son, "us"
II. 1:5-7:28—Historical prologue, governed and bracketed by Pss 2 and 110
   A. 1:5-2:4—Heavenly history: God, Son, and angels (w/ WARNING)
   B. 2:5-18—Incarnational history: Jesus brother of humans
   C. 3:1-4:13—Israelite history: Moses, wilderness, Joshua (w/ WARNING)
   D. 4:14-5:10—Jesus' history on earth: victory through suffering
   E. 5:11-6:12—Current history: WARNING to the audience against lethargy
   F. 6:13-7:28—The future of history: God's oath to Jesus = believers' hope
III. 8:1-10:18—Statement of substance (Jer 31:31-34) ratified in blood
IV. 10:19-39—Stipulations with threat of curse
   A. 10:19-25—Communal/ethical stipulations
   B. 10:26-39—WARNING against willful disobedience
V. 11:1-40—Invocation of witnesses lends credence to the new paradigm
VI. 12:1-29—New covenant blessings with threats of curse (WARNING)
VII. 13:1-25—Further stipulations with epistolary ending[7]

(This figure is reprinted by permission of the author. All rights reserved.)

According to the above structure of Hebrews, since Clary defends that Heb 8:1-10:18 is the heart of Hebrews as a covenant document,[8] one can now explain why *Auctor* waits until half way through his material to present his doctrinal ground for its center of priesthood in Heb 8. Put simply, *Auctor* introduces the doctrinal ground (Heb 8:1-5) immediately after completing the preamble and historical prologue (Heb 1:1-7:28). As a matter of fact, the doctrinal ground together with its center (8:1-5) occurs immediately after *Auctor* indicates the necessity and significance for a revelatory change of dispensation (7:11-28) in light of Christ's priesthood but prior to the discussion of the relation between the Old and New Covenants (8:6-13).

In the same vein, since the historical prologue is introductory to the heart of Hebrews (Heb 8:1-10:18), one should understand *Auctor*'s discussion about the qualification for Christ's priesthood in Heb 5 as preparatory and basic. Moreover, *Auctor*'s doctrinal goal is to argue that Jesus functions as a *heavenly*

---

[6] See David Mark Allen, "'Deuteronomic Re-Presentation in a Word of Exhortation': An Assessment of the Paraenetic Function of Deuteronomy in the Letter to the Hebrews" (Ph.D. diss., University of Edinburgh, 2007), 235. This work is published in 2008.

[7] Clary, "Hebrews," 205.

[8] Clary writes: "The high point of the entire book is in 8:1-10:18, joining God's action of grace in Christ for followers of the new covenant" (ibid., 224).

priest, not merely a priest (Heb 8:4).[9] In other words, it is unnecessary for *Auctor* to reveal the doctrinal ground for Christ's ministry in *heaven* as a heavenly priest (8:1-5) when his emphasis in Heb 5 is simply to explain what God has done in the salvation history to prepare Christ on *earth* as a priest in *heaven*.

Hebrews 4:14-5:10 is part of *Auctor*'s introductory portion of his covenant renewal document and it belongs to the ongoing salvation history in the reason of nature on earth.[10] In Heb 8:1-2, according to Müller, *Auctor* summarizes his main point "*before* specifically turning to the covenant, the sanctuary, and the sacrifice."[11] After presenting his doctrinal center of Christ's priesthood in the heavenly sanctuary (8:1-2), *Auctor* actually does not delay but immediately presents his ontological ground, which is the spatiotemporality of the heavenly sanctuary. Thus presented, his doctrinal center comes to the fore in Heb 8:5 as the *first* mention of τῶν ἁγίων (the spatiotemporal heavenly sanctuary and its holy of holies) occurs in Heb 8:2.[12]

The presentation of the ontological ground is also important for *Auctor*'s subsequent discussion about the New Covenant (8:6-13) because covenant and sanctuary are inseparable.[13] Clary rightly argues that the blood of Christ is the substance for ratifying the New Covenant from the continuity-renewal perspective (8:1-10:18). However, he fails to note that the blood of the New Covenant can only be grounded ontologically via the spatiotemporality of the heavenly sanctuary (12:24; cf. 9:12-25; 10:4, 19, 29; 13:20).

Before moving on, it is necessary to show the relation between Christ's heavenly priesthood and His sonship. In Heb 1-7, *Auctor*'s repeated usage Pss 2:7 and 110:4 provides literary evidence for such a relation. Clary provides the following diagram to explain the significance of the two Psalms.[14] He demonstrates that *Auctor* utilizes the two texts (Pss 2:7 and 110:4) in the preamble and historical prologue (Heb 1-7) to confirm the divine appointment of Jesus to the dual roles of sonship and priesthood in salvation history. He argues that "Hebrews 5:5-6 unite sonship and priesthood by quoting Pss 2:7 and 110:4."[15]

---

[9] See Paul Vernon Hydon, "The Priesthood of Jesus as Presented by the Hebrews" (Ph.D. diss., Boston University, 1941), 158-59.

[10] Clary declares, "Heb 1-7 is history *par excellence*" (Clary, "Hebrews," 214).

[11] Ekkehardt Müller, "Jesus and the Covenant in Hebrews," in *"For You Have Strengthened Me": Biblical and Theological Studies in Honor of Gerhard Pfandl in Celebration of His Sixty-Fifth Birthday*, ed. Martin Pröbstle, Gerald A. Klingbeil, and Martin G. Klingbeil (St. Peter am Hart, Austria: Seminar Schloss Bogenhofen, 2007), 207, emphasis added. Müller adopts the continuity-renewal perspective to interpret the relation between the Old and New Covenants (ibid., 208).

[12] For the grammatical significance of τῶν ἁγίων in Heb 8:2, see 127-30 (supra).

[13] See 130-32(supra).

[14] Clary, "Hebrews," 214.

[15] Ibid., 219.

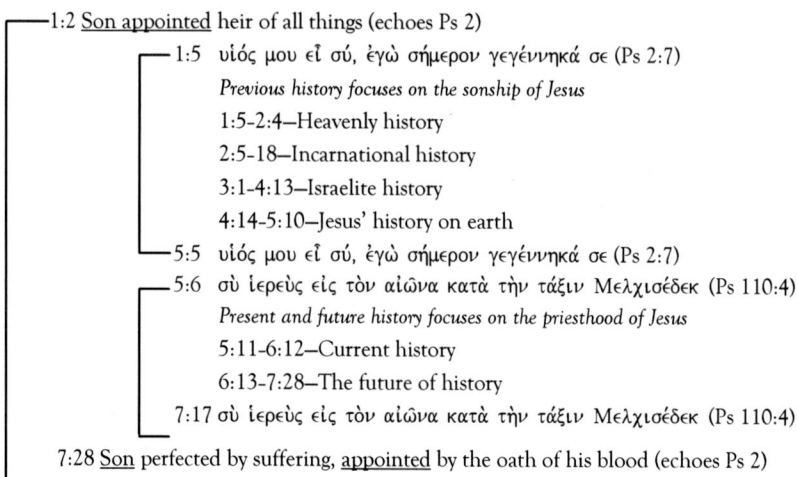

Figure 18. Significance of Psalms 2 and 110 in Hebrews

- 1:2 Son appointed heir of all things (echoes Ps 2)
  - 1:5 υἱός μου εἶ σύ, ἐγὼ σήμερον γεγέννηκά σε (Ps 2:7)
    - Previous history focuses on the sonship of Jesus
    - 1:5-2:4–Heavenly history
    - 2:5-18–Incarnational history
    - 3:1-4:13–Israelite history
    - 4:14-5:10–Jesus' history on earth
  - 5:5 υἱός μου εἶ σύ, ἐγὼ σήμερον γεγέννηκά σε (Ps 2:7)
  - 5:6 σὺ ἱερεὺς εἰς τὸν αἰῶνα κατὰ τὴν τάξιν Μελχισέδεκ (Ps 110:4)
    - Present and future history focuses on the priesthood of Jesus
    - 5:11-6:12–Current history
    - 6:13-7:28–The future of history
  - 7:17 σὺ ἱερεὺς εἰς τὸν αἰῶνα κατὰ τὴν τάξιν Μελχισέδεκ (Ps 110:4)
- 7:28 Son perfected by suffering, appointed by the oath of his blood (echoes Ps 2)

(This diagram is reprinted by permission of the author. All rights reserved.)

However, the dual roles of Jesus should not be construed to support that *Auctor*'s doctrinal center is dual in terms of sonship and priesthood. Instead, *Auctor* employs the hermeneutic of dual roles to bring out the functional (economic) and ontological (immanent) significance of Jesus as heavenly priest because Christ's priesthood derives its superiority (eminence) from sonship.[16] This connection is also supported by the way *Auctor* uses Ps 2:7 (a passage speaking clearly of Jesus' sonship) in relation to Ps 110:4. Clary observes:

> Psalm 2:7 is here [in Heb 5:5-6] quoted for the second and last time; it brackets the history of the Son in the world. This allows 5:6 to shift the emphasis properly to priesthood with its quote of Ps 110:4; this is the first direct quotation of that verse. Psalms 110:4 becomes the guiding text through 7:28 and is alluded to four more times in Heb 8-12. Hebrews 5:7-10 gives the historical and theological bases for Jesus' "designation" (προσαγορευθεὶς) as high priest–his "reverent submission" (εὐλαβείας). His loyalty and devotion to the Father won him a covenant of grant–a kingdom and priesthood.[17]

---

[16] Simon Kistemaker, *The Psalm Citations in the Epistle to the Hebrews* (Amsterdam: Wed. G. van Soest, 1961), 135-36.

[17] Clary, "Hebrews," 219.

In other words, *Auctor*'s repeated citations of Ps 2:7 in Heb 1-7 function primarily to bring out the significance of Jesus as heavenly priest whose qualifications are irreproachable by acclaiming Jesus first and foremost as Son.[18]

Autopistic vis-à-vis Axiopistic Hermeneutic

We have seen that *Auctor*'s pedagogy is biblical pedagogy or Bible-centered hermeneutics.[19] Under biblical pedagogy, the object of investigation is the Scripture and hermeneutics is ontologically (and epistemologically) prior to the Scripture. To support this understanding, Canale writes:

> The English dictionary tells us that "to interpret" means "to conceive in the light of belief, judgment, or circumstance." Key to the notion of interpretation is the "light" in which we see things. In technical jargon, the "light" in which we see things is made up by the presuppositions or context we assume when attempting to understand data, information or facts.[20]

Since thinking is presuppositional and knowledge is derived from one's act of interpreting data, the process of interpretation in hermeneutics is prior to that which is to be interpreted. In this vein, Canale says, "interpreters do not 'invent' the light or presuppositions they need to understand their objects of study, but they assume it from the objects themselves, based on previous knowledge or experience."[21] Hence, it is possible that *Auctor* follows an axiopistic hermeneutic (process of understanding a text)—the use of external sources or criteria not internal to the object of investigation (i.e., Scripture).

The axiopistic hermeneutic is reflected in the Jewish Background and Apostolic School.[22] This school interprets *Auctor*'s hermeneutic as axiopistic because he is assumed to utilize Scriptures and the intertestamental works.[23] In other words, *Auctor*'s sources include "the Septugiant (LXX); Targums; Rabbinic literature . . . DSS; and Philo's writings."[24] On the other hand, the auto-

---

[18] This is the thesis of David Wallace, "Texts in Tandem: The Coalescent Usage of Psalm 2 and Psalm 110 in Early Christianity" (Ph.D. diss., Baylor University, 1995), 199.

[19] See chapters four and six (supra, 80-83, 112-113).

[20] Fernando Canale, *Basic Elements of Christian Theology: Scripture Replacing Tradition* (Berrien Springs, MI: Andrews University Lithotech, 2005), 19.

[21] Ibid., 20.

[22] Herbert W. Bateman IV, "Dispensationalism Yesterday and Today," in *TCICD*, ed. Herbert W. Bateman IV (Grand Rapids: Kregel Publications, 1999), 41. Bateman has presented a concise description of the Jewish Background and Apostolic School in his dissertation. Idem, "Jewish and Apostolic Hermeneutics: How the Old Testament Is Used in Hebrews 1:5-13" (Ph.D. diss., Dallas Theological Seminary, 1993), 62-71. The major representative of the Jewish Background and Apostolic School is Richard Longenecker (ibid., 62). For a selected writing of Longenecker, see ibid., 62, n.1. Bateman's dissertation is published as *Early Jewish Hermeneutics and Hebrews 1:5-13*, American University Studies (New York: Peter Lang Publishing, 1997).

[23] Bateman, "Dispensationalism Yesterday and Today," 41.

[24] Bateman, "Hebrews 1:5-13," 63.

pistic hermeneutic is reflected in the Divine Intent-Human Words School.[25] This school interprets *Auctor*'s hermeneutic as autopistic because he is assumed to confine his epistemological realm of investigation to Scripture.

Can one ascertain whether *Auctor*'s hermeneutic is autopistic or axiopistic? The answer can be uncovered by a study of (1) *Auctor*'s epistemological realm of investigation for formulating his doctrinal center (X)—Christ's heavenly priesthood, and (2) his epistemological realm revealed by his use of Exodus (Y). Table 6 below summarizes the possible outcomes.

Table 6. Autopistic vis-à-vis Axiopistic Hermeneutic

Auctor's Hermeneutic in Light of His Hermeneutical Use of Exodus	
Auctor's hermeneutic is axiopistic • When X > Y (Scope of Source X > Scope of Source Y)	*Auctor*'s hermeneutic is autopistic • When X = Y (Both Sources are the Same) or • When X < Y (Scope of Source X < Scope of Source Y)

We have seen that *Auctor*'s pedagogical use of Exod 3:14 reveals that his epistemological realm (Y) is the Scripture via the analysis of *Auctor*'s reception of the history of the interpretive influence of Exodus.[26] Now what remains is to investigate the epistemological source (X) for formulating *Auctor*'s heavenly priesthood. To achieve this objective, it is necessary to investigate *Auctor*'s cultic vocabulary for depicting Christ as heavenly priest. I have already demonstrated that *Auctor* utilizes the cutic vocabulary of Exodus (e.g., priests, covenant, sanctuary, or tabernacle) as the primary (in the sense of foundational and sufficient) inter-textual source to describe the relationship between the Old and New Covenant forms of worship in terms of the Aaronic and Melchizedean priesthoods respectively.[27]

In short, the cultic vocabulary from Exodus is foundational and sufficient for constructing *Auctor*'s doctrinal center—the heavenly priesthood of Christ. Hence, *Auctor*'s hermeneutic is autopistic because the scope of source X is within the scope of source Y (i.e., X < Y). In other words, *Auctor*'s hermeneutical use of Exodus indicates that he constructs his doctrinal center autopistically instead of axiopistically. *Auctor*'s autopistic hermeneutic actually explains why he cares nothing for the temple and its cultus in Jerusalem.

---

[25] Bateman, "Dispensationalism Yesterday and Today," 39. For a concise discussion of the Divine Intent-Human Words School (or the Divine Intent-Human Author School), see idem, "Hebrews 1:5-13," 39-61. The key representative of the Divine Intent-Human Words School is Elliott Johnson (ibid., 39). For some selected work of Elliott Johnson, see ibid., 39 n.2.

[26] See chapter six

[27] See chapter two (supra 37-48).

One may charge that the thesis can only be accepted tentatively because it is necessary to validate it by examining whether there is indeed a conceptual difference of priesthood in Hebrews and second temple Judaism. If there is a difference, it means that the thesis is validated. Otherwise, the thesis cannot be supported. There are at least two reasons why this validation is not necessary.

First, it is obvious that there is always a conceptual difference of priesthood in Hebrews and second temple Judaism in the context of a high Christology. This concept holds except if the intertestamental Jewish writers were to adopt the same Christocentric-typological use of Exod 25:40 in Hebrews.[28] The fact of the matter is that it is impossible for non-elect intertestamental Jewish writers to accept that Jesus Christ is a real man and yet completely God. They reject the Christocentric-typological use of Exod 25:40. Wyschogrod writes:

> Unlike Christianity, Judaism does not believe that the central event of its history or of human history has taken place. This central event, the advent of the Messiah and the redemption of Israel and the world, has not yet taken place.[29]

Consequently, non-elect Jewish writers do not have the definite divine ontological ground to activate the Christocentric-typological use of Exod 25:40. This is so because, according to Martin, "the incarnation of God in Jesus Christ whose life, death, and resurrection is the definitive reality that manifests the unity of created existence with its ontological grounding in God."[30] This means that a conceptual or theological difference of priesthood in Hebrews and second temple Judaism always exists.

Second, scholars have already investigated the difference. However, there is a crisis of belief when one examines the conceptual difference of priesthood in Hebrews and second temple Judaism. When scholars conduct such comparative analyses of priesthood presented between Hebrews and intertestamental literature, their conclusions can be classified into four major positions: (1) *Auctor*'s concept of Christ's priesthood is of uncertain origin;[31] (2) the comparison reveals close parallels (i.e., *Auctor*'s work is coherent with extra-

---

[28] See *Auctor*'s typological use of Exod 25:40 in chapter seven.

[29] Michael Wyschogrod, *The Body of Faith: God and the People of Israel*, 2nd ed. [1st published as *The Body of Faith: Judaism as Corporeal Election*. New York: Seabury Press, 1983] (Northvale, NJ: Jason Aronson, 1996), 225.

[30] Robert K. Martin, *The Incarnate Ground of Christian Faith: Towards a Christian Theological Epistemology for the Educational Ministry of the Church* (Lanham, MD: University Press of America, 1998), 69.

[31] This is the thesis of Hayne Preston Griffith Jr., "An Investigation into the Origin of the High Priest Christology in the Epistle to the Hebrews" (Ph.D. diss., University of Aberdeen, 1978), 292.

biblical writings);[32] (3) the comparison reveals many differences (i.e., *Auctor*'s work is not coherent with extra-biblical writings);[33] and (4) others. The fourth category represents various proposals. For example, Henderson and Giles argue a close parallel between Hebrews and John.[34] On the other hand, Theißen and Grässer follow Käsemann's thesis and argue for a Gnostic context for understanding the high priestly Christology in Hebrews.[35] Such varied assessments of the conceptual difference of priesthood in Hebrews and second temple Judaism should be expected because they do not start with the authorial reading of Christ as Yahweh in Hebrews. In conclusion, *Auctor*'s use of Exodus indicates that he constructs his doctrinal center autopistically.

Comparative Analysis of *Auctor*'s Hermeneutics

Auctor's Christocentric-typological use of Exod 25:40 enables him to move the doctrinal center beyond a functional model toward an ontological one. To achieve this objective, it is necessary to demonstrate that (1) scholars' valuations of *Auctor*'s hermeneutics for doing Christology can be classified as either deductive or inductive; (2) *Auctor*'s Christology should be understood and constructed within the boundary of a functional model when *Auctor*'s Christocentric-typological use of Exod 25:40 is not recognized; (3) *only* the Christocentric-typological use of Exod 25:40 can enable *Auctor* to construct Christology ontologically *and* functionally. My goal here is to defend the third

---

[32] This is the thesis of Eric Farrel Mason, "The Concept of the Priestly Messiah in Hebrews and Second Temple Judaism" (Ph.D. diss., University of Notre Dame, 2005), 184. This work is published as '*You Are a Priest Forever*': *Second Temple Jewish Messianism and the Priestly Christology*, Studies on the Texts of the Desert of Judah, ed. Florentino García Martínez (Leiden: Brill, 2008).

[33] This is the thesis of Grothe and McCullough. See Jonathan F. Grothe, "Was Jesus the Priestly Messiah? A Study of the New Testament's Teaching of Jesus' Priestly Office against the Background of Jewish Hopes for a Priestly Messiah" (Th.D. diss., Concordia Seminary, St. Louis, 1981), 181; J. C. McCullough, "Hebrews and the Old Testament: A Comparison of the Use Which the Author of the Epistle to the Hebrews Makes of the Old Testament, with the Use Made by Other Writers of His Day" (Ph.D. diss., Queen's University of Belfast, 1971), 478.

[34] See Marion W. Henderson, "The Priestly Ministry of Jesus in the Gospel of John and the Epistle to the Hebrews" (Th.D. diss., Southern Baptist Theological Seminary, 1965), 260. Giles has written a published massive M.A. thesis (283 pages excluding bibliography) for Manchester University under the supervision of F. F. Bruce to defend a similar thesis. Pauline Giles, *Jesus the High Priest* (Bognor Regis, UK: New Horizon, 1984).

[35] See Gerd Theißen, *Untersuchungen zum Hebräerbrief*, SNT, ed. Günter Klein, Willi Marxsen, and Wolfgang Schrage, vol. 2 (Gütersloh: Gütersloher Verlagshaus Gerd Mohn, 1969), 151-52; Erich Grässer, "Das wandernde Gottesvolk: Zum Basismotiv des Hebräerbriefes," ZNW 77 (1986): 160-79.

mini-thesis because Williams has already demonstrated the first two mini-theses in his doctoral dissertation.[36]

Scholars' Valuations of *Auctor*'s Hermeneutics for Constructing Christology

There are two interpretive paradigms for Christology: functional (low or economic) and ontological (high or immanent) model. Hurst says:

> That two types of Christology (known by the labels "low" and "high" and "functional" and "ontological") developed side by side within early Christianity must be remembered.[37]

The inductive and deductive logics are necessarily associated with the hermeneutical methodology of doing functional (economic) and ontological (immanent) christologies respectively. It is important to note that the functional model is called "low" Christology simply because this inductive model starts by observing how the spatiotemporal life of the human Jesus functions as the Messiah or high priest in salvation history *from below* (earth to heaven).[38] Hence, one can still reach an exalted (elevated) or "high" status of Christ from the functional (low) perspective.

On the other hand, high Christology starts with the assumed fact or confession that Jesus is God from the beginning. The ontological model is called high Christology because this deductive model starts by presupposing a certain divine ontology to explain *how* the divine Christ (Son) *from above* becomes the human Jesus on earth and returns to heaven as the Messiah or high priest (heaven to earth to heaven). The ontological model is constructed deductively since one must presuppose a certain divine ontology whereby one can ground his understanding about the unseen (mysterious) reality of God.

This section demonstrates that (1) scholars' valuations of *Auctor*'s hermeneutics for doing Christology can be classified as either deductive or inductive; (2) *Auctor*'s Christology should be understood and constructed within the boundary of the functional model when *Auctor*'s Christocentric-typological use

---

[36] Arthur Hayes Williams Jr., "An Early Christology: A Systematic and Exegetical Investigation of the Traditions Contained in Hebrews, and of the Implications Contained in Their Later Neglect" (Th.D. diss., Johannes Gutenberg University of Mainz, 1971), 27.

[37] L. D. Hurst, "The Christology of Hebrews 1 and 2," in *The Glory of Christ in the New Testament: Studies in Christology in Memory of George Bradford Caird*, ed. L. D. Hurst and N. T. Wright (Oxford: Clarendon Press, 1987), 163. Low Christology can also be subdivided into two types: "the 'evolutionary' and the 'developmental'" (Andrew Chester, *Messiah and Exaltation*, WUNT, ed. Jörg Frey et al., vol. 207 [Tübingen: Mohr Siebeck, 2007], 21).

[38] Richard Bauckham, "The Sonship of the Historical Jesus in Christology," *SJT* 31, no. 3 (1978): 258.

of Exod 25:40 is not recognized.[39] *Auctor*'s hermeneutics should be seen in light of his use of Exodus autopistically since I have demonstrated above that *Auctor* constructs his doctrinal center autopistically instead of axiopistically. I am indebted to Williams who has already defended the two sub-theses in light of *Auctor*'s autopistic hermeneutic. However, it is important to note that Williams, like many scholars in the past, still has failed to recognize the prescriptive significance of *Auctor*'s Christocentric-typological use of Exod 25:40.

Auctor regards the Torah as sufficient and foundational for constructing his Christology even concerning the novel idea of Christ as royal high priest.[40] Williams argues that one of the reasons why Greek ontology is almost universally presupposed by Christian traditions to understand *Auctor*'s doctrinal center in the context of ontological Christology is because Christian theologians have historically understood Hebrews as an anti-Jewish document.[41] We have seen that this anti-Jewish attitude understands *Auctor*'s theology of revelation from the discontinuity perspective which is ontologically inconsistent with his ontology.[42]

Further, Hebrews reflects "an early Christology" because *Auctor*'s ontology is free from any ontological import exerted from later Christian traditions or Greek creeds.[43] Williams cogently charges that ontological (high) "christologies" made by later traditions (schemes of Christology) are speculative and anachronistic (i.e., reading Greek ontology into Hebrews); these Christian traditions attempt to explain how it is possible for certain (immanent) actions of God (e.g., the Incarnation) to happen by way of extra-biblical divine ontology.[44] In short, Williams demonstrates that theologians should not interpret *Auctor*'s Christological hermeneutic by ontological-deductive hermeneutics because such knowledge about God cannot be reached by human reason.[45] Likewise, Canale argues that silence in the divine reality (ontology) is golden: "Since this knowledge [of divine reality] belongs to the inner essence of the

---

[39] We have demonstrated that *Auctor*'s Christocentric-typological use of Exod 25:40 is not even recognized by scholars focusing on the use of Exodus in Hebrews (see supra, 90-94).

[40] See Williams, "An Early Christology," 27.

[41] Ibid., 1.

[42] See chapter seven of this study, supra, 138.

[43] Williams, "An Early Christology," ix.

[44] Ibid., xiii-xiv. Williams' view (about the relation between divine ontology and epistemology in the context of constructing Christology within the classical and modern Christian traditions) is shared by another reformed theologian, Bruce L. McCormack, "The Actuality of God: Karl Barth in Conversation with Open Theism," in *Engaging the Doctrine of God: Contemporary Protestant Perspectives*, ed. Bruce L. McCormack (Grand Rapids: Baker Academic, 2008), 187.

[45] Williams, "Early Christology," xiv.

Godhead, created beings cannot achieve it now, nor will the redeemed have access to it throughout eternity."[46]

According to Williams, since divine immanent reality (ontology) is speculative, one should only observe the divine Trinitarian spatiotemporal (economic or functional) *life* revealed in the Bible via inductive exegesis of Hebrews. In other words, when *Auctor*'s Christocentric-typological use of Exod 25:40 is not recognized, Williams argues that scholars' valuations of *Auctor*'s hermeneutics for doing Christology will be classified as either deductive or inductive. *Auctor*'s Christology should be understood within the boundaries of the functional model because *Auctor* constructs his Christology autopistically and inductively from function to status (e.g., as Christ and priest in heaven).

On the one hand, I would agree with Williams' proposal if *Auctor* did not use Exod 25:40 christocentric-typologically. Why did Williams miss the prescriptive use of Exod 25:40 in Hebrews? This is not difficult to answer because the prescriptive power of Exod 25:40 in Hebrews cannot be activated unless the prescriptive power of Exod 3:14 is activated. Otherwise, one cannot identify the correct ontological valuation of Exod 25:40 in Heb 8:5. I will argue later why *Auctor*'s christocentric-typological use of Exod 25:40 enables him to construct an autopistic-ontological-functional Christology.

On the other hand, Williams is right because divine ontology is in fact speculative. Due to the speculative nature of divine ontology, this study only presupposes one divine reality: Christ is Yahweh. This presupposed divine reality affirms both the oneness and the plurality of God revealed in the Bible. I have demonstrated that this theo-onto-logical approach to Christology is consistent with *Auctor*'s ontological framework which is contrary to the doctrinal systems derived from the classical (traditional) and from liberal (modern or Kantian) Christian theology influenced by extra-biblical philosophy.[47]

The authorial reading of Christ as Yahweh gives priority to the ontology revealed in Scripture. In other words, this presupposed divine reality affirms both the oneness and the plurality of God revealed in the Bible. This is contrary to classical and modern theologians who presuppose that true ultimate

---

[46] Fernando L. Canale, "Doctrine of God," in *Handbook of Seventh-day Adventist Theology*, ed. Raoul Dederen, CRS, ed. George W. Reid, vol. 12 (Washington, DC: Review and Herald Publishing Association, 2000), 114.

[47] Recall that there are three types of theological projects in the history of interpretation: (1) classical or traditional (e.g., Augustine, Thomas Aquino), (2) liberal or modern (e.g., the open view of God, Rudolf Bultmann), and (3) historical-cognitive or biblical (e.g., Canale, Norman Gulley).The first project constructs theology via the axiom that the reality (nature or essence) of God is timeless—a timeless reality that does not exist in the future-present-past flux of time and cannot experience anything new. The second project assumes that the nature of God is simultaneously timeless and temporal. The third one presupposes that God is a temporal-historical Being: one can only know God's spatiotemporal life revealed in Scripture because any theory about God's nature (divine ontology) is speculative. See Canale, *Revelation-Inspiration*, 75-160.

(divine) reality is simple and without space, that is, it has no parts and is therefore indivisible. Canale rightly declares:

> Theologians who start from a conception of God's oneness [simplicity] tend to see in the Trinitarian revelation presented in the Bible a problem to be solved rather than a characteristic of God to be integrated in our understanding about the very life and being of God. Thus, classical [and modern/Kantian] theology starts with the conception of God as One (*Deo uno*) and only then does it deal with the Trinitarian God (*Deo Trino*) witnessed in the Bible.[48]

The present theo-onto-logical approach gives primacy to the Trinitarian God revealed in the Bible so that divine ontology controls epistemology not vice versa.[49]

Ontological Significance of Exodus 25:40 for Constructing Christology in Hebrews

Only the Christocentric-typological use of Exod 25:40 can enable *Auctor* to construct his doctrinal center ontologically and functionally. To defend this thesis, I integrate the findings of Arthur Williams's dissertation in light of the pedagogy-oriented analysis done in chapters three to seven. When *Auctor's* Christocentric-typological use of Exod 25:40 is not recognized, according to Williams, scholars of Hebrews employ either deductive or inductive hermeneutics to construct (and understand) *Auctor's* Christology. *Auctor's* Christology should be understood within the boundaries of the functional model through inductive hermeneutics since using deductive hermeneutics to explain Christ's ontology would be speculative.[50] Put simply, in light of *Auctor's* autopistic hermeneutic, silence is golden when we talk about divine ontology.[51] I would fully agree with Williams' thesis if there were no Christocentric-typological use of Exod 25:40 in Heb 8:5 (see Table 7).

---

[48] Fernando Canale, *Basic Elements of Christian Theology: Scripture Replacing Tradition* (Berrien Springs, MI: Andrews University Lithotech, 2005), 78.

[49] McCormack, "Actuality of God," 187. See supra, 74.

[50] Williams, "An Early Christology," x. Though Williams has only illustrated why ontological Christology is speculative by focusing on *how* the kenotic theory is used by theologians to explain the Incarnation via extra-biblical ontology (ibid., xi-xv), the speculative nature of ontological Christology is evident when one recognizes that there are various competing theories to explain the Incarnation. According to Givens, there are at least three major ontological hypotheses developed by theologians for explaining the incarnational motifs when they utilize Christ as hermeneutical center in doctrinal construction: (1) logos motif; (2) incarnational motif; and (3) kenotic motif. Jimmy McMath Givens Jr., "Christ as Hermeneutical Referent: An Analysis of the Extension of Christological Motifs within the Theologies of A. H. Strong, E. Y. Mullins, and W. T. Conner" (Ph.D. diss., Southwestern Baptist Theological Seminary, 2000), 95-123.

[51] See Williams, "Early Christology," 292. Canale defends the same position. See Canale, "Doctrine of God," 118.

Like other scholars in the past, Williams missed the ontological significance of the heavenly sanctuary in Hebrews. In other words, it is *only* the Christocentric-typological use of Exod 25:40 which can enable *Auctor* to construct the doctrinal center ontologically and functionally (see Case G). The table below demonstrates why it is necessary to update Williams' thesis here in light of the pedagogy-oriented analysis (cf. chapters 3 to 7). Here are laid out various possible scenarios of the relation between hermeneutic, hermeneutics, and Christology in Hebrews.

Table 7. Scholars' Valuations of *Auctor*'s Hermeneutics and Hermeneutic

Auctor's Hermeneutical Methodology according to Arthur Hayes Williams				
Scholars' Valuations of *Auctor*'s Hermeneutic ↓	Scholars' Valuations of *Auctor*'s Hermeneutics		Nature of *Auctor*'s Christology Constructed According to Respective Hermeneutics	
	Deductive ↓	Inductive ↓	Ontological ↓	Functional ↓
Autopistic (Case A)	N/A	Inductive study without premise	No	Yes
Axiopistic (Case B)	N/A	Inductive study without premise	No	Yes
Autopistic (Case C)	Jesus Christ = Messiah (Functional Premise)	N/A	No	Yes
Axiopistic (Case D)	Jesus Christ = Messiah (Functional Premise)	N/A	No	Yes
Axiopistic (Case E)	Jesus Christ = Yahweh (Ontological Premise)	N/A	No	Yes
Autopistic (Case F)	Jesus Christ = Yahweh (Ontological Premise)	N/A	No	Yes
Auctor's Hermeneutical Methodology in Light of His Christocentric-Typological Use of Exod 25:40				
Autopistic (Case G)	Jesus Christ = Yahweh (Ontological Premise)	N/A	Yes	Yes

"N/A" in Table 7 means that both inductive and deductive hermeneutics involve the use of the grammatico-historical approach to study the Bible. Inductive hermeneutics differs from the deductive approach only in one aspect: the former does not entail an *explicit* use of a universal premise (either ontological or functional) as the reading strategy to arrive at the meaning of a text. This is true even if the interpreter adopting inductive approach may believe that Jesus Christ is Yahweh (God) (ontological premise) or/and the Messiah (functional premise). Deductive approach is rejected by modern (Kantian) pedagogy. According to modern pedagogy, the use of a universal premise to read the text is considered as uncritical.

Christology constructed under Cases A and B is functional (economic or from below) because there is no ontological ground to serve as the starting point for constructing ontological Christology. The functional Christology of Cases A and B can result in either an exalted or depreciated functional status of Christ.[52] Christology constructed under Cases C and D is not ontological because the universal premise about divine ontology (*theos*) is functional (i.e., not reflecting the divine reality from the side of God). Though the interpreters of Case C correctly understand *Auctor* hermeneutic as autopistic, the starting point for constructing ontological Christology has to be a presupposition about divine ontology. The functional premise (e.g., Jesus = Messiah, Priest, or King) can only construct Christology in a functional sense (i.e., within the realm of nature in our world).

Christology constructed under Case E should be functional because one could deduce that Christ is the Messiah (or the heavenly Priest) using the premise about Christ as Yahweh. Then, one could use such a functional premise to construct his functional Christology. However, an explicit use of the ontological premise (Christ = Yahweh) is incapable of constructing a genuine ontological Christology in the biblical sense when *Auctor*'s hermeneutic is incorrectly presupposed to be axiopistic. The axiopistic hermeneutic is onto-theo-logical and thus uses the notion of reality or being (*ontos*) to determine both divine ontology (*theos*) and methodology (*logia*). McCormack correctly describes the axiopistic (onto-theo-logical) hermeneutic as follows:

> That is to say, though the being of God is above and prior to the being of all else that exists (and therefore first in the "order of being"), our knowledge of God proceeds from a prior knowledge of some aspects or aspects of creaturely reality (and therefore the knowledge of God follows knowledge of the self or the world in the "order of knowing"). The consequence of this methodological decision is that the way taken to knowledge of God controls and determines the kind of God-concept one is able to generate; thus epistemology controls and determines divine ontology.[53]

In other words, the Christology of Case E should not be considered as ontological Christology because it is not derived from *Auctor*'s (autopistic or biblical) view of divine ontology but from an extra-biblical natural theology (i.e., the knowledge of the self or the world).

For Case F, the ontological premise about God (Christ = Yahweh) should enable an interpreter to deduce that Christ is the Messiah. This functional premise then enables *Auctor* to construct a functional Christology via inductive hermeneutics. However, it is also impossible for Case F to construct onto-logical-functional Christology. Before we revise Williams' thesis, one needs to appreciate his contribution in the context of the present study: there is no ontology except for a functional Christology in Hebrews when the Christocen-

---

[52] For example, Hydon seems to reach a depreciated valuation of Christ's status as heavenly priest via inductive exegesis free from the use of any explicit ontological or functional presupposition to reach the meaning of Hebrews. See Paul Vernon Hydon, "The Priesthood of Jesus as Presented by the Hebrews" (Ph.D. diss., Boston University, 1941), 195.

[53] McCormack, "Actuality of God," 187.

tric-typological significance of the sanctuary (tabernacle) typology of (Heb 8:5) is not recognized. In other words, in light of Williams' work and the prescriptive power of Exod 25:40 for constructing *Auctor*'s metanarrative,[54] one can safely posit that it is *only* the Christocentric-typological use of Exod 25:40 which can enable *Auctor* to construct the doctrinal center ontologically and functionally (see Case G). Without the spatiotemporal revelation of the heavenly sanctuary in Exod 25:40, *Auctor* is unable to find a definite autopistic-ontological ground in the realm of nature that also reflects paradoxically *divine* ontology in the realm of supernature, whereby *Auctor* can ground a genuine (biblical) ontological-functional Christology.

In the past, Hebrews scholars neither recognized nor utilized the ontology of sanctuary (tabernacle) typology to bridge the transcendental gap between earth (nature) and heaven (supernature) when formulating *Auctor*'s Christology. This is why Canale rightly says, "Scripture speaks clearly of the transcendence of God from the starting point of His immanence in the sanctuary."[55]

In summary, there is only one possible scenario (valuation) for understanding *Auctor*'s hermeneutical methodology in light of his Christocentric-typological use of Exodus (see Case G): *Auctor* constructs his Christology autopistically, ontologically, and functionally in the context of the theo-ontological structure of reason via the divine ontological presupposition of Christ as Yahweh *and* he uses sanctuary typology to develop the highest possible view of Christology in early Christianity.

Though Christology high (immanent) or low (economic) belongs to systematic theology as a scholarly discipline, scholars' valuations of *Auctor*'s Christology have never been truly ontological in the biblical sense because these scholars in the past did not recognize *Auctor*'s Christocentric-typological use of Exod 25:40 in Heb 8:5. It is easy to miss the prescriptive power of Exod 25:40 for constructing divine ontology in Hebrews because such power cannot be activated unless the prescriptive power of Exod 3:14 is activated *and Auctor*'s pedagogical use of Exod 3:14 is recognized.[56]

Why such recognition is so important ontologically? This is because, according to Canale, "'thinking' and 'Being' belong together."[57] More specifically, God's ontic presence and His Being are different and *inseparable* according to Exod 3:14.[58] Hence, the thinking (reading strategy) of understanding Christ as Yahweh ensures God's ontic presence (His appearance) in one's hermeneu-

---

[54] See chapter seven (supra, 130-37).

[55] The sanctuary typology is unique in the Bible (see supra, 130-31).

[56] See supra, 117-19.

[57] Fernando Luis Canale, *A Criticism of Theological Reason: Time and Timelessness as Primordial Presuppositions*, AUSDDS, vol. 10 (Berrien Springs, MI: Andrews University Press, 1987), 35.

[58] Ibid., 352-54.

tic whereas the theo-onto-logia recognizes God's Being as the starting point for understanding the nature of reality (*ontos*) and method (*logia*) in one's hermeneutics.

By recognizing the pedagogical use of Exod 3:14 in Hebrews, one can understand why *Auctor* is able to construct the autopistic-ontological-functional doctrinal center by the Christocentric-typological use of Exod 25:40 reading Christ as Yahweh in the context of the theo-onto-logical structure of reason. Therefore, Williams's dissertation should be updated in light of Canale's revolutionary dissertation done twelve years later. The dissertations of Williams and Canale were completed in 1971 and 1983 respectively. When one updates the work of Arthur Williams, Bauckham's significant thesis that one should construct NT Christology by thinking Christ as Yahweh plays only a secondary role because Bauckham's method can only identify Case E and F (in Table 7 above) as the most likely scenarios (valuations) to understand *Auctor*'s relation between hermeneutic, hermeneutics, and Christology.[59] Bauckham cannot identify Case G as the correct valuation because he presupposes onto-theo-logia to do theology.[60]

Summary

The purpose here is to highlight the hermeneutical significance of Exodus in Hebrews. I briefly examined the works of Martin Emmrich, Kiwoong Son, and Gabriella Gelardini in chapter five.[61] Their works can now be given a more critical assessment in light of the hermeneutical significance of Exodus in Hebrews. Put simply, the arguments of Son, Emmrich, and Gelardini should be rejected because they assume that *Auctor*'s hermeneutic is axiopistic—*Auctor*'s doctrine has been adapted to the literary sources external to the Scripture, and to the culture/philosophy of the day.

For example, Gelardini interprets *Auctor*'s theology of revelation in relation to the Old and New Covenants in light of rabbinic sources.[62] As a result,

---

[59] See Richard Bauckham, *God Crucified: Monotheism and Christology in the New Testament* (Cumbria, UK: Paternoster Press, 1998).

[60] See Richard Bauckham, "Tradition in Relation to Scripture and Reason," in *Scripture, Tradition, and Reason: A Study in the Criteria of Christian Doctrine*, ed. Richard J. Bauckham and Benjamin Drewery (Edinburgh: T & T Clark, 1988), 140-45.

[61] Martin Emmrich, "Pneumatological Concepts in Hebrews" (Ph.D. diss., Westminister Theological Seminary, 2001); Kiwoong Son, "Sinai and Zion Symbolism and the Hermeneutics of Hebrews: Heb. 12:18-24 as an Interpretative Key to the Epistle" (Ph.D. diss., Brunel University, 2004); Gabriella Gelardini, "«Verhärtet eure Herzen nicht» Der Hebräer, eine Synagogenhomilie zu *Tischa be-Aw*" (Ph.D. diss., University of Basel, 2004).

[62] Ibid., 134; idem, "Hebrews, an Ancient Synagogue Homily for *Tisha be-Av*: Its Function, Its Basis, Its Theological Interpretation," in *Hebrews: Contemporary Methods—New Insights*, ed.

she suggests that Hebrews was most likely a homily on the occasion of fasting for *Tisha be-Av*.[63] Gelardini cites evidence from Zech 8:19 and rabbinic literature (Mishnah, Tosefta, and Talmudim) for supporting her thesis.[64] However, there is only one fast required by Mosaic Law (Lev 16). Commenting on the observance of the fastings mentioned in Zech 7-8, Merrill writes:

> A particular problem with the observance was that it had no [Mosaic] sanction in Israel's ancient religious traditions as did other holy days. Was it appropriate, then, to create holy days to observe occasions that had arisen in the post-Mosaic period? It obviously was being done de facto, but until the ecclesiastical authority structures were back in place in Jerusalem it was impossible to get an official ruling.[65]

In order to support Gelardini's thesis, one must interpret *Auctor*'s use of Exodus from the perspective of the axiopistic hermeneutic. Son also understands *Auctor*'s ontology of the heavenly Zion in light of the Jewish apocalyptic literature.[66] Finally, Emmrich expounds *Auctor*'s doctrine of the Holy Spirit in light of rabbinic sources.[67] In summary, the axiopistic hermeneutic of Son, Emmrich, and Gelardini are speculative and not warranted because *Auctor* constructs his doctrine autopistically by deductive hermeneutics by the authorial reading of Christ as Yahweh and the divine ontology of the heavenly sanctuary.

We have also seen that *Auctor* utilizes Exod 25:40 to construct his doctrinal center in the context of autopistic-ontological-functional Christology. This is significant because *Auctor* actually sets a paradigmatic model of how to construct divine ontology for the NT scholars. *Auctor*'s hermeneutics indicates that one's approach to constructing an ontological Christology should be autopistic via the sanctuary (tabernacle) typology and the authorial reading of Christ as Yahweh. Without the spatiotemporal revelation of the heavenly tabernacle (sanctuary) to reflect divine ontology from the side of God, one's divine ontology is inevitably speculative and changing.

In fact, scholars have recently recognized the significance of deductive hermeneutics in relation to the traditional quest of the historical Jesus.[68] Due

---

Gabriella Gelardini, BIS, ed. R. Alan Culpepper and Ellen van Wolde, vol. 75 (Leiden: Brill, 2005), 119.

[63] Ibid., 107.

[64] Ibid., 118-123.

[65] Eugene H. Merrill, *An Exegetical Commentary: Haggai, Zechariah, Malachi* (Chicago: Moody Press, 1994), 208.

[66] Kiwoong Son, *Zion Symbolism in Hebrews: Hebrews 12:18-24 as a Hermeneutical Key to the Epistle*, Paternoster Biblical Monographs, ed. I. Howard Marshall et al. (Waynesboro, GA: Paternoster Press, 2005), 184; idem, "Sinai and Zion," 227.

[67] Emmrich, "Pneumatological Concepts," 205-206.

[68] For a chronological overview of the research about the historical Jesus, see Craig A. Evans, "Chronological Table," in *The Historical Jesus: Critical Concepts in Religious Studies*, ed. Craig

to the inductive nature of the traditional quest, Loewe observes that "research on the historical Jesus currently offers a wide array of historical images of Jesus."[69] Scholars have recently realized that "the historical Jesuses" are actually personal constructs "discovered" by scholars.[70] Piper describes the inductive approach to reconstruct a portrait of Jesus as "an illusion because by definition the method adopted only offers fragments without immediate context."[71] Piper continues to say, "That means the mind of the scholars, not the reality of Jesus, is governing the reconstruction."[72]

By an appropriate use of assumed divine ontology for biblical exegesis, one's deductive approach to construct Christology is better because an exhaustive inductive examination cannot be carried out in practice to eliminate all alternative explanations and interpretations.[73] Hence, Tilley proposes that the deductive approach should replace the traditional inductive quest of the "historical Jesuses."[74] The deductive hermeneutics should be adopted because "Jesus does not fit our familiar categories; we need to acknowledge his strangeness to us."[75] This study acknowledges Jesus' strangeness and argues that the ontological-functional Christology in Hebrews has to be deductively formulated via the authorial reading of Christ as Yahweh and the *divine* ontology of the heavenly sanctuary.

A. Evans, vol. 1 (London: Routledge, 2004), xix-xxviii. Evans' overview spans from 1846 to 2001.

[69] William P. Loewe, "From the Humanity of Christ to the Historical Jesus," *TS* 61 (June 2000): 330.

[70] Terrence W. Tilley, "Remembering the Historic Jesus—A New Research Program?" *TS* 68 (March 2007): 1, n. 1.

[71] John Piper, *What Jesus Demands from the World* (Wheaton, IL: Crossway Books, 2006), 33-34.

[72] Ibid., 34.

[73] See Greg L. Bahnsen, "Inductivism, Inerrancy, and Presuppositionalism," *JETS* 20 (December 1977): 301.

[74] Tilley, "Historic Jesus," 1.

[75] Ibid., 6.

• CHAPTER NINE •

Conclusion

By reading Christ as Yahweh in Hebrews, this study appears to be the first to unravel one of the most mysterious riddles in Hebrews—why the author focuses not on the temple rituals in Jerusalem but only on the biblical cultus of the tabernacle from the Torah. In order to solve the riddle, I investigated how *Auctor* understands the religious language of "analogy" ontologically. Put simply, he utilizes analogy to construct his metanarrative. His construction is from vision to system which is encapsulated by his metanarrative as a portrait of the vision. This study posits that a proper understanding of how *Auctor* utilizes the canonical revelation from Exodus can provide readers with an epistemological lens from Exodus to identify the correct interpretation of other passages within Hebrews, for example Heb 9:22-23, which was discussed in the opening chapter. This chapter applies the preceding results of prescriptive analysis to resolve indeterminacy of Heb 9:22-23. This chapter has three parts: (1) summary of descriptive and prescriptive analyses; (2) correct interpretation of Heb 9:22-23; (3) suggestions for future research.

Summary of Descriptive and Prescriptive Analyses

Since I have already provided a summary for each chapter, this section will only provide an overall highlight. The use of Exod 3:14 and 25:40 by *Auctor* reflects the significant explanatory, theological, and hermeneutical role that Exodus played in the development of *Auctor*'s thought. The explanatory (rhetorical) significance of Exodus is demonstrated by a text-oriented analysis (chapter 2). *Auctor*'s dependence on Exodus is significant, both through his rehearsal of key cultic vocabulary and through his choice of citations. Thus, the reader who cannot connect *Auctor*'s audience to the Exodus generation via the Book of Exodus will certainly be insufficiently guided in terms of the significance of the high-priestly ministry of Christ in the heavenly sanctuary.

The goal of rhetorical (descriptive) analysis is to identify the significant hermeneutical and ontological markers. Exodus 3:14 and 25:40 have been identified as significant markers which are then examined in the pedagogy-oriented analysis. The prescriptive significance of Exodus in Hebrews is examined by the pedagogy-oriented analysis (chapters 3 to 7). By recognizing *Auctor*'s pedagogical use of Exod 3:14, one is able to identify *Auctor*'s preferred ontological framework whereby he understands the ontology of the heavenly sanctuary revealed in Exod 25:40 (Heb 8:5). This preferred ontological framework (Mosaic-biblical metanarrative) then serves as the ground to understand how *Auctor* utilizes Exod 25:40 from the level of the pedagogy-oriented analysis. The prescriptive power of Exod 25:40 is revealed by *Auctor*'s Christocentric-typological exegesis of Exod 25:40. This use of Exod 25:40 prescribes *Auctor*'s metanarrtive—the benchmark of his doctrinal system. Under *Auctor*'s Christocentric-typological exegesis of Exod 25:40, intertextual borrowing produces a message of arresting import, evoking canonical images of God's love and His commitment to Israel via the sanctuary-covenant metanarrative, and heightening divine commitment to His people to an eschatological level. The prescriptive use of Exod 25:40 also identifies the correct valuation of *Auctor*'s theology of revelation concerning the relation between the Old and New Covenants. It points to the continuity-renewal perspective as the correct theological model whereby the Old Covenant is related to the New Covenant Christologically.

The hermeneutical significance of Exodus is demonstrated from three levels: (1) text-oriented analysis; (2) pedagogy-oriented analysis; (3) methodological analysis. This trio reveals an order of investigation to be followed carefully throughout this study because I attempt to interpret Hebrews using a theological precondition—the authorial reading of Christ as Yahweh. This reading moves from a higher level of cognitive specificity to a lower one (see Figure 19).

Figure 19. Levels of Cognitive Specificity in Connection with the Theologcal Precondition

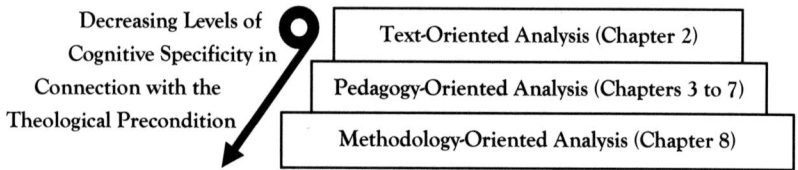

The theological precondition is supported in light of the rhetorical context of Hebrews. The methodological analysis is preceded by the pedagogy-oriented analysis because the former is the least determinative and specific to one's theological precondition in terms of cognitive specificity. The pedagogy-oriented analysis is preceded by the text-oriented analysis because the latter one is a descriptive (rhetorical) analysis of how *Auctor* engages his readers theologically.

The results of the text-oriented analysis and the pedagogy-oriented analysis are utilized for the methodology-oriented analysis (chapter 8). From the perspective of hermeneutics, the text-oriented analysis indicates that Exod 3:14 and 25:40 are significant ontological and hermeneutical markers respectively. Exodus 3:14 and 25:40 are then utilized in the pedagogy-oriented analysis to demonstrate that *Auctor*'s hermeneutics is Christocentric-typologcial biblical pedagogy. Moreover, the text-oriented analysis indicates that Exod 32-34 is the controlling revelation in *Auctor*'s hermeneutic whereas the pedagogy-oriented analysis reveals that his hermeneutic is theo-onto-logical. Finally, the methodology-oriented analysis indicates that *Auctor* constructs his doctrinal center (Christ's heavenly priesthood) autopistically (instead of axiopistically), functionally (economically), and ontologically (immanently).

Correct Interpretation of Hebrews 9:22-23

We have seen the diversity of theological positions of Heb 9:22-23 in chapter one. Now, we know *Auctor*'s pedagogy is a biblical pedagogy, we can use this as the ontological benchmark to decide which theological valuations of scholars are ontologically consistent with *Auctor*'s doctrinal system. In other words, we can now uncover whether scholars' valuations of *Auctor*'s pedagogy are founded or unfounded, regardless of their theological perspectives (see Table 8).

Table 8. Scholars' Valuations of *Auctor*'s Pedagogy Reflected by the Various Interpretations of Heb 9:22-23

Scholars	How should one understand the reality of the heavenly sanctuary?	Scholars' Valuations of Auctor's Pedagogy
Harold W. Attridge	Metaphorical (immaterial) sanctuary	Classical Pedagogy
F. F. Bruce	Presence of God in heaven	Classical Pedagogy
Peter T. O'Brien	Metaphorical (immaterial) sanctuary	Classical Pedagogy
Ceslas Spicq	Cannot be understood	Modern Pedagogy
Hugh Montefiore	Cannot be understood	Modern Pedagogy
Alberto Treiyer	Spatiotemporal sanctuary	Biblical Pedagogy
Kevin Conner	Spatiotemporal sanctuary	Biblical Pedagogy

Spicq and Montefiore cannot understand the reality of the heavenly sanctuary and why the "heavenly things" needing to be purified because they presuppose that *Auctor*'s pedagogy is modern or Kantian. They assume that only the things in the earthly realm needed to be purified. Even though the things in heavenly realm needed to be purified, they argue that this understanding uniquely belongs to *Auctor* and it should be rejected. This is because human reason can never attain to the heavenly reality.

Obviously, believers should reject the theologcal perspective of Spicq and Montefiore because they incorrectly presuppose that *Auctor*'s predagogy is modern. Under modern pedagogy, believers are unable to affirm absolutely that their life is spatiotempotal or real in the heaven. In other words, believers cannot be completely sure that their fellowship and walk with God is spatiotemporal. In fact, divine cognitive communication cannot take place in the realm of nature (earth). Kant argues that the real content of faith does not include knowledege originated from the supernatural realm because supernatural knowledge is always dogmatic.[1] Hence, beleivers should neither accept supernatural reality revealed by the Scripture nor believe that their reason can enter into the non-spatiotemporal realm of heaven.

Figure 20. Non-Spatiotemporal Heavenly Sanctuary according to Classical Pedagogy

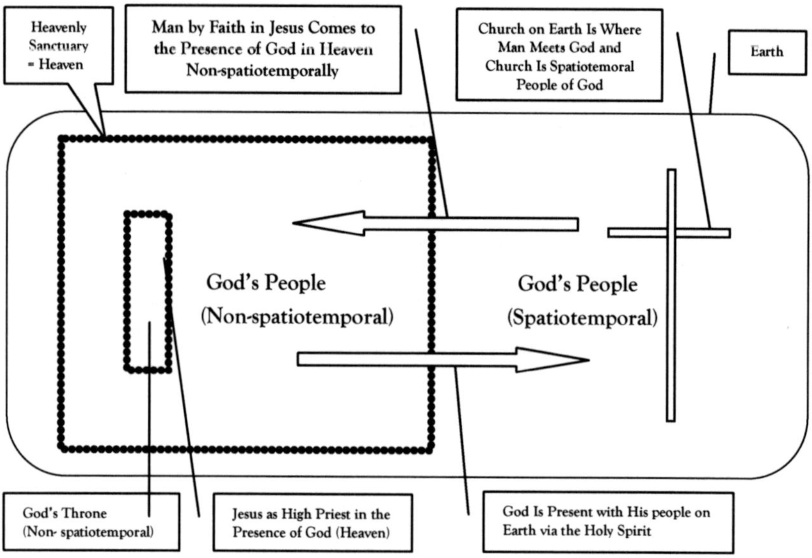

| Heavenly Sanctuary = Heaven | Man by Faith in Jesus Comes to the Presence of God in Heaven Non-spatiotemporally | Church on Earth Is Where Man Meets God and Church Is Spatiotemoral People of God | Earth |

God's People (Non-spatiotemporal)

God's People (Spatiotemporal)

| God's Throne (Non- spatiotemporal) | Jesus as High Priest in the Presence of God (Heaven) | God Is Present with His people on Earth via the Holy Spirit |

Under the influence of classical pedagogy, most schoalrs interpret Heb 9:22-23 like Attridge, Bruce, and O'Brien. Since they presuppose that the heavenly sanctuary or tabernacle is a timeless and nonhistorical reality (see Figure 20), I use the dotted line to indicate its ultimate reality in heavenly realm. The heavenly sanctuary is the heaven itself. The narrow line indicates

---

[1] Immanuel Kant, "Preface to Second Edition," in *Critique of Pure Reason*, trans. Werner S. Pluhar (Indianapolis: Hackett, 1996), 25.

the realm of nature according to classical pedagogy because the earthly reality is not ultimate but is changing and transient. Since spatiotemporal reality is not ultimate according to classical pedagogy, scholars argue that Heb 9:23 refers to the cleanisng of non-spatiotemporal realities. These scholars ususally argue that these realites needing to be cleansed, but some options are human consciences, spirits, or souls. As a result, classical theologians tend to emphasize the pursuit of divine and human union or encounter in spirits or souls via the mediation of the Scripture. The human body is often understood as an obstacle to reaching complete union with God. This spiritual impedance occurs not only when one sins but also the body is ontologically inferior to soul and spirit. That is, at death, the spatiotemporal body cannot continue to exist like soul and spirit. Believers therefore are encouraged to achieve a higher level of spirituality by pursuing an intimate relationship between God and their spirits (souls) in the timeless and nonhistorical realm. Under this pedagogy, the importance of holy living in spatiotemporal realm is easily neglected and believers become consciously or unconsciously accustomed to a dualistic way of Christian living.

Figure 21. Spatiotemporal Heavenly Sanctuary according to Biblical Pedagogy

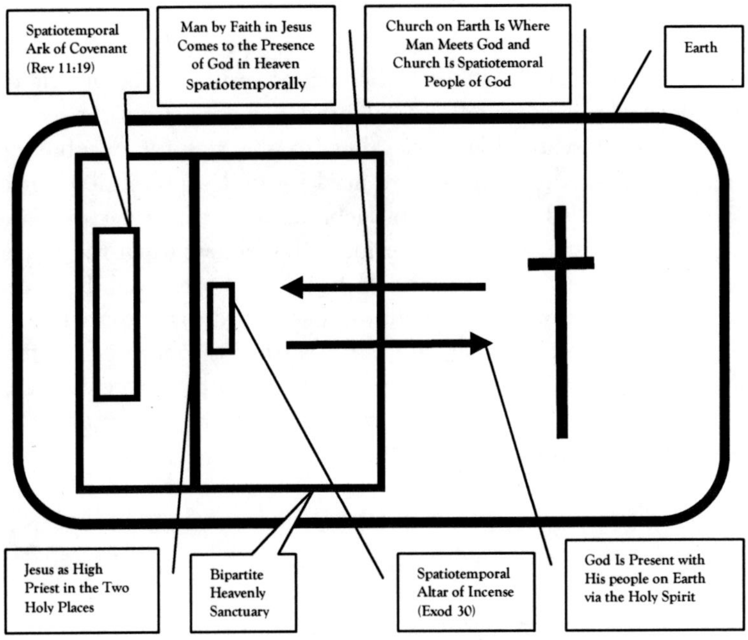

On the contrary, Figure 21 shows the spatiotemporal heavenly sanctuary according to biblical pedagogy. To indicate that the realms of earth and heaven are spatiotemporal, I use the shaded line. Treiyer and Conner correctly interpret Heb 9:22-23 ontologically even though they do not recognize the prescriptive significane of Exodus in Hebrews. In order to conduct a descriptive analysis of Hebrews, it is necessary for them to maintain an ontology as their ground for exegeisis. Their ontology is now identifed as the correct one by the present study because it is consistent with *Auctor*'s ontology or pedagogy.

Suggestions for Future Study

Since this book appears to be the first study to investigate the use of Exodus in Hebrews using the authorial reading of Christ as Yahweh, it is obvious that the same methodology can be extended to other biblical books. This study is also the first to *apply* biblical ontology to the study of a NT book whereas Canale's dissertation is the first to *derive* biblical ontology from Exodus. I suggest more work be done on other biblical books in the future reading through the lens of biblical ontology. Biblical ontology provides a new road to explore Scripture, and it provides a way to construct biblical theology independent of philosophical ontology.

Also, more works should be done on every stream (e.g., Christology, eschatology, soteriology) of systematic theology according to the biblical or temporal analogy of being (*analogia entis*). Christian doctrinal systems have always been constructed synthetically according to the classical or philosophical *analogia entis*. This points up the dire need for philosophical deconstruction. This need is amplified in the case of Hebrews since I have demonstrated the ontological inconsistency especially evident in Hebrews when the audience is understood to be Jewish Christians. Hence, Wyschogrod rightly argues that "philosophy in the sense of the tradition that started with pre-Socratics, Plato and Aristotle, is a foreign enterprise as far as Israel is concerned."[2] After philosophical deconstruction, one is then ready to reconstruct systematic theology according to the temporal or biblical *analogia entis*. This will be an unfamiliar but rewarding journey for many students of the Bible.

---

[2] Michael Wyschogrod, *The Body of Faith: God and the People of Israel*, 2nd ed. [1st published as *The Body of Faith: Judaism as Corporeal Election*. New York: Seabury Press, 1983] (Northvale, NJ: Jason Aronson, 1996), 80.

Bibliography

Books

Allen, David M. *Deuteronomy and Exhortation in Hebrews: A Study in Narrative Re-presentation.* Wissenschaftliche Untersuchungen zum Neuen Testament, ed. Jörg Frey et al., vol. 238. Tübingen: Mohr Siebeck, 2008.

Attridge, Harold W. *The Epistle to the Hebrews: A Commentary on the Epistle to the Hebrews.* Hermeneia, ed. Helmut Koester et al. Philadelphia: Fortress Press, 1989.

Bateman, Herbert W. IV. *Early Jewish Hermeneutics and Hebrews 1:5-13.* American University Studies. New York: Peter Lang Publishing, 1997.

Bauckham, Richard. *God Crucified: Monotheism and Christology in the New Testament.* Cumbria, UK: Paternoster Press, 1998.

Bauckham, Richard. *Jesus and the God of Israel: God Crucified and Other Studies on the New Testament's Christology of Divine Identity.* Grand Rapids: Eerdmans, 2008.

Belcher, Richard P. *A Comparison of Dispensationalism and Covenant Theology.* Southbridge, MA: Crowne Publications, 1986.

Biblia hebraica stuttgartensia. Edited by K. Ellinger and W. Rudolph, 4th corrected ed. Stuttgart: Deutsche Bibelgesellschaft, 1990.

Brown, Raymond E. *The Gospel according to John I-XII.* Anchor Bible, ed. William Foxwell Albright and David Noel Freedman, vol. 29. New York: Doubleday, 1966.

Brown, Stephen J. *The World of Imagery: Metaphor and Kindred Imagery.* London: Kegan Paul, Trench, Trubner & Co., 1927. Reprint, New York: Russell and Russell, 1966.

Bruce, F. F. *The Epistle to the Hebrews: Revised.* Rev. ed. New International Commentary on the New Testament, ed. Gordon D. Fee. Grand Rapids: William B. Eerdmans Publishing Company, 1990.

Buchanan, George Wesley. *To the Hebrews: Translation, Comment, and Conclusions.* Anchor Bible, ed. William Foxwell Albright and David Noel Freedman, vol. 36. New York: Doubleday, 1972.

Canale, Fernando L. *Back to Revelation-Inspiration: Searching for the Cognitive Foundation of Christian Theology in a Postmodern World.* Lanham, MD: University Press of America, 2001.

Canale, Fernando L. *Basic Elements of Christian Theology: Scripture Replacing Tradition.* Berrien Springs, MI: Andrews University Lithotech, 2005.

Canale, Fernando. *The Cognitive Principle of Christian Theology.* Berrien Springs, MI: Andrews University Lithotech, 2005.

Canale, Fernando. *Creation, Evolution, and Theology: The Role of Method in Theological Accommodation.* Berrien Springs, MI: Andrews University Lithotech, 2005.

Canale, Fernando Luis. *A Criticism of Theological Reason: Time and Timelessness as Primordial Presuppositions.* Andrews University Seminary Doctoral Dissertation Series, vol. 10. Berrien Springs, MI: Andrews University Press, 1987.

Caneday, Ardel B., and Thomas R. Schreiner. *The Race Set before Us: A Biblical Theology of Perseverance & Assurance*. Downers Grove, IL: InterVarsity Press, 2001.

Chester, Andrew. *Messiah and Exaltation: Jewish Messianic and Visionary Traditions and New Testament Christology*. Wissenschaftliche Untersuchungen zum Neuen Testament, ed. Jörg Frey et al., vol. 207. Tübingen: Mohr Siebeck, 2007.

Clowney, Edmund P. *Preaching and Biblical Theology*. Grand Rapids: William B. Eerdmans Publishing Company, 1961.

Cody, Aelred. *Heavenly Sanctuary and Liturgy in the Epistle to the Hebrews: The Achievement of Salvation in the Epistle's Perspective*. St. Meinrad, IN: Grail Publications, 1960.

Conner, Kevin J. *The Book of Hebrews*. Vermont, VIC: KJC Publications, 2002.

Cullmann, Oscar. *Christ and Time: The Primitive Christian Conception of Time and History*. Translated by Floyd V. Filson. Rev. ed. Philadelphia: Westminster Press, 1962.

Cullmann, Oscar. *Immortality of the Soul or Resurrection of the Dead? The Witness of the New Testament*. London: Epworth Press, 1958; reprint, New York: Macmillan Co., 1964.

D'Angelo, Mary Rose. *Moses in the Letter to the Hebrews*. Society of Biblical Literature Dissertation Series, ed. Howard C. Kee and Douglas A. Knight, vol. 42. Missoula, MT: Scholars Press, 1979.

Davidson, Richard M. *Typology in Scripture: A Study of Hermeneutical τύπος Structure*. Andrews University Seminary Doctoral Dissertation Series, vol. 2. Berrien Springs, MI: Andrews University Press, 1981.

DeSilva, David A. *Perseverance in Gratitude: A Social-Rhetorical Commentary on the Epistle "to the Hebrews"*. Grand Rapids: William B. Eerdmans Publishing Company, 2000.

Docherty, Susan E. *The Use of the Old Testament in Hebrews: A Case Study in Early Jewish Bible Interpretation*. Wissenschaftliche Untersuchungen zum Neuen Testament, ed. Jörg Frey, Friedrich Avemarie, Markus Bockmuehl, and Hans-Josef Klauck. Tübingen: Mohr Siebeck, 2009.

Dray, William H. *Philosophy of History*. Foundations of Philosophy Series, ed. Monroe Beardsley and Elizabeth Beardsley. Englewood Cliffs, NJ: Prentice-Hall, 1964.

Dulles, Avery. *Models of Revelation*. 2nd ed. Maryknoll, NY: Orbis Books, 1992.

Dunnill, John. *Covenant and Sacrifice in the Letter to the Hebrews*. Society for the New Testament Studies Monograph Series, ed. Margaret E. Thrall, vol. 75. Cambridge: Cambridge University Press, 1992.

Dupont-Sommer, A. *The Dead Sea Scrolls: A Preliminary Survey*. Translated by E. Margaret Rowley. Oxford: Basil Blackwell, 1952.

Durham, John I. *Exodus*. Word Biblical Commentary, ed. David A. Hubbard and Glenn W. Barker, vol. 3. Waco, TX: Word Books, 1987.

Eisele, Wilfried. *Ein unerschütterliches Reich: Die mittelplatonische Umformung des Parusiegedankens im Hebräerbrief*. Beihefte zur Zeitschrift für die neutestamentliche Wissenschaft, ed. James D. G. Dunn et al., vol. 116. Berlin: Walter de Gruyter, 2003.

Ellingworth, Paul. *The Epistle to the Hebrews: A Commentary on the Greek Text*. New International Greek Testament Commentary, ed. I. Howard Marshall and W. Ward Gasque. Grand Rapids: William B. Eerdmans Publishing Company, 1993.

Emmrich, Martin. *Pneumatological Concepts in the Epistle to the Hebrews: Amtscharisma, Prophet, & Guide of the Eschatological Exodus*. Lanham, Maryland: University Press of America, 2003.

Exodus. Edited by John William Wevers. Septuaginta: Vetus Testamentum Graecum, ed. auctoritate Academiae Scientiarum Gottingensis, vol. 2. Göttingen: Vandenhoeck & Ruprecht, 1991.

Farrer, Austin. *Finite and Infinite: A Philosophical Essay*. 2nd ed. Seabury Library of Contemporary Theology. London: Dacre Press; New York: Seabury Press, 1979.

Fee, Gordon D. *Pauline Christology: An Exegetical-Theological Study*. Peabody, MA: Hendrickson Publishers, 2007.

Fuhrmann, Sebastian. *Vergeben und Vergessen: Christologie und Neuer Bund im Hebräerbrief*. Wissenschaftliche Monographien zum Alten und Neuen Testament, ed. Günther Bornkamm and Gerhard von Rad, vol. 113. Neukirchen-Vluyn: Neukirchener Verlag, 2007.

Gäbel, Georg. *Die Kulttheologie des Hebräerbriefes: Eine exegetisch-religionsgeschichtliche Studie*. Wissenschaftliche Untersuchungen zum Neuen Testament, ed. Jörg Frey et al., vol. 212. Tübingen: Mohr Siebeck, 2006.

Gane, Roy E. *Cult and Character: Purification Offerings, Day of Atonement, and Theodicy*. Winona Lake, IN: Eisenbrauns, 2005.

Gane, Roy E. *Ritual Dynamic Structure*. Gorgias Dissertations: Religion, vol. 14. Piscataway, NJ: Gorgias Press, 2004.

Gadamer, Hans-Georg. *Truth and Method*. 2d rev. ed. Translated by Joel Weinsheimer and Donald G. Marshall. N. p.: Sheed and Ward, 1975; reprint, New York: Continuum Publishing Co., 1989.

Gelardini, Gabriella. *Verhärtet Eure Herzen Nicht: Der Hebräer, Eine Synagogenhomilie Zu Tischa be-Aw*. Biblical Interpretation Series. Edited by Ellen van Wolde and R. Alan Culpepper. Leiden: Brill, 2007.

Giles, Pauline. *Jesus the High Priest*. Bognor Regis, UK: New Horizon, 1984.

Goldingay, John E. *Approaches to Old Testament Interpretation*. Downers Grove, IL: InterVarsity Press, 1981.

Grässer, Erich. *Der Alte Bund im Neuen*. Wissenschaftliche Untersuchungen zum Neuen Testament, ed. Joachim Jeremias et al., vol. 35. Tübingen: J. C. B. Mohr (Paul Siebeck), 1985.

Grässer, Erich. *Der Glaube im Hebräerbrief*. Marburger theologische Studien, ed. Werner Georg Kümmel and Hans Graß, vol. 2. Marburg: N. G. Elwert, 1965.

Green, Joel B. *Body, Soul, and Human Life: The Nature of Humanity in the Bible*. Grand Rapids: Paternoster/Baker Academic, 2008.

Greenlee, J. Harold. *An Exegetical Summary of Hebrews*. Dallas, TX: Summer Institute of Linguistics, 1998.

Grelot, Pierre. *The Language of Symbolism: Biblical Theology, Semantics, and Exegesis*. Translated by Christopher R. Smith. Peabody, MA: Hendrickson Publishers, 2006.

Grenz, Stanley J. *The Named God and the Question of Being: A Trinitarian Theo-Ontology*. Louisville, KY: Westminster John Knox Press, 2005.

Gulley, Norman R. *Prolegomena*. Vol. 1 of *Systematic Theology*. Berrien Springs, MI: Andrews University Press, 2003.

Guthrie, Donald. *New Testament Introduction*. 4th ed. Downers Grove, IL: InterVarsity Press, 1990.

Ha, Hong Pal. *Heb 1:2-3: The Threefold Characterization of the Person of Christ as Prerequisite for the Fulfillment of a Complete Atonement*. Korean Sahmyook University Monographs: Doctoral Dissertation Series, vol. 4. Seoul, Korea: Institute for Theological Research, 1996.

Ha, John. *Genesis 15: A Theological Compendium of Pentateuchal History*. Beihefte zur Zeitschrift für die alttestamentliche Wissenschaft, ed. Otto Kaiser, vol. 181. Berlin: Walter de Gruyter, 1989.

Hafemann, Scott J. *Paul, Moses, and the History of Israel: The Letter/Spirit Contrast and the Argument from Scripture in 2 Corinthians 3*. Paternoster Biblical Monographs, ed. I. Howard Marshall and Richard J. Bauckham. Waynesboro, GA: Paternoster, 2005.

Hagner, Donald A. *Hebrews*. New International Biblical Commentary, ed. W. Ward Gasque. Peabody, MA: Hendrickson Publishers, 1990.

Hahn, Scott. *Kinship by Covenant: A Canonical Approach to the Fulfillment of God's Saving Promises*. Anchor Yale Bible Reference Library, ed. John J. Collins. New Haven: Yale University Press, 2009.

Hanson, Anthony Tyrell. *Jesus Christ in the Old Testament*. London: SPCK, 1965.

Harmon, Jerry R. *Exodus 34:6-7: A Hermeneutical Key in the Openness Debate*. Studies in Biblical Literature, ed. Hemchand Gossai. New York: Peter Lang, 2008.

Harrisville, Roy A. *Fracture: The Cross as Irreconcilable in the Language and Thought of the Biblical Writers*. Grand Rapids: William B. Eerdmans Publishing Company, 2006.

Hartmann, Nicolai. *New Ways of Ontology*. Translated by Reinhard C. Kuhn. Chicago: Henry Regnery Co., 1953.

Harvey, A. E. *The New English Bible: Companion to the New Testament*. Oxford: Oxford University Press, 1970.

Hays, Richard B. *Echoes of Scripture in the Letters of Paul*. New Haven: Yale University Press, 1989.

Heppenstall, Edward. *Our High Priest: Jesus Christ in the Heavenly Sanctuary*. Washington, DC: Review and Herald Publishing Association, 1972.

Hofius, Otfried. *Katapausis. Die Vorstellung vom endzeitlichen Ruheort im Hebräerbrief*. Wissenschaftliche Untersuchungen zum Neuen Testament, ed. Joachim Jeremias and Otto Michel, vol. 11. Tübingen: J. C. B. Mohr (Paul Siebeck), 1970.

Hofius, Otfried. *Der Vorhang vor dem Thron Gottes: Eine exegetisch-religionsgeschichtliche Untersuchung zu Hebräer 6,19f. und 10,19f*. Wissenschaftliche Untersuchungen zum Neuen Testament, ed. Joachim Jeremias and Otto Michel, vol. 14. Tübingen: J. C. B. Mohr (Paul Siebeck), 1972.

Holladay, Carl R. *A Critical Introduction to the New Testament: Interpreting the Message and Meaning of Jesus Christ*. Nashville, TN: Abingdon Press, 2005.

Hughes, Graham. *Hebrews and Hermeneutics: The Epistle to the Hebrews as a New Testament Example of Biblical Interpretation*. Society for New Testament Studies Monograph Series, ed. R. McL. Wilson and M. E. Thrall, vol. 36. Cambridge: Cambridge University Press, 1979.

Hughes, Philip Edgcumbe. *A Commentary on the Epistle to the Hebrews.* Grand Rapids: William B. Eerdmans Publishing Company, 1977.

Hurst, L. D. *The Epistle to the Hebrews: Its Background of Thought.* Society for the New Testament Studies Monograph Series, ed. G. N. Stanton, vol. 65. Cambridge: Cambridge University Press, 1990.

Iser, Wolfgang. *The Implied Reader: Patterns of Communication in Prose Fiction from Bunyan to Beckett.* Baltimore, MD: Johns Hopkins University Press, 1974.

Johnson, Luke Timothy. *Hebrews: A Commentary.* New Testament Library, ed. C. Clifton Black and John T. Carroll. Louisville, KY: Westminster John Knox Press, 2006.

Johnsson, William G. *In Absolute Confidence: The Book of Hebrews Speaks to Our Day.* Anvil Biblical Studies, ed. Gerald Wheeler. Nashville, TN: Southern Publishing Association, 1979.

Joslin, Barry C. *Hebrews, Christ, and the Law: The Theology of Mosaic Law in Hebrews 7:1–10:18.* Paternoster Biblical Monographs, ed. I. Howard Marshall et al. Colorado Springs, CO: Paternoster Press, 2008.

Karrer, Martin. *Der Brief an die Hebräer. Kapitel 5,11–13,25.* Ökumenischer Taschenbuchkommentar zum Neuen Testament, ed. Rudolf Hoppe and Michael Wolter, vol. 20. Gütersloher: Gütersloher Verlagshaus, 2008.

Käsemann, Ernst. *The Wandering People of God: An Investigation of the Letter to the Hebrews.* Translated by Roy A. Harrisville and Irving L. Sandberg. Minneapolis, MN: Augsburg Publishing House, 1984.

Käsemann, Ernst. *Das wandernde Gottesvolk.* Göttingen: Vandenhoeck & Ruprecht, 1938.

Kim, Lloyd. *Polemic in the Book of Hebrews.* Princeton Theological Monograph Series, ed. K. C. Hanson, vol. 64. Eugene, OR: Pickwick Publications, 2006.

Kistemaker, Simon. *The Psalm Citations in the Epistle to the Hebrews.* Amsterdam: Wed. G. van Soest, 1961.

Koester, Craig R. *Hebrews.* Anchor Bible, ed. William Foxwell Albright and David Noel Freedman, vol. 36. New York: Doubleday, 2001.

Kreeft, Peter. *The Philosophy of Jesus.* South Bend, IN: St. Augustine's Press, 2007.

Lane, William L. *Hebrews 1–8.* Word Biblical Commentary, ed. David A. Hubbard and Glenn W. Barker, vol. 47A. Dallas, TX: Word, 1991.

Lane, William L. *Hebrews 9–13.* Word Biblical Commentary, ed. David A. Hubbard and Glenn W. Barker, vol. 47B. Dallas, TX: Word, 1991.

Laub, Franz. *Bekenntnis und Auslegung: Die paränetische Funktion der Christologie im Hebräerbrief.* Biblische Untersuchungen, ed. Jost Eckert and Josef Hainz, vol. 15. Regensburg: Verlag Friedrich Pustet, 1980.

Leach, Edmund. *Culture and Communication: The Logic by Which Symbols Are Connected.* Themes in the Social Sciences, ed. Jack Goody and Geoffrey Hawthorn. Cambridge: Cambridge University Press, 1976.

Lindars, Barnabas. *The Theology of the Letter to the Hebrews.* Cambridge: Cambridge University Press, 1991.

Loader, William R. G. *Sohn und Hoherpriester: Eine traditionsgeschichtliche Untersuchung zur Christologie des Hebräerbriefes*. Wissenschaftliche Monographien zum Alten und Neuen Testament, ed. Günther Bornkamm and Gerhard von Rad, vol. 53. Neukirchen-Vluyn: Neukirchener Verlag, 1981.

Lyttkens, Hampus. *The Analogy between God and the World: An Investigation of Its Background and Interpretation of Its Use by Thomas of Aquino*. Uppsala: Almqvist and Wiksells Boktryckeri, 1952.

Manson, William. *The Epistle to the Hebrews: A Historical and Theological Reconsideration, the Baird Lecture, 1949*. London: Hodder and Stoughton, 1951.

Marías, Julián. *History of Philosophy*. Translated by Stanley Appelbaum and Clarence C. Strowbridge New York: Dover Publications, 1967.

Marion, Jean-Luc. *God without Being: Hors-Texte*. Translated by Thomas A. Carlson. Religion and Postmodernism, ed. Mark C. Taylor. Chicago: University of Chicago Press, 1991.

Martin, Robert Keith. *The Incarnate Ground of Christian Faith: Towards a Christian Theological Epistemology for the Educational Ministry of the Church*. Lanham, MD: University Press of America, 1998.

Mason, Eric Farrel. *'You Are a Priest Forever': Second Temple Jewish Messianism and the Priestly Christology*. Studies on the Texts of the Desert of Judah, ed. Florentino García Martínez. Leiden: Brill, 2008.

McDonough, Sean M. *YHWH at Patmos: Rev. 1:4 in Its Hellenistic and Early Jewish Setting*. Wissenschaftliche Untersuchungen zum Neuen Testament, ed. Martin Hengel and Otfried Hofius, vol. 107. Tübingen: Mohr Siebeck, 1999.

McGowan, A. T. B. *The Divine Spiration of Scripture: Challenging Evangelical Perspectives*. Nottingham, England: Apollos, 2007.

Merrill, Eugene H. *Deuteronomy*. New American Commentary, ed. E. Ray Clendenen, vol. 4. Nashville, TN: Broadman & Holman Publishers, 1994.

Merrill, Eugene H. *An Exegetical Commentary: Haggai, Zechariah, Malachi*. Chicago: Moody Press, 1994.

Miller, Ted. *Refuting Liberation Theology's Use of the Exodus with Hebrews 3-4*. Bob Jones University Seminary Publication. Greenville, SC: Bob Jones University Press, 2009.

Mills, Watson E. *Hebrews*. Bibliographies for Biblical Research: New Testament Series, ed. Watson E. Mills, vol. 20. Lewiston, NY: Mellen Biblical Press, 2001.

Mitchell, Alan C. *Hebrews*. Sacra pagina Series, ed. Daniel J. Harrington, vol. 13. Collegeville, MN: Liturgical Press, 2007.

Moberly, R. W. L. *At the Mountain of God: Story and Theology in Exodus 32-34*. Journal for the Study of the Old Testament: Supplement Series, ed. David J. A. Clines, Philip R. Davies, and David M. Gunn, vol. 22. Sheffield: JSOT Press, 1983.

Moltmann, Jürgen. *Theology of Hope: On the Ground and the Implications of a Christian Eschatology*. Translated by James W. Leitch. New York: Harper & Row, Publishers, 1967.

Montefiore, Hugh. *A Commentary on the Epistle to the Hebrews*. Harper's New Testament Commentaries, ed. Henry Chadwick. New York: Harper & Row, 1964. Reprint, Peabody, MA: Hendrickson Publishers, 1987.

Nash, Ronald H. *The Meaning of History*. Nashville, TN: Broadman & Holman Publishers, 1998.

Ninow, Friedbert. *Indicators of Typology within the Old Testament: The Exodus Motif*. Friedensauer Schriftenreihe, ed. Wolfgang Kabus et al., vol. 4. Frankfurt am Main: Peter Lang, 2001.

Nixon, R. E. *The Exodus in the New Testament*. London: Tyndale Press, 1963.

Nota, John H. *Phenomenology and History*. Translated by Louis Grooten and John H. Nota Chicago, IL: Loyola University Press, 1967.

Novum Testamentum Graece. Edited by Barbara and Kurt Aland, Johannes Karavidopoulos, Carlo M. Martini, and Bruce M. Metzger. 27th rev. ed. Stuttgart: Deutsche Bibelgesellschaft, 1993.

O'Brien, Peter T. *The Letter to the Hebrews*. Pillar New Testament Commentary, ed. D. A. Carson. Grand Rapids: Wm. B. Eerdmans Publishing Co., 2010.

Oxford Latin Dictionary. Edited by P. G. W. Glare. Oxford: Clarendon Press, 1982.

Pfitzner, Victor C. *Hebrews*. Chi Rho Commentary, ed. Everard Leske. Street Adelaide, South Australia: Lutheran Publishing House, 1979.

Phillips, Richard D. *Hebrews*. Reformed Expository Commentary, ed. Richard D. Phillips and Philip Graham Ryken. Phillipsburg, NJ: P&R Publishing, 2006.

Piper, John. *What Jesus Demands from the World*. Wheaton, IL: Crossway Books, 2006.

Powers, Daniel G. *Salvation through Participation: An Examination of the Notion of the Believers' Corporate Unity with Christ in Early Christian Soteriology*. Contributions to Biblical Exegesis and Theology, ed. Tj. Baarda et al., vol. 29. Leuven: Peeters, 2001.

Rabinowitz, Peter J. *Before Reading: Narrative Conventions and the Politics of Interpretation*. Ithaca, NY: Cornell University Press, 1987.

Reinhartz, Adele. *Why Ask My Name? Anonymity and Identity in Biblical Narrative*. New York: Oxford University Press, 1998.

Rice, Richard. *Reason and the Contours of Faith*. Riverside, CA: La Sierra University Press, 1991.

Rissi, Mathias. *Die Theologie des Hebräerbriefs*. Wissenschaftliche Untersuchungen zum Neuen Testament, ed. Joachim Jeremias et al., vol. 41. Tübingen: Mohr Siebeck, 1987.

Saucy, Robert L. *The Case for Progressive Dispensationalism: The Interface between Dispensational & Non-Dispensational Theology*. Grand Rapids: Zondervan Publishing House, 1993.

Schenck, Kenneth L. *Cosmology and Eschatology in Hebrews*. Society for New Testament Studies: Monograph Series, ed. John M. Court, vol. 143. Cambridge: Cambridge University Press, 2007.

Scholer, John M. *Proleptic Priests: Priesthood in the Epistle to the Hebrews*. Journal for the Study of the New Testament: Supplement Series, ed. David E. Orton, vol. 49. Sheffield: JSOT Press, 1991.

Schröger, Friedrich. *Der Verfasser des Hebräerbriefes als Schriftausleger*. Biblische Untersuchungen, ed. Otto Kuss, vol. 4. Regensburg: Verlag Friedrich Pustet, 1968.

Schunack, Gerd. *Der Hebräerbrief*. Zürcher Bibelkommentare, ed. Hans Heinrich Schmid and Hans Weder, vol. 14. Zürich: TVZ, Theologischer Verlag, 2002.

Seitz, Christopher R. *Figured out: Typology and Providence in Christian Scripture*. Louisville, KY: Westminster John Knox Press, 2001.

Selby, Rosalind M. *The Comical Doctrine: An Epistemology of New Testament Hermeneutics*. Paternoster Biblical Monographs, ed. I. Howard Marshall et al. Waynesboro, GA: Paternoster, 2006.

Septuaginta: Id est Vetus Testamentum graece iuxta LXX interpretes. Edited by Alfred Rahlfs. Stuttgart: Deutsche Bibelgesellschaft, 1979.

Son, Kiwoong. *Zion Symbolism in Hebrews: Hebrews 12:18-24 as a Hermeneutical Key to the Epistle*. Paternoster Biblical Monographs, ed. I. Howard Marshall et al. Waynesboro, GA: Paternoster Press, 2005.

Sontag, Frederick. *How Philosophy Shapes Theology: Problems in the Philosophy of Religion*. New York: Harper & Row, Publishers, 1971.

Spicq, Ceslas. *L'Épître aux Hébreux*. 3d ed. Etudes bibliques, ed. Th. Camelot, P. J. de Menasce, and V. Ducatillon, 2 vols. Paris: J. Gabalda, 1952-1953.

Stanley, Christopher D. *Arguing with Scripture: The Rhetoric of Quotations in the Letters of Paul*. New York: T & T Clark International, 2004.

Strobel, August. *Der Brief an die Hebräer*. Das Neue Testament Deutsch: Neues Göttinger Bibelwerk, ed. Hans Conzelmann et al., vol. 13. Göttingen: Vandenhoeck & Ruprecht, 1991.

Synge, Francis Charles. *Hebrews and the Scriptures*. London: S.P.C.K., 1959.

Telscher, Guido. *Opfer aus Barmherzigkeit: Hebr 9,11-28 im Kontext biblischer Sühnetheologie*. Forschung zur Bibel, ed. Rudolf Schnackenburg and Josef Schreiner, vol. 112. Würzburg, Germany: Echter Verlag, 2007.

Theißen, Gerd. *Untersuchungen zum Hebräerbrief*. Studien zum Neuen Testament, ed. Günter Klein, Willi Marxsen, and Wolfgang Schrage, vol. 2. Gütersloh: Gütersloher Verlagshaus Gerd Mohn, 1969.

Thomson, Iain D. *Heidegger on Ontotheology: Technology and the Politics of Education*. Cambridge: Cambridge University Press, 2005.

Thurén, Lauri. *Argument and Theology in 1 Peter: The Origins of Christian Paraenesis*. Journal for the Study of the New Testament: Supplement Series, ed. Stanley E. Porter et al., vol. 114. Sheffield: Sheffield Academic Press, 1995.

Thyen, Hartwig. *Der Stil der jüdisch-hellenistischen Homilie*. Forschungen zur Religion und Literatur des Alten and Neuen Testaments, ed. Rudolf Bultmann, vol. 65. Göttingen: Vandenhoeck & Ruprecht, 1955.

Thomas, C. Adrian. *A Case for Mixed-Audience with Reference to the Warning Passages in the Book of Hebrews*. New York: Peter Lang, 2008.

Timmer, Daniel C. *Creation, Tabernacle, and Sabbath: The Sabbath Frame of Exodus 31:12-17; 35:1-3 in Exegetical and Theological Perspective*. Forschungen zur Religion und Literatur des Alten und Neuen Testaments, ed. Detrick-Alex Koch et al. Göttingen: Vandenhoeck & Ruprecht, 2009.

Treiyer, Alberto R. *The Day of Atonement and the Heavenly Judgment: From the Pentateuch to Revelation*. Siloam Springs, AR: Creation Enterprises International, 1992.

Übelacker, Walter G. *Der Hebräerbrief als Appell: Untersuchungen zu Exordium, Narratio und Postscriptum (Hebr 1-2 und 13,22-25)*. Coniectanea biblica: New Testament Series, vol. 21. Stockholm: Almqvist and Wiksell International, 1989.

Van Seters, John. *The Life of Moses: The Yahwist as Historian in Exodus-Numbers.* Louisville: Westminster/John Knox Press, 1994.

Van Wijk-Bos, Johanna W. H. *Making Wise the Simple: The Torah in Christian Faith and Practice.* Grand Rapids: William B. Eerdmans Publishing Company, 2005.

Vanhoye, Albert. *Old Testament Priests and the New Priest: According to the New Testament.* Translated by J. Bernard Orchard. Studies in Scripture, ed. Cyril Karam, Mary Clare Vincent, and Leonard Maluf. Petersham, MA: St. Bede's Publications, 1986.

Walter, Nikolaus. *Praeparatio Evangelica: Studien zur Umwelt, Exegese und Hermeneutik des Neuen Testaments.* Wissenschaftliche Untersuchungen zum Neuen Testament, ed. Wolfgang Kraus and Florian Wilk, vol. 98. Tübingen: J. C. B. Mohr (Paul Siebeck), 1997.

Webb, William J. *Returning Home: New Covenant and Second Exodus as the Context for 2 Corinthians 6.14-7.1.* Journal for the Study of the New Testament: Supplement Series, ed. Stanley E. Porter et al., vol. 85. Sheffield: JSOT Press, 1993.

Westcott, Brooke Foss. *The Epistle to the Hebrews: The Greek Text with Notes and Essays.* 3rd ed. London: Macmillan and Co., 1903.

Williamson, Ronald. *Philo and the Epistle to the Hebrews.* Arbeitern zur Literatur und Geschichte des hellenistischen Judentums, ed. K. H. Rengstorf, vol. 4. Leiden: E. J. Brill, 1970.

Wolterstorff, Nicholas. *On Universals: An Essay on Ontology.* Chicago: University of Chicago Press, 1970.

Wyschogrod, Michael. *The Body of Faith: God and the People of Israel.* 2nd ed. [1st published as *The Body of Faith: Judaism as Corporeal Election.* New York: Seabury Press, 1983] Northvale, NJ: Jason Aronson, 1996.

Zimmermann, Heinrich. *Die Hohepriester-Christologie des Hebräerbriefes: Vortrag beim Antritt des Rektorats und zur Eröffnung des Studienjahres 1963/64 der Philosphisch-Theologischen Akademie zu Paderborn, gehalten am 22. Oktober 1963.* Paderborn: Ferdinand Schöningh, 1964.

Articles and Periodicals

Averbeck, Richard E. "זָבַח." In *New International Dictionary of Old Testament Theology and Exegesis,* ed. Willem A. VanGemeren, vol. 1, 1066-73. Grand Rapids: Zondervan Publishing House, 1997.

Averbeck, Richard E. "חַטָּאת." In *New International Dictionary of Old Testament Theology and Exegesis,* ed. Willem A. VanGemeren, vol. 2, 93-103. Grand Rapids: Zondervan Publishing House, 1997.

Averbeck, Richard E. "עֹלָה." In *New International Dictionary of Old Testament Theology and Exegesis,* ed. by Willem A. VanGemeren, vol. 3, 405-15. Grand Rapids: Zondervan Publishing House, 1997.

Bahnsen, Greg L. "Inductivism, Inerrancy, and Presuppositionalism." *Journal of the Evangelical Theological Society* 20 (December 1977): 289-305.

Bateman, Herbert W., IV. "Dispensationalism Tomorrow." In *Three Central Issues in Contemporary Dispensationalism: A Comparison of Traditional and Progressive Views,* ed. Herbert W. Bateman IV, 307-17. Grand Rapids: Kregel Publications, 1999.

Bateman, Herbert W., IV. "Dispensationalism Yesterday and Today." In *Three Central Issues in Contemporary Dispensationalism: A Comparison of Traditional and Progressive Views*, ed. Herbert W. Bateman IV, 21-60. Grand Rapids: Kregel Publications, 1999.

Bauckham, Richard. "Biblical Theology and the Problems of Monotheism." In *Out of Egypt: Biblical Theology and Biblical Interpretation*, ed. Craig Batholomew and Anthony Thiselton. Scripture and Hermeneutics Series, ed. Craig Bartholomew, vol. 5, 187-229. Grand Rapids: Zondervan Publishing House, 2004.

Bauckham, Richard. "Monotheism and Christology in Hebrews 1." In *Early Jewish and Christian Monotheism*, ed. Loren T. Stuckenbruck and Wendy E. S. North. *Early Christianity in Context*, ed. John M. G. Barclay. Journal for the Study of the New Testament: Supplement Series, ed. Mark Goodacre, vol. 263, 167-85. London: T & T Clark International, 2004.

Bauckham, Richard. "Reading Scripture as a Coherent Story." In *The Art of Reading Scripture*, ed. Ellen F. Davis and Richard B. Hays, 38-53. Grand Rapids: William B. Eerdmans Publishing Company, 2003.

Bauckham, Richard. "The Sonship of the Historical Jesus in Christology." *Scottish Journal of Theology* 31, no. 3 (1978): 245-60.

Bauckham, Richard. "The Throne of God and the Worship of Jesus." In *The Jewish Roots of Christological Monotheism: Papers from the St. Andrews Conference on the Historical Origins of the Worship of Jesus*, ed. Carey C. Newman, James R. Davila, and Gladys S. Lewis. Supplements to the Journal for the Study of Judaism, ed. John J. Collins, vol. 63, 43-69. Leiden: Brill, 1999.

Bauckham, Richard J. "Tradition in Relation to Scripture and Reason." In *Scripture, Tradition, and Reason: A Study in the Criteria of Christian Doctrine*, ed. Richard J. Bauckham and Benjamin Drewery, 117-45. Edinburgh: T & T Clark, 1988.

Behm, Johannes. "θύω." In *Theological Dictionary of the New Testament*, ed. Gerhard Kittel, trans. and ed. Geoffrey W. Bromiley, vol. 3, 180-90. Grand Rapids: Wm. B. Eerdmans Publishing Company, 1965.

Bergman, J., B. Lang, and H. Ringgren. "זָבַח." In *Theological Dictionary of the Old Testament*, ed. G. Johannes Botterweck and Helmer Ringgren, trans. David E. Green, vol. 4, 8-29. Grand Rapids: William B. Eerdmans Publishing Company, 1980.

Bird, Chad L. "Typological Interpretation within the Old Testament: Melchizedekian Typology." *Concordia Journal* 26 (January 2000): 36-52.

Canale, Fernando L. "Deconstructing Evangelical Theology?" *Andrews University Seminary Studies* 44 (Spring 2006): 95-130.

Canale, Fernando L. "Doctrine of God." In *Handbook of Seventh-day Adventist Theology*, ed. Raoul Dederen. Commentary Reference Series, ed. George W. Reid, vol. 12, 105-59. Washington, DC: Review and Herald Publishing Association, 2000.

Canale, Fernando L. "From Vision to System: Finishing the Task of Adventist Biblical and Systematic Theologies—Part II." *Journal of the Adventist Theological Society* 16 (Spring 2005): 114-42.

Canale, Fernando L. "From Vision to System: Finishing the Task of Adventist Theology—Part III: Sanctuary and Hermeneutics." *Journal of the Adventist Theological Society* 17 (Autumn 2006): 36-80.

Canale, Fernando L. "Interdisciplinary Method in Christian Theology?" *Neue Zeitschrift für systematische Theologie und Religionsphilosophie* 43, no. 3 (2001): 366-89.

Canale, Fernando L. "Philosophical Foundations and the Biblical Sanctuary." *Andrews University Seminary Studies* 36 (Autumn 1998): 183-206.

Canale, Fernando L. "The Quest for the Biblical Ontological Ground of Christian Theology." *Journal of the Adventist Theological Society* 16 (Spring 2005): 1-20.

Capes, David B. "Pauline Exegesis and the Incarnate Christ." In *Israel's God and Rebecca's Children: Christology and Community in Early Judaism and Christianity, Essays in Honor of Larry W. Hurtado and Alan F. Segal*, ed. David B. Capes et al., 135-53. Waco, TX: Baylor University Press, 2007.

Capes, David B. "YHWH Texts and Monotheism in Paul's Christology." In *Early Jewish and Christian Monotheism*, ed. Loren T. Stuckenbruck and Wendy E. S. North. *Early Christianity in Context*, ed. John M. G. Barclay. Journal for the Study of the New Testament: Supplement Series, ed. Mark Goodacre, vol. 263, 120-37. London: T & T Clark International, 2004.

Carlston, Charles Edwin. "Eschatology and Repentance in the Epistle to the Hebrews." *Journal of Biblical Literature* 78 (1959): 296-302.

Chan, Mark L. Y. "Following Jesus as the Truth: Postmodernity and Challenges of Relativism." *Evangelical Review of Theology* 31 (October 2007): 306-19.

Davidson, Richard M. "Typology in the Book of Hebrews." In *Issues in the Book of Hebrews*, ed. Frank B. Holbrook. *Daniel & Revelation Committee Series*, ed. Frank B. Holbrook, vol. 4, 121-86. Silver Spring, MD: Biblical Research Institute, 1989.

Davies, Graham I. "The Exegesis of the Divine Name in Exodus." In *The God of Israel*, ed. Robert P. Gordon, 139-56. University of Cambridge Oriental Publications, vol. 64, 139-56. Cambridge: Cambridge University Press, 2007.

Delio, Ilia. "Theology, Metaphysics, and the Centrality of Christ." *Theological Studies* 68 (June 2007): 254-73.

DeVaux, Roland. "The Revelation of the Divine Name YHWH." In *Proclamation and Presence: Old Testament Essays in Honour of Gwynne Henton Davies*, ed. John I. Durham and J. R. Porter, 48-75. Richmond, VA: John Knox Press, 1970.

Duke, R. K. "Priests, Priesthood." In *Dictionary of the Old Testament: Pentateuch*, ed. T. Desmond Alexander, and David W. Baker, 646-55. Downers Grove, IL: InterVarsity Press, 2003.

Eisenbaum, Pamela. "Heroes and History in Hebrews 11." In *Early Christian Interpretation of the Scriptures of Israel: Investigations and Proposals*, ed. Craig A. Evans and James A. Sanders. Studies in Scripture in Early Judaism and Christianity, ed. Craig A. Evans and James A. Sanders, vol. 5. Journal for the Study of the New Testament: Supplement Series, ed. Stanley E. Porter, vol. 148, 380-96. Sheffield: Sheffield Academic Press, 1997.

Erickson, Millard J. "Presuppositions of Non-Evangelical Hermeneutics." In *Hermeneutics, Inerrancy, and the Bible*, ed. Earl D. Radmacher and Robert D. Preus, 593-612. Grand Rapids: Academie Books, 1984.

Esler, Philip Francis. "Collective Memory and Hebrews 11: Outlining a New Investigative Framework." In *Memory, Tradition, and Text: Uses of the Past in Early Christianity*, ed. Alan Kirk and Tom Thatcher. Society of Biblical Literature: Semeia Studies, ed. Gale A. Yee, vol. 52, 151-71. Atlanta, GA: Society of Biblical Literature, 2005.

Evans, C. F. "The New Testament in the Making." In *From the Beginning to Jerome*, ed. C. F. Evans and P. R. Ackroyd. *Cambridge History of the Bible*, ed. C. F. Evans et al., vol. 1, 232-84. Cambridge: Cambridge University Press, 1970.

Evans, Craig A. "Chronological Table." In *The Historical Jesus: Critical Concepts in Religious Studies*, ed. Craig A. Evans, vol. 1, xix-xxviii. London: Routledge, 2004.

Evans, Craig A. "The Old Testament in the New." In *The Face of New Testament Studies: A Survey of Recent Research*, ed. Scot McKnight and Grant R. Osborne, 130-45. Grand Rapids: Baker Academic, 2004.

Fanning, Buist M. "A Classical Reformed View." In *Four Views on the Warning Passages in Hebrews*, ed. Herbert W. Bateman IV, 172-219. Grand Rapids: Kregel Publications, 2007.

Fanning, Buist M. "A Theology of Hebrews." In *A Biblical Theology of the New Testament*, ed. Roy B. Zuck and Darrell L. Bock, 369-415. Chicago: Moody Press, 1994.

Fiorenza, Elisabeth S. "Cultic Language in Qumran and in the NT." *Catholic Biblical Quarterly* 38 (January 1976): 159-77.

Fisher, John. "Covenant Fulfillment and Judaism in Hebrews." In *The Enduring Paradox: Exploratory Essays in Messianic Judaism*, ed. John Fisher, 37-60. Baltimore, MD: Lederer/Messianic Jewish Publishers, 2000.

France, R. T. "The Writer of Hebrews as a Biblical Expositor." *Tyndale Bulletin* 47 (November 1996): 245-76.

Freedman, D. N., and M. P. O'Connor. "יהוה." In *Theological Dictionary of the Old Testament*, ed. G. Johannes Botterweck and Helmer Ringgren, trans. David E. Green, vol. 5, 500-521. Grand Rapids: William B. Eerdmans Publishing Company, 1986.

Freedman, David Noel, and David Miano. "People of the New Covenant." In *The Concept of the Covenant in the Second Temple Period*, ed. Stanley E. Porter and Jacqueline C. R. De Roo. Supplements to the Journal for the Study of Judaism, ed. John J. Collins, vol. 71, 7-26. Leiden: Brill, 2003.

Geisler, Norman L. "Analogy: The Only Answer to the Problem of Religious Language." *Journal of the Evangelical Theological Society* 16 (Summer 1973): 167-79.

Gelardini, Gabriella. "Hebrews, an Ancient Synagogue Homily for *Tisha be-Av*: Its Function, Its Basis, Its Theological Interpretation." In *Hebrews: Contemporary Methods—New Insights*, ed. Gabriella Gelardini. Biblical Interpretation Series, ed. R. Alan Culpepper and Ellen van Wolde, vol. 75, 107-27. Leiden: Brill, 2005.

Gieschen, Charles A. "Listening to Intertextual Relationships in Paul's Epistles with Richard Hays." *Concordia Theological Quarterly* 70 (January 2006): 17-32.

Gieschen, Charles A. "The Real Presence of the Son before Christ: Revisiting an Old Approach to Old Testament Christology." *Concordia Theological Quarterly* 68 (April 2004): 105-26.

Gleason, Randall C. "A Moderate Reformed View." In *Four Views on the Warning Passages in Hebrews*, ed. Herbert W. Bateman IV, 336-77. Grand Rapids: Kregel Publications, 2007.

Godzieba, Anthony J. "Ontotheology to Excess: Imagining God without Being." *Theological Studies* 56 (March 1995): 3-20.

Gorman, Frank H., Jr. "Ritual Studies and Biblical Studies: Assessment of the Past; Prospects for the Future." *Semeia* 67 (1994): 13-36.

Grässer, Erich. "Der Hebräerbrief 1938-1963." *Theologische Rundschau* 36 (October 1964): 138-236.

Grässer, Erich. "Das wandernde Gottesvolk: Zum Basismotiv des Hebräerbriefes." *Zeitschrift für die neutestamentliche Wissenschaft* 77 (1986): 160-79.

Greenhaw, David M. "The Formation of Consciousness." In *Preaching as a Theological Task: World, Gospel, Scripture in Honor of David Buttrick*, ed. Thomas G. Long and Edward Farley, 1-16. Louisville, KY: Westminster John Knox Press, 1996.

Grier, James M., Jr. "The Apologetical Value of the Self-Witness of Scripture." *Grace Theological Journal* 1 (Spring 1980): 71-76.

Guthrie, George H. "Hebrews' Use of the Old Testament: Recent Trends in Research." *Currents in Biblical Research* 1 (April 2003): 271-94.

Haight, Roger. "Jesus and Salvation: An Essay in Interpretation." *Theological Studies* 55 (June 1994): 225-51.

Hanson, A. T. "Hebrews." In *It Is Written: Scripture Citing Scripture, Essays in Honour of Barnabas Lindars, SSF*, ed. D. A. Carson and H. G. M. Williamson, 292-302. Cambridge: Cambridge University Press, 1988.

Hanson, A. T. "The Gospel in the Old Testament according to Hebrews." *Theology* 52 (July 1949): 248-52.

Harnack, Adolf. "Probabilia über die Adresse und den Verfasser des Hebräerbriefs." *Zeitschrift für die neutestamentliche Wissenschaft* 1 (1900): 16-41.

Hart, Trevor. "Tradition, Authority, and a Christian Approach to the Bible as Scripture." In *Between Two Horizons: Spanning New Testament Studies and Systematic Theology*, ed. Joel B. Green and Max Turner, 183-204. Grand Rapids: William B. Eerdmans Publishing Company, 2000.

Hartog, Paul. "The 'Rule of Faith' and Patristic Biblical Exegesis." *Trinity Journal* 28 (Spring 2007): 65-86.

Heckl, Raik. "Die Religionsgeschichte als Schlüssel für die Literargeschichte: Eine neu gefasste Überlieferungskritik vorgestellt am Beispiel von Ex 32." *Theologische Zeitschrift* 63, no. 3 (2007): 193-215.

Hegermann, Harald. "Christologie im Hebräerbrief." In *Anfänge der Christologie: Festschrift für Ferdinand Hahn zum 65. Geburtstag*, ed. Cilliers Breytenbach and Henning Paulsen, 337-51. Göttingen: Vandenhoeck & Ruprecht, 1991.

Heidegger, Martin. "The Onto-Theo-Logical Constitution of Metaphysics." In *Identity and Difference*, trans. Joan Stambaugh. Martin Heidegger Works, ed. J. Glenn Gray, 42-74. New York: Harper & Row, 1969.

Heidegger, Martin. "The Principle of Identity." In *Identity and Difference*, trans. Joan Stambaugh. Martin Heidegger Works, ed. J. Glenn Gray, 23-41. New York: Harper & Row, 1969.

Hendrix, Ralph E. "מִשְׁכָּן and אֹהֶל מוֹעֵד: : Etymology, Lexical Definitions, and Extra-Biblical Usage." *Andrews University Seminary Studies* 29 (Autumn 1991): 213-23.

Hilber, John W. "Theology of Worship in Exodus 24." *Journal of the Evangelical Theological Society* 39 (June 1996): 177-89.

Himmelfarb, Martha. "The Torah between Athens and Jerusalem: Jewish Difference in Antiquity." In *Ancient Judaism in Its Hellenistic Context*, ed. Carol Bakhos. Supplements to the Journal for the Study of Judaism, ed. John J. Collins, vol. 95, 113-29. Leiden: Brill, 2005.

Hofius, Otfried. "Biblische Theologie im Lichte des Hebräerbriefes." In *New Directions in Biblical Theology: Papers of the Aarhus Conference, 16-19 September 1992*, ed. Sigfred Pedersen. Supplements to Novum Testamentum, ed. C. K. Barrett et al., vol. 76, 108-25. Leiden: E. J. Brill, 1994.

Hübner, Hans. "New Testament Interpretation of the Old Testament." In *From the Beginnings to the Middle Ages (until 1300)*, ed. Chris Brekelmans, Menahem Haran, and Magne Sæbø. *Hebrew Bible / Old Testament: The History of Its Interpretation*, ed. Magne Sæbø, vol. 1, pt. 1, Antiquity, 332-72. Göttingen: Vandenhoeck & Ruprecht, 1996.

Hughes, John J. "Hebrews 9:15ff and Galatians 3:15ff: A Study in Covenant Practice and Procedure." *Novum Testamentum* 21 (January 1979): 27-96.

Hultgren, Arland J. "Liturgy and Literature: The Liturgical Factor in Matthew's Literary and Communicative Art." In *Texts and Contexts: Biblical Texts in Their Textual and Situational Contexts*, ed. Tord Fornberg and David Hellholm, 659-73. Oslo: Scandinavian University Press, 1995.

Hurst, L. D. "The Christology of Hebrews 1 and 2." In *The Glory of Christ in the New Testament: Studies in Christology in Memory of George Bradford Caird*, ed. L. D. Hurst and N. T. Wright, 151-64. Oxford: Clarendon Press, 1987.

Johnson, Elliott E. "Premillennialism Introduced: Hermeneutics." In *The Coming Millennial Kingdom: A Case for Premillennial Interpretation*, ed. Donald K. Campbell and Jeffrey L. Townsend, 15-33. Grand Rapids: Kregel Publications, 1997.

Johnsson, William G. "Defilement/Purification and Hebrews 9:23." In *Issues in the Book of Hebrews*, ed. Frank B. Holbrook. Daniel & Revelation Committee Series, ed. Frank B. Holbrook, vol. 4, 79-104. Silver Spring, MD: Biblical Research Institute, 1989.

Johnsson, William G. "The Heavenly Sanctuary: Figurative or Real?" In *Issues in the Book of Hebrews*, ed. Frank B. Holbrook. Daniel & Revelation Committee Series, ed. Frank B. Holbrook, vol. 4, 35-51. Silver Spring, MD: Biblical Research Institute, 1989.

Johnsson, William G. "The Pilgrimage Motif in the Book of Hebrews." *Journal of Biblical Literature* 87 (June 1978): 239-51.

Kant, Immanuel. "Preface to Second Edition." In *Critique of Pure Reason*, trans. Werner S. Pluhar. Indianapolis: Hackett, 1996.

Kellermann, D. "עלה." In *Theological Dictionary of the Old Testament*, ed. G. Johannes Botterweck, Helmer Ringgren, and Heinz-Josef Fabry, trans. David E. Green, vol. 11, 96-113. Grand Rapids: William B. Eerdmans Publishing Company, 2001.

Koch, K. "חטא." In *Theological Dictionary of the Old Testament*, ed. G. Johannes Botterweck and Helmer Ringgren, trans. David E. Green, vol. 4, 309-19. Grand Rapids: William B. Eerdmans Publishing Company, 1980.

Koptak, Paul E. "Intertextuality." In *Dictionary for Theological Interpretation of the Bible*, ed. Kevin J. Vanhoozer, 332-34. Grand Rapids: Baker Academic, 2005.

Bibliography

Kraus, Wolfgang. "Neuere Ansätze in der Exegese des Hebräerbriefs." *Verkündigung und Forschung* 48, no. 2 (2003): 65-80.

Laansma, Jon C. "Hebrews, Book of." In *Dictionary for Theological Interpretation of the Bible*, ed. Kevin J. Vanhoozer, 274-81. Grand Rapids: Baker Academic, 2005.

Lefkovitz, Lori Hope. "Creating the World: Structuralism and Semiotics." In *Contemporary Literary Theory*, edited by G. Douglas Atkins and Laura Morrow, 60-80. Amherst: University of Massachusetts Press, 1989.

Lategan, Bernard C. "History, Historiography and Hermeneutics." In *Philosophical Hermeneutics and Biblical Exegesis*, ed. Petr Pokorný and Jan Roskovec. Wissenschaftliche Untersuchungen zum Neuen Testament, ed. Jörg Frey, Martin Hengel, and Otfried Hofius, vol. 153, 204-18. Tübingen: Mohr Siebeck, 2002.

Lategan, Bernard C. "Introduction: Coming to Grips with the Reader." *Semeia* 48 (1989): 3-17.

Lee, Patrick. "Language about God and the Theory of Analogy." *New Scholasticism* 58 (Winter 1984): 40-66.

Leithart, Peter J. "Womb of the World: Baptism and the Priesthood of the New Covenant in Hebrews 10.19-22." *Journal for the Study of the New Testament* 78 (June 2000): 49-65.

Lincoln, Andrew T. "Hebrews and Biblical Theology." In *Out of Egypt: Biblical Theology and Biblical Interpretation*, ed. Craig Batholomew and Anthony Thiselton. Scripture and Hermeneutics Series, ed. Craig G. Batholomew, vol. 5, 313-38. Grand Rapids: Zondervan Publishing House, 2004.

Loewe, William P. "From the Humanity of Christ to the Historical Jesus." *Theological Studies* 61 (June 2000): 314-31.

Löhr, Hermut. "›Umriß‹ und ›Schatten‹ Bemerkungen zur Zitierung von Ex 25,40 in Hebr 8." *Zeitschrift für die neutestamentliche Wissenschaft* 84, no. 3/4 (1993): 218-32.

Lombard, H. A. "Κατάπαυσις in the Letter to the Hebrews." *Neotestamentica* 5 (1971): 60-71.

Lutzer, Erwin W. "A Response to Homiletics and Hermeneutics." In *Hermeneutics, Inerrancy, and the Bible*, ed. Earl D. Radmacher and Robert D. Preus, 833-37. Grand Rapids: Academie Books, 1984.

Luz, Ulrich. "Der alte und der neue Bund bei Paulus und im Hebräerbrief." *Evangelische Theologie* 27 (1967): 318-36.

Mach, Michael. "Concepts of Jewish Monotheism during the Hellenistic Period." In *The Jewish Roots of Christological Monotheism: Papers from the St. Andrews Conference on the Historical Origins of the Worship of Jesus*, ed. Carey C. Newman, James R. Davila, and Gladys S. Lewis. Supplements to the Journal for the Study of Judaism, ed. John J. Collins, vol. 63, 21-42. Leiden: Brill, 1999.

Mackie, Scott D. "Confession of the Son of God in Hebrews." *New Testament Studies* 53 (January 2007): 114-29.

MacLeod, David John. "The Doctrinal Center of the Books of Hebrews." *Bibliotheca sacra* 146 (July-September 1989): 291-300.

Masson, Robert. "Analogy and Metaphoric Process." *Theological Studies* 62 (September 2001): 571-96.

Master, John R. "The New Covenant." In *Issues in Dispensationalism*, ed. Wesley R. Willis and John R. Master, 93-110. Chicago: Moody Press, 1994.

McCann, J. Clinton, Jr. "Exodus 32:1-14." *Interpretation* 44 (July 1990): 277-81.

McCarthy, Dennis J. "Exod 3:14: History, Philosophy and Theology." *Catholic Biblical Quarterly* 40 (July 1978): 311-22.

McCormack, Bruce L. "The Actuality of God: Karl Barth in Conversation with Open Theism." In *Engaging the Doctrine of God: Contemporary Protestant Perspectives*, ed. Bruce L. McCormack, 185-242. Grand Rapids: Baker Academic, 2008.

McCormack, Bruce L. "What's at Stake in Current Debates over Justification? The Crisis of Protestantism in the West." In *Justification: What's at Stake in the Current Debates*, ed. Mark Husbands and Daniel J. Treier, 81-117. Downers Grove, IL: InterVarsity Press, 2004.

McCullough, J. C. "Hebrews in Recent Scholarship (Part 2)." *Irish Biblical Studies* 16 (July 1994): 108-20.

McKnight, Edgar V. "Presuppositions in New Testament Study." In *Hearing the New Testament: Strategies for Interpretation*, ed. Joel B. Green, 278-99. Grand Rapids: William B. Eerdmans Publishing Company, 1995.

McKnight, Scot. "The Warning Passages of Hebrews: A Formal Analysis and Theological Conclusions." *Trinity Journal* 13 (Spring 1992): 21-59.

Michalson, Carl. "The Real Presence of the Hidden God." In *Faith and Ethics: The Theology of H. Richard Niebuhr*, ed. Paul Ramsey, 245-67. New York: Harper & Brothers, 1957.

Michel, Otto. "ὁμολογία." In *Theological Dictionary of the New Testament*, ed. Gerhard Friedrich, trans. and ed. Geoffrey W. Bromiley, vol. 5, 215-20. Grand Rapids: Wm. B. Eerdmans Publishing Company, 1967.

Moberly, R. W. L. "Exodus, Book of." In *Dictionary for Theological Interpretation of the Bible*, ed. Kevin J. Vanhoozer, 211-16. Grand Rapids: Baker Academic, 2005.

Moe, Olaf. "Der Gedanke des allgemeinen Priestertums in Hebräerbrief." *Theologische Zeitschrift* 5 (March-June 1949): 161-69.

Morris, Leon. "Hebrews." In *The Expositor's Bible Commentary*, ed. Frank E. Gaebelein, vol. 12, 3-158. Grand Rapids: Zondervan Publishing House, 1981.

Motyer, Stephen. "The Psalm Quotations of Hebrews 1: A Hermeneutic-Free Zone?" *Tyndale Bulletin* 50, no. 1 (1999): 3-22.

Muilenburg, James. "The Biblical View of Time." *Harvard Theological Review* 54 (October 1961): 225-52.

Müller, Ekkehardt. "Jesus and the Covenant in Hebrews." In *"For You Have Strengthened Me": Biblical and Theological Studies in Honor of Gerhard Pfandl in Celebration of His Sixty-Fifth Birthday*, ed. Martin Pröbstle, Gerald A. Klingbeil, and Martin G. Klingbeil, 189-208. St. Peter am Hart, Austria: Seminar Schloss Bogenhofen, 2007.

Neusner, Jacob. "The Idea of History in Rabbinic Judaism: What Kinds of Questions Did the Ancient Rabbis Answer?" In *Historical Knowledge in Biblical Antiquity*, ed. Jacob Neusner, Bruce D. Chilton, and William Scott Green, 139-74. Blandford Forum, UK: Deo Publishing, 2007.

Newing, Edward George. "A Rhetorical and Theological Analysis of the Hexateuch." *South East Asia Journal of Theology* 32 (1981): 1-15.

Neyrey, Jerome H. "'Without Beginning of Days or End of Life' (Hebrews 7:3): Topos for a True Deity." *Catholic Biblical Quarterly* 53 (July 1991): 439-55.

Olbricht, Thomas H. "Analogy and Allegory in Classical Rhetoric." In *Early Christianity and Classical Culture: Comparative Studies in Honor of Abraham J. Malherbe*, ed. Thomas H. Olbricht, John T. Fitzgerald, and L. Michael White. Supplements to Novum Testamentum, ed. C. K. Barrett et al., vol. 110, 371-89. Leiden: Brill, 2003.

Osborne, Grant R. "A Classical Arminian View." In *Four Views on the Warning Passages in Hebrews*, ed. Herbert W. Bateman IV, 86-128. Grand Rapids: Kregel Publications, 2007.

Oudersluys, Richard C. "Exodus in the Letter to the Hebrews." In *Grace upon Grace: Essays in Honor of Lester J. Kuyper*, ed. James I. Cook, 143-52. Grand Rapids: William B. Eerdmans Publishing Company, 1975.

Parry, Robin. Review of *Back to Revelation-Inspiration: Searching for the Cognitive Foundation of Christian Theology in a Postmodern World*, by Fernando L. Canale. *Evangelical Quarterly* 76 (April 2004): 186-89.

Piper, Otto A. "Unchanging Promises." *Interpretation* 2 (January 1957): 3-22.

Porter, Stanley E. "Further Comments on the Use of the Old Testament in the New Testament." In *The Intertextuality of the Epistles: Explorations of Theory and Practice*, ed. Thomas L. Brodie, Dennis R. MacDonald, and Stanley E. Porter. New Testament Monographs, ed. Stanley E. Porter, vol. 16, 98-110. Sheffield: Sheffield Phoenix Press, 2006.

Procksch, Otto. "ἅγιος." In *Theological Dictionary of the New Testament*, ed. Gerhard Kittel, trans. and ed. Geoffrey W. Bromiley, vol. 1, 88-97. Grand Rapids: Wm. B. Eerdmans Publishing Company, 1964.

Rabinowitz, Peter J. "Whirl without End: Audience-Oriented Criticism." In *Contemporary Literary Theory*, ed. G. Douglas Atkins and Laura Morrow, 81-100. Amherst: University of Massachusetts Press, 1989.

Rice, George E. "Apostasy as a Motif and Its Effect on the Structure of Hebrews." *Andrews University Seminary Studies* 23 (Spring 1985): 29-35.

Rice, George E. "Hebrews 6:19: Analysis of Some Assumptions Concerning *Katapetasma*." In *Issues in the Book of Hebrews*, ed. Frank B. Holbrook, *Daniel & Revelation Committee Series*, ed. Frank B. Holbrook, vol. 4, 229-34. Silver Spring, MD: Biblical Research Institute, 1989.

Richard, Ramesh P. "Premillennialism as a Philosophy of History: Part 1, Non-Christian Interpretations of History." *Bibliotheca sacra* 138 (January-March 1981): 13-21.

Richard, Ramesh P. "Premillennialism as a Philosophy of History: Part 2, Elements of a Biblical Philosophy of History." *Bibliotheca sacra* 138 (April-June 1981): 108-18.

Rodríguez, Angel Manuel. "Sanctuary Theology in the Book of Exodus." *Andrews University Seminary Studies* 24 (Summer 1986): 127-45.

Ruffatto, Kristine J. "Polemics with Enochic Traditions in the *Exagoge* of Ezekiel the Tragedian." *Journal for the Study of the Pseudepigrapha* 15 (May 2006): 195-210.

Sahlin, Harold. "The New Exodus of Salvation according to St. Paul." In *The Root of the Vine*, ed. Anton Fredrichsen, 81-95. New York: Philosophical Library, 1953.

Salom, Alwyn P. "*Ta Hagia* in the Epistle to the Hebrews." In *Issues in the Book of Hebrews*, ed. Frank B. Holbrook, *Daniel & Revelation Committee Series*, ed. Frank B. Holbrook, vol. 4, 219-27. Silver Spring, MD: Biblical Research Institute, 1989.

Schrenk, Gottlob. "ἀρχιερεύς." In *Theological Dictionary of the New Testament*, ed. Gerhard Kittel, trans. and ed. Geoffrey W. Bromiley, vol. 3, 265-83. Grand Rapids: Wm. B. Eerdmans Publishing Company, 1965.

Shultz, Gary L., Jr. "God's Purposes in the Atonement for the Nonelect." *Bibliotheca sacra* 165 (April-June 2008): 145-63.

Siegert, Folker. "Early Jewish Interpretation in a Hellenistic Style." In *From the Beginnings to the Middle Ages (until 1300)*, ed. Chris Brekelmans, Menahem Haran, and Magne Sæbø. *Hebrew Bible / Old Testament: The History of Its Interpretation*, ed. Magne Sæbø, vol. 1, pt. 1, Antiquity, 130-98. Göttingen: Vandenhoeck & Ruprecht, 1996.

Skarsaune, Oskar. "Jewish Believers in Jesus in Antiquity—Problems of Definition, Method, and Sources." In *Jewish Believers in Jesus: The Early Centuries*, ed. Oskar Skarsaune and Reidar Hvalvik, 3-21. Peabody, MA: Hendrickson Publishers, 2007.

Smillie, Gene R. "Contrast or Continuity in Hebrews 1.1-2?" *New Testament Studies* 51 (October 2005): 543-60.

Spieckermann, Hermann. "Barmherzig und gnädig ist der Herr . . ." *Zeitschrift für die alttestamentliche Wissenschaft* 102, no.1 (1990): 1-18.

Spiegelberg, Herbert. "The 'Reality-Phenomenon' and Reality." In *Philosophical Essays: In Memory of Edmund Husserl*, ed. Marvin Farber, 84-105. New York: Greenwood Press, 1968.

Stanley, Christopher D. "The Rhetoric of Quotations: An Essay on Method." In *Early Christian Interpretation of the Scriptures of Israel: Investigations and Proposals*, ed. Craig A. Evans and James A. Sanders. Studies in Scripture in Early Judaism and Christianity, ed. Craig A. Evans and James A. Sanders, vol. 5. Journal for the Study of the New Testament: Supplement Series, ed. Stanley E. Porter, vol. 148, 44-58. Sheffield: Sheffield Academic Press, 1997.

Stählin, Gustav et al. "ἁμαρτάνω." In *Theological Dictionary of the New Testament*, ed. Gerhard Kittel, trans. and ed. Geoffrey W. Bromiley, vol. 1, 267-316. Grand Rapids: Wm. B. Eerdmans Publishing Company, 1964.

Sterling, Gregory E. "The First Theologian: The Originality of Philo of Alexandria." In *Renewing Tradition: Studies in Texts and Contexts in Honor of James W. Thompson*, ed. Thomas H. Olbricht, Mark W. Hamilton, and Jeffrey Peterson. Princeton Theological Monograph Series, ed. K. C. Hanson, vol. 65, 145-62. Eugene, OR: Pickwick Publications, 2007.

Sterling, Gregory E. "Hellenistic Philosophy and the New Testament." In *Handbook to Exegesis of the New Testament*, ed. Stanley E. Porter. New Testament Tools and Studies, ed. Bruce M. Metzger and Bart D. Ehrman, vol. 25, 313-58. Leiden: Brill, 1997.

Sterling, Gregory E. "'The Jewish Philosophy': The Presence of Hellenistic Philosophy in Jewish Exegesis in the Second Temple Period." In *Ancient Judaism in Its Hellenistic Context*, ed. Carol Bakhos. Supplements to the Journal for the Study of Judaism, ed. John J. Collins, vol. 95, 131-53. Leiden: Brill, 2005.

Sterling, Gregory E. "'Philo Has Not Been Used Half Enough': The Significance of Philo of Alexandria for the Study of the New Testament." *Perspectives in Religious Studies* 30 (Fall 2003): 251-69.

Stockhausen, Carol L. Review of *Echoes of Scripture in the Letters of Paul (Yale University Press: New Haven, 1989)*, by Richard B. Hays. *Journal of Biblical Literature* 111 (Spring 1992): 155-57.

Suleiman, Susan R. "Introduction: Varieties of Audience-Oriented Criticism." In *The Reader in the Text: Essays on Audience and Interpretation*, ed. Susan R. Suleiman and Inge Crosman, 3-45. Princeton, NJ: Princeton University Press, 1980.

Sweeney, Marvin A. "The Wilderness Traditions of the Pentateuch: A Reassessment of Their Function and Intent in Relation to Exodus 32-34." In *Society of Biblical Literature: 1989 Seminar Papers*, ed. David J. Lull. Society of Biblical Literature Seminar Papers, ed. David J. Lull, no. 28, 291-99. Atlanta: Scholars Press, 1989.

Swetnam, James. "On the Literary Genre of the 'Epistle' to the Hebrews." *Novum Testamentum* 11 (October 1969): 261-69.

Thiele, F. "θύω." In *New International Dictionary of New Testament Theology*, ed. Colin Brown, trans. Colin Brown et al., vol. 3, 417-38. Grand Rapids: Zondervan Publishing House, 1986.

Thiessen, Matthew. "Hebrews and the End of the Exodus." *Novum Testamentum* 49, no. 4 (2007): 353-69.

Thompson, James W. "The Structure and Purpose of the Catena in Heb 1:5-13." *Catholic Biblical Quarterly* 38 (July 1976): 352-63.

Tilley, Terrence W. "Remembering the Historic Jesus—A New Research Program?" *Theological Studies* 68 (March 2007): 3-35.

Travers, Michael E. "The Use of Figures of Speech in the Bible." *Bibliotheca sacra* 164 (July-September 2007): 277-90.

Vanhoye, Albert. "Longue marche ou accès tout proche? Le contexte biblique de Hébreux 3,7-4,11." *Biblica* 49, no. 1 (1968): 9-26.

Verbrugge, Verlyn D. "Towards a New Interpretation of Hebrews 6:4-6." *Calvin Theological Journal* 15 (April 1980): 61-73.

Vervenne, Marc. "Current Tendencies and Developments in the Study of the Book of Exodus." In *Studies in the Book of Exodus: Redaction, Reception, Interpretation*, ed. Marc Vervenne. Bibliotheca Ephemeridum Theologicarum Lovaniensium, vol. 126, 21-59. Leuven: Leuven University Press, 1996.

Walvoord, John F. "The Theogoical Context of Premillennialism." *Bibliotheca sacra* 150 (October-December 1993): 387-96.

Wenkel, David H. "*Gezerah Shawah* as Analogy in the Epistle to the Hebrews." *Biblical Theology Bulletin* 37 (Summer 2007): 62-68.

White, Roger. "Notes on Analogical Predication and Speaking about God." In *The Philosophical Frontiers of Christian Theology: Essays Presented to D. M. MacKinnon*, ed. Brian Hebblethwaite and Stewart Sutherland, 197-226. Cambridge: Cambridge University Press, 1982.

Williams, Donald L. "The Israelite Cult and Christian Worship." In *The Use of the Old Testament in the New and Other Essays: Studies in Honor of William Franklin Stinespring*, ed. James M. Efird, 110-24. Durham, NC: Duke University Press, 1972.

Williamson, Ronald. "Platonism and Hebrews." *Scottish Journal of Theology* 16 (March 1963): 415-24.

Willi-Plein, Ina. "Some Remarks on Hebrews from the Viewpoint of Old Testament Exegesis." In *Hebrews: Contemporary Methods–New Insights*, ed. Gabriella Gelardini. Biblical Interpretation Series, ed. R. Alan Culpepper and Ellen van Wolde, vol. 75, 25-35. Leiden: Brill, 2005.

Witherington, Ben, III. "Jesus as the Alpha and Omega of New Testament Thought." In *Contours of Christology in the New Testament*, ed. Richard N. Longenecker. McMaster New Testament Studies, ed. Stanley E. Porter, 25-46. Grand Rapids: William B. Eerdmans Publishing Company, 2005.

Wolf, Herbert. "זָבַח." In *Theological Wordbook of the Old Testament*, edited by R. Laird Harris, Greason L. Archer Jr., and Bruce K. Waltke, vol. 1, 233-35. Chicago: Moody Press, 1980.

Unpublished Works

Akao, John Osemeikhian. "The Burning Bush: An Investigation of Form and Meaning in Exodus 3 and 4." Ph.D. diss., University of Glasgow, 1985.

Allen, David Mark. "'Deuteronomic Re-Presentation in a Word of Exhortation': An Assessment of the Paraenetic Function of Deuteronomy in the Letter to the Hebrews." Ph.D. diss., University of Edinburgh, 2007.

Balentine, George L. "The Concept of the New Exodus in the Gospels." Th.D. diss., Southern Baptist Theological Seminary, 1961.

Bateman, Herbert W., IV. "Jewish and Apostolic Hermeneutics: How the Old Testament Is Used in Hebrews 1:5-13." Ph.D. diss., Dallas Theological Seminary, 1993.

Beavis, Mary Ann Lilian. "A Study of the Relation of the Old and New Covenants in the Epistle to the Hebrews, in the Light of Scholarship 1938-1980." M.A. thesis, University of Manitoba, 1981.

Blanton, Thomas R., IV. "Constructing a New Covenant: Discursive Strategies in the Damascus Document and Second Corinthians." Ph.D. diss., University of Chicago, 2006.

Borland, James Allen. "Christophanies: Old Testament Appearances of Christ in Human Form." Th.D. diss., Grace Theological Seminary, 1976.

Bristol, Lyle Osborne. "The Logos Doctrine of Philo Judaeus and the Epistle to the Hebrews." Th.D. diss., Victoria University, Toronto, 1947.

Brueggemann, Dale A. "The Use of the Psalter in John's Apocalypse." Ph.D. diss., Westminister Theological Seminary, 1995.

Buck, Daniel E. "The Rhetorical Arrangement and Function of OT Citations in the Book of Hebrews: Uncovering Their Role in the Paraenetic Discourse of Access." Ph.D. diss., Dallas Theological Seminary, 2002.

Buerger, Martin A. "Judgment and Grace in the Wilderness Narrative." Ph.D. diss., Concordia Seminary, 1985.

Canale, Fernando Luis. "Exodus 3:14: Toward a Biblical Ontology." Unpublished report presented for [course] OTST850 Theology of Pentateuch and [course] OTST890 Directed Reading in Old Testament Studies. Andrews University. April 1981.

Canale, Fernando Luis. "Toward a Criticism of Theological Reason: Time and Timelessness as Primordial Presuppositions." Ph.D. diss., Andrews University, 1983.

Casey, Jay Smith. "Exodus Typology in the Book of Revelation." Ph.D. diss., Southern Baptist Theological Seminary, 1981.

Clary, Henry Walter. "Hebrews as a Covenant Document: A New Proposal." Ph.D. diss., Southwestern Baptist Theological Seminary, 2007.

Cotton, Roger. "An Exegetical Analysis of the Torah Collection of the Pentateuch (Exodus 20-23; Leviticus 17-27; Deuteronomy 12-26): A Description of Their Expressions of Theological Ideas Based on an Analysis of Their Principles of Rhetorical and Thematic Organization." Th.D. diss., Concordia Seminary, 1983.

Cox, Ronald R. "By the Same Word: The Intersection of Cosmology and Soteriology in Hellenistic Judaism, Early Christianity and 'Gnosticism' in the Light of Middle Platonic Intermediary Doctrine." Ph.D. diss., University of Notre Dame, 2005.

Darnell, David Rancier. "Rebellion, Rest, and the Word of God (An Exegetical Study of Hebrews 3:1-4:13)." Ph.D. diss., Duke University, 1973.

DeSouza, Elias Brasil. "The Heavenly Sanctuary/Temple Motif in the Hebrew Bible: Function and Relationship to the Earthly Counterparts." Ph.D. diss., Andrews University, 2005.

Dukes, James Graydon. "Eschatology in the Epistle to the Hebrews." Th.D. diss., Southern Baptist Theological Seminary, 1956.

Eichhorst, William R. "Man in the Image of God: Created and Renewed." Th.D. diss., Grace Theological Seminary, 1973.

Ellingworth, Paul. "The Old Testament in Hebrews: Exegesis, Method and Hermeneutics." Ph.D. diss., Aberdeen University, 1977.

Ellis, Nicholas J. "Hebrews 6:4-6 and Divine Repentance." M.A. thesis, Trinity Western University, 2006.

Emmrich, Martin. "Pneumatological Concepts in Hebrews." Ph.D. diss., Westminister Theological Seminary, 2001.

Fowler, Sam Whittemore. "The Visual Anthropomorphic Revelation of God." Th.D. diss., Dallas Theological Seminary, 1978.

Fowler, William G. "The Influence of Ezekiel in the Fourth Gospel: Intertextuality and Interpretation." Ph.D. diss., Golden Gate Baptist Theological Seminary, 1995.

Friederichsen, Douglas W. "Hermeneutics of Typology." Th.D. diss., Dallas Theological Seminary, 1970.

Galenieks, Ēriks. "The Nature, Function, and Purpose of the Term שְׁאוֹל in the Torah, Prophets, and Writings." Ph.D. diss., Andrews University, 2005.

Gelardini, Gabriella. "«Verhärtet eure Herzen nicht» Der Hebräer, eine Synagogenhomilie zu Tischa be-Aw." Ph.D. diss., University of Basel, 2004.

Givens, Jimmy McMath, Jr. "Christ as Hermeneutical Referent: An Analysis of the Extension of Christological Motifs within the Theologies of A. H. Strong, E. Y. Mullins, and W. T. Conner." Ph.D. diss., Southwestern Baptist Theological Seminary, 2000.

Glanz, Oliver. "Time, Reason, and Religious Belief: A Limited Comparison, Critical Assessment, and Further Development of Herman Dooyeweerd's Structural Analysis of Theoretical Thought and Fernando Canale's Phenomenological Analysis of the Structure of Reason and Its Biblical Interpretation." M.A. thesis, Vrije Universiteit Amsterdam, 2006.

Glanz, Oliver. "Who Is Speaking? Who Is Addressed? A Critical Study into the Conditions of Exegetical Method and Its Consequences for the Interpretation of Participant Reference-Shifts in the Book of Jeremiah." Ph.D. diss., Vrije Universiteit Amsterdam, 2010.

Gonzales, Alexander R. "The Divine Proclamation Formula as the Basis for Renewal of the Sinaitic Covenant: A Literary Exposition of Exodus 34:6-7." S.T.M. thesis, Dallas Theological Seminary, 2005.

Gotaas, David Stanley. "The Old Testament in the Epistle to the Hebrews, the Epistle of James, and the Epistle of Peter." Th.D. diss., Northern Baptist Theological Seminary, 1958.

Griffith, Hayne Preston, Jr. "An Investigation into the Origin of the High Priest Christology in the Epistle to the Hebrews." Ph.D. diss., University of Aberdeen, 1978.

Grothe, Jonathan F. "Was Jesus the Priestly Messiah? A Study of the New Testament's Teaching of Jesus' Priestly Office against the Background of Jewish Hopes for a Priestly Messiah." Th.D. diss., Concordia Seminary, St. Louis, 1981.

Hahn, Scott Walker. "Kinship by Covenant: A Biblical Theological Study of Covenant Types and Texts in the Old and New Testaments." Ph.D. diss., Marquette University, 1995.

Harmon, Jerry R. "Exodus 34:6-7: A Hermeneutical Key in the Open Theism Debate." Ph.D. diss., Mid-America Baptist Theological Seminary, 2005.

Henderson, Marion W. "The Priestly Ministry of Jesus in the Gospel of John and the Epistle to the Hebrews." Th.D. diss., Southern Baptist Theological Seminary, 1965.

Hoehner, Harold W. "The Reinstitution of Sacrifices in the Millennium." Th.M. thesis, Dallas Theological Seminary, 1962.

Hre Kio, Stephen. "Exodus as a Symbol of Liberation in the Book of the Apocalypse." Ph.D. diss., Emory University, 1985.

Hullinger, J. M. "A Proposed Solution to the Problem of Animal Sacrifices in Ezekiel 40-48." Th.D. diss., Dallas Theological Seminary, 1993.

Hung, Emmanuel Yun-wing. "Relationship and Rebirth: A Literary Study of the Exodus Motif in Jeremiah." Ph.D. diss., Westminster Theological Seminary, 2001.

Hydon, Paul Vernon. "The Priesthood of Jesus as Presented by the Hebrews." Ph.D. diss., Boston University, 1941.

Jelinek, John Anthony. "The Contribution of the City Metaphor toward an Understanding of the New Jerusalem." Th.D. diss., Grace Theological Seminary, 1992.

Johnsson, William G. "Defilement and Purgation in the Book of Hebrews." Ph.D. diss., Vanderbilt University, 1973.

Joslin, Barry Clyde. "The Theology of the Mosaic Law in Hebrews 7:1-10:18." Ph.D. diss., Southern Baptist Theological Seminary, 2005.

Keesmaat-de Jong, Sylvia Christine. "Paul's Use of the Exodus Tradition in Romans and Galatians." Ph.D. diss., Worcester College, 1994.

Kirby, John Charles. "The Exodus in the New Testament." S.T.M. thesis, McGill University, 1957.

Bibliography

Kitchens, James A. "The Death of Jesus in the Epistle to the Hebrews." Th.D. diss., New Orleans Baptist Theological Seminary, 1964.

Larson, Duane Howard. "The Temporality of the Trinity: A Christian Theological Concept of Time and Eternity in View of Contemporary Physical Theory." Ph.D. diss., Graduate Theological Union, 1993.

Lee, Young-Jae. "A Study in the Composition of the Unit Exodus 31.18–34.35 as the Centre of the Centre of the Pentateuch: A Synchronic and Diachronic Reading of the Text." Ph.D. diss., Aberdeen University, 2004.

Lloyd, Gwilym George. "The Treatment of the Mosaic Law in the Epistle to the Hebrews with Some Comparison of the Pauline Attitude." Ph.D. diss., University of Edinburgh, 1944.

Luther, James Henry, Jr. "The Use of the Old Testament by the Author of Hebrews." Ph.D. diss., Bob Jones University, 1977.

MacLeod, David John. "The Theology of the Epistle to the Hebrews: Introduction, Prolegomena, and Doctrinal Center." Th.D. diss., Dallas Theological Seminary, 1987.

Manuel, Donald Gordon. "The Religious Identity of the Recipients of the Epistle to the Hebrews." Th.D. diss., New Orleans Baptist Theological Seminary, 1965.

Martin, Robert Keith. "The Incarnate Ground of Christian Education: The Integration of Epistemology and Ontology in the Thought of Michael Polanyi and Thomas F. Torrance." Ph.D. diss., Princeton Theological Seminary, 1994.

Marty, William Henry. "The New Moses." Th.D. diss., Dallas Theological Seminary, 1984.

Mason, Eric Farrel. "The Concept of the Priestly Messiah in Hebrews and Second Temple Judaism." Ph.D. diss., University of Notre Dame, 2005.

McCullough, J. C. "Hebrews and the Old Testament: A Comparison of the Use Which the Author of the Epistle to the Hebrews Makes of the Old Testament, with the Use Made by Other Writers of His Day." Ph.D. diss., Queen's University of Belfast, 1971.

McGahey, John F. "An Exposition of the New Covenant." Th.D. diss., Dallas Theological Seminary, 1957.

McKenzie, Tracy J. "An Analysis of the Innertextuality between Exodus 32:7-20 and Deuteronomy 9:12-21." Ph.D. diss., Southeastern Baptist Theological Seminary, 2006.

McNickle, Alan A. "The New Jerusalem in Amillennial Theology." Th.D. diss., Dallas Theological Seminary, 1984.

McNicol, Allen James. "The Relationship of the Image of the Highest Angel to the High Priest Concept in Hebrews." Ph.D. diss., Vanderbilt University, 1974.

Measell, James S. "Development of the Concept of Analogy in Philosophy, Logic, and Rhetoric to 1850." Ph.D. diss., University of Illinois at Urbana-Champaign, 1970.

Mickelsen, A. Berkeley. "Methods of Interpretation in the Epistle to the Hebrews." Ph.D. diss., University of Chicago, 1950.

Miller, Russell E., Jr. "The Doctrine of Rest in Hebrews 3-4 and Its Implications for Liberation Theology's Use of the Exodus." Ph.D. diss., Bob Jones University, 2004.

Mintek, Shawn Joseph. "Rationality and Absolute Presuppositions." Ph.D. diss., University of Washington, 1977.

Morrison, Michael Duane. "Rhetorical Function of the Covenant Motif in the Argument of Hebrews." Ph.D. diss., Fuller Theological Seminary, 2006.

Ninow, Friedbert. "The Indicators of Typology within the Old Testament: The Exodus Motif." Ph.D. diss., Andrews University, 1999.

Nixon, Hilary Arthur. "Typology of the Mosaic Tabernacle and Its Articles as Interpreted by Authors of the Nineteenth and Twentieth Centuries." Ph.D. diss., Drew University, 1984.

Pao, David Wei Chun. "Acts and the Isaianic New Exodus." Ph.D. diss., Harvard University, 1998.

Phillips, W. Gary. "Apologetics and Inerrancy: An Analysis of Select Axiopistic Models." Th.D. diss., Grace Theological Seminary, 1985.

Pigott, Susan Marie. "'God of Compassion and Mercy': An Analysis of the Background, Use, and Theological Significance of Exodus 34:6-7." Ph.D. diss., Southwestern Baptist Theological Seminary, 1995.

Powers, Philip Edwards. "Prefigurement and the Hermeneutics of Prophetic Typology." Ph.D. diss., Dallas Theological Seminary, 1995.

Rankin, Jeffrey Jay. "An Intertextual Reading of the Inclusio around the $lm hwhy Psalms." Ph.D. diss., New Orleans Baptist Theological Seminary, 2006.

Rayburn, Robert Stout. "The Contrast between the Old and New Covenants in the New Testament." Ph.D. diss., Aberdeen University, 1978.

Reynolds, James E. "A Comparative Study of the Exodus Motif in the Epistle to the Hebrews." Th.D. diss., Southwestern Baptist Theological Seminary, 1976.

Russell, Brian Douglas. "The Song of the Sea: The Date and Theological Significance of Exodus 15:1-21." Ph.D. diss., Union Theological Seminary and Presbyterian School of Christian Education, 2002.

Sanford, Carlisle Junior. "The Addressees of Hebrews." Th.D. diss., Dallas Theological Seminary, 1962.

Sexton, James Hardy. "The Knowledge of Yahweh Motif in the Book of Exodus." Ph.D. diss., New Orleans Baptist Theological Seminary, 1999.

Shea, William H. "The Significance and Function of *Ton Hagion* in Hebrews 8-10." Unpublished paper collected by the Center for Adventist Research, 1989.

Showers, Renald E. "The New Nature." Th.D. diss., Grace Theological Seminary, 1975.

Smillie, Gene. "Living and Active: The Word of God in the Book of Hebrews." Ph.D. diss., Trinity Evangelical Divinity School, 2000.

Smith, Billy O. "The Reconciliation of the Moral Attributes of Yahweh as Revealed in Exodus 34:6-7." Th.D. diss., New Orleans Baptist Theological Seminary, 1953.

Son, Kiwoong. "Sinai and Zion Symbolism and the Hermeneutics of Hebrews: Heb. 12:18-24 as an Interpretative Key to the Epistle." Ph.D. diss., Brunel University, 2004.

Stine, Donald Medford. "The Finality of the Christian Faith: A Study of the Unfolding Argument of the Epistle to the Hebrews, Chapters 1-7." Th.D. diss., Princeton Theological Seminary, 1964.

Stuart, Streeter Stanley, Jr. "The Exodus Tradition in Late Jewish and Early Christian Literature: A General Survey of the Literature and a Particular Analysis of the Wisdom of Solomon, II Esdras and the Epistle to the Hebrews." Ph.D. diss., Vanderbilt University, 1973.

Tetley, Joy D. "The Priesthood of Christ as the Controlling Theme of the Epistle to the Hebrews." Ph.D. diss., University of Durham, 1987.

Theron, Stanley Winter. "Paraenesis in the Epistle to the Hebrews." D.Div. diss., University of Pretoria, 1984.

Timmer, Daniel C. "Creation, Tabernacle and Sabbath: The Function of the Sabbath Frame in Exodus 31:12-17; 35:1-3." Ph.D. diss., Trinity Evangelical Divinity School, 2006.

Tomesch, Harald. "Genre and Outline: The Key to the Literary Structure of Hebrews." Th.D. diss., Concordia Seminary, St. Louis, 1996.

Treiyer, Alberto R. "Le Jour des Expiations et la Purification du Sanctuaire." Ph.D. diss., University of Strasbourg, 1982.

Wallace, David. "Texts in Tandem: The Coalescent Usage of Psalm 2 and Psalm 110 in Early Christianity." Ph.D. diss., Baylor University, 1995.

Watts, James Washington. "The Meaning of Yahweh in Exodus." Ph.D. diss., Southern Baptist Theological Seminary, 1933.

Watts, Rikki E. "The Influence of the Isaianic New Exodus on the Gospel of Mark." Ph.D. diss., Cambridge University, 1990.

Williams, Arthur Hayes, Jr. "An Early Christology: A Systematic and Exegetical Investigation of the Traditions Contained in Hebrews, and of the Implications Contained in Their Later Neglect." Th.D. diss., Johannes Gutenberg University of Mainz, 1971.

Woodring, Hoyt C., Jr. "Grace under the Mosaic Covenant." Th.D. diss., Dallas Theological Seminary, 1956.

Subject Index

A
Abraham, 15, 37
Acts, 7, 8n7, 12, 15, 27
allusion, 3, 11, 28, 35, 48-49, 65
Ambrose, 109n113
analogia entis, 6, 84-85, 174
analogy, 6, 62n33, 69n1, 71, 76-79, 83-84, 85n68, 98, 114, 123, 130, 141n57, 169, 174
analogy of being, 6, 76-77, 79, 83
angel, 20n41, 82, 85, 152
antitype, 26, 132, 133
apostasy, 6, 16-17, 26-27, 29-33, 137, 144
Aquino, Thomas 76, 161n47
Aristotle, 74, 83, 174
atonement, 5, 17, 43, 45-46, 132, 135-136, 143, 145
Augustine, 21, 77, 161
autopistic-ontological-functional Christology, 161, 167
autopistic system, 73, 85
axiopistic system, 73, 84

B
baptism, 129n10, 131n21
Barth, Karl, 95n38, 160n44
biblical ontology, 56, 60, 69, 73, 77-78, 113, 115, 121-124, 127, 132n28, 174
biblical pedagogy, 74, 77-78, 81-84, 124-126, 132, 134, 141, 150, 155, 171, 173-174
blood, 4, 43-44, 89, 130, 136, 141, 142, 145-146, 152-154
burning bush, 113n7, 115, 125

C
Christ as Yahweh, 13, 19-27, 30, 36, 61, 66, 90, 93, 104-105, 125, 137, 150, 158, 161, 164-170, 174
Christ event, 3, 6, 24, 26, 60, 62, 71, 87, 88-89, 94n33, 97-98, 105, 109-110, 122, 124, 126-127, 135, 145
Christology, 6, 13n6, 19-21, 22n51, 23, 25nn61-62, 26-27, 61, 70, 107n102, 110, 150, 157-168, 174
Christophany, 104, 106-107, 109
church, 5n4, 16, 58-60n27, 63, 83-84, 95, 109n113, 157n30, 172-173
comparative-prescriptive analysis, 138, 144
confession, 19, 22-25, 36, 110, 118, 137, 145, 159
confessional continuity, 21, 26, 26n65, 31, 38, 47
consciousness, 5, 105
cosmology, 54, 81n51-82n55, 97, 121nn34-35, 123n40
Covenant
    biblical, 131
    blessings, 145, 152
    Mosaic, 29n80, 31, 32n99, 45, 144
    New, 6, 8n7, 9, 25-27, 31-32, 44-49, 62-63, 96-102, 104, 110, 129n10, 131, 137-147, 151-153, 156, 166, 170
    Old, 26, 30, 32, 39, 43-45 48, 98-99, 102-104, 131, 137, 139-142, 144-146, 170
    promise, 137
    Sinai, 26, 32, 41, 45n162, 49
    curses, 145
covenant renewal, 26, 41, 102, 144, 153
creation, 3-4, 29n77-30n82, 71, 73, 79, 82, 84-85, 87-89, 103n86, 107, 112n3
crisis of faith, 5, 9, 59-60, 121
criticism
    audience-oriented, 13, 13nn7-8, 17-19, 24, 53, 55, 60-61, 125
    form, 14n11

of theological reason, 6, 7, 7n5, 27n70,
35n112, 53, 54n3, 56, 62, 74n15,
88n7, 113n6, 165n57
process of, 54, 95
rhetorical, 13, 61
textual, 38
theological, 56
cultus, 34, 38, 43, 47-48, 102, 110, 131,
138, 145, 156, 169

D

Day of Atonement, 5n3, 45n162, 46n169,
135n39, 136n42, 143n64, 145
death, 3, 21, 26, 32n100, 47-49, 63, 81-82,
102, 105, 141, 145, 157, 173
deconstruction
need of, 79, 95
of classical analogy of being, 78
philosophical, 73, 88, 94-95, 174
deductive hermeneutics, 150, 160, 162-
163, 167
descriptive analysis, 4, 7-9, 11, 13, 27, 53,
60-61, 67, 70, 73, 88, 94, 97-98, 103,
121, 138, 144, 174
Deuteronomy, 28n73, 41nn141-142,
65n43, 134n34, 151, 152n6
dispensational
hermeneutic, 56, 62, 135n37
perspective, 62
position, 63
theology, 62n35
divine ontology, 92-93, 95, 114, 150, 159-
162, 164-165, 167-168

E

earth, 90, 133, 153, 159, 165, 172-174
Egypt, 19n35, 21n45, 105n91
Enoch, 22
Esdras, 8n9, 99n58
eisegesis
anachronistic, 109
ontological, 119
spiritual, 109

exegesis
Auctor's, 60, 104-106, 108, 125
biblical, 7, 81n49, 110n116, 168
Christocentric, 71, 88-89, 106-110,
112, 124
Christocentric-typological, 170
inductive, 161n52
Jewish, 118, 118n27
method-oriented, 60-62
natural, 108
NT, 107n102
of Scripture, 54, 117
of the divine name, 113n7
OT, 47n178
Pauline, 21n43
text-oriented, 60-61, 149
typological, 105n96, 130n15
Enoch, 22n46
epistemological lens, 9, 169
epistemology, 5, 27, 41, 54n6, 57, 58, 59-
60n27, 67, 75, 83, 95, 106, 157n30,
160n44, 162, 164
eschatology, 26, 30n87, 62, 70, 78n34,
81n51, 91n17, 93n27, 102, 121n34,
123n40, 139, 174
Exagoge of Ezekiel, 22
Exodus
Mosaic, 146
new, 8n7, 26n66, 145-146
paradigm, 146
Ezekiel, 32, 63n38, 65n43

F

faith, 3, 5-6, 9, 13n10, 15-17, 23, 24n58,
27, 28n72, 33, 36, 47, 59-60, 77, 81,
83n59, 90-91, 93n30, 105, 106n101,
110n116, 116, 121, 140, 142, 146n79,
157nn29-30, 172-173, 174n2
fast, 23-25, 167
Father (God), 23, 25, 109n113, 154
foreknowledge, 73, 85
functional Christology, 163-164

Subject Index

G

golden calf, 26-31, 144-145, 150
Gospels, 7, 8n7, 143
grace, 8n8, 29, 29nn79-80, 31-32, 43, 152n8
ground
    biblico-ontological, 60
    doctrinal, 151-153
    epistemological, 95
    for divine ontology, 114
    Incarnate, 5n4, 83n59, 157n30
    metaphysical, 59
    of being, 113
    ontological, 4, 9, 54-55, 63-64, 67, 69-70, 72, 76, 83, 90, 107, 132-135, 137, 153, 157, 163, 165
    philosophical, 77
    spiritual, 133
grounding analysis, 71, 88n5, 89, 97, 103, 104n90
grounding role, 70, 88, 110
grounding source(s), 70-71, 74, 78, 108, 112, 131, 137

H

Haggai, 167n65
haphtarah, 102
heaven, 80, 90, 125, 129, 133, 153, 159, 165, 172, 174
heavenly priest, 152-156, 164
Heidegger, 5, 55n7, 58-59, 91n13, 114
hermeneutic, 18n33, 56, 60, 62-64, 80, 82-84, 135n37, 149-151, 154-156, 160, 162-164, 166-167, 171
hermeneutics, 9n9, 53n2-54, 61n30-62n35, 77, 81n49, 82-85n67, 87n2, 92n22, 97n49, 99n58, 105-106, 107n104, 110n117, 116n19, 130n15, 131nn19-22, 137n45, 139nn49-50, 140n55, 142n59, 147n83, 149-151, 155, 158-164, 166-168, 171
history of the interpretive influence, 56, 59, 71, 111-113, 115, 117-125, 156

Holy of Holies, 128, 142, 153
holy place, 39, 89, 128-130, 134-136, 173
Holy Spirit, 24, 82, 87, 101, 137, 167, 172-173
homily, 12-13n6, 102, 166n62, 167

I

idolatry, 30, 145
immortality, 82
Incarnation, 21, 26, 44n158, 79, 88, 89, 106, 114, 135, 157, 160, 162n50
Incarnational history, 152, 154
inductive hermeneutics, 150, 162-164
intertextuality, 28n73, 29, 65, 65nn43-46, 66, 66n48, 67
Israel, 20-24, 27, 29-32, 35-36, 39, 41-42, 45, 61n31, 63, 81n52, 87, 91-93n30, 101-102, 105n96, 107, 109, 113n7, 116nn16-18, 131, 137, 143, 145-146, 147n81, 157, 167, 170, 174

J

Jeremiah, 32, 146
Jerusalem, 119n27, 135n37, 136n40, 140, 156, 167, 169
Jesus, 6, 15, 19-27, 30, 32n100, 35, 40, 61, 70, 89-90n9, 92-93, 97n50, 101-102, 105-107n102, 109-110, 123, 125, 135-137, 142-143, 145, 152-155, 157-159, 163-164, 167-168
Judaism, 15, 17, 20-21n43, 24, 36n116, 61n31, 81n52, 92n24-93n30, 116n16, 118-119, 121n35, 138, 144nn65-66, 146n79, 157-158, 174n2
judgment, 5n3, 9, 24, 29n79, 31, 79, 103, 121, 135n39, 136n42, 138, 143n64, 155
justification, 95n38, 113

K

Kant, 73, 74, 75, 77, 78, 88, 161, 172-172n2
Kantian
    framework, 88
    ontology, 73

204 Subject Index

pedagogy, 163, 171
theology, 161-162
knowledge
  historical, 66, 92n24
  human, 54, 76
  modern, 81
  new, 83
  nonhistorical, 75, 84
  personal, 30, 82
  previous, 155
  prior, 83, 164
  real, 75
  scriptural, 3
  spatiotemporal, 81, 83
  supernatural, 172

L
liturgy, 3, 4, 33, 47, 49, 138n47
logia, 55-56, 61, 63, 78, 91, 137, 164, 166
logos, 78-80, 121n35, 162n50
LXX, 11-12, 35, 37-38, 39n128, 40nn134-139, 41nn145-146, 42, 42n147, 44, 44nn159-160, 45n162, 64, 96, 117-118, 155

M
Malachi, 167n65
Masoretic Text, 12
Melchizedek, 40n139
Melchizedekian
  priest, 40n139
  typology, 105n97
Messiah, 157-159, 163-164
metanarrative, 79, 82, 97, 110-111, 115-119, 122, 125, 127, 130-140, 142-143, 147, 165, 169-170
metaphysics, 49, 54-56, 58n21, 83, 91, 94, 97n50, 131
methodology, 20, 54-56, 61, 65-66, 82-83, 90, 96, 149-150, 159, 163-165, 174
methodology-oriented analysis, 170-171
methodology-oriented study, 150
millennium, 63, 135n37, 136nn40-42, 146

Moab, 41
monotheism, 21n45-22n51, 24n59, 25, 166n59
Mosaic dispensation, 63
Mosaic Law, 104n88, 131, 146n80, 167
Mosaic legislation, 63
Moses, 15, 22n46, 28n73, 29-30, 30n92, 32, 34-35, 37, 39, 41, 44, 46, 71, 109n113, 119, 125, 133, 136-137, 143, 152

N
name, 15n20, 21-25, 27, 35, 37, 82, 105, 113, 114n10, 119n32
Neoplatonism, 77

O
offering, 40n140, 41-48
ontic Christology, 35
ontic presence, 35-36, 165
ontological Christology, 160, 162n50-164, 167
ontological consistency, 112, 138
ontological distension, 114
ontological eisegesis, 109, 119
ontological ground, 4, 9, 54-55, 60, 63-64, 67, 69-70, 72, 76, 83, 90, 107, 132-135, 137, 153, 157, 163, 165
ontological inconsistency, 113-114, 138-139, 142-143, 147, 174
ontological influence, 88, 112, 118
ontological valuation(s), 95, 111-115, 117-120, 122-123, 133, 161
ontology
  biblical, 27, 56, 60, 69, 73, 77-78, 84, 113, 115, 118, 121-124, 127, 132n28, 162n50, 174
  classical, 93, 96, 107
  extra-biblical, 84, 162n50
  Greek, 37, 56, 58, 60, 73, 75, 93, 113, 119, 121-123, 125, 160
  mixed, 73, 115-116, 119, 121-123
  modern, 73, 89
  Parmenidean, 117

Subject Index

Philonic, 36
philosophical, 174
ontos, 55-56, 61, 78-79, 91, 124, 137, 164, 166
onto-theo-logia, 54-56, 58, 60-61, 64, 73, 166
onto-theo-logy, 59
ontotheology, 55n7, 78n35
onto-theo-logical
    constitution, 58n21, 59n25
    hermeneutic, 164
    matrix or framework, 60, 107, 114
    model, 94, 97, 113, 115-117, 120-121
    philosophy, 91
    presupposition, 65,
    structure of reason, 78-79, 82, 103
ousia, 118

P

Parmenides, 58-59, 95, 115-117
Paul [the apostle], 6, 8n7, 21, 25, 26n66, 30n83, 65-67
Pauline Epistles, 7, 20, 66
pedagogy,
    biblical, 74, 77-78, 80-84, 125-126, 132, 134, 141, 150, 155, 171, 173-174
    classical, 74-76, 78-79, 82, 84, 141, 171-173
    modern, 74-76, 78-79, 163, 171-17
Pentateuch, 5n3, 28-29, 29n76, 38, 40, 40n139, 41nn142-144, 44nn159-160, 45-46, 78n32, 135n39
Philo, 36-37, 119, 119n30 121n35, 122n39, 141, 155
philosopher, 54, 58, 90
philosophy,
    biblical, 113
    extra-biblical, 161
    Greek (popular), 118, 119
    Hellenistic, 118n27, 121n35, 122n38
    human, 55-56, 82
    Jewish, 118n27, 119n31

    of history, 71, 88-89, 90-91, 94, 97, 106-110, 112, 124
    of Jesus, 21n44
    of modern Western view, 92
    of religion, 77n31, 96n45
    of the day, 166
    onto-theo-logical, 91
    Parmenidean, 114
    Philonic, 49,
    Platonic, 49
Plato, 75, 83, 119, 174
Platonism, 77, 118-119, 122, 123n40
postmodernity, 59, 75, 97n50
prayer, 47-48
preaching, 61, 105
precondition, 7, 21, 26, 56, 109-110, 170
predestination, 73, 85
pre-existence
    of Christ, 107-108
    timeless, 133
premillennialism, 62n35, 90n12, 91n16
prescriptive analysis, 6-9, 53-54, 62, 64, 67, 69-70, 73, 90, 96, 98, 111-112, 120, 127, 144, 169
prescriptive-descriptive analysis, 138, 142, 143
prescriptive power, 98-99, 120-121, 123, 125, 127, 147, 161, 165, 170
presupposition
    absolute, 117n21
    functional, 164n52, 165
    hermeneutical, 56
    methodological, 53-54, 62, 65, 94
    of prescriptive analysis, 53
    ontological, 54, 55, 60, 65, 98
    primordial, 7n5, 27n70, 54n3, 74n15, 88n7, 113n6, 165n57
    shared, 26
    theological, 77, 103
pre-understanding, 54, 74, 111-113, 117-118, 120

priest
  better, 130
  great, 40
  heavenly, 142, 153-156, 164, 164n52
  high, 20n41, 22-23, 34, 40, 43n153, 129, 136, 142, 145, 154, 157n31-159, 160, 172-173
  new, 16n25, 42n153, 45n164, 46n168, 47n177, 48n180
  proleptic, 136
priesthood, 39n133, 40, 45, 48, 64, 100, 131n21, 133, 136-137, 151-154, 156-158, 164, 171
professed
  believers, 147
  Christian(s), 25, 125, 144-145
  faith in Christ, 17
  Jewish believers, 17
  Jewish Christians, 16, 36
profession of faith, 16
prophet(s), 21, 82n55, 91, 99n58, 105, 146
providence, 25n60, 27n69, 36n115, 71, 73, 87-88, 118n26
purification, 43n154, 46n169, 132nn26-27

Q
Qumran, 38n124
quotation(s), 3, 11, 18n33, 24, 33, 33n103, 41, 42n153, 44n159, 48-49, 61n31, 67n51, 72, 109n113, 128n2, 151n4, 154

R
reality
  complex, 98
  conflicting views of, 116
  consistent view of, 112
  creaturely, 164
  definitive, 157
  divine, 72-73, 78, 85, 89-90, 106-107, 109, 137, 160-162, 164
  divine relation to, 124
  earthly, 89, 173
  heavenly, 133-135, 172
  historical, 107, 109
  immanent, 161
  in heaven, 143
  in the heavenly homeland, 3
  index of, 103n86, 112, 117, 123
  logic of, 94
  mixed view of, 117
  nonhistorical, 116, 172
  notion of, 79, 164
  of Christ's ministry, 137
  of God (God's), 3-6, 85, 94, 116, 159, 161n47
  of history, 93, 115
  of Jesus, 168
  of nature, 75, 166
  of the (heavenly) sanctuary, 4, 132, 137, 171
  one's view of, 55, 72
  ontological, 106, 132, 138
  perspectives of, 17
  relational, 34
  respective, 80
  sacred entities, 34
  spatiotemporal, 134, 140, 173
  supernatural, 172
  timeless, 75, 161n47
  true, 116
  ultimate, 56, 74, 76, 84, 112, 115-118, 120n33, 133, 162, 172
reason
  Auctor's structure of, 67
  classical, 55, 97
  classical structure of, 97
  contemporaneous, 6
  human, 75-76, 160, 172
  modern, 78
  onto-theo-logical structure of, 79, 82, 103
  theological, 6-7, 20, 27n70, 35n112, 53, 54n3, 55n8, 56, 56n11,

Subject Index

58nn20-23, 62, 70, 74n15, 78nn32-33, 80n43, 85nn66-70, 88n7, 97n51, 113n6, 114n8, 116n17, 118n28, 165n57
   theo-onto-logical structure of, 80, 82, 124, 150, 165-166
redemption, 21, 45, 73, 92, 157
resurrection, 21, 26, 82, 106, 157
revelation
   anthropomorphic, 109n111
   authoritative, 6
   bearer of, 101n61
   biblical, 62, 84
   canonical, 9, 169
   cognitive, 58
   continuum of, 139
   controlling, 40, 149-150, 171
   divine, 26, 31, 97, 139
   general, 55-56, 64, 79, 82
   natural, 55, 58-59, 64
   new, 98-99, 103
   of God (God's), 93-94
   of the divine name, 119n32
   of the Word of God, 140
   ontological continuity of, 139
   particular, 84
   progress of, 124
   progressive, 139
   sources of, 70, 74, 78-79, 82, 89, 108
   spatiotemporal, 165, 167
   special, 55, 82, 84
   theology of, 59, 62-63, 71, 88-89, 94, 96-97, 99, 101-103, 110-111, 138-139, 142-143, 147, 160, 166, 170
   Trinitarian, 162
   various moments of, 139
   whole, 101n61

S

Sabbath, 13, 15, 29, 29n77

sacrifice, 3, 4, 6, 26, 32-33, 38, 40-49, 63n38, 102, 130, 136, 140, 142, 144n68, 145, 153
sacrificial system, 42, 43, 46
salvation
   eschatological, 146
   history, 114, 153, 159
   in Christ, 109
   loss of, 15, 33
   means of, 15
   nature of, 16n25
   new Exodus of, 26n66
   of Christ, 6
   of Israelites, 63
   paradigm, 145-146
   plan of, 105, 131
   possibility of, 82
sanctuary
   earthly, 38-39, 131-133, 135-136, 143, 145-146
   heavenly, 4, 30, 38-39, 71, 97, 129-142, 145, 153, 163, 165, 167-174
   millennial, 136, 141, 145
   Mosaic, 141
Scripture(s), 3-4, 6, 11, 11n1, 12, 14n14, 16, 16n25, 19-21, 24, 25n60, 26n67, 28-29, 30n83, 36n116, 54-59, 61, 61n31, 64-67, 72, 77, 79-85, 87-88, 92-96, 101n67, 105-110, 110n117, 116-119, 130n15, 132, 133n30, 139n52, 155-156, 161, 161n47, 162n48, 165, 166n60, 172-174
second temple Judaism, 157-158
sidrah, 102
sin(s), 30, 41-43, 82, 141, 173
Sinai, 9n9, 26, 32, 36, 41, 45n162, 49, 99-103, 166n61, 167n66
sin-offering, 41-42, 44nn158-160
Sitz im Leben, 14, 42
sonship, 64, 151, 153-154, 159n38
soul(s), 47, 74-76, 78, 81-82, 173
spatiotemporality, 153

starting point, 7, 11, 12, 59, 64-67, 73, 163-166
supernature, 76-77, 80-81, 123-124, 137, 141, 147, 165

T

tabernacle
    earthly, 34, 127, 133, 141
    heavenly, 34, 49, 121, 123, 130, 133, 142, 145, 167
    Mosaic, 34, 49, 98n54, 130n15, 132n28-133n32, 136n42, 145
temple, 20, 23-24, 34, 38, 39n127, 63, 102, 118n27, 156-158, 169
Tetragrammaton, 23, 27
theo-onto-logia, 53-56, 58, 61, 64-66, 73, 80, 122-123, 166
theophany, 71, 81, 88-89, 104, 106-108, 137
theology
    autopistic, 73
    axiopistic, 73
    biblical, 4, 14n14, 15n20, 19n35, 21n45, 22n46, 26n65, 72, 92n20, 93, 104n91, 105nn91-95, 136n42, 174
    natural, 55, 56, 61, 76, 77, 82, 83, 91, 164
    onto-theo-logical, 95
    systematic, 26n67, 57n17-58, 60, 70, 84-85, 116n20, 136n42, 147, 150n2, 165, 174
theos, 55-56, 61, 78-79, 91, 124, 137, 164
Tisha be-Av, 12n5, 102, 166n62, 167
Torah, 28, 29, 31, 41n142, 42, 46, 82n55, 116, 119, 135n37, 141, 160, 169
tradition(s), 6-7, 8nn7-9, 13n6, 17, 19, 22n46, 24, 26, 26n67, 28, 28n74, 36nn117-120, 56, 58, 58n22, 60, 74, 77, 81n53, 85n69, 88, 92n26, 93-95, 95n40, 99n58, 100n59, 107n105, 110n117, 113-114, 116, 119, 140, 155n20, 159n36, 160, 162n48, 166n60, 167, 174
Trinity, 24, 29n77, 85n71, 89
truth, 4, 21, 47, 54, 67, 75, 80, 84, 97n50, 111n1, 116, 135
typology
    Christological, 105
    complementary, 140
    double, 140-141
    Exodus, 8n7
    ground for, 71
    horizontal, 101, 141
    prefigurative, 130n15
    prophetic, 127, 130n15, 146n74
    sanctuary, 130-132, 134-137, 141, 165
    tabernacle, 130n15, 133, 165, 167

V

veil, 32, 129, 130

W

Wirkungsgeschichte, 111, 111n1
worship, 3, 6, 13, 23-27, 30, 39, 42-49, 131, 135n37, 137, 156

Y

Yahweh, 13, 19-32, 36, 39, 41, 45, 56, 61, 63, 66, 71, 90, 92-93, 101, 104-106, 114, 115, 125, 137, 144n67, 145, 149-150, 158, 161, 163-170, 174
YHWH, 24, 25n61, 27-28, 113n7, 117n23, 119n32

Z

Zechariah, 167n65
Zion, 9n9, 34n108, 99n58-100n59, 102, 102nn76-77, 103, 166n61, 167, 167n66

Author Index

A
Akao, John Osemeikhian, 109, 111
Allen, David Mark, 65n43, 134, 134n34 152, 152n6
Attridge, Harold W., 4, 5n3, 33n103, 171-172
Averbeck, Richard E., 42, 42nn147-152

B
Bahnsen, Greg L., 168n73
Balentine, George L., 8n7
Bateman, Herbert W. IV, 27n71, 33n101, 63, 63n36, 146n73, 155nn22-24, 156n25
Bauckham, Richard, 20-24, 29, 29n78, 30n83, 159n38, 166, 166nn59-60
Beavis, Mary Ann Lilian, 98-101n60, 103, 103n84
Behm, Johannes, 42n148, 44n159
Belcher, Richard P., 62n35
Bergman, J., 41, 41n143
Bird, Chad L., 105, 105n97
Blanton, Thomas R. IV, 144n68
Borland, James Allen, 106, 106n100
Bristol, Lyle Osborne, 121, 121n35, 122, 122n37
Brown, Raymond E., 20, 20n38
Brown, Stephen J. M.., 84, 84n63
Bruce, F. F., 4, 5n3, 33n103, 158n34, 171-172
Brueggemann, Dale A., 65, 65n44, 66n50
Buchanan, George Wesley, 142, 143n61
Buck, Daniel E., 42n153
Buerger, Martin A., 29n79

C
Canale, Fernando Luis, 7, 7n5, 12, 12n2, 27, 27n70, 34, 34n105, 35, 35nn110-112, 36, 36n114, 49n186, 53-58, 60, 60nn28-29, 69-70, 72nn10-11, 73-78, 80-83, 85, 85nn66-71, 88-89, 92-97, 98n53, 103n86, 107-108, 110n117, 112-118, 131, 131n22, 137, 137n45, 142n59, 144, 144n65, 147, 147n83, 149n1, 155, 155n20, 160-162, 165-166, 174
Caneday, Ardel B., 15n20
Capes, David B., 21n43, 25, 25n61
Carlston, Charles Edwin, 30n87
Casey, Jay Smith, 8n7
Chan, Mark L. Y., 97n50
Chester, Andrew, 155, 159n37
Clary, Henry Walter, 151-154
Clowney, Edmund P., 105, 105n95
Cody, Aelred, 138, 138n47
Conner, Kevin J., 4, 5n3, 171, 174
Conner, W. T., 162n50
Cotton, Roger D., 41n142
Cox, Ronald R., 121, 121n35
Cullmann, Oscar, 78, 78n34, 81, 82nn55-56, 93n32

D
D'Angelo, Mary Rose, 125, 125n45
Darnell, David Rancier, 30n88
Davidson, Richard M., 105n96, 130n15, 132-134,
Davies, Graham I., 113-115
de Jong, Christine Keesmaat, 8n7
Delio, Ilia, 55n7
Delling, Gerhard, 42n153
deSilva, David A., 33n103
deSouza, Elias Brasil, 39n127
deVaux, Roland, 119, 119n32
Docherty, Susan E., 104n87
Dray, William H., 91, 91nn14-18
Duke, R. K., 39, 39n133
Dukes, James Graydon, 93n27, 123n40, 139n49
Dulles, Avery, 97, 98n52
Dunnill, John, 144n68

Dupont-Sommer, A., 102n82
Durham, John I., 30n84, 119n32
E
Ellis, Nicholas J., 146n73
Eichhorst, William R., 142n60
Eisele, Wilfried, 35n109
Eisenbaum, Pamela, 36n116
Ellinger, K., 12
Ellingworth, Paul, 22n48, 33n103, 35n109, 107, 107nn103-104, 140n55
Emmrich, Martin, 8n9, 99n58, 100-101, 146n73, 166-167
Erickson, Millard J., 53-54
Esler, Philip Francis, 36, 36n117
Evans, C. F., 123, 123n42
Evans, Craig A., 36n116, 61n31, 105n93, 106n98, 167n68
F
Fanning, Buist M., 14n14, 33n101
Farley, Edward 5, 105n93
Farrer, Austin, 84n64
Fee, Gordon D., 5n3, 20-21, 25, 25n62, 33n103
Fisher, John, 144, 144nn66-70
Fiorenza, Elisabeth S., 38, 38n124, 48n181
Fowler, Sam Whittemore., 109n111
Fowler, William G., 65n43
France, R. T., 61, 62n32
Freedman, David Noel, 20n38, 23, 23n53, 33n103, 102nn74-82, 143n61
Friederichsen, Douglas W., 130n15
Fuhrmann, Sebastian, 104n87
G
Gäbel, Georg, 103n87, 110n115
Gadamer, Hans-Georg, 111n1
Galenieks, Ēriks, 82nn55-56
Gane, Roy E., 46, 46nn169-172, 48, 48n182
Geisler, Norman L., 77n29
Gelardini, Gabriella, 9n9, 12n5, 13n6, 28, 28n75, 47n178, 99-102, 144n68, 166-167

Gieschen, Charles A., 22, 22n51, 66n46, 107n102, 108-109
Givens, Jimmy McMath Jr., 162n50
Glanz, Oliver, 57, 57n17, 85n71
Glare, P. G. W., 3n1
Gleason, Randall C., 146n73
Godzieba, Anthony J., 78n35
Goldingay, John E., 88n3
Gonzales, Alexander R., 144n69
Gorman, Frank H. Jr., 46, 46n173
Gotaas, David Stanley, 145n72
Grässer, Erich, 35n109, 87n1, 96n47, 122n37, 139n51, 158n35
Green, Joel B., 26n67, 57n14, 81, 81n54
Greenhaw, David M., 105n93
Greenlee, J. Harold, 22n48
Grelot, Pierre, 91, 92n20, 105, 105n92
Grenz, Stanley J., 23, 23n54, 55n7, 109n113
Grier, James M. Jr, 11, 11n1
Griffith, Hayne Preston Jr., 157n31
Grothe, Jonathan F., 158n33
Gulley, Norman R., 57, 57n17, 60n29, 85n71, 95, 116n20, 161n47
Guthrie, Donald, 14, 14n16, 15, 15n19
Guthrie, George H., 12n3, 104n91
H
Ha, Hong Pal, 132, 132n26, 136n41
Ha, John, 32n99
Hafemann, Scott J., 31, 31n95
Hagner, Donald A., 35n109
Hahn, Scott, 145, 145n71
Haight, Roger, 106, 106n99
Hanson, Anthony Tyrell., 101n67, 106n101, 107n102, 143, 143n62
Harmon, Jerry R., 31, 31nn90-93
Harnack, Adolf, 14n13
Harrisville, Roy A, 89, 89n8, 140n53
Hart, Trevor, 26n67
Hartmann, Nicolai, 69, 69n3, 95n37
Hartog, Paul, 110, 110n116
Harvey, A. E., 13, 13n9
Hays, Richard B., 29n78, 65-66

Author Index

Heckl, Raik, 30n83
Hegermann, Harald, 110, 110n115
Heidegger, Martin, 5, 55n7, 58, 58n21, 59, 59nn25-26, 91n13, 114
Henderson, Marion W., 158, 158n34
Hendrix, Ralph E., 39n128
Heppenstall, Edward, 136n42
Hilber, John W., 45nn163-165
Himmelfarb, Martha, 119, 119n29
Hobbs, Edward Craig, 8n7
Hoehner, Harold W., 136n40
Hofius, Otfried, 81n49, 104n91, 113n7, 129nn8-10
Holladay, Carl R., 89, 90n9
Hre Kio, Stephen, 8n7
Hübner, Hans, 24, 24n57, 39, 39n132, 72, 72n8, 109, 109n114, 110
Hughes, John J., 96, 96n46
Hughes, Graham, 61, 61n30, 87n2, 139, 139nn49-50
Hughes, Philip Edgcumbe, 33, 33n103
Hullinger, J. M., 63n38
Hultgren, Arland J., 47n176
Hung, Emmanuel Yun-wing, 146n73
Hurst, L. D., 3n1, 159, 159n37
Hydon, Paul Vernon, 153n9, 164n52

I
Iser, Wolfgang, 18n31

J
Jelinek, John Anthony, 135n37
Johnson, Elliott E., 62n35, 156n25
Johnson, Luke Timothy, 33n103
Johnsson, William G., 43, 43n154, 131n17, 133, 133nn31-33
Joslin, Barry Clyde, 146, 146n80

K
Kant, Immanuel, 73-75, 77-78, 161, 172, 172n2
Karrer, Martin, 104n87
Käsemann, Ernst, 100, 100n60, 101n61, 139, 140n53, 158
Keesmaat-de Jong, Sylvia Christine, 8n7
Kellermann, D., 44n159

Kim, Lloyd, 104n87
Kirby, John Charles, 8nn7-8
Kistemaker, Simon, 154n16
Kitchens, James A., 32n100
Koch, K., 42, 42n151, 43n156
Koester, Craig R., 33n103
Koptak, Paul E., 66, 66n48
Kraus, Wolfgang, 110n115, 138n48
Kreeft, Peter, 21, 21n44

L
Laansma, Jon C., 14n13, 93, 93n33
Lane, William L., 3n2, 33, 33nn103-104, 35n109
Lang, B., 41, 41n143
Larson, Duane Howard, 85n71
Lategan, Bernard C., 14n11, 18n32, 81, 81n49
Laub, Franz, 23, 24n56
Leach, Edmund, 48n185
Lee, Patrick, 76n26
Lee, Young-Jae, 28-29, 29nn76-77, 31
Lefkovitz, Lori H., 18, 18n30
Leithart, Peter J., 129n10, 131, 131n21
Lincoln, Andrew T., 19, 19n35, 26n65, 105n91
Lindars, Barnabas, 70n4, 101n67
Lloyd, Gwilym George, 104n88, 131n18
Loader, William R. G., 22n49
Loewe, William P., 168, 168n69
Löhr, Hermut, 128n28
Lombard, H. A., 142, 146n78
Longenecker, Richard, 19n37, 155n22
Luther, James Henry Jr., 63n37
Lutzer, Erwin W., 92n22
Luz, Ulrich, 93, 94n33, 138, 138n47
Lyttkens, Hampus, 76n26

M
Mach, Michael, 25n64
Mackie, Scott D., 22, 22nn47-49
MacLeod, David John, 14, 14nn13-15, 20n42, 64n40, 70n4, 96-97, 97n48, 147n82, 151, 151n3
Manson, William, 125n45

Manuel, Donald Gordon, 96n47
Marías, Julián, 115, 116n15
Marion, Jean-Luc, 78-79, 79n37
Martin, Robert Keith, 5, 5n4, 60n27, 83, 83n59, 157, 157n30
Marty, William Henry, 30n83
Mascall, E. L., 84n65
Mason, Eric Farrel, 158n32
Masson, Robert, 69n1
Master, John R., 62, 62n34
McCann, J. Clinton Jr., 29, 29n79
McCarthy, Dennis J., 37n123, 78, 78n34
McCormack, Bruce L., 95, 95nn38-41, 160n44, 162n49, 164, 164n53
McCullough, J. C., 12n5, 158n33
McDonough, Sean M., 113n7, 117, 117n23, 118
McGahey, John F., 63n37
McGowan, A. T. B., 64n41
McKenzie, Tracy J., 28n73
McKnight, Edgar V., 56, 57n14
McKnight, Scot, 15n20, 105n93
McNickle, Alan A., 136n40
McNicol, Allen James, 20n41
Measell, James S., 83, 83n60
Merrill, Eugene H., 41n141, 167, 167n65
Miano, David, 102nn74-82
Michalson, Carl, 106n101
Michel, Otto, 19, 19n36, 128n8
Mickelsen, A. Berkeley, 121-123
Miller, Ted (Russell E. Jr.), 9n9, 99n58, 100, 100n59, 101, 101n69
Mills, Watson E., 8n7
Mintek, Shawn Joseph, 117, 117n21
Mitchell, Alan C., 33n103
Moberly, R. W. L., 30, 30n85, 31n93
Moe, Olaf, 42n153
Moltmann, Jürgen, 78, 78n34
Montefiore, Hugh, 4, 5n3, 171-172
Morris, Leon, 33n103
Morrison, Michael Duane, 15n18, 98nn54-55, 131n20
Motyer, Stephen, 18, 18n33

Muilenburg, James, 81, 81n47
Müller, Ekkehardt, 153n11
Mullins, E. Y., 162n50
N
Nash, Ronald H., 90, 90n11, 92, 92n21, 93n32
Neusner, Jacob, 92, 92n24
Newing, Edward George, 32, 32n97
Neyrey, Jerome H., 35, 35n111
Ninow, Friedbert, 38, 38n127, 39n127, 105n96
Nixon, Hilary Arthur, 98n54, 130n15, 132n28, 133n32, 136n42
Nixon, R. E., 8nn7-8
Nota, John H., 81n50, 92, 92n23
O
O'Brien, Peter T., 4, 5n3, 171-172
O'Connor, M. P., 23, 23n53
Olbricht, Thomas H., 141, 141n57
Osborne, Grant R., 27n71, 105n93
Oudersluys, Richard C., 8n8
P
Pao, David Wei Chun, 8n7
Parry, Robin, 57, 57n15
Pfitzner, Victor C., 35n109
Phillips, Richard D., 35n109
Phillips, W. Gary, 64n41, 150n2
Pigott, Susan Marie, 31, 31n94
Piper, John, 168, 168n71
Piper, Otto A., 7, 7n6, 8n7
Porter, Stanley E., 14n12, 19n37, 36n116, 61n31, 65, 65n46, 102n74, 121n35
Powers, Daniel G., 16n25
Powers, Philip Edwards, 130n15, 146n74
Procksch, Otto, 38, 38n126
R
Rabinowitz, Peter J., 13, 13n7, 18, 18nn29-34, 26n68
Rahlfs, Alfred, 12
Rankin, Jeffrey Jay, 65, 65n44, 66n50, 91n19
Rayburn, Robert Stout, 62, 62n34
Reinhartz, Adele, 23, 23n55

Author Index

Reynolds, James E., 8n9, 99n58, 100, 100n59
Rice, George E., 27n71, , 129n11
Rice, Richard, 90, 90n10
Richard, Ramesh P., 90, 90n12, 91, 91n16, 92n25, 94, 94n34
Ringgren, H., 41, 41n143
Rissi, Mathias, 70n4
Rodríguez, Angel Manuel, 137, 137n46
Roth, E. M., 14, 14n13
Rudolph, W., 12
Ruffatto, Kristine J., 22n46
Russell, Brian Douglas, 65n43

S

Sahlin, Harold, 26n66
Salom, Alwyn P., 39n131, 128, 128nn1-5, 129n7
Sanford, Carlisle Junior, 15n18
Saucy, Robert L., 63n35
Schenck, Kenneth L., 81n51, 82n55, 121, 121n34, 123n40
Scholer, John M., 136, 136n43
Schreiner, Thomas R., 15n20
Schrenk, Gottlob, 40, 40n138
Schröger, Friedrich, 33n104
Schunack, Gerd, 103n87
Seitz, Christopher R., 25, 25n60, 27, 27n69, 36, 36n115, 118, 118n26
Selby, Rosalind M., 54n6, 83, 83n61
Sexton, James Hardy, 144n67
Shea, William H., 128-129, 134n35, 135n38
Showers, Renald E., 141n56
Shultz, Gary L. Jr, 17n26
Siegert, Folker, 37, 37n122
Skarsaune, Oskar, 25, 25n63
Smillie, Gene R., 99, 99n56, 112n2
Smith, Billy O., 31nn89-92
Son, Kiwoong, 9n9, 34n108, 99n58, 100, 138, 166, 166n61, 167n66
Sontag, Frederick, 77n31, 96, 96n45
Spicq, Ceslas, 4, 5n3, 142n58, 171-172
Spieckermann, Hermann, 31, 31n91

Spiegelberg, Herbert, 72, 72n12
Stählin, Gustav, 42-43, 44n159-45n166, 48n180
Stanley, Christopher D., 61n31, 67n51
Sterling, Gregory E., 36, 36n120, 118n27, 119, 119nn30-31, 121-123
Stine, Donald Medford, 13n10
Stockhausen, Carol L., 65-66
Strobel, August, 121, 121n35
Strong, A. H., 162n50
Stuart, Streeter Stanley, Jr., 8n9, 99n58, 100, 100n59
Suleiman, Susan R., 13n8, 17, 17n27
Sweeney, Marvin A., 28, 28n74
Swetnam, James, 12n5
Synge, Francis Charles, 14n14, 139n52

T

Telscher, Guido, 104n87
Tetley, Joy D., 64n40, 151, 151n3
Theißen, Gerd, 35
Theron, Stanley Winter, 81n51, 124n43
Thiele, F., 40-41, 42n148, 44n159
Thiessen, Matthew, 8n8, 146, 146n75
Thomas, C. Adrian, 15-16
Thompson, James W., 22n49, 36n120
Thomson, Iain D., 55n7
Thurén, Lauri, 14, 14n12
Thyen, Hartwig, 12n5
Tilley, Terrence W., 168, 168nn70-74
Timmer, Daniel C., 29-31
Tomesch, Harald, 13n6
Travers, Michael E., 83, 83n62
Treiyer, Alberto R., 4, 5n3, 132, 132nn26-27, 135, 135n39, 136n42, 143, 143n64, 171, 174

U

Übelacker, Walter G., 36n118

V

van Seters, John, 28n73
van Wijk-Bos, Johanna W. H., 28, 28n72
Vanhoye, Albert, 8n7, 16n25, 22, 22n50, 40, 40n135, 42n153, 45n164, 46, 46n168, 47, 47n177, 48n180

Verbrugge, Verlyn D., 16-17
Vervenne, Marc, 28n73
W
Wallace, David, 155n18
Walter, Nikolaus, 110, 110n115
Walvoord, John F., 62n35
Watts, James Washington, 29n81
Watts, Rikki E., 8n7
Webb, William J., 8n7
Wenkel, David H., 62n33
Westcott, Brooke Foss, 22n48, 36, 36n119, 43n153, 143, 143n63
Wevers, John William, 12n4
White, Roger, 79n41
Williams, Arthur Hayes Jr., 13n6, 159-166
Williams, Donald L., 42n149, 43, 43n155, 47, 47n175, 48n185
Williamson, H. G. M., 101n67
Williamson, Ronald, 121, 121n35, 122-123, 123n40
Willi-Plein, Ina, 47, 47n178
Witherington, Ben III, 19, 19n37
Wolf, Herbert, 44n161
Wolterstorff, Nicholas, 124, 124n44
Woodring, Hoyt C. Jr., 29n80, 32n99
Wyschogrod, Michael, 24, 24n58, 81, 81n52, 93, 93n30, 116, 116nn16-18, 146n79, 147n81, 157, 157n29, 174, 174n2
Z
Zimmermann, Heinrich, 87n1, 140, 140n54

Studies in Biblical Literature

This series invites manuscripts from scholars in any area of biblical literature. Both established and innovative methodologies, covering general and particular areas in biblical study, are welcome. The series seeks to make available studies that will make a significant contribution to the ongoing biblical discourse. Scholars who have interests in gender and sociocultural hermeneutics are particularly encouraged to consider this series.

For further information about the series and for the submission of manuscripts, contact:

> Peter Lang Publishing
> Acquisitions Department
> P.O. Box 1246
> Bel Air, Maryland 21014-1246

To order other books in this series, please contact our Customer Service Department:

> (800) 770-LANG (within the U.S.)
> (212) 647-7706 (outside the U.S.)
> (212) 647-7707 FAX

or browse online by series at:

> WWW.PETERLANG.COM